FREEDOM'S FRONTIER

Atlantic Union Now

FREEDOM'S FRONTIER

Atlantic Union Now

by CLARENCE K. STREIT

This is what I have learnt from America—
it is the amount, and it I teach again.
Whitman, *By Blue Ontario's Shore*

HARPER & BROTHERS, PUBLISHERS, NEW YORK

FREEDOM'S FRONTIER

Copyright © 1940, 1961 by Clarence K. Streit

Printed in the United States of America

Library of Congress catalog card number: 61-9817

To My Grandchildren

VALERIE STREIT SCHROTH
PIERRE ALEXANDRE ROHATYN
NICOLAS STREIT ROHATYN

and to yours
that they may be
"freer than all that has been before"

Contents

INTRODUCTION: This Book's Aim ix

BOOK I

1. What Doest Thou Here? 3
2. The NATO Nations as Founders of the Union 29
3. Confederation Next—Not Federation Now? 56
4. The U. S. Experiments with Confederation and Federation 69
5. British Riddle, French *Mystère,* American Enigma 80
6. Cancer Cell No. 1 in the Free Body Politic 90
7. Two American Revolutions Made You Sovereign 99
8. How the Civil War Kept You Sovereign 119
9. The Sovereignty You Gain by Atlantic Union 129
10. *Union Now,* the U. N. and World Government 142
11. We Must—Like William Tell—Aim High 149
12. Fourfold Fulfillment 157
13. Time for an Heroic Step Ahead 173
    Last Word 181

BOOK II—UNION NOW
The Basic Chapters of the 1940 Concise Edition

INTRODUCTIONS:

I To This Edition—*Senator Estes Kefauver* 187
II To the 1949 Postwar Edition—*Oscar Jaszi* 189

PROPOSAL

I What This Book Is About 191
VI How to Organize the Democracies 209
VII League or Union? Three Tests 215
IX Isolation of the Germ 237
X The Union 240
XII To Get the Union Now 252

PHILOSOPHY

XIII Of Freedom and Union   261

POEM

Man   286

ANNEXES

Annex 1: Illustrative Constitution   287

Annex 2: My Own Road to Union   296

Last Word   306

INDEX   309

Introduction: This Book's Aim

If you would be freer than all that has been before,
come, listen to me.—*Whitman,* By Blue Ontario's Shore

Twenty-one years after *Union Now* was first published, its basic idea reached the Rubicon. The idea was summed up in the book's sub-title: "A Proposal for a Federal Union of the Democracies of the North Atlantic." The Rubicon took the form of an Act of Congress in the summer of 1960, authorizing the calling of a Convention of "representative citizens" of North Atlantic nations to explore how to advance their freedom by greater political and economic unity, and report by January 31, 1962. The fact that it is patterned on the 1787 Convention which worked out the world's first Federal Union —the revolutionary United States Constitution—seems evidence enough that the turning point which the Atlantic community and the *Union Now* proposal have now reached is indeed significant.

To add to its significance, Senator John F. Kennedy, after voting for this Act, won the White House under the banner of "the new frontier," on a platform pledging "the Atlantic Community" a "broader partnership" . . . while Vice President Richard M. Nixon, who almost won, urged a "North Atlantic Confederation." These developments are dealt with further in this book, notably in Chapters 1, 3 and 11.

Earlier, the State High School Debate Leagues had, with singular foresight, voted to make free world security their topic for the 1960-61 scholastic year, with the No. 1 debate proposition under it: "Resolved: That the North Atlantic Treaty Organization be transformed into a federal government." As a result more than 50,000 students in some 10,000 American high schools are already debating the subject which will face some 100 leaders from NATO nations when the Atlantic Convention meets in 1961.

The high school decision led Dr. Bower Aly, Executive Secretary of the National Committee on Debate Materials for these students, to write: "I wish I knew some man with money and enough perception to supply a copy of *Union Now* to each high school debate squad in the United States. It is the best single book for our purposes." He found this man in the person of F. Gilbert Lamb, President of Lamb-Weston, Inc., of Weston, Oregon. He generously offered to give a copy to all the 10,000 debate squads—but there were only 200 copies of the 1949 Postwar edition left in print.*

In these circumstances, it was decided that another edition should be published, with the five Postwar chapters replaced with others written now. The political developments thereafter led me to change plans and write this new book, to which I have added the basic parts of *Union Now*. The result is virtually two books in one. Because of the debaters' demand for *Union Now*, I had to write this book more rapidly than I would have liked. It is, however, the product of research, study, experience and thought through more than a quarter-century. In it I aim at three targets—yea four, as the ancient Hebrews loved to say.

First (in order of appearance), I have considered afresh the proposal and philosophy of *Union Now* in the light of the world changes since 1939. Then I have tried to do the three things I think most need doing if we are to realize our present opportunity—or even escape catastrophe—namely, a) to clear away the confusion over sovereignty which keeps the free divided and fog-bound, b) to clarify the misunderstood but momentous and inspiring lessons of American history on sovereignty and Union, and c) to provide the powerful motive force needed for the free to reach the new world to which they alone can lead mankind.

The fog over sovereignty has kept the free circling for fifty years in a sea of troubles—instead of sailing on to make this the century of individual freedom-and-union in an even higher, broader degree than was the period from 1776 to 1910. We cannot remove this fog by removing dictatorship; we ourselves create it—the confusion lies in us. I have done my best to clarify the subject of sovereignty, and show that it centers in no body politic but equally in our individual selves or, more accurately, in the intangible self that Tocqueville called "the angel in man."

To do this, I have turned perforce to the history of the United States. I say *perforce* for four reasons: 1) The history of no other people has so much to teach on sovereignty; here, as an English author taught me, one can see its workings as one may study "bees in a glass hive." 2) No people is more

* This was the last of *Union Now's* seven editions for the United States: my private one (1938), Unabridged (printed in France for Harper & Bros., 1939), Unabridged (printed in the United States by Harper & Bros., 1939), Concise (1940), Book-of-the-Month Dividend (1941), Wartime, with three new chapters (1943), Postwar, with five new chapters (1949). Also exhausted are the foreign editions: Jonathan Cape, London; Librairie de Medicis, Paris, (*Union ou Chaos*); and Natur och Kultur, Stockholm (*Union Nu*), all in 1939. More than a quarter million copies in all have been sold, not counting a pirated edition in China and a Dutch edition in Indonesia in 1941.

befogged now over sovereignty. 3) To clarify Americans on it is essential; while they remain fog-bound, the Atlantic Community cannot sail on. 4) The best way to de-fog us is through fresh air from our own history—which also helps make others understand us.

To lift a fog is not enough; all can be clear and yet one can stay becalmed, or fail to move fast enough to reach port in time. But as the breeze that lifts a fog can drive a ship ahead, so what clarifies confusion may not only give us our direction but help us reach it. By nature the sovereign—whether king, nation, or citizen—must seek to exercise his sovereignty and grow in power. When we recognize ourselves as sovereigns, we feel more impellingly the need, and responsibility, to develop ourselves, to free our persons in the myriad ways liberty requires, to fulfill our potentialities. No one else can do this for us—yet no one can free or fulfill himself alone.

Heaven itself needs more than one star, more than a galaxy or Milky Way, to be Heaven and "declare the glory of God." To be sovereign, to be all we each can be, each man and woman requires the help of a myriad men and women. Each is weak in more ways than strong—but we are so richly varied that there are always others who fulfill themselves by supplying what we lack, as we each do for them.

This subject is vast; in this book I am concerned only with some phases, particularly the political and moral. I have tried to indicate how, by extending our sovereignty to create a Union of the Free, each can fulfill himself in four of our embodiments—as part of mankind, as a member of the free world, as one of our nation, and (I would add, above all) in our individual self—as *homo sapiens,* citizen, patriot and person, or soul. By Atlantic Union we develop ourselves, the country we love, the freedom we cherish and the whole human species—everything we are and belong to.

To this end I have sought to bring out better than I have before the positive rather than the negative motive in the philosophy of freedom-and-union and in the proposal of Federation of the Free. To be against and to seek to escape danger are natural motives, but they are not the things that move us in the highest measure. We cannot be ourselves without being for something. To be a man is to act, create, do. Our eyes are not aimed sidewise and backward, as a fly's, to flee with. Our eyes look forward; our hands and feet are shaped to move ahead; we must turn to see pursuers. Man is made to hunt rather than be hunted; his genius lies in building rather than letting alone, or destroying.

Like all living creatures we are often moved by fear; un-

like them we are also moved by faith. And it is faith that has
moved Man to do all the great things he has done, and all the
minor things that he is proud of, too—everything that he
calls manly, womanly, humane, heroic. And the more prodigious his achievement, the more sublime was his faith. In
the end, faith moves men more than fear.

We know this almost instinctively. We often prove it by our
action. Yet more often we speak as if we believed the contrary, at least about our fellows. I must confess I have. What
set and kept me working for Union of the Free, for twenty-
seven years now, was not merely the dangers from dictatorship, depression and war that result from disunion; it was,
much more, the freer, fuller, better individual life and greater
civilization that would result from the creation of this
Union. As I have continued in this endeavor, I have been
strengthened in this faith by experiencing the freer, fuller,
better life which even the continued effort to help create this
Unior. brought me personally—and seeing many others en-
gaged in it with me enjoy these rewards, too.

Yet I have written and talked of Union of the Free much
more in terms of the dangers of disunion we could escape
than in terms of the advantages we would gain, individually
and collectively. It is no excuse to say that this is common
practice. (Certainly the major reason given by those who hope
to realize quickly such things as disarmament or world government is that it is "a matter of survival." They expect to
work stupendous miracles by invoking the fearful animal in
man, rather than the stuff that miracles and men are made on
—willingness to sacrifice the body to the spirit and risk survival in order to do what one believes in.)

Compared to disarmament, which so many practical politicians and newspapers treat as if it could be achieved in a
few years, Atlantic Union requires only a minor miracle.
Though I have not tried to bring it about by appealing to
fear of non-survival, I have appealed too much to fear of
dictatorship and war, and not enough to the faith that moved
me, myself. Nor is it an excuse to say that the dangers of disunion seem immediate and concrete, while the rewards of
Union are relatively distant, or intangible.

It was not fear, but far greater faith than Atlantic Union
now requires that made Mecca, Mecca. Since we all move
from low as well as high motives, both to escape the club and
to reach the carrot, it seems to me necessary to invoke both,
to achieve any political aim. But realism requires me also to
admit that, the greater the miracle one seeks to make, the
more we need to arouse faith rather than fear. And so I have

sought—particularly in Chapters 12 and 13 and in the Last Word—to correct this balance.

BOOK II—*Union Now*

Book II gives the basic parts of *Union Now.* I have drawn them from the condensed version of the original 1939 text which I made for the Concise edition in 1940. To present the proposal and philosophy of that book in that text separately, yet combined with this new book, permits those who read *Union Now* years ago to refresh their memory easily. It is no less convenient for those who have heard of *Union Now,* read reviews or digests of it, and—I like to think—meant to read it but left this intention unfulfilled (as I so often have with other books). Most of all I hope that Book II will introduce *Union Now* to those who have never heard of it, particularly to the generation still unborn when it appeared, or too young to read when the 1949 edition was published.

The twenty-one years since its first publication permit readers now to put it to a far more searching test than any other proposal in the field, *provided* the author resists the temptation to revise the text as hindsight may suggest. Readers rarely can put any idea to such a test. Many, I think, will find this experience more interesting than they anticipated. Those who assume that any book that appeared even a year ago must be too dated now to waste time on, can easily test that theory by turning to Book II and scanning the opening paragraphs of 1939.

Certainly I believe the greatness of our present opportunity, and danger, justify the severest test of any proposal and philosophy for meeting them. We live in a time when the world grows incessantly more complex, confusing. Long before change became so widespread, Lord Acton warned that "political calculations are so complex that we cannot trust theory, if we cannot support it by experience." But how are we to distinguish sound theory from false today? How to reduce the cost, and danger, of learning by trial and error when time rockets, and error may annihilate? How to cleave to reason when leaders in whom we trust are so often proven wrong, once their policies are tried? "To govern is to foresee," a French king said. But how are we to know foresight in time?

The surest way we can hope for is by some test of time. A policy that met changing conditions in the past five, ten, twenty, fifty, 150 years better than alternatives offers sounder hope of meeting future needs than do policies that permit no such test, that are pure theory, or that have just been tried and failed, or have never worked in history. Yet how seldom do we—or can we—apply any test of time before we try proposals in the present field. Pause for a moment to think of the many policies for advancing peace and freedom that we have tried in the past fifty, twenty, ten, five years—only to find their foresight false, their reasoning unsound, and freedom and peace in greater danger than before . . .

. . . And now pause again—perhaps we read too rapidly and think too little while reading—and let your mind roam over the many solutions that were not tried out but did gain much attention because they had behind them men of high position or great wealth, or mass media, respected institutions, important organizations. Try to recall at least one of these proposals that had their day on Page 1, or in the halls of learning, and are now mercifully forgotten . . .

. . . Is it surprising that through these fifty years we have seemed to go in circles, yet really spiraled downward . . . that so many lament today "a lack of purpose"? How can we hope for better while we give so little thought to the test of time? Some say that I attach too much importance to the lessons of experience that American history teaches. Since I do weigh heavily the time factor in human affairs, and since the proposal and philosophy of *Union Now* have had to face some test of time, I think it only right that you should have the opportunity Book II gives of applying to Book I a more searching test than most books permit.

I wish, indeed, there were space to include all of *Union Now,* but various factors limit this volume. And so I have had to omit six chapters and one annex, and some paragraphs in others. The parts omitted deal with conditions that no longer obtain, such as American neutralism, or that I consider secondary. All that is basic has been retained, with no change whatever in the original text.

I regret, too, that there is no space to mention by name even some of the many to whom I am deeply indebted for their part in this enterprise, and book. I hope I have made clear in the Last Word of Book I, and in Chapter XIII of *Union Now,* how grateful I am to each of them. I must mention one: Without my wife, Jeanne Defrance, I could not have done my part in this work, nor have the proof I have of the truth and beauty of freedom-and-union.

C.K.S.

Armonk, New York, November 10, 1960

BOOK I

The time is ripe for these nations to build an Atlantic Community.—*Atlantic Congress, Final Declaration, June 10, 1959.*

We stand today on the edge of a new frontier . . . a frontier of unknown opportunities and perils . . . it holds out the promise of more sacrifice instead of more security . . . Beyond that frontier are uncharted areas of science and space, unsolved problems of peace and war, unconquered pockets of ignorance and prejudice . . . The times demand invention, innovation, imagination, decision. I am asking each of you to be pioneers on that new frontier.—*Senator John F. Kennedy, accepting the Democratic nomination for President, July 15, 1960.*

We are ready to go ahead and explore new approaches. We are a society of individuals. Our institutions project outward from the people, not downward to the people.—*Vice President Richard M. Nixon in* Life, *August 29, 1960.*

A period of crisis is always a period of opportunity. . . . It may mark the beginning of a period of steady deterioration, ending, so far as human intelligence can foresee, in tragedy. Or it may be the beginning of better things.—*Prime Minister Harold Macmillan, of Great Britain, United Nations Assembly, September 29, 1960.*

Something must be done. We cannot . . . sit helplessly watching the world drift in a direction which can only end in catastrophe.—*Prime Minister Jawaharlal Nehru of India, United Nations Assembly, October 3, 1960.*

To my mind, Atlantic Union is an absolute and early necessity . . . an excellent idea. And the sooner we move, the better it is.—*Dr. Edward Teller, "father of the H-Bomb," November 12, 1960.*

Where once we could unite only in fear, I believe we can now unite in courage and hope to do more noble works than men have ever done before . . . We can go beyond allaying fears to fulfilling dreams.—*Vice President-elect Lyndon B. Johnson at the* NATO *Parliamentarians Conference, Paris, November 22, 1960.*

Was then the American Revolution effected . . . was the blood of thousands spilt, and the hard-earned substance of millions lavished, not that the people of America should enjoy peace, liberty and safety, but that the government of the individual States . . . might enjoy a certain extent of power, and be arrayed with certain dignities and attributes of sovereignty? We have heard of the impious doctrine in the Old World, that the people were made for kings, not kings for the people. Is the same doctrine to be revived in the New in another shape—that the solid happiness of the people is to be sacrificed to . . . political institutions of a different form? . . . As far as the sovereignty of the States cannot be reconciled to the happiness of the people, the voice of every good citizen must be, Let the former be sacrificed to the latter. *James Madison, No. 45 of* The Federalist, *1788.*

If there is a country in the world where the doctrine of the sovereignty of the people can be fairly appreciated . . and where its dangers and advantages may be judged, that country is assuredly America * * * The people reign in the American political world as the Deity does in the universe. They are the cause and the aim of all things; everything comes from them and everything is absorbed in them.—*Tocqueville,* Democracy in America, *Vol 1, chapter IV 1835* (my translation).

We must appeal to the sober sense and patriotism of the people. We will make converts day by day; we will grow strong by calmness and moderation; we will grow strong by the violence and injustice of our adversaries. And, unless truth be a mockery and justice a hollow lie, we will be the majority after a while, and the revolution which we will accomplish will be none the less radical from being the result of pacific measures. The battle of freedom is to be fought out on principle.—*Abraham Lincoln in his "Lost Speech," May 19, 1856.*

What Doest Thou Here?

> And Elijah came unto all the people, and said, How
> long have ye been between two opinions? If the Lord
> be God, follow him; but if Baal, then follow him.
> And the people answered him not a word. * * * And
> (Elijah fled) for his life . . . into the wilderness. * * *
> And, behold . . . a great and strong wind rent the
> mountains, and brake in pieces the rocks . . . but the
> Lord was not in the wind; and after the wind an earth-
> quake; but the Lord was not in the earthquake; and
> after the earthquake, a fire; but the Lord was not in
> the fire; and after the fire a still small voice . . .
> came . . . and said, What doest thou here, Elijah?—
> *I Kings, 18:21; 19; 3, 11-13.*

Avoidable catastrophe and missed opportunity, both immense, have marked the years since *Union Now* appeared in
1939. Change—violent and peaceful—has also been immense. Yet the fundamentals faced in the opening pages of
this book still face us now. The basic lines of the picture
have grown in magnitude rather than changed in nature.
The stakes are higher, the need for action—sound and
bold—much more urgent. The same catastrophes knock at
the door, and the same opportunity. If there seems cause
for despair, there is greater cause for the faith that moves
mountains.

The catastrophes have been much greater than I anticipated. So too have been not only man's deafness to opportunity, but his—and opportunity's—capacity for survival.
From all this I draw greater faith in the soundness of the
fundamental philosophy and principles of Union of the
Free, and a greater sense of the *nowness* of *Union Now*,
and the federal union of North Atlantic democracies it proposed. (*To avoid repetition I would suggest that the reader
who is not familiar with that proposal turn now to Book II,
Chapter 1, and read the first ten paragraphs, which give
its essence.*)

ENTER, THE ATLANTIC CONVENTION

One change in the picture, which has seemed too slight or too recent to be noted yet by the general public, seems to me so significant as to give in itself reason enough for new faith in freedom's future, and for this new effort to advance it. On September 7, 1960, President Eisenhower signed an act of Congress authorizing a United States Citizens Commission on NATO to organize and participate in a Convention of Citizens of North Atlantic Democracies with a view to exploring fully and recommending concretely how to unite their peoples better. Before an Atlantic Federal Union can be formed, such a Convention must meet. The meeting does not mean that such a Union will be formed, but it does open the door to this.

The fact that it has taken twenty years to open this door is proof of its importance. Other facts increase it. One is that the Senate approved the Convention on June 15, 1960, by the narrow majority of 51 to 44—but with the support of both candidates for President and the Majority Leader. Another is that, despite the close Senate vote, the House— whose shorter term requires its members to assess current and coming public opinion more accurately—gave overwhelming approval, 288 to 103, after three hours of debate on August 24. In between came the Democratic Platform pledge of a "broader partnership" in "the Atlantic Community," and the Rockefeller-Nixon proposal that the United States "should promptly lead toward the formation" of a North Atlantic "Confederation."

Delegates from the other NATO nations had already joined with those of the United States in unanimously recommending—both at the NATO Parliamentarians Conferences in 1957 and 1959 and at the Atlantic Congress in 1959—that such a Convention be called. The latter Congress of some 700 eminent citizens, from all the NATO nations except Iceland went much further. It not only made the unanimous Declaration cited on the opening page of this book, but it also approved the unanimous report of its Political Committee, which stressed that the Convention should tackle the problem of Atlantic unification "as a whole" and face, too, "the important question of principles" it involves. The preamble, written by the committee's rapporteur, Maurice Faure of France, added:

> One solution would be to bring about some form of political federation of all our states. The idea of such

a federation at this time should not be ruled out, but we must face up to the possibility that it may be psychologically premature. In any event we must proceed beyond the stage of an alliance. In other words what we must do is to create a genuine community.

This will not be an easy task. What it requires is an entirely new enterprise for which there is no precedent * * The traditional concept of the sovereignty of our countries must not be regarded as something unalterable, as Holy Writ. * * * It must also be realized that in our democratic society, the rights of the individual * * are limited by law in order to preserve the freedom of other individuals, or to secure social progress in accordance with technical progress. Hence the need for us to accept limitations of the sovereignty of our States; limitations which are urgently called for by the over-riding needs of our defense, our well-being and our unity. * * *

It is clear that we are living in an era when safeguarding the freedom of Man—which is the highest good—will be impossible to ensure without far-reaching structural reforms. The time has come for this need to be fully understood, for the peril is becoming more serious as well as more general * * * NATO must prepare itself to meet all these threatening perils. But NATO can only do this if * * * it builds up stronger institutions which will effectively place the whole of its means at the service of a policy of closer union which will lead mankind to the new era made possible by scientific, industrial, political and moral progress.

A STILL GREAT PATTERN, AND A STILL SMALL VOICE

One more significant fact needs be added. The Atlantic Convention's approach to the problem of unification is patterned on that of the Federal Convention in 1787—notably in that the members are free from official instructions, each able to act as his individual experience, vision and conscience advise. This procedure, which is unprecedented in the field of international relations (as the debate in the United States Congress on the Atlantic Convention resolution brought out) produced the most prodigious and enduring success in the history of conferences among sovereign states —the United States Constitution.

Yet the Federal Convention began in Philadelphia amid skepticism much stronger than the Atlantic Congress' fear lest Atlantic federation be "psychologically premature" today.

George Washington himself asked on March 10, 1787: "Is the public mind matured for such an important change . . . ? What would be the consequences of a premature attempt?" And after he arrived at the Convention on the day set for it to open—May 14—and had to wait ten days for apathy to permit a quorum, he went further and forecast: "It is too probable that no plan we propose will be adopted. Perhaps another dreadful conflict is to be sustained." But in the next breath he added: "If, to please the people, we offer what we ourselves disapprove, how can we afterward defend our work? Let us raise a standard to which the wise and the honest can repair; the event is in the hand of God."

Thanks to the heroic faith and efforts of Washington and the other Founding Fathers, out of that Convention came, not another dreadful conflict, but the world's first Federal Union of the Free. There is, of course, no certainty that the Atlantic Convention will thus rise to the occasion . . . but it can. It may indeed produce only unneeded proof that democracy moves almost always "too little and too late." It will fail thus, miserably, if its members and the press and public do not see with much more clearness and act with much more courage than has marked Atlantica's past twenty years. The fact remains that free men now, at last, are in position, at least, to grasp the vast opportunity that has been vainly knocking at their door.

Like the ancient Hebrews they have remained since 1939 between two opinions, uncertain whether their highest Truth was the Sovereign Citizen or the Sovereign Nation—whether their Lord was God or Baal. Like Elijah they sought escape in . . . a wilderness. There, in those twenty-one years, they have, dumbfounded, witnessed hurricane, earthquake, holocaust. But their Truth came not out of the wind of war that rent mountains of states. Nor did it come out of the earthquake of science, nor out of the fire that consumed empires.

Their highest Truth *can* come out of the Atlantic Convention, however still and small its voice may seem today. It will come out if the Convention brings home to enough free men and women the question with but one answer which, through the ages, has moved the individual conscience to assert its sovereign power, and led man to make his many miracles: . . . "What doest thou here, Elijah?" To help make this voice heard is the present purpose.

THE REWARDS OF BAAL, THROUGH TWO DECADES

Let us begin by following the lead that Lincoln gave when he said on June 17, 1858: "If we could first know where we are, and whither we are tending, we could better judge what to do, and how to do it." To adapt his next sentence to the present occasion I have changed a few words to those italicized: "We are now far into the *twenty-first* year since *policies were* initiated with the avowed object and confident promise of putting an end to *our problem.* Under the operation of *those policies,* that *problem* has not only not ceased, but it has constantly augmented." The proof is evident, but not its accumulating effect—judging from the failure to reverse these policies. In the 1949 edition of *Union Now* its new chapters began by reporting on the situation ten years after the book's appearance, and noted first that the policies that had prevailed since 1939 had left this result:

> Still disunited, the democracies still confront a formidable dictatorship. It is armed with a great army, and a militant dogma that violently subordinates man to the state. It is bent on driving individual freedom off the earth, and enslaving all mankind under its tyrannical world government.

In the decade since, the Communist dictatorship has added to its arsenal all the other four arms that we then practically or completely monopolized. It has now a very powerful air force. Its sea power is much stronger than Hitler had—most of all in submarines to which the free are doubly vulnerable, because of their Atlantic life-lines and because their great cities and industrial areas are much closer to the coast than Russia's, more exposed to bombardment by the aerial "torpedoes" submarines can fire today. Out of the devastation of Russia has risen, too, since 1949, a mighty industrial plant, keyed to producing arms rather than electric kitchens. Moscow has also broken the one complete monopoly we had; its stockpiles of atomic bombs now balance ours. On top of this, it is armed with rocket power that surpasses ours in intercontinental guided missiles and in thrust into Space.

Nor is this all: By being first to send a satellite into orbit round the planet, this dictatorship has armed itself with the prestige in the field of science and invention that Atlantica had almost monopolized for the previous two centuries.* Moreover, Communist dictatorship has consolidated its hold over 600,000,000 Chinese since 1949. It is arming itself there under even more ruthless pressure than in Russia . . . at a time in history when the methods of mass production

---

* See *Freedom Against Itself* by the author (Harpers 1954), Chapter 4 and Annex 1, which lists "1,012 Major Inventions, Discoveries and Innovations since 1750," and shows that 95 per cent came from Atlantica, 2 per cent from Russia.

and mass destruction give an advantage to the country with the greatest masses of men.

The Postwar edition of *Union Now* continued, in its report on the 1939-49 decade:

> Still without a central government, the free Atlantic community still invites economic collapse and another World War.

We have continued through another decade to escape the depression that sooner or later has invariably followed great wars in the past. Our escape has been only partly due to the "built-in" stabilizers to the economy which so many trust will prevent another great depression. It has also resulted partly from the market provided by such great undertakings as the Marshall Plan's reconstruction of Europe, and "Point 4" and other programs for aiding underdeveloped nations.

But perhaps the main reason for our escape thus far is that—as Felix Morley succinctly put it in his *Freedom and Federalism*: "We have avoided the depression that normally follows war by the unusual expedient of avoiding peace." In an important sense the war period has not yet ended; while the line-ups have changed, it has continued in cold fury rather than hot—but at a total cost to the United States alone that surpasses its expenditures in World War II. Meanwhile there have been building up inflationary and other economic strains that make for a collapse much more dangerous to freedom than was the Great Depression.* And now for the first time we face an autocracy that can hope to win not merely by war but by using economic arms—all of which it monopolizes as we monopolize only military arms— to advance its aims in all the Cubas and the Congos, and to try to deepen any Atlantic economic recession into a serious depression.

Since 1949 the Soviet dictatorship has already gained significant economic beachheads in the Mideast, in Africa and at the doorsill of the United States. Meanwhile the people of Atlantica have not yet begun to form a common government through which to meet common dangers by the common sense of common policies. True, the European shore of the ocean community has regained its productive power through joint efforts that are to the honor of all the Atlantic people. But this restoration of national competing power, with no means of regulating it for the common purpose, can be as productive of depression now as it was in the 1920s. True again, the "Six Nations" of the Continent

---

* *Freedom Against Itself,* pp. 150-172.

have formed a common Coal and Steel Authority and a Common Market; but this advance has left Western Europe dangerously divided—literally at "Sixes and Sevens"—to say nothing of the far more dangerous economic division between Atlantica's European and American shores.

While the United States spent billions rebuilding Western European nations into such independent Daniels that they already beard the automobile lion in his Detroit den, Communist Russia has tightened its grip on the nations of Eastern Europe. By "specializing" their economies, it has tied them to its system to a degree and at a speed that make the integrating efforts of Western Europe's audacious "Six" seem trivial.

BALKANIZING THE WORLD FOR NATIONALISM'S BAAL

Since 1939 only the Russian and Chinese empires have strengthened their grip on the peoples they conquered in past centuries, and extended their empires. In this period the Atlantic countries have transformed practically all their empires into dozens of new sovereign nations. These have been admitted to the United Nations with all sides rejoicing for a cacophony of reasons. This reached its peak when the 1960 Assembly admitted fourteen new member nations, and Prime Minister Diefenbaker of Canada rose to ask: "How many human beings have been liberated by the U.S.S.R.?"—after he had proudly pointed out:

> Since the last war seventeen colonial areas and territories, comprising more than forty million people, have been brought to complete freedom by France. In the same period fourteen colonies and territories, comprising half a billion people have achieved complete freedom within the Commonwealth. Taken together some 600 million people in more than thirty countries, most of them now represented in this Assembly, have attained their freedom—this with the approval, the encouragement and the guidance of the United Kingdom, the Commonwealth and France.

This is indeed a record unique in the annals of empire, with such overtones of virtue in all concerned as to have drowned any discordant doubts. And yet . . . and yet . . . forty million divided by seventeen results in seventeen new nations with an average population of a bit more than two million each. Subtracting India and Pakistan from the 600 million, one finds that the population of the other dozen new Commonwealth nations averages only five million each.

Put together, these twenty-nine new nations sprung from the British and French empires average only 3.5 million people—only half the population of Balkan Bulgaria. In all the words that have welcomed these new nations, precious few have paused at these ominous facts.

Yet, great as is the virtue in this act of creation, the still unseen economic and political vice accompanying it is so plain that, to be seen, it needs but be stated: This "complete freedom" has also created dozens of new national barriers to trade and production, dozens of dubious new currencies, dozens of new visas and other vexations to commerce and travel, dozens of new doubts, uncertainties and new reasons to make private investors reluctant to risk their savings in potential Congos and Cubas. Dozens and dozens of these balkanizations of business have come, in freedom's name, to enshackle the economic growth which freedom requires. They have been added pell-mell to the super-abundance of these on the planet. Even in the 1920s there were enough to help bring on the recession that produced Mussolini, and the depression that put Hitler in power—even in nations as advanced as Italy and Germany.

The dragon's teeth which the United States sowed in those years by adding new barriers to the free flow of men, money and goods are now being scattered over the Earth as never before. There is every reason to fear that the example which the oldest democracies still set in economic nationalism will be followed with enthusiasm by the new nations, to their grief, and ours. These trappings of unlimited national sovereignty are no aid to them in their efforts to overcome their true foes—ignorance, disease and poverty—nor to us in our hopes of helping them win this war on which their true freedom depends. All these nationalistic bedevilments to their economies and ours serve only the ends of dictatorship.

They breed Lumumbas and Castros—or rather, they convert ambitious idealists into national dictators who fall easy prey to the Communist dictatorship. They encourage leaders in under-developed countries to believe their best hope for developing them quickly is to follow the methods that seem to have succeeded so well in backward Russia, rather than the free principles—political and economic—that led the British and the Americans to advance so much further against ignorance, disease and poverty. They lead these beginners to seek to make themselves strong by eating the swift-rising but poisonous mushroom, and shunning the fruit of the slow-growing, enduring Tree of Liberty and Life.

To think that the people of Atlantica can cope with this

huge problem while remaining as blind to these factors as
are our political leaders, pundits and press,—and while continuing to set the anarchic example around their own ocean,
and also while lacking the vision to call for Atlantic Union,
as Kwame Nkrumah calls for African Federation—this is
folly indeed.

"Those whom the gods would destroy they first make
mad"—and this is that kind of madness. The god that has
afflicted Atlantica with it is the Baal of unlimited national
sovereignty, on whose bloody, barren altars we have sacrificed so many of our finest hours, and men, and whose worship we have spread around the world far more than our
true religion. For our God lies in no collective form of
man, in no body politic—whether nation, state or tribe—but
in the only human body endowed with soul and conscience . . . individual man.

* * *

To turn back to my 1949 review of the preceding decade:

> Meanwhile, science and engineering have released
> atomic power and developed radar, the robot rocket,
> the jet plane, supersonic speed, germ warfare, and
> things still secret. At the same time free enterprise has
> further expanded mass production. Man has immensely
> magnified his power, both to build a far better world
> and to destroy civilization. Never did man's future
> seem so vast as it does today. Never did more massive
> catastrophe threaten to cut us all from it.

In the decade since, there have come sputniks orbiting the
Earth, Moon and Sun. They are witnesses enough to prove
that this awesome race has continued to accelerate. All too
clearly the dangers of "depression, dictatorship, false recovery and war are hemming us in" still, as when those
words appeared on page 1 of *Union Now* in 1939. Like
shadows they have stuck with us through political hurri-
canes, economic earthquakes and volcanic social eruptions.
And like shadows they have lengthened as we moved away
from our true direction—the West—and let our Light sink in
the heavens, lower and lower.

ALWAYS IGNORED, OPPORTUNITY TOO HAS REMAINED

For there to be shadow there must be light. And so let
us turn now to the opportunity that has also clung to us . . .
always ignored, while we followed our shadow, instead, to-

ward the idols of the East. At the start of the 1939-1949 decade, we Americans put our trust in neutralism and then in measures "short of war," while the British and French put theirs in alliance. When this combination of policies cost freedom the Continent, I wrote *Union Now with Britain* in 1940 to bring out the opportunity which that emergency offered. That book proposed that we form immediately a provisional union with the English-speaking democracies that then stood alone. The aim: To make sure that freedom would not only win the war but secure the peace by creating, while the iron was hot, the nucleus of the broader Atlantic federation that *Union Now* had proposed. The answer: No, this would bring us into the war. Six months later Hitler invaded Russia. When he was at the gates of Moscow while we stood petrified, an emboldened Japan Pearl Harbored us into the war we had sought to avoid by disunion of the free.

Now we Americans had the white heat of war to help leaders form the nuclear Atlantic Union which could win it with less loss of life, and greater assurance of peace and freedom. This opportunity, too, went begging. Japan and Hitler, in allying us to the Isles that had flowered then through (and in) Churchill, had tied us also to Stalin's Siberia—and we sought to achieve peace by treating them both on a par, and replacing the League of Nations with the United Nations league. The fatal defect of the former, people said, was not the one which *Union Now* set forth in chapter VII, but Washington's absence from Geneva. A league that began with both the United States and Soviet Russia could not but succeed. Remember?

While this policy was forming, the Wartime Edition of *Union Now* appeared in 1943, with three new chapters. They held that it was folly to trust either in a league that had no Atlantic Union in it, or in a dictatorship, even though it was our ally. To quote from the first of these chapters, entitled, "Again in Vain?"

> Now, once more, many think we are out of danger, but the end is not in sight. We Americans are hoping to secure peace by merely defeating and disarming the other side, or by establishing some kind of international organization, no matter what, just so it is backed by force, does not really limit our national sovereignty, and does not stir us too much from our mental ruts.
>
> America and all the United Nations are still far from applying the principles of *Union Now*. Yet, if one grants that *Union Now* has isolated the germ and pro-

vided the serum, then it must follow that peace cannot be had by other principles any more than malaria
can be ended by chasing butterflies. * * * Victory must
be disastrous if it is victory really for the anarchy of
national sovereignty among the democracies.

The second chapter agreed there was need for a universal
league, but took issue with those who put their hopes in
it, alone. It opposed alike those who urged this whether,
"in the name of idealism, universal union or nothing, the
brotherhood of man or bust," or as appeasers—"only now
it is Stalin before whom they would have the democracies
bow and scrape for fear he might do business with Germany, Japan or China"; or as "realists" who advocate alliance "as just as good and much cheaper" than union.
The chapter added: "The free can listen to these Pied
Pipers of 'idealism,' 'appeasement,' and 'realism'—but God
help their children if they do."

Wartime Warning Against the Communist Ally

"Russian hopes of expansion lie in the least developed
area of Europe," this 1943 edition noted, in warning against
trusting in dictatorship. "The only serious possibility of
Soviet Russia quickly over-running the world lies in the
continued disunion among the democracies. *The Soviet
Union, of course, has great potential power, and so have
China and India. But this power is potential. The power
of the democracies is immediate; they do not need precious
years to develop it. They need only unite to enjoy, in the
decisive years immediately following this war, the same great
opportunities to secure enduring peace in freedom that they
had in 1938.*" (Italics in original.)

"Suppose we of Atlantica form no Union now," the last
of these 1943 chapters concluded. "Suppose that all we do
is to organize, nation-to-nation, the United Nations. * * *
Now for the first time in Europe we have to reckon with
a great power whose possibilities of expansion do not solely
depend on the old European methods of conquest . . . Let
us assume the best. Let us assume that the Soviet Government in dissolving the Comintern definitely abandoned all
idea of spreading Communism, all idea of world revolution
. . . But suppose . . . that the very reasons that keep them
[the Atlantic democracies] from forming a Union now—
their prejudices, mutual distrust . . . wishful thinking, apathy, lack of political courage and vision—suppose all this
keeps them from working together on . . . complex prob-

lems better than they did before the war. The result—nothing essential is done and chaos rules. * * *

"Under this hypothesis . . . there is no Union of Democracies in which any people who desired to try our free way of life could hope to enter, or even turn to for support in their early struggles. Could you blame the Soviet Union for spreading thus willy nilly through Eastern Europe, Germany . . . China, the Americas? Nature abhors a vacuum not only in physics but also in politics. It was this kind of democratic vacuum that led to the Nazis spreading through Europe. And today, as in 1939, *Union Now* calls attention to the cause of the vacuum and the danger in it.

DEMOCRACY BETRAYED FOR DISUNION

"You can still dismiss *Union Now* as alarmist or visionary. You can still listen to those who see under its covers all manner of ghosts and goblins. You can defer action on it until it is no longer possible. You can make alliances or try half-measures such as the proposed United Nations organization. * * * But you cannot thereby keep other nations and other forces from organizing the world that the airplane and mass production imperatively demand. You cannot beat somebody with nobody, or with a semi-body.

"This war is a tremendous testing ground for all the various ways of life offered to humanity. Why has the prestige of the Soviet way risen so remarkably? Because Communist Russia has proved stronger than most people expected . . . Why has the prestige of the free gone down so badly? Because they disappointed expectations. Because they sold their opportunities for a mess of nationalism. Because they wrangled when they should have wrought. Because they identified democracy with disunion. * * *

"Where the success of the Soviet armies and factories have redounded to the prestige of Communism, even the successes of democracy in production, transportation and on the battlefield have redounded more to the credit of the U.S.A. or Britain than to democracy. They have served to keep nationalism alive rather than to give freedom itself the prestige it would have gained had merely these two peoples worked and fought as a Union of the Free.

"How can you expect our freedom to inspire the Russians . . . others, as it is? Take yourself. Have we yet achieved or undertaken anything in this war that stirred you to the soul, raised you out of your ordinary self, left you inspired? . . . The Founding Fathers knew that feeling. Hear James

Madison telling the Federal Convention: 'The government we mean to erect is intended to last for ages.' . . . Thirteen little democracies in a world ruled by great hereditary despots . . . Don't you think that all Americans want to share that sublime faith of the Founding Fathers, once before they die?

"If all the tears we shed, and cause others to shed in this war, are tears of grief and frustration, if none of them is a tear of joy—one of those heart-warming tears that well to the eyes when we see men do great good against great odds—if we have no such tears of joy to shed before this war is over, then God pity us in the bitter years to come."

THE POSTWAR OPPORTUNITY THE ATOM BROUGHT

That wartime opportunity was lost; instead of winning by the courage of statesmen and the proverbial power of union we won by the courage of millions of young men and the diabolic power of the atom bomb. Its explosion blew public opinion in the United States toward the view that peace was more important than freedom. Peace, by this view, must and could be gained only on a universal basis—by strengthening the United Nations with such steps toward universal world government as the atomic energy plan which the United States proposed—or the more radical steps in that direction that many Americans urged. In these conditions the Postwar edition of *Union Now* appeared with five new chapters. They pointed to ten such fallacies in current thought as these:

> The atomic weapon has made the need for world government much more urgent; therefore it has made all nations ripe for this . . . Every nation willing to try the free way of life is able to practice it; therefore there is no danger that the great mass of humanity that has never succeeded, in fact, in achieving free self-government will swamp the small minority that has achieved this, if these two groups should be united together in a world government.

Experience since then has made it no longer necessary to argue this. Nor does there seem need now to restate the major case the 1949 edition made, namely, that "freedom is the key to peace," that we must put it first, not second, or take it for granted, that freedom is "in a dangerous minority," that "mere European Union"—in which so many hopes then were placed—would leave freedom's cards dangerously divided between Europe and the United States, but that Atlantic Union could still give freedom the decisive power needed to preserve both itself and peace. True, so few yet understand all this that I wish there were room here for those pages in the Postwar edition—particularly those that explain why the principles and institutions of individual liberty make for peace as those of dictatorship make for war. Since the formation of the Atlantic alliance a few months after the appearance of that 1949 edition, however, we have at least been acting on the principle that the free Atlantic community *is* the citadel of peace.

Those postwar years when (be it repeated) we possessed a monopoly of atomic power—and practically of air, sea and production power—gave us another great opportunity to assure by Atlantic Union that freedom would shape the future. Again we let it slip through our hands—and again the event proved that the national advantages on which we counted were far less durable, and the price of disunion far higher, than any of us imagined. In the decade that began in 1950, dictatorship, we have noted, soon broke our atomic monopoly, and was challenging us in air and sea power, and boasting of "burying" us by its production in another decade. Instead of uniting the great scientific and technical resources of the Atlantic Community to advance freedom's lead, we sought to do this by keeping our scientific secrets as rigorously from the free as from dictatorship—and within nine years we were ignominiously trailing the latter in Space. Meanwhile we saw China's traditional friendship for us propagandized into unbelievable hatred.

THE LOST CHANCE TO SAVE THE GOOD IN EMPIRE

Meanwhile, too, we lost another great opportunity that Atlantic Union offered—that of developing democracy's non-self-governing territories as the Thirteen States did theirs—into new states in the Union. *Union Now* put this opportunity thus in chapter X:

> The Union's policy should be to train them [colonial territories] for admission to the Union as fully self-governing nations. It is true that one can destroy democracy by seeking to spread it too quickly and over-loading the state with too many voters untrained for self-government. It is also true, however, that the only way to acquire such training is to practise self-government, and that an old and well-trained democracy can safely and even profitably absorb a much greater proportion of inexperienced voters than seems theoretically possible.

Only Atlantic Union gave this possibility of liberating all the peoples in the Western empires, both as persons and nations, without the losses and dangers to them, and to freedom and peace that, it is all too evident now, were inherent in the policy followed. That policy was no doubt the better remaining alternative, but it destroyed the good with the bad in empires. Union allowed the bad to be eliminated while retaining the advantages for all concerned that unity in certain fields brings. Such unity would have hastened building the sound political and economic foundations that are needed, even by the most experienced democratic peoples, to maintain freedom.

Out of Atlantica came more than the principles of individual and of national freedom to which all the world pays at least lip service now. Out of it came also the federal union way to combine individual and national freedom to the advantage of both, and save them from the twin dangers of anarchy and tyranny to which each remains always exposed.

Around 1950 the people of the United States faced a choice between these two concepts they had fathered—a choice much more crucial than anyone realized then. Their Declaration of Independence had already encouraged every colonial people to seek its combination of democratic government and national sovereignty. By leading the way with Atlantic Union while the empires of Western Europe still held vast territories in trust, the American people could have worked out the problems of imperialism with them the federal way—and thus established through all this great area the higher democratic pattern of free federation. Unlike imperialism, federal union gives an equal status to every citizen and an equal dignity and independence to every state, large or small, developed or undeveloped, old or new, Founder or Fiftieth State—whether it be Texas or Delaware, New York or Alaska, Virginia or Hawaii.*

THE WAY OF HAWAII AND THE WAY OF THE CONGO

The multiracial people of Hawaii provide an enlightening example of the difference—as regards status, preparation for self-government, guarantees of freedom, economic development and political future—between the territory of a free federation and that of the freest of imperial powers. Even before their admission to statehood in the Union, the Hawaiians enjoyed far greater advantages in all these respects

* See "Federalism's Expansion Principle," chapter 20, *The New Federalist* by Publius II (Harper & Bros., 1950).

than the peoples to whom imperialism points as its star exhibits.*

While still a territory, the people of Hawaii enjoyed practically every advantage the people of any state enjoyed, with this major exception—they had no voice in electing the President of the United States and no voting representation in Congress. Statehood put them on a par in these respects with every citizen and every state in the Union. One of their two United States Senators is an American of Chinese origin, while their Representative in the House is one of Japanese descent. Each has precisely the same great power that each of his white, and black, colleagues possesses—the power of casting the single vote that often makes a majority and thus decides the policy of the United States on the gravest issues.†

All the dignity, freedom and self-government that each colonial people rightly sought could have been assured them by the time-tested way that delivered all this, and much more besides, to each of the Thirteen Colonies and all the Fifty United States—without the fearful price which the balkanizing alternative inevitably costs. By pledging themselves in an Atlantic Constitution to prepare each people in their trust for self-government and admission to the Union as early as practicable as a fully self-governing state,‡ the people of Atlantica could have given, on a world scale, an object lesson in the immense advantages of free federation in solving the problem that underdeveloped peoples present.

Instead, we Americans let all our weight continue behind the last paragraph in the Declaration of Independence—and therefore against its great opening principles and the Federal Constitution they produced. And so the people of Atlantica went dizzily down the road that gave the Congo the costly illusions of national independence, an equal but powerless vote in the United Nations and a precarious choice at home between domestic and foreign dictatorship. With never an effort to set humanity the higher goal we had found, we prided ourselves more than ever on making "complete free-

---

* That these advantages for Hawaii resulted from the virtues of free federal union rather than from any national superiority seems evident from the fact that race prejudice afflicts many more white Americans than Frenchmen, or Britons.

† Incidentally, the Senate Foreign Relations Committee approved the Atlantic Convention on Feb. 10, 1960, by a vote of eight to seven. Had this majority of one been the other way, the measure would not have reached the Floor and action would have been deferred to the new Congress, meeting in 1961.

‡ As *Union Now* proposed in Article II, sections 2 and 4, of its "Illustrative Constitution." (See Book II, first annex.)

dom" mean only complete national sovereignty. The more un-prepared the people for self-government and the greater the consequent danger of continued poverty, disease, ignorance, dictatorship and war, the more we speeded the world's balkanization. Faced with a faltering United Nations league, we sought to save it by saddling it helter-skelter with still spinier problems to be solved by more and more inexperienced, sovereign nations.

Granted, the problems European empires left were much harder to solve the federal way than those the American Union solved. Even so, the Balkan way was no answer, but only a jump from the frying pan into the fire. Granted, we still have an opportunity to make free federal union the world's future pattern. The continents of Latin America and Africa, and much of Asia may still be to a North Atlantic Union what the Far West was to the Union of the Thirteen States, namely, a vast area capable of immense development, politically and economically, to the equal advantage of all concerned, by the federal principle uniting it in generations ahead—whether as new states in the union of the Free, or through the growth first of federations in Latin America, Africa, Asia, or by mixture of the two procedures. True, this great opportunity is still ours—but it is no less true that our balkanization of the world has made the problem infinitely harder, and more urgent and dangerous, than it was twenty years ago, or ten, or one.

Some Europeans Who Kept Opportunity With Us

Despite all the missed opportunities, opportunity has re-mained within reach of the free because they have thrown overboard enough impedimenta to stay in the race—though not enough to keep the lead they still had in the early 1950s, nor to keep from falling more and more behind since then. By my standards, the greatest contributions that kept At-lantica in the running were made before and during the war by the British, and since then by the Six Nations of Western Europe, and the United States and Canada. (These standards of mine are not merely the principles of *Union Now:* They include those of *noblesse oblige*—how far a people justifies its privileges, lives up to its responsibilities and ideals, turns its assets to the greatest good. I would add to the parable of the talents this thought: From him who hath the most ad-vantages, the most can rightfully be required, and to him who hath the most handicaps, relatively more honor should go for what he achieves.)

For almost a year and a half the British stood up, alone,

for all Atlantica. Like the French in World War I they bore
the brunt of the battle and held the Verduns until reinforce-
ments arrived. After heroic efforts, whether moral or physical, anyone needs rest. Perhaps that explains why the French
failed in 1940 to live up to their great name as soldiers, and
why the British since 1945 have clung to their most outworn
ideas, and have done relatively so little to build free government (the field they once led), on the scale of the ocean
that cradled their power.

Since the war the Dutch and the Belgians, though handicapped by their small numbers, and by neutrality's sterile
traditions combined with invasion's embittering disillusionment, have lighted the way of the future with Benelux.

The French, whose Jean Monnet and Charles de Gaulle
were the first to propose the 1940 offer of Franco-British
Union * that Churchill made a little too late, were also the
first to propose officially the creation of an Atlantic alliance.
General Pierre Billotte in 1946-47 persuaded the Paris Government to authorize him to urge on General George C.
Marshall (who proved very receptive) a much more advanced
organization than NATO is even now.

The French also led the fight for European Union that
Churchill launched but did not long continue. They, who
alone were burdened with emotions piled high by three invasions since 1870, threw off the most impedimenta. Under
the leadership of Robert Schuman, Edouard Herriot, Georges
Bidault, Vincent Auriol, Guy Mollet, Paul Reynaud, Maurice Schumann—and now Charles de Gaulle—they have carried reconciliation with the Germans the farthest toward
union, in the establishment of the Council of Europe and
the much more advanced Coal and Steel Community,
Euratom and the Common Market of the Six Nations.

Reconciliation and union require more than one nation.
These achievements could not have been done without
Benelux, and such Belgians as Paul-Henri Spaak, Frans van
Cauwelaert, and Paul Van Zeeland, such Dutchmen as J. W.
Beyen, Henri Brugmans and Paul Rykens. Nor without Italy.
It has had the handicap of *fascismo* to overcome—but demo-
cratic statesmen of the calibre of Count Sforza, Alcide de
Gasperi, Gaetano Martino, to restore its true glory.

The Western Germans merit special praise for throwing
off so soon the worst poisons and humiliations that any Atlantic people has suffered. Rising from rubble and cigarette

* See "De Gaulle Urged Federal Union on Churchill in 1940," July
1958 *Freedom & Union,* a research report based on their memoirs
and other sources. A reprint of this may be had from *Freedom &
Union* for 10¢.

currency, their economic genius not only led in Europe's re-
covery, but—more important—the spirit that created the free
Hanseatic cities produced incredibly, from the ruins of
Cologne and Berlin, three mayor-made Gibraltars of free-
dom: The towering Konrad Adenauer, the heroic Ernest
Reuter and Willy Brandt.

THE CONTRIBUTIONS THE U. S. HAS MADE TO ATLANTICA

Let us turn now to the American people. Their isolationism and neutralism had made them the one absentee at the
Geneva League which their own Woodrow Wilson had
founded; they threw off this incubus in 1945 and entered the
United Nations. Under President Truman they continued to
discard other impedimenta in a swift series of moves, each
an immense break with the past—however inadequate
from the standpoint of the immediate future. First came
1947's bold guarantee of the Greeks and the once "terrible"
Turks—at the point of Europe most remote from Washington and most touchy for Moscow. That year ended with the
far-sighted Plan that Will Clayton conceived, General Marshall fathered and Britain's Ernest Bevin mid-wifed—a Plan
so generous that only Moscow's *nyet* kept it from restoring
Eastern as well as Western Europe, and Russia besides.

Then in 1949—thanks to Stalin's blockade of Berlin, the
one city where the squabbling Americans, British and French
had joint vital interests, and forces—the United States threw
overboard its historic injunctions against entering "entangling
alliances" with Europe. It followed President Truman and
Secretary Acheson and Senator Vandenberg in forming (with
powerful assists from Britain's Ernest Bevin and Canada's
Lester Pearson*) the North Atlantic Treaty Organization.
Thereafter came the arming of NATO—under the leadership
of General Eisenhower and General Gruenther—with the
most entangling and advanced form of international force
ever achieved in a military alliance. There followed (with
Secretary Dulles leading, and Secretary Generals Ismay and
Spaak doing the groundwork) the development of the NATO
Council into an instrument of political consultation which set
another new high for the alliance system. Thereafter came,

---

* Mr. Pearson fathered the most constructive provision in the
North Atlantic Treaty, Article 2 by which the Parties pledge "further development of peaceful and friendly international relations by
strengthening their free institutions, by bringing about a better understanding of the principles upon which these institutions are founded, and by promoting conditions of stability and well-being," and
by seeking "to eliminate conflict and encourage economic collabor-
ation."

too, the establishment in 1955, of the annual NATO Parliamentarians Conference, fathered by the Speaker of the Canadian Senate, Wishart McL. Robertson, Finn Moe, M.P. of Norway, and these members of the United States Congress: Senators Estes Kefauver and Guy Gillette, Representatives James P. Richards and Wayne Hays.

By this series of moves toward Atlantic Union, Western Europe was restored, the Atlantic Community was made aware of itself, and Communism's advance in Europe was halted. Thus freedom survived, and its great opportunity remains at the door. And now the United States has put forward a hand—the Atlantic Convention—that can unlock the door and seize the opportunity.

WHAT IS THE KEY CAUSE OF IT ALL?

When all credit is given, troubling questions remain. What brought on us the hurricane, earthquake, holocaust? Why have such vast danger and opportunity moved us too little, too slowly? Freedom-and-union blessed us Atlanticans with the greatest advantages—why have we done no more with them? Why have we, the community that is still far more advanced politically and economically than any other on earth, advanced so gropingly, so timidly, so snailishly through these fifteen postwar years? How does it come that Russia, burdened by the poverty and ignorance of unbroken ages of tyranny, has risen so much faster from the war that left Russia in ruins . . . and America intact? Have the people of Atlantica lost their purpose and grown soft . . . through the high standards of living democracy brought them? Is that the answer? Long ago Tocqueville warned:

> While men devote themselves to this honest and legitimate search for a better material life, they need beware lest they finish by losing the use of their most sublime faculties and, in seeking to improve their surroundings, end by degrading themselves. There, and not elsewhere, lies the danger. * * *

> When the materialists have proved sufficiently that they are not brutes, they seem as proud as though they had proved themselves gods.

> Materialism is everywhere a dangerous disease of the human spirit, but it is to be guarded against particularly by a democratic people, for it combines marvellously with their common vice. Democracy encourages a taste for material satisfactions. This taste, if it becomes

excessive, leads men soon to believe that matter alone counts; materialism, in turn, leads them to pursue material satisfactions with a senseless ardor. Such is the vicious circle into which democratic nations are pulled. To hold themselves back, they need to see this danger.*

To say that our high standards of living have thus softened us for the kill would be a bleak answer indeed. All the new nations, and all humanity, are now eager to gain the material comforts we have attained; they seek these much more avidly than the high moral principle of freedom-and-union which brought us these fruits. What draws them most to Moscow is that the Communist dictatorship seems to have found a shortcut by which under-developed nations can more quickly attain greater material rewards. But Tocqueville also pointed out:

> Man has risen above the beasts because he used his soul to gain the material goods they gain by instinct only. The angel in man taught the beast in him the art of satisfying his needs. It is because Man is capable of rising above the body and sacrificing his own life [for what he believes in]—a quality that beasts have no conception of—that he has found out how to multiply his bodily satisfaction to a degree that they can not conceive of either.†

If we who have proved this most by our respect for the "angel in man"—if we have already fallen victims of materialism to the point where we can no longer surpass the Communist dictatorship, then what hope can there be for humanity in the triumph of the system that begins by making materialism its god, and denies each human being the spark of God that makes him a man?

LOOKING UP TO HEAVEN, NOT MERELY UP TO SPACE

There is much to make one believe that where our Founding Fathers looked up to Heaven, we look up to Space. But there is more to persuade me, for one, that this bleak answer is not the key cause of our present problem. The free people of Atlantica need to be more vigilant against materialism—but they have by no means succumbed to it. They are not soft, nor have they lost their high purpose. Look at the

* Tocqueville, *Democracy in America*, Part IV, chapter 15 (my translation).
† *Ibid.*, Part IV, chapter 16 (my translation).

way they have responded to all the highest and hardest appeals their leaders have made to them. Look how the British rose to the faith that Churchill had in them . . . Remember the response of the French to de Gaulle . . . the Germans to Adenauer . . . the Italians to de Gasperi . . .

Consider the prodigious efforts we Americans made in the war and—more important—how our people responded to every effort our leaders asked of us then, and since then, no matter how great the break with our past or how heavy the sacrifice.* Entry into the United Nations . . . sacrifice of sovereignty in the Acheson atomic plan . . . guaranty of Turkey and Greece . . . Marshall Plan . . . Atlantic alliance . . . upholding the United Nations by war in Korea . . . carrying a heavy unending taxation burden for foreign aid—there has not been a single great thing asked of the American people since the war that they and their representatives in Congress have not promptly delivered, no matter how much power was divided between the parties, between the Houses, and between the Congress and President.

Compare this recent record with that which followed World War I—the Senate's rejection of the Covenant inspired by so great a President as Woodrow Wilson, and the people's return to "normalcy" with Harding, and their appearance as "Uncle Shylock," with Coolidge's "they hired the money." Compare the two postwar periods . . . and then say whether the fault since 1939 lies in the people having too many gadgets, and too many mass media . . . or in their leadership seeing too many ghosts, and having too little faith in themselves, and in their fellow-citizens ever to look up to, instead of down on, the American people—ever to ask them to seize the great opportunity there at the door.† . . .

Henry L. Stimson in his memoirs, *On Active Service,* which he wrote in the third person, thus characterized his own role in the period between World Wars I and II: "To himself he seemed adventurous." In reviewing the book in *The New York Times Book Review,* Gerald W. Johnson noted:

* I shall never forget hearing Will Clayton, Joseph Grew and Justice Owen J. Roberts stress this fact to Dean Acheson, then Secretary of State, when he received one afternoon a delegation of Atlantic Unionists I was privileged to be in.

† For my part, I confess I would have despaired, had not my direct and widespread knowledge of the American people always kept me looking up to them, and expecting greatness from them—not 13-year-old mentalities. This may seem strange, in view of the time it has taken to get even an Atlantic Convention called, but the answer is that it would have been called much sooner had Presidents whom the people trusted had my own trust in the American people.

It is sufficient commentary on the failure of state-craft in the Long Armistice that a man doing the obviously prudent and necessary thing should have seemed adventurous to himself. "The political history of Postwar Europe," he [Stimson] comments bitterly, can easily be read as a series of great hopes meanly lost. Stimson emphatically refuses to try and exculpate himself or his colleagues as they blundered from war to war.

"The besetting sin of the nations was nationalism, that of the statesmen was timidity," Stimson concluded. To themselves they all seemed adventurous, but the most courageous among them ended by finding they were, in fact, cowards.

There is much to make one believe that their continued rash caution is the cause of the disasters that we have suffered, the opportunities we have missed, the plight we are in. But to me this, like our sins of materialism, is only a contributing factor. There are many such factors, of course. It may seem foolhardy to single out one as the key cause, but to do this is essential—as essential as it was for Pasteur to single out one invisible microbe, when anthrax slew the sheep. If we are not venturesome enough to try to do this, we are cowards indeed, and doomed to fail.

The Master Key to Pandora's Hotel: Confusion over Sovereignty

Amid the hotel-keeper's mass of keys, there is a master key that seems no more important than the rest, but does open all the doors. There is also a master key, I believe, to our disasters, our missed opportunities, our balkanization of continents, our suicidal policies, and to the timidity of our leaders, the fear of popular opposition that prevents them from doing what they know is right, and the sense of hopelessness that keeps so many, in politics, diplomacy, press and the public, from tackling openly—or at all—the dragon ahead that is blocking us all.

The key cause, I believe, is the continuing confusion of the free over sovereignty. That this confusion should continue is only too understandable, for the democratic concept of sovereignty does leave the people, like the subjects of Baal's Jezebel, between two opinions. Looked at the old way, the sovereign is the nation, the state. The sovereign is collective man, whether federation, kingdom, city republic or tribe, and whether the body politic be incarnated in a divine right autocrat or in a tribal divinity—a Baal whom man was made to serve. Looked at the democratic way, the sovereign is the citizen—equally each of the people who make the state, and make it to serve life, liberty, and greater happiness to them *individually*—and who count on "the angel" in each of them to make this concept work.

So much does this concept count, in fact, on the God in every soul that Rousseau found that "democracy is a government for gods, but unfit for men"—and put his faith instead in the older idea, which he disguised as *la volonté générale*—"the general will." * It is more often known today as the "national interest," "the collective will," "the dictatorship of the proletariat," the "totalitarian state."

The confusion over the democratic concept begins when a number of democratic states arise in a region, for then all these free people must answer the question: Which is our true sovereign, which shall we recognize as supreme, in our dealings with one another—the state or the citizen, our nation or our soul? They must answer, in short, the probing question Elijah put to the Hebrews: Which is the Lord—Baal, or the God who speaks with a still, small voice inside each individual? Between them we have remained . . . with two opinions. We Atlanticans have kept God above Baal within each of our nations, and have kept Baal above God in our Atlantic community. We still seek to serve both Jesus and Jezebel.

For twenty-seven years now I have tried, in books, articles, talks, to end this confusion. The only clear result is that I have not done so. Nor have better men. There is some little comfort in noting how confused, and confusing, so many great men of the past have been on this subject—and I shall share with you in chapter 7 some of this comfort. No matter from what angle you approach the democratic concept of sovereignty, you soon find that it is not the simple thing it seemed at first. And yet, like all great truths, it must be simple.

The confusion surrounding it is a most difficult fog to see through, and clear away. Yet I am completely convinced that until, and unless, this subject of sovereignty is clarified greatly, there will be, and can be, only stumbling little steps foredoomed to disaster—and no possibility whatever of our grasping in time our immense opportunity. After pondering all that has happened since *Union Now* appeared, and studying how I might contribute most at this stage to its program, principle and philosophy, I came to this conclusion: Freedom, peace and man's vast future will all stand or fall on how clearly we understand our democratic concept of sovereignty.

* Felix Morley has much to say on this in his book, *Freedom and Federalism* (Regnery 1960) which one should read.

And so I threw out the work I had done on concrete questions, and have devoted most of the chapters in this book to this subject.

In them I try to clarify sovereignty by approaching it from several angles, but mainly by throwing on it the searching light that American history provides. I concentrate so much on the latter for two reasons (plus those in the Introduction): A) My deep respect for Europe's many achievements includes admiration for the rare grasp a few Europeans have had even of United States history and federalism—fields in which Europe generally is not at its best. In other words, I agree with Tocqueville and other exceptional European observers that democratic sovereignty is the subject on which everyone can learn most from United States history. B) Finally, I agree with Lord Acton, and the British in general, that in questions so complex as political ones, example and experience provide the wisest guides.

In writing *Union Now* originally, I studied much more American history than its few references to this might suggest. I thought I had also gained an understanding of sovereignty in my ten years covering the League of Nations. Since then I have learned far more than I then knew about both sovereignty and its history in America. This has confirmed but clarified the basic view of sovereignty I gave in *Union Now.** This is true, too, of the chapters that follow. In writing them, I have added so much to my own understanding, at least, as to make me comprehend better why Sir Isaac Newton said that he was but picking up pebbles on the seashore of truth.

Yet if one picks up the right pebble, and aims it as truly as David, Goliath himself can be conquered. It is time that he should fall.

CONTINUED TRAGEDY—OR TRIUMPHANT ENDING?

So swiftly have the years flown for me since *Union Now* appeared, that it comes as a shock to realize that children who were born then are old enough to vote today—the boys to bear arms, the girls to bear children. A new generation has risen that was too young to read the editions of 1939, 1940, 1941, and 1943. Millions of new human beings who were just learning to read fairy tales when the last edition appeared in 1949 are in high school today—old enough to take part in the current interscholastic debate on Atlantic Union. The generation I addressed on page 52 of *Union Now* in 1939—

* See especially chapters VI, VII, IX, XIII in Book II.

those with whom I played cowboy and hide-and-go-seek—
they are grandparents now, as I am. And our grandchildren
are the ones who will die Communists—if Mr. Khrushchev
is right, and his concept of sovereignty continues to divide
the free.

"Some day . . . something like what Mr. Streit suggests
will have to come to pass, either now or after we and our
children's children have waded anew through flowing rivers
of blood." So wrote the historian, James Truslow Adams, in
reviewing *Union Now* in *The New York Times* in 1939.
Nothing like it was done by parents then. Their children
went to war as they came of age. Must their children's children continue to fulfill that prophecy—because parents continue to be "too busy to read" or to help assure that something like what *Union Now* suggests will be tried—*now?*

"The reader of *Union Now*," Mr. Adams continued, "will
feel Fate marching on with the inevitable footfalls of a Greek
tragedy as the author takes up one alternative after another
and shows the certain futility of them all . . . If all alternatives are futile and this solution is impossible, what
then? The answer—misery, chaos, untold horror—lends a
tragic and poignant emotion to the slow moving, but states-
manlike pages of *Union Now*."

Now the stage is set at the Atlantic Convention for the
greatest act in this drama. For my part, I am not discouraged
by democracy's painful process of trying error always first.
I believe that, with freedom-and-union now, we can not
only bury Communism, as completely as we did Hitler, but
do it without world war. I see our children's children—and
even us grandparents—enjoying a higher civilization than
we dream of . . . no utopia, but something as real as the
immense advance that men have made since the principle of
freedom-and-union began its miracles on this continent in
1789.

My faith that this will come about is not blind faith. It is
lit by the most lucid thought I am capable of. If this book
should succeed in making this reasoning clear and simple
enough for anyone to understand, then this faith should be
contagious . . . and we shall, together, bring the long tragedy
of our century to a triumphant ending. But faith is shown
by works, not words. In the end, all depends on how we
each answer the double-barbed question which a still small
Voice put to Elijah, when he too had fled to the wilderness
. . . "What doest thou here?"

The NATO Nations as Founders of the Union

With firmness in the right, as God gives us to see the right.—*Abraham Lincoln.*

If I were revising or re-writing *Union Now,* what changes would I make? None in its poem (to follow the chronological order in which its three parts were originally written*), none in its philosophy, and some in its proposal—even though none even there that I consider to be major changes. I say this at the risk of being considered rigid, and criticized as suffering an acute case of author's pride. Two principles, however, have long guided me, and proved their worth so well that I shall stick to them. One I got from Descartes in my teens and have confirmed from experience, namely, that it is wise never to cease subjecting even one's firmest convictions, conclusions or working hypotheses to reconsideration in the light of greater knowledge, events, failures, shortfalls, and criticism by oneself and others.

To know or feel in my heart that an idea is the offspring of fallacious reasoning, or of ignorance of certain facts, and yet to cling to it because I was the first to be seduced by it, or am publicly identified with it—this does not appeal to me. I find it more satisfying, and exciting, to keep on guard against one of our common fallacies, which Georges de la Fouchardière pointed out in 1918 to this reader of his column in *L'Oeuvre.* He wrote that, with ideas as with other property, once we acquire them—and no matter how we happen to get them—we defend them with our life's blood, and the devil's readiest weapons, whenever anyone tries to take them from us.

The other guiding principle I got as a boy, when learning to shoot a rifle, and later had hammered into me as a newspaper reporter, namely, the importance of trying always to be accurate. To make a virtue of understatement seems to

---

* The poem and the chapter on the philosophy "Of Freedom and Union" were written, the former in 1928, the latter (in first draft) in 1932, for other books that I have never finished. After the basic idea of Atlantic Union of the Free came to me, late in 1933, and grew into *Union Now,* I rewrote and expanded the philosophy behind it, and later added the poem, which seemed to me to fit in this picture, too.

me as wrong as to practise over-statement (unless humor is one's purpose). The aim should be to hit the target, not to shoot over it, or under. We all need to know the facts just as they are. This requires that they be expressed as accurately as one can humanly present them, neither swollen nor shrunken so as to make the speaker or writer appear the better, or to enable him to "play it safe."

WHERE I WOULD ALTER *Union Now*

When I say that I would not change any of what I consider to be the fundamentals in *Union Now,* I would like this statement to be understood as the product of those two guiding thoughts. I would add that although frequent reconsideration of the fundamentals in *Union Now* in the light of events, criticisms, alternative proposals, and further study, has strengthened my belief in them, this does not mean that if I were re-writing *Union Now* today it would be the same throughout—apart from obvious differences between 1960 and 1939. There would be a number of changes, some of which others might consider major. To me they are secondary, and would tend mainly to bring out more clearly and strongly the basic principles of the original, put them in better perspective by more accurate evaluations, and adapt them better to practical application in the present and looming situations.

In the Postwar edition I dealt with nine of these changes in new Chapter 3, "Were I Re-Writing *Union Now.*" I would refer those interested to it—particularly to understand why I now attach even greater value to individual freedom as the key to peace and to production, and would emphasize even more the importance of power to freedom and peace, and why I now think that free federal principles are likely to spread gradually around the world in a different way than I originally suggested.

Even more now than in 1949, I believe that the immense impulse toward free federation, resulting from the creation of the Atlantic Union, will lead not merely to our Union's expansion through the admission of new member nations, but also to the creation of regional free federations by other nations—for example, in Southern Asia, among the Arab nations, in Africa and in Latin America, I believe, too, that it will encourage the long suffering Chinese and Russian peoples eventually to transform those dictatorships into free unions themselves. As all these processes gradually develop, as present difficulties are lessened and better means of overcoming them acquired, and as men profit from the incalculable and increasing moral and material power that these Unions of the Free would produce, one could reasonably expect the latter to federate with each other. Or they could be transforming meanwhile the United Nations—to which they would all belong—gradually into a federation.

All this is, as the Germans would say, music of the future. But consider how man's scientific and technical development has continued to confirm through both decades since 1939 what *Union Now* noted then on page 49:

> If we compare each decade of the past thirty years with the decade before it, we shall have some clue to the accumulating speed with which the machine will be making our world one during the next decade—if our failure to provide the machine with a governor does not meanwhile wreck it and us.

If we have the creative imagination needed to keep this factor in mind, we may find that Tennyson's "Parliament of Man," which now seems as far distant as going to the Moon seemed in 1950, may not be in fact so far ahead.

THE FOUNDERS OF THE ATLANTIC UNION

The main change I would make in *Union Now* relates to the founders, and results from the establishment of NATO since the Postwar edition appeared. This brings us to one of these necessities that keep recurring in human affairs— the necessity of marrying the ideal and the practical if anything living is to be created in good time—and the promising progress toward free government in the past to last, and the offspring to flourish. And so I would first emphasize now, even more than in 1939, the principles underlying nuclear union of the free. I would continue to stress the importance of proposing a concrete list of founders. But I would make clearer that it is no hard and fast list, and that adjustments can, and should, be made according to conditions obtaining at the time of action.

The essentials continue to me to be that (a) the nucleus of the Union should be composed of relatively few nations, (b) these should be strong enough in both material and moral power and ties, to assure the Union from the start enough power for it to have a reasonable hope of winning, without war, against dictatorship, depression and disintegration, and (c) the ratio of experienced to inexperienced democratic peoples or "problem" nations among the founders should be great enough to give a stronger guaranty of individual freedom than any practical alternative can.

From the standpoint of experience in free government—to which I continue to attach decisive importance—the fifteen founders I suggested in *Union Now* remain in my opinion the ideal list. I have long believed that one should aim clearly at what one finds to be ideal, *and* that this aim in itself rules out the possibility of achieving the ideal at the outset. One cannot seek an objective and at the same time have it in hand. To move toward the ideal, and to achieve it completely in the end,* one must start with less than the ideal, because of the practical considerations that always necessarily affect any attempt to translate thought into action, and turn ideals into realities.

The practical question we must always face in the present enterprise is: Just which of the ideal list of peoples experienced in free government offers the most reasonable hope of forming, with just which other peoples, a sound nuclear Union of the Free at any given time? The answer is bound to vary with conditions prevailing at the time one must answer it.

It was one thing when Hitlerian Germany, militarist Japan and Fascist Italy formed the most imminent danger facing all of the fifteen I nominated as founders in 1939. When Communist Russia made its pact with Nazi Germany and enabled Hitler to conquer all the experienced democracies on the Continent, except Switzerland and Sweden, which dictatorship surrounded, one had to start with the seven English-speaking democracies that remained, if one were to start at all. In these circumstances I proposed in 1940-41 in *Union Now with Britain* that these seven form a provisional union to meet this emergency. I stressed that this smaller nucleus was meant to grow into the larger Union with the liberation of the other democracies, but the book's title has led many to assume that *Union Now* aims at an exclusively English-speaking Union—a project which that book rejected.

THE NATO FIFTEEN AND *Union Now*'S FIFTEEN

With the liberation and victory I returned to the broader original proposal. After the North Atlantic alliance was formed by the United States, Canada, Britain, France, the

---

* One must achieve, in fact, more than the ideal in the end, for one's standards and means of attaining them improve in the process of seeking to attain the original goal.

Netherlands, Belgium and Luxemburg, I urged that these seven form the nucleus for an Atlantic Union, too. I supported the Atlantic Union resolutions that were introduced in Congress in the sessions of 1949, 1951 and 1955; they solved the problem of the nucleus by inviting the seven sponsors of the Atlantic alliance to send delegates to a convention which would be authorized to explore how they might best form a union, and to invite "such other democracies" as they thought wise to join them in the work of the convention.

Meanwhile, NATO grew larger, and a variety of other factors made it increasingly difficult to restrict the Convention nucleus to the seven sponsors, and increasingly practical to begin with all the fifteen NATO nations. Although the number—fifteen—is the same as *Union Now* proposed in 1939, the composition is quite different. Of the original *Union Now* fifteen, the fifteen NATO nations include only eight—the United States, Canada, Britain, France, Belgium, the Netherlands, Denmark and Norway. My other seven —Australia, Eire, Finland, New Zealand, Sweden, Switzerland and the Union of South Africa—are replaced in the NATO fifteen by Iceland, Luxemburg, the German Federal Republic, Greece, Italy, Portugal and Turkey. Clearly the last five are much less experienced in free government than are the missing seven of the *Union Now* list—with the exception of the Union of South Africa, where a most undemocratic racism has ruled in recent years.

Facing this choice between the "more ideal" and the "more practical," my weighing of the various factors involved leads me to conclude that we should aim now at an Atlantic Union composed of the NATO fifteen. The Atlantic Convention allows this possibility to be explored without further delay. I believe it can work out a plan to federate these fifteen to what I consider a minimum but decisive degree.

If this does not prove possible, one must re-examine the problem—perhaps even in the Convention—in the light of the situation then obtaining. Events may make it practical to try to federate a more ideal group more fully. Or they may make it imperative to try to start on a less ideal basis. All that we can be sure of now is that by making the most of the opportunity which the Convention offers, we shall learn more than we could learn otherwise, and be more likely to succeed thereafter.

Having stated this conclusion, I would now give some of the reasoning that has gone into it. To me the important question is this: Is the NATO group sufficiently loaded on the side of democratic experience, and community of background and interest, to make it reasonably possible to federate these nations on a sound free basis? I find the answer is clearly, Yes. The question is one of ratio. So long as the percentage of inexperience and other weakening factors is considerably less than half, or as small as in the present instance, I think it is safe. Perhaps a comparison—however odious comparisons may be—will clarify the point.

ATLANTIC UNION AND EUROPEAN UNION: EXPERIENCE VS. INEXPERIENCE

Much as I applaud the Six Nations of Europe for the Common Market they have achieved, I find that in these Six the ratio of inexperience to experience in free government is dangerously high for sound political union. The three members that have the longest record in stable free government—those of Benelux—form only 11 per cent of the total population. In a free federal Union, population is, in final analysis, the long term dominating factor. The twenty million people of Benelux cannot possibly suffice to keep on the side of liberty a union with a total population of 170 millions.

Free government in France has had so checkered a career as to make some doubtful of it, but personally I would readily include France with Benelux, as an experienced democracy. The many and magnificent contributions to freedom the French have made since the 18th century, leave no uncertainty in my mind about them. But when we add the French to Benelux, the combined population of those experienced in freedom remains a minority in the Six Nations. The Germans and Italians would form the majority, with 105 million of its 170 million population. Though they have made very promising progress toward free government in the past century, and particularly since World War II, who can forget how the Italian democracy gave way to Fascist dictatorship in the early 1920s—or how the German democracy succumbed to a far more sinister dictatorship in 1933?

An individual needs to learn to know his weaknesses and be on guard against them in his own interest; so it is with nations, too. The great majority of Germans and Italians want their present experiment in democracy to succeed. They have suffered much more than the rest of us from dictatorship. And so they have even more reason than I to doubt that a political union of the Six Nations would provide sufficient brakes against a recurrence of dictatorship when it faced such crises as depression or war. Certainly it is not surprising that many people in Benelux and France are reluctant to convert their economic union into a political one. They realize that such a Union, even with federation's checks against majority rule, would expose their heroically won liberties to a government where the majority would be composed of peoples whose efforts to govern themselves in freedom have not yet withstood the strain of any major emergency. This illustration will serve to show why I am chary of any Union where the factor of experience in free government is not very strong from the outset.

But whereas inexperience would dominate from the start in a European Six Nation Union, it would be in a minority in an Atlantic Union. Add Portugal, Greece and Turkey to West Germany and Italy, and still this group would form less than one-third of the population of an Atlantic Union composed of the fifteen NATO nations, which would total 471,000,000—with 322,000,000 of them long experienced in free government.

In such an Atlantic Union the United States, Britain and Canada would form more than half (249,000,000) of its total population. The majority of its people from the start would thus contribute to its success the world's longest experience in maintaining stable free government, and a two-party system, on a vast scale of population and area. From the start, too, it would have another advantage—more than 40 per cent of its population could contribute the long experience in maintaining vast, free federal unions that the United States and Canada have. All this would help assure that the constitution of such a Union would be soundly built—and that its statesmen could meet the dangers and difficulties of its early, formative years more successfully than a Union of the Six Nations could.

Add to this solid center the experience and varied contributions to free government that Belgium, Denmark, France, Iceland, Luxemburg and Norway offer, and this core expands into a two-thirds majority of the Union, in number of nations as well as in population—in both its Senate and House. This would also be the proportion of people and peoples in it who would contribute another important asset to success—the fact that they had never fought each other for nearly a century and a half. This contrasts sharply with the emotional volcano that may still be smouldering under the European Six, 65,000,000 of whom were fighting the other 105,000,000 less than twenty years ago—with the majority advantage on the side of the two peoples whose governments attacked, and lost.

This may suffice to show why such an Atlantic Union

would inspire more confidence all around—and confidence
is a most important consideration. The factors that cause
distrust and fear would insidiously contribute to unsoundness in the drafting of a federal constitution for the European Six, and to friction and weakness in its functioning.
The reasons for confidence and faith that come, when
this group is broadened into an Atlantic Union, would also
work in many ways to assure it the firm constitutional
foundation, and the cooperative, give-and-take spirit, that
such a venture needs to survive its early years.

(It should also be noted that the factor of experience would
be increased by the first nations that were admitted to the
Atlantic Union, once it was established. I would hope
that these would include Australia, New Zealand, the Philippines, Austria, Eire, Sweden, Switzerland, and some of
the stabler Latin American Republics. Their admission, and
that of others, would, of course, also strengthen the Union
in other ways.)

With such a strong nucleus, and in such a favorable climate, the problem which Germany, Italy, Portugal, Greece
and Turkey present should not be dangerously difficult. In
fact, one could reasonably hope that an Atlantic federal
union with them would suffice to remove all real danger
from the problem, and lessen its intrinsic difficulties considerably. Its solution thus would add considerable elements
of strength and stability to the union. In all these five peoples,
except Portugal, free government has made very promising
progress in recent years against great odds. Membership in
an Atlantic Union would lessen these odds. It would not
only remove negative factors but provide the positive conditions and incentive needed to speed the solid growth of free
government in these nations, and assure its success.

Renaissance, Reformation, Age of Discovery, Athens
and Ataturk—Revived and Harnessed to Freedom by
Atlantic Union

And what great possibilities they offer! Think of hitching
securely to the star of freedom-and-union, or adding to it:
. . . the astonishing energies of the Germans—everlastingly
resurgent, from the days of Julius Caesar down to the swift
recovery we ourselves witnessed after both World Wars. . . .
the mixture of poetry, philosophy and power that produced such giants as Beethoven, Braun, Bunsen, Charlemagne, Clausewitz, Daimler, Diesel, Duerer, Einstein,
Goethe, Helmholtz, Heine, the I. G. Farben, Kant, Koch,
Luther, Mommsen, Mozart, Ranke, Schiller, Schubert . . .

... And adding the rare qualities which the people of Italy have shown in so many fields (for so many centuries since the rise of Rome, resurgent in the glories of medieval Florence, Venice, Genoa, and then of the *Risorgimento*), and in the geniuses they gave mankind,—Bruno, Caesar, Cavour, Cicero, Columbus, Dante, la Duse, Fabius, Ferrero, Galileo, Garibaldi, and the Grachii, Horace, Leonardo, Machiavelli, Marconi, Marcus Aurelius, Petrarch, Pliny the Elder and Younger, Raphael, St. Francis d'Assisi, Savonarola, Titian, Virgil, Volta ...

... And adding the fabulous creative abilities of the people of Greece—long dormant but still fertile—who gave us heroes of the stature of Aeschylus, Alexander, Archimedes, Aristides, Aristophanes, Aristotle, Demosthenes, Euclid, Euripides, Herodotus, Hippocrates, Homer, Leonidas, Miltiades, Pericles, Phidias, Pindar, Plato, Praxiteles, Pythagoras, Sappho, Socrates, Sophocles, Thucydides, Xenophon ...

... And adding the less known (to the West) but obvious abilities that enabled the Turks to create an empire which stretched from Persia to Morocco, from Mecca to Vienna, and to maintain it—despite all its conflicting religions and medley of peoples, and without benefit of railway, steamship or telegraph—much longer * than the empires of Britain and France have survived, and to hold for centuries the name of the "Grand Turk," and give such proofs of it as Mohammed the Conqueror and Suleiman the Magnificent, Sinan the architect and Sudi the scholar, and, in our day, Ataturk, Ismet Inonu, Halidé Edib and Ahmed Emin Yalman ...

... And adding, too, the venturing spirit that has slept so long among the Portuguese since the years when Vasco da Gama sailed first to India, and Magellan's expedition sailed round the planet—but that Atlantic Union could well awaken ...

One needs but thus skim the surface to see how great a re-

---

* Even in the 17th century this Empire's duration led the English diplomat, Ricaut, stationed in Constantinople when the British Empire was only beginning, to write a book to explain what made the Turkish Empire endure. In it he exclaimed: "To discover the maxims of government of the best established Republics, such as those founded on reason and on religion, is no easier than to decipher an enigma and explain a mystery. . . . When I consider the Turkish manner of governing, I cannot but admire the long duration of this great and vast Empire, and I can attribute its immovable firmness inside and its expansion through the constant progress of its arms only to some supernatural cause rather than to ordinary political maxims." This is my translation from the French edition of his book, entitled, *l'Etat Présent de l'Empire Ottoman*, published by Jean Lucas in Rouen in 1687, which I bought in the Istanbul bazaar in 1923.

birth is possible in these five peoples alone when Union of the
Free rekindles those who led the Renaissance, the Reformation, the Age of Discovery; those whose Athens first sowed
the seed of the West, and whose Ataturk, linking Europe and
Asia, led in the westernizing movement that has now swept
through all Islam, and in the emancipation of women that
has advanced so far in Asia and Africa. Here are potentialities to fire the imagination—mighty intangibles that
freedom-and-union would harness together, and would also
unite with all that the Americans, British, French, Belgians,
Canadians, Dutch and Scandinavians have to contribute.
These things of the spirit, when touched by the magical
power that union adds, will—if we are right in our faith that
puts man and his soul above matter—soon replace the losses
in relative material power that Atlantica has suffered since
1939.

OUR FINEST KNOWHOW, WHICH WE FAIL TO TEACH

To harness securely to freedom the five peoples of NATO
who are least experienced in maintaining democratic government would in itself be justification enough for Atlantic
Union, if only because it would turn us to the task we have
too long overlooked—that of learning by experience how to
teach better to others the best knowhow we have to teach,
namely democratic government. This is the hardest technique
to teach because it is the hardest for men to learn. Soviet Russia and China can teach the knowhows in technology and
science in which we have put our pride and concentrated our
Point Four programs, to our increasing danger. We have already so perfected these techniques that it is infinitely easier
to teach people how to operate and make the most complicated (and destructive) machines than to govern themselves
in freedom. That the latter should be—at best—so much
harder to teach and to learn may seem a paradox. Yet it is
self-evident that man (whom we so often call "little") is a far
more powerful and unpredictable atom than the atoms that
make our bombs or intercontinental missiles and sputniks,
since it is self-evident that it is man who created all these
wonders, and weapons.

Man can accurately foretell what atoms will do under
given conditions, but no atom and no man can predict
what this or that human individual will do, can do—how
feeble or how great he will prove at the test, of what base
clay he is really made, or of what divine spirit. And so it is
a far harder and worthier achievement for man to govern
himself than for him to govern matter, dictate to atoms, or

even to other men. It is also a much more rewarding achievement.

The acme of this achievement is not for Robinson Crusoe to govern himself on a lonely island, but for millions of Robinson Crusoes to govern themselves together in freedom.

Each civil liberty democracy has gained its strength by proving capable of doing what the people of Soviet Russia have not yet begun to do. All these democracies are living proof that their citizens can govern themselves on a basis of individual freedom and equality—that it *is* possible for men to achieve this marvel: Establish and maintain a system whereby each of these unpredictable individuals of incalculable potential power for both evil and good is helping govern all the others, while being governed equally at the same time by each and all of them.*

In comparison to this marvel, how petty and pitiful is the spectacle of one man governing other men by terror and force, even though the dictator keeps hundreds of millions of his fellow-men in enslavement, much as a scientist keeps in subjection a myriad of atoms . . . bloodless, mindless, heartless, soul-less atoms.

Too long our aim has been centered on releasing the energy that lies in atoms. Too long have we neglected the field where our greatest genius lies, that of releasing the far greater energy that comes from freeing men from the prejudice, and ignorance, and fear, and lack of faith in themselves and their fellows, that has kept so much of humanity, through so much of its history, from gaining for themselves and all mankind, living and unborn, the unbelievable rewards that have always followed the Union of Free Men.

The danger to freedom in our success in teaching underdeveloped peoples to industrialize and arm themselves, while failing to teach them democratic government, should be evident enough in Japan's swift rise to Pearl Harbor, and Russia's to Sputnik. The first necessity is to make clear to the new nations why freedom is the key to peace; why the institutions of individual liberty give the strongest human guarantees against war—and particularly against the surprise attack which atomic weapons make everyone fear—whereas the institutions of dictatorship are loaded for war and treacherous attack; and why individual liberty is also the key to the productive power the new nations seek. All this is not so

* For a much fuller discussion of all this, see the author's *Freedom Against Itself* (Harper 1954) especially Chapters 9, "The Cinderella Science", 14, "How Freedom Arms Dictatorship," and 15, "Freedom is Hardest to Govern."

hard to prove,* but the 1960 United Nations Assembly makes it only too evident that our official spokesmen have failed to persuade the new nations that the peace and prosperity they desire should lead them, because of the nature of the institutions involved, to help strengthen those of civil liberty in the great powers, not those of dictatorship.

FREEDOM IS IN A DANGEROUS MINORITY

Freedom requires a political ability that the human race all too evidently is slow to acquire. It is so hard for people to govern themselves with equal individual liberty that I find only about one-eighth of mankind has succeeded in doing this as independent nations, even fairly well, for so short a period as fifty years. Ominously, while the world's population has been "exploding" in numbers, this small, fairly "free" fraction has grown even smaller in the past decade; since 1950 it has shrunk from one-seventh of humanity to one-eighth. Half of that eighth is supplied by the United States—and its shortcomings, particularly on the racial side, are obvious. The other half, no less imperfect, is weakly divided into a dozen sovereign nations: The United Kingdom, France, Switzerland, Belgium, Luxemburg, the Netherlands, Denmark, Norway, Sweden, Canada, Australia, New Zealand. Some of these have been practising freedom for many generations; others, you may say, hardly meet my low fifty-year test. If you find other nations that you think meet them all, you can add them to your list; the fraction will remain small. We have already noted that by no means all the members of NATO meet this test. And even the NATO fifteen put together have a population of only 471,000,000—or one-sixth of the 2,850,000,000 persons now† on earth.

At best, one must agree that, for the great bulk of humanity, individual liberty is very young indeed, is in a very vulnerable minority in a huge mass long habituated to despotism. One must agree, too, that modern techniques in mass deception, mass subjugation and mass destruction fearfully increase the danger to the one-eighth of mankind who have governed themselves with a fair degree of equal individual freedom for the past fifty years. If you agree that freedom makes for peace and production, then you must

---

* Reasons why freedom is the key to peace, and to production are set forth concisely on pages 268-273 of the Postwar edition of *Union Now*.

† *Now* (October 13, 1960) on earth.

conclude that the present danger to the tiny free minority is a danger to all mankind, too.

So hard it is for men to practice the free way of life that individual liberty, to rise at all and to survive long enough for men to become conditioned to it from childhood, hitherto required the protection of inanimate Nature. So ill-adapted is it to making war, and so vulnerable to attack do its philosophy and institutions make it, that freedom, to grow up at all, needed such defenses as the mountains of Switzerland, the lowlands of Holland, the English Channel and the oceans of America.

With the development of the jet plane, the guided missile, the atomic bomb, *nothing in Nature remains now to protect liberty anywhere—nothing but the best in human nature, the wisdom, courage, kindness and spirit that give freedom the power that lies in Union of the Free.*

The protection that Nature no longer gives, the peoples most experienced in freedom must themselves provide, both to defend their own liberty and to shield nascent liberty in other countries long enough for it to take root.

THE IMPORTANCE OF POWER TO FREEDOM AND PEACE

If we agree that the freest nation is the least aggressive and the most productive, the problem of peace, both on its political and economic sides, boils down to the question: *How to put more and more of the world's power under freedom? How to put enough moral and material power behind it soon enough to eliminate present dangers, and long enough to enable the host of young nations to develop themselves educationally, industrially, and politically, and to permit freedom to spread and grow all over the world?*

To abolish the United Nations veto or try to change the United Nations into a world government now is clearly no answer to this problem. Such policies merely shift to the seven-eighths of mankind, who are inexperienced in freedom, more voice in the control of the power that the free eighth now divide.

Nor can the problem be answered by the free militarizing themselves as they are now doing, giving the government more and more power over the citizen, resorting in peacetime to propaganda, spying and secrecy—going, in short, the way of dictatorship.

In the game with dictatorship that we must win, freedom obliges the free to play with cards face up against an opponent whose cards are face down. To govern ourselves freely we must know what our government is doing. But there is no way whereby we can keep an eye on it without everyone on earth—and the Kremlin first of all—knowing everything we learn. We can know what the Canadians, British, French and other democratic governments are doing because their people have institutions like ours for keeping tabs on their governments. But none of us can know what is happening under the Communist dictatorship any more than can its slaves.

And so the free must win in a game for keeps, where the cards of Uncle Sam, John Bull, Marianne de France are face up on the table, with the searchlight of the press and opposition parties playing not only on the cards but up the sleeves of the players and under their part of the table to make sure that nothing phony is going on—and trying . . . vainly . . . to reach the other end of the table where the master of the Kremlin sits with his cards hidden in his hand.

There is only one possible way to win in such a game, and that is to have so strong a hand that no dictator can challenge it. Clearly freedom can not hold such a hand while its cards are divided as they are now.

How can the free gain such a hand? There is only one way: By ceasing to leave freedom's cards divided among fifteen "sovereign" players. By ceasing to play their aces and trumps against each other. By putting their cards together in one hand, played by a Federal Union government representing all the free.

In other terms, the answer is that of *Union Now: Federate the freest fraction of mankind in a Great Union of the Free, and thereafter extend this federal relationship to other nations as rapidly as this proves practicable, until the whole world is thus eventually governed by freedom and union.*

No halfway Union, whether in powers or members, will answer the problem of giving freedom decisive power without sacrificing liberty in the process.

THE FIVE-ACE UNION

Only by fully federating *all* the free fraction can the free gain the decisive power they need, morally, militarily, politically, to save themselves and world peace. The postwar *Union Now* pointed out in 1949:

> Such is the power that freedom produces through union that this small minority need only federate for

their Union to hold all four aces, and the joker—the hand that can be played face up, and win.

The ace of clubs, or armed power: Union would make them far stronger in land power, give freedom the bulk of the world's air power, 91 per cent of the world's naval tonnage, 100 per cent atomic power, and strategic bases all over the globe.

The ace of spades, or productive power: Tangled up though they are with their tariffs and currencies, the free seventh has long out-produced all the rest of the world—and how freedom's production would soar if the free nations all had one currency and formed one free-trade market as the forty-eight United States do!

The ace of diamonds, or raw material power . . .

The ace of hearts, or moral power: This Union would unite all the peoples toward whom the rest of humanity has long looked for refuge from oppression, and leadership toward liberty. Union, by giving it every ace, would add irresistible power to freedom's appeal.

All four aces, and the joker, too—the Union's power to grow: The Union need only admit other nations to it as they proved their freedom to keep on increasing its overwhelming power.

Never was so great an opportunity offered to a free people as that which history offers now to the citizens of the United States.

In 1952 General Eisenhower confirmed this in his NATO report: "Visible and within our grasp we have the possibility of building such military, economic and moral strength as the Communist world would never dare challenge." And he added: "Then the Atlantic Community will have proved worthy of its history and its God-given endowments. We shall have proved our union the world's most potent influence toward peace."

We put our trust, however, in alliance, not in union. So did he as President, although in the same report he had said: "Peacetime coalitions throughout history have been weak and notoriously inefficient."

The resulting weakness has led us inevitably to begin turning down our cards, too, little by little. Let us fool ourselves no longer. As the U-2 spy plane affair showed all the world so luridly, we are copying dictatorship when we seek strength by spying, secrecy, giving more power to the Executive, making the people depend blindly on the Government.

True, one must fight fire with fire at times—but one can burn oneself badly that way. Must we burn ourselves worse than with the U-2 before we fight fire with less dangerous means?

With the Soviet space-ship orbiting above every 91 minutes as I write, some may fear that the proverbial power that lies in union can no longer give freedom the unchallengeable hand that was in our grasp in 1952. If so, it is still true that the more strength we gain that way the safer we shall be. For my part, I believe that we can still thus gain the unbeatable hand we need . . . but we have no time to lose.

THE "BALANCE OF TERROR" IN ARMED POWER

Armed power was about the only important thing in which the combined strength of the dictatorships, compared to that of the democracies, was relatively high before World War II, as reflected in the tables in *Union Now*. The fact that nations so poor and so weak in so many other respects should be so heavily and expensively armed by dictatorship, while democracy kept the richest and strongest peoples from spending relatively so much on arming, tells its own story. And the tragic story began six months after *Union Now* appeared. Today, armed power is still, significantly, the thing that dictatorship has built up out of all proportion to its strength in other respects, the thing in which it is in relatively the best position to challenge the NATO fifteen now. So much more is kept secret now than then, that it seems useless to try to pin any comparison of relative strength down to figures. Two great differences with 1939 need to be noted: a) atomic, missile, air and submarine power has grown so enormously on both sides that b) there is now much stronger agreement all round that each is able to destroy the other, no matter who starts, and that therefore a "balance of terror" has been reached which serves as a powerful deterrent to war. The point was well put by Dr. Harold C. Urey, the atomic scientist who won the Nobel Prize, when he said at the University of Southern California on August 10, 1960:

> At present, estimates have been made that there exist stored within the various countries of the world explosives equivalent to the order of ten tons of TNT for

every man, woman and child on the surface of the earth. Never before have men stored such enormous quantities of explosives. Rockets have been developed capable of delivering hydrogen bombs one-third of the way around the earth, and there is no certainty that the end is in sight at all.

What I wish to emphasize is that the magnitude of these changes is so great that it involves a change in the quality of the modern world. For the first time in history, no country is large enough to maintain within its border a relatively secure heartland which can be regarded as free from attack.

It is often stated that the idea of overwhelming strength on the part of the democracies of the world as opposed to the Communist bloc is impossible since both sides have atomic and hydrogen bombs, and this makes any disparity in military strength impossible. I think this is true, or that it will be true in a short time.

But it is also stated, and I believe correctly, that neither side can use these immensely powerful weapons for they will surely destroy both sides in a major conflict. I rather think that this is understood by the people of the United States and those who represent us in Washington. I also think that it is realized by the Soviet Union. It is not so certain that Communist China appreciates the situation, but it is to be hoped that she will before long. As a practical matter of pursuing the policies of these individual groups, it is not possible to use these great weapons.

All of us, therefore, must fall back on something else. In fact, it appears that the Soviet Union is actively pursuing a policy of disruption in any part of the world where it can exert influence—Cuba, Africa, the Middle East, the Far East—and attempts are made to promote disorder and misunderstanding in Europe and between Europe and the United States. In other words, it is pursuing other means of waging modern conflict than the use of atomic bombs. This means that the West must strengthen its means of waging its war along similar lines. The Union of the democratic countries of the West in a Federal Government would promote great strength along these other lines.

Union Increases Our Atomic Power in Four Ways

Before considering the non-military power factors in the problem, let us note that Atlantic Union would greatly strengthen the position of the free as regards atomic and other modern weapons. It would do this in at least four ways.

First, Union would give Atlantica two tremendous strategic advantages: 1) Its territory and industrial and military centers would be much more widely dispersed than those of the United States or Soviet Russia, and 2) it would have dependable bases much nearer to Communism's citadel than the United States has, or than the Kremlin has to the Union's citadel in North America. True, the United States now has bases in Western Europe, but whether these can be used at the showdown is very doubtful. This doubt is inherent in the alliance system. It had been increased by agreements that give each country, on whose soil these bases are situated, a veto over American use of certain weapons. The uncertainty is growing greater in Britain as a result of the rise of unilateral atomic disarmament, anti-American and neutralist sentiment, particularly in the left wing of the Labor Party. It is growing in France, as a result of President de Gaulle's "nationalistic" policies. The uncertainty regarding American bases in Europe inevitably encourages Communist aggression. Merely by replacing this doubt with certainty, Atlantic Union would immensely strengthen Freedom's hand while saving at least $10 billions a year*—and discouraging the Kremlin and Peking from risking atomic war.

Experience shows that dictators are highly unlikely to attack unless they believe they have a good chance to win not merely the opening battle but the war, without suffering more destruction themselves than the prize is worth. The present "balance of terror" already acts as powerful deterrent; the more impossible we make it for Moscow to wipe out our means of devastating retaliation to any attack it launches, the stronger this deterrent becomes. Those who still fear that the Kremlin would attack this gigantic, widely dispersed Union, should fear even more that it will attack the United States, or any European Union.

It is important to note, too, that both strategic advantages which Atlantic Union brings would increase as it admitted other nations to it—and we have already seen that one could hope for the first of these to include far-flung countries from all around the globe.†

Secondly, Atlantic Union would immensely and immediately advance Atlantic development of all modern weapons. It would do this also in two ways. First, it would eliminate the shocking waste of money and time, and of scientific and engineering minds and knowledge that is inevitable in the

---

* See Chapter 9 for this estimate by P. F. Brundage, former Director of the United States Budget Bureau.
† See the end of this chapter and also Chapter 12, for further reassurance Atlantic Union would give against Communist aggression.

present system, or in any alternative short of Atlantic federation. The latest example of this financial waste is the current decision of President de Gaulle to spend $2.4 billion more on arming France atomically. It seems to me idle to single him out for censure because of this, or to blame him alone for "excessive nationalism," or as being "obsessed" with the idea of French "grandeur." It was no less wasteful and nationalistic for Britain to make its own atomic bombs. The primary responsibility for all this, however, lies not in London or Paris, but in Washington. It set the nationalistic example, and by its policy of not sharing its secrets with its friends it practically forced these proud powers to take the course they took. If the situation were reversed, and France were in our position and the United States and Britain were in that of France, would not we and the British insist as strongly as President de Gaulle does on having our own atomic bombs, and an equal voice with France on world policy?

My own view is that President de Gaulle's "excessive nationalism" results, in last analysis, from his believing, not that this is wiser for France than an Atlantic Union, but that nationalism and "power politics" are in control in Washington, and therefore the only realistic policy for France is to follow suit. I believe that this assumption is based on a profound misconception of the American people, but I can understand why this view of the United States is widely held in West Europe. One of the strong driving forces behind many supporters of European Union is the belief that, to stand up to Washington, one must have power, and the only way to get enough power to deal with it as an equal is to federate Western Europe. Because of this reasoning, European Union is often urged as an essential first step to Atlantic Union, if not the only way, to bring the United States in.

During the war, General de Gaulle had no little cause to conclude that, in last analysis, only power counts with Washington and London. Commenting on the absence of his government at Yalta—where Roosevelt and Churchill went to accommodate a dictator who had gained his power by atrocious purges—I wrote in the March 1945 *Federal Union World:*

> In 1939 when France was heavily armed it had a full voice in Big Power meetings. Now it is weak, and snubbed. Though much of the war is being fought on its soil, decisions of vital interest to it are taken without consulting it. The lesson is plain to every Frenchman . . . if you would have the position you had before,

then arm, arm, arm . . . If you cannot equal the U. S.
in power, you can hope to equal Britain. It does not
matter what you do to gain power . . . if the end result
is to give you great armed power, then Uncle Sam and
John Bull will come knocking deferentially at your
door. That is the lesson Yalta teaches, and to peace it
is poison.

The Yalta poison is still working.

Even worse than the waste of money our atomic policy
has caused, is the waste of time, knowledge, scientists, tech-
nicians, and prestige. We have deprived the best scientists
and engineers in Western Europe of facts and techniques we
have learned, and have diverted many of them into trying
to learn secrets which the less scrupulous Communists already know. By Union we would have had them helping push
forward the frontiers of science. We thus contributed heavily
to Moscow's gaining the prestige Sputnik gave it. If we are
making the British and French learn the hard way some of
our "secrets," they are making us learn just as wastefully
certain secrets they have each discovered. Atlantic Union
would reverse this idiotic policy. It would pool all of Atlantica's secrets and scientists. These are by no means limited
to the Americans, British and French; witness the part that
Danes, Germans, Italians and others played in the atomic
breakthrough. The gain that would result for all of us
from positively uniting our best scientific and engineering
knowledge and brains is incalculable.

GREATER ATOMIC SECURITY THROUGH UNION

*Thirdly, Atlantic Union would assure better security for
our secrets* than present United States policy, which was
adopted primarily for reasons of security. Once all the
secrets of the Americans, British, French and other members
of an Atlantic Union were transferred to the Union government, there would no longer be the danger of leaks in this
or that nation there is now. All the people of the Union
would have a voice in determining policy in this field, but
their national governments would no longer have anything
to do with it—no more than the Tennessee state government
now has any control over atomic plants on its territory,
or any knowledge of Washington's secrets. The security
advantages of Atlantic Union were pointed out by Dr. Urey
long before Soviet Russia learned our atomic secrets. He
wrote in the July 1947 *Freedom & Union:*

>We would not give the atomic secrets to France, to England, to Holland, any more than we give our present secrets to the state of Illinois. There might be citizens of other countries (in the Union) who would know these secrets, but if so, they would be controlled by law, just as are the citizens of the state of Illinois at present.

Before the Fuchs case proved him right, Dr. Urey went on to warn: "There are people in England, France, Denmark, who know a great deal about our atomic secrets. We have no control over their actions by any legal methods." The Union plan, he continued, "would replace the situation in which we have no legal control over people who know atomic bomb secrets, with one in which some sort of control would be set up, and thus from the standpoint of military secrets, the situation would be improved." Whatever leaks might occur through Union, he added, "would not be as important as the greatly increased military strength of such a federal union."

Fourthly, Atlantic Union would ease the problem of securing atomic agreement with the nations outside the Union, particularly Russia. Here again the Union would be much better off than is the United States today. It would need merely to admit other nations to it to extend its Atomic Authority's jurisdiction. As this increased its gigantic power in every field, the Kremlin's position would be made so weak that it might well prefer to reach atomic agreement with the Union soon after its creation, just as it buried the hatchet with Hitler when it felt relatively weak.

Fifthly, Atlantic Union would reduce the number of atomic powers from four to two, and end the danger of Germany entering that club.

ATLANTIC NON-MILITARY POWER IN 1939 AND NOW

Meanwhile, the "balance of terror," while requiring the free to keep up their guard militarily, makes the non-military factors in power all the more important.

Atlantica clearly does not have the same degree of non-military material power that *Union Now* showed in Chapter V * it had in 1939. Nor does the addition of Western Ger-

* This chapter had to be omitted in Book II from lack of space in this volume but its results may be found in summary form in Chapter I, third section, entitled "Fifteen Founder Democracies."

many, Italy, and the other NATO countries suffice to compensate for all the material power lost. Even so, I am convinced that the NATO fifteen, by federating their strength, would still gain material power, to an overwhelming degree, compared to the combined strength of Russia and China, and moral power even more.

The addition of Germany and Italy to the *Union Now* group increases, of course, the relative world power of Atlantica in the Chapter V measurements that concern manufacturing, transportation and finance. The losses are mainly in raw materials, area and population; they result from the transformation of the Belgian, British, Dutch and French Empires into more than thirty new sovereign nations. These losses, however, are more apparent than real, for the simple reason that, if these peoples are to raise their standards as they wish, the great bulk of their products must be exchanged in Atlantica for the latter's manufactured goods and stored capital. This is inevitable for the coming years, at least (and Atlantic Union would make it inevitable indefinitely), because only Atlantica has the surplus financial and manufacturing power they need, and the merchant marine to carry their goods to market and bring back their purchases.

The low living standards and other domestic needs of Russia and China will not permit them for a number of years to do more than score economic propaganda points such as they have made in Cuba. They can make a showing in a few commodities in a few countries, but if this ever led all—or many of—the new countries to turn, like Castro and Lumumba, their hands to the Communist empires for salvation, and their backs to Atlantica, they would soon learn to their grief what a mirage Russia and China really present. Atlantica has the further immense advantage that nearly all the leaders of these new countries were educated in America, Britain and France, and speak—and what is more important—think in English or French. Add Spanish and Portuguese, and all these considerations apply also to Latin America. All this immense raw material power is so much, by the nature of the situation, on the side of Atlantica, that it could lose this only by continuing the folly of the past twenty years.

These realities belie the apparent changes that national independence has introduced into the picture as presented in 1939. Because of this, and because figures for Soviet Russia and China are always doubtful and propagandistic, and completely lacking on some things (such as—significantly—gold), it has not seemed to me worthwhile to revise now in detail the tables in Chapter V. Moreover, I think that the basic points in that chapter can be proved without revising its tables, and that the space can be better used to do two things that I did not develop there. These are the fact (which I have already touched on) that the strength that union brings is far greater than the sum of its parts, and—particularly—the fact that the mere power that the mere act of union gives the free would daunt the Communists much more than superiority in material power.

WHY UNION'S PROVERBIAL POWER MOST IMPRESSES MOSCOW

Rate freedom's existing power as you will, by federating it politically and economically we would make it much greater than that of the United States alone. Mr. K could no longer hope to surpass it by 1970, or 2000. Moreover, in that period federation would immensely stimulate the growth of freedom's power in every field—not only in per capita production and standards of living, but on the political, military, scientific, educational and moral sides. These factors are so interrelated that, when combined the Federal Union way, their power becomes immensely greater than by any other combination of them. Federation raises their power as a straight flush does that of five cards.

You may think that instead of five aces—as in 1939 and 1949—freedom now holds only an ace, king, queen, jack and ten. If those cards are combined the alliance or confederation way, in different "sovereign" suits, you have only a "straight," which is not too hard to beat in the poker game the world is in.

If, however, all five cards belong to the same suit, this one change, which seems so slight, makes the hand 255 times stronger—an unbeatable royal flush. Similarly, when freedom's power is no longer divided among different nations but united in one Atlantic Federal Union, its hand becomes unbeatable.

The Atlantic community has not yet begun to gain the strength that comes from organic Union. Here is our vast reservoir of unused power. It costs us nothing to harness this power—except the loss of prejudices and ideas that are contrary to our basic free principles. The power Atlantica would gain is not only the cheapest, but the kind that would most impress Moscow, and Peking, for three reasons:

First, the Communists have made a fetish of unity. They have carried their "monolithic" unity to the extreme of tyranny. They bank on this extreme unity, which is inherent in Communism, and on the extreme disunity which they believe is inherent in free enterprise and individual liberty, to deliver our grandchildren to their system. The glasses that we Atlanticans wear magnify for us even microscopic dangers and difficulties to freedom in union—but those that the Communists wear magnify immensely in their eyes the proverbial strength and other advantages that Atlantic Union would bring us.

Secondly, the Communists know that they cannot possibly begin to compete with us in the kind of power that union brings. For one thing, they have already practically exhausted this resource, which we Atlanticans have hardly started to harness. They have carried unity to such extremes that the Kremlin is now trying to decentralize industry to some degree to increase efficiency. And they know that whereas the assets they had, or have, are relatively half-developed, the nations of Atlantica include the most highly-developed ones on earth; they have the kind of assets whose power can be most quickly multiplied by the inherent magic of union.

Atlantic Union would most impress the Communists because, thirdly, it would come with the force of surprise as would nothing else we could do. One reason why may suffice. The creation of this Union by common agreement would prove that a basic Marxist dogma is unfounded. The Communists believe that "greed for profits" must inevitably drive the capitalist countries into cut-throat competition and conflict for markets. This has all too often been true, but the Thirteen States, by their great experiment in Federal Union, proved that free enterprise states can—by applying between them their basic principles instead of sacrificing them—create a much richer common market. From it everyone benefits, by the elimination of trade barriers and other nationalistic rivalry, and by the continued competition of free enterprise. The latter requires that the competition be the peaceful, healthy one between citizens or corporations. The unhealthy, war-producing competition of nations results from the doctrine of national sovereignty—not from the principles of capitalism. The latter are, in fact, contrary to that doctrine.

By taking the road to Atlantic Federation we knock out this keystone of Communist ideology. We prove that "St." Lenin and "St." Marx were completely wrong in their teachings on this essential point. We cannot deliver a blow that is more bewildering and devastating to the Marxists, inside and outside Russia, than this is.

The downgrading of Stalin opened a door to revolution

in Eastern Europe. But he was attacked for the terroristic means he employed (and that are inevitable in the Communist system)—not for error in his Marxist thinking. All that Mr. Khrushchev did was to slap Stalin's bloody hands. Atlantic Union, by peacefully uniting the capitalist nations, would hit straight at the heart of Leninism and Marxism.

REVOLUTIONIST VALUES, LENIN'S LOW POINT
—AND THE SPIRIT OF '76 AND '87

When Chairman Khrushchev made his first visit to the United States, the type of American mind that counts on Sears Roebuck catalogs rather than on Whitman's "By Blue Ontario's Shore" to impress revolutionists, fondly believed that the sight of our many material achievements would daunt Mr. K. The event confirmed instead what I wrote in the September *Freedom & Union* just before he came:

> More probably it will be a stimulating challenge to him. Why? Because he has what we do not seem to have any more at the top levels—the revolutionist's standard of values, which ranks idea-power far above material power. The revolutionist is a man who believes his idea is so powerful that he is willing to tackle incredible material odds.

> In his *Lenin,* David Shub writes: "Isolated from events in Russia, deserted by many of his early followers, struggling to pay his modest living expenses, seeking in vain to rally Socialists of other lands to his slogan of international civil war, Lenin, at the end of 1916, was hitting the bottom rung of his ladder. Never did his words seem to attract fewer followers."

> Utter weakness on his side, plus the fact that on the other side all the armed power of Russia was mobilized under the Czar, did not suffice to daunt Lenin—and ten months later he was in control of Russia. This is the kind of spirit that has been glorified in Russia, not merely by propaganda but by what it has achieved before the eyes of living men. It is bound to affect particularly the values and judgments of those who have reached the top, as has Mr. K, by their natural aggressiveness, ruthlessness.

> We Americans once put will power and political ideas far above material strength . . back in the days when Tom Paine wrote of a ragged militia confronting all the armed might of Great Britain: "We have it in our

power to begin the world over again," and James Wilson told his fellow-delegates at the 1787 Convention, "we are laying the foundations for a building, which is to last for ages." But we have drifted so far from this "Common Sense" of 1776 that our hopes of impressing Mr. K are now put in electric kitchens, rather than in electrifying thought and action.*

WHAT BROUGHT MOSCOW'S ONLY CONCESSIONS

The best proof of the decisive strength that still lies for Atlantica in Union may be found in Moscow's reactions to the steps already taken in this direction. In 1948, our atomic monopoly, plus our superior sea and air power, plus the contrast between our intact industrial plant and the devastation the war still left in Russia—all this did not keep Moscow from daring to blockade Berlin then. *But* when that led us to form the Atlantic alliance in 1949, even this "notoriously inefficient" type of unity (to quote again General Eisenhower's 1952 NATO report) caused Stalin himself to abandon that blockade, immediately. Moscow, moreover, left Berlin tranquil for the next ten years. When we moved to strengthen Atlantic unity still more by admitting the German Federal Republic to NATO, and permitting it to rearm, Moscow made all manner of threats to prevent this, but when this was carried through in 1955, the Kremlin—where Mr. Khrushchev was then in power with Mr. Bulganin—promptly withdrew from Austria.

No other moves we have made since the war have brought such important—and unilateral—concessions as did these, the only important steps to strengthen Atlantic unity that we have taken in those fifteen years.

Surely this is proof enough that the power that union brings Atlantica impresses Moscow more than any other power we can get. It should also suffice to reassure those who agree that Union would put overwhelming power behind freedom, but who fear it would make Communism's future so hopeless that the Kremlin would seek to block it by "getting tough," or even by launching a preventive war. The fact is that, whether or not the "balance of terror" suffices to deter attack—and it will not if by continued disunion we let that balance become too unfavorable—Atlantic Union is

---

* Fortunately, Vice President Nixon's experience with Mr. K at the kitchen door seems to have awakened him to the need of fighting ideas with better ones, judging from his masterly TV speech to the Soviet audience,—and even more from the Atlantic Confederation proposal he later joined Governor Rockefeller in making (which we shall discuss in the next chapter).

our surest hope not merely to prevent war, but to put, and keep, the Communist empires in a conciliatory mood.

MOSCOW IN THE LION'S CAGE

When we see a man with a whip and a chair alone in a cage of lions, we are amazed that these kings of the jungle haven't sense enough to unite their immensely superior strength against the tamer, who exploits their common inner weakness to their humiliation. Similarly, we can count on the Communists to see how overwhelmingly powerful the Sovereign Nations of Atlantica would be if only they united, and to be amazed that we haven't sense enough to see this ourselves. They have seen us act so senselessly so long in the name of freedom that one can hardly blame them for concluding that we are no more intelligent than the animals our nations put their pride in—lions, eagles, fighting cocks. The most convinced Communists will probably be the last to believe that we free Atlanticans are really capable of being rational men. And so, whatever Mr. K may rule the Kremlin, he cannot but believe that all he needs to do is bluff with a whip, flourish an empty chair, and toss us —when we all growl in too ominous a chorus—enough raw meat to keep our "Sovereign Nations" snarling at each other. In other words, if the animals of the Atlantic jungle should show any symptoms of common sense, the Communist leaders, though inwardly aware that this—if continued— would mean the end of their dreams, could not believe that it could possibly continue, if they tossed us in time a juicy concession. Communists simply cannot remain true to Communist thinking and believe that capitalist peoples can really organically unite. And the success they have thus far had in checking Atlantic unification by quick concessions must strengthen them in this belief.

WHY UNION WOULD MAKE MOSCOW
CONCILIATORY, NOT WARLIKE

Why did Moscow drop the Berlin blockade when we made the Atlantic alliance? To remove our incentive to unite further. And it worked. Instead of moving on toward Union, we Atlanticans were soon growling at each other over Korea, China, Indo-China. No wonder Premier Malenkov chortled on August 8, 1953: "If today, in conditions of tension in international relations, the North Atlantic bloc is rent by internal strife and contradictions, the lessening of this tension may lead to its disintegration." A little later he was thrown out by Mr. Khrushchev—but not his lion-tamer strategy. For when the Atlantic Sovereign Nations began to think enough like men to strengthen NATO with West Germany in 1955, his successor tossed them the Soviet withdrawal from Austria. This worked so well that Atlantica, instead of uniting effectively, within a year was near "its disintegration" over Suez.

To folksy Mr. K, this must have confirmed the wisdom not only of Marxist thinking but of the old Russian custom of throwing meat to the wolves. Folk memories of Russians run to wolves rather than lions. That is another reason to believe that concessions will be the Russian response when they find the lions of the Atlantic jungle gaining the degree of intelligence the wolves of the steppes show by hunting in packs.

If an Atlantic Convention moves boldly toward Union, the intra-Atlantic tensions and difficulties that stand in the way will still encourage Moscow to continue a conciliatory policy, aimed at increasing the obstacles and lessening incentive to unite, rather than to risk a warlike attitude that would increase that incentive and lessen the difficulties facing Union. It will take time to make an Atlantic Union, and in the earlier stages success is bound to seem most problematical; when the Rubicon is crossed it will seem insignificant compared to the mountains ahead. As Atlantica advances toward Union, success will always remain in doubt. This will help keep Moscow trying to stop it with bigger and better concessions. One can be sure that through the Convention stage, and even more during the stage of ratifying a Union constitution, we Atlanticans will ourselves give plenty of reason to believe that we will never be men enough to achieve Union without war. And so our doubts, and their wishful thinking, will combine to lead the Communists to destruction. Once Atlantic Union confronts them—a *fait accompli* that proves that Marx's basic belief about us was false—they will be as helplessly vulnerable as the trainer who suddenly finds that his whip, his chair and his chunk of meat no longer work.

CHAPTER 3

Confederation Next—Not Federation Now?

To our friends and associates in the Atlantic community: We propose a broader partnership that goes beyond our common fears, to recognize the depth and sweep of our common political, economic, and cultural interests. We welcome the recent heartening advances toward European unity. In every appropriate way, we shall encourage their further growth within the broader framework of the Atlantic community.—*Democratic Platform, July 12, 1960.*

The vital need of our foreign policy is new political creativity, leading and inspiring the formation, in all great regions of the free world, of confederations, large enough and strong enough to meet modern problems and challenges. We should promptly lead toward the formation of such confederations in the North Atlantic community and in the Western hemisphere.—*Point Two of the Nixon-Rockfeller Agreement, July 23, 1960.*

The advance toward Atlantic Union reached a new high mark in 1960 when Governor Nelson Rockefeller proposed a "North Atlantic Confederation" in his address to the Binghamton (N. Y.) Rotary club on June 21.* It rose still higher on July 12 when the Democrats adopted a platform promising a "broader partnership" in "the Atlantic Community" than NATO; the terms were broader and the volume of support was greater. And then the advance reached still another peak on July 23 when Richard M. Nixon agreed to the Rockefeller proposal's Point Two in their joint statement.

The climax came when the Democratic party, which has long been the one more favorable to Atlantic Union, won the White House and both Houses of Congress. This puts it in position to achieve, as far as the United States is concerned, its promise of a "broader partnership"—a term that does not exclude Atlantic Union. Its responsibility to do this is the greater, since it cannot fear opposition to this from Vice President Nixon—and he ran so far ahead of the Congressional candidates of his party that he nearly won the White House, and surely won their respect. Nor need President Kennedy fear opposition from Governor Rockefeller and his wing of the Republican party. To advance Atlantic unification through Congress in these conditions would seem easy, compared to some of the legislative feats that those master Congressional leaders, Vice President Lyndon Johnson and Speaker Sam Rayburn, have already accomplished.

Their party being split as it is, the Republican candidate for President and Governor Rockefeller deserve hearty applause for the refreshing courage they have shown in pro-

* See July-August *Freedom & Union* for the full text of his proposal.

posing American leadership toward a North Atlantic Confederation. In the American mind, "confederation," is inevitably associated with two highly significant experiences in American history: The Articles of Confederation, ratified by the Thirteen States in 1783, which formed a system more advanced than NATO, and the Confederate States of America, set up by the South in 1861, which was practically a federation (as Chapter 8 will bring out).

Parties tend to steal each other's thunder (rather than lightning), and Confederacy may understandably appeal more than Union to Southern Democrats. Before we attach too much importance to this emotional factor, however, or to the Nixon-Rockefeller use of the term, let us see what they mean by confederation, and try to define the basic difference between confederation and federation, both in principle and in American practice. Then let us assess the results achieved by the American experiments with both systems, and draw all the advantage we can from the lessons they have now for us, and all Atlantica—and the world.

"Albert Kolonji, a Baluba tribal leader," Russell Howe reported from Elisabethville in the *Washington Post* on August 10, 1960, "called for a confederal type of association in the Congo but seemed hazy about the difference between federation and confederation. He said he was studying the constitutions of Canada, the United States and Switzerland." His confusion is all too widespread, and may even be increased by the examples he is studying. All three are clear examples of federations, but the Swiss style theirs the "Helvetian Confederacy." One may gain more clarity by studying the examples of both systems which the history of the United States gives.

WHAT DID NIXON AND ROCKEFELLER MEAN?

First let us see what light the authors of the Nixon-Rockefeller agreement throw on the meaning they attach to "confederation." The latter, while leaving its substance vague, has given some significant hints. The most far-reaching came when Curtin Winsor asked the Governor this question from the floor, after his talk on "The Third Century" to the Philadelphia World Affairs Council on April 22, 1960: "Do you think that it is possible that these regional groupings (such as the Atlantic one) might get together into full federation, at some time in the future?"

Governor Rockefeller answered: "I would think, myself, that that would be, at some point, a very logical conclusion. Certainly the experience of the United States has been one of the most exciting and thrilling in the history of the world. I know that some of us are concerned about states rights, and we do our best to preserve them. Yet I think the federal system has proven its tremendous strength and vitality. So I do not see why—where regions exist, with compatible objectives on the part of the people—they should not ultimately lead to confederation."

These words suffice to show that he has been thinking in terms of federal union and does not shy at the thought of trying this solution "at some point." The last two sentences indicate, moreover, that he then used "federal" and "confederation" as synonymous, that when he spoke of ultimate "confederation" in the last sentence, he had in mind "the federal system" he had cited just before. How could the reverse be true—how could he have meant confederation in its usual sense when he spoke of "federal," since he had said "the federal system has proven its tremendous strength and vitality," and he had already called "the experience of the United States . . . most exciting"? Its trial of the Articles of Confederation proved, as Governor Rockefeller knows, the feebleness and futility of confederation.

On the other hand, one must remember that Governor Rockefeller was then speaking "off the cuff." Although such speaking often throws more light on a political leader's real thinking than do his formal statements, the latter show much better what he considers to be "practical politics."

The little light he gives on the meaning he attaches to confederation strongly indicates that he uses the term in its usual, non-federal sense. "The work of moving toward confederation does not involve any super-states," he explained at Binghamton. He made clearer that he did not mean federation when he proposed in the same speech that the United States should enter not only a North Atlantic but also a Western Hemisphere confederation. No state in the United States—or in any federal union—can belong at the same time to another federation, or enter into any confederation, league, alliance or treaty with any foreign nation. Nor could any member do this in the Confederation originally set up by the Thirteen States; the Confederation stipulated in Article VI: "No state without the Consent of the united states (*sic*) in congress assembled, shall send any embassy to, or receive any embassy from, or enter into any conference, agreement or alliance or treaty with any King, prince or state." Apparently Governor Rockefeller uses confederation in a much looser sense than did these Articles.

The only significant hints added by Governor Rockefeller's statement of July 23 to which Mr. Nixon agreed lay

in the words, "vital," "strong," "promptly"—"the vital need
. . . of confederations, large enough and strong enough to
meet modern problems and challenges. We should promptly
lead toward the formation of such confederations in the
North Atlantic community and in the Western Hemisphere."

Vice President Nixon, in his major campaign speech on
foreign policy on October 14, strongly pledged himself to
push energetically, if elected, "toward confederation"—a
term he twice repeated. "I would ask the NATO governments to consider the feasibility of still closer ties," he said,
and added a little later, in a way that covered both Atlantica
and Latin America, "Such regional action, moving toward
confederation, is an imperative of our times."

He threw no light on what he meant by confederations, but
the context suggested that he shared the Rockefeller view as
indicated above—except that he made no mention of either
super-state or federal union.

From the available evidence, one may well conclude either
that Vice President Nixon and Governor Rockefeller have
not thought out what they mean by confederation (although
there is good reason to believe they have long given thought
to both confederation and federation), or that they have made
only an opening move which will be spelled out later. Certainly one must conclude from the public evidence now that
the confederation they are talking about is a system stronger
in structure than the present NATO alliance—but much
weaker than confederation in the historic American sense,
though capable of "gradual and evolutionary" growth (to
quote from the Binghamton speech) into something similar
to the latter.

To clarify this vital question further, let us turn now to
the dictionary, see if its definitions can be bettered, and then
pin them down more realistically by comparing NATO with the
Articles of Confederation, and the latter with the federation which the Federal Constitution formed. Webster distin-
guishes thus between confederation and federation:

> *Confederacy* and *confederation* . . . [apply] specif-
> ically to a union by treaty or compact of independent
> states under a government to which powers are
> delegated for dealing with common external rela-
> tions; of the two, confederation, perhaps, now implies
> the closer or more permanent association; as the
> Southern Confederacy, the Articles of Confederation,
> the Germanic Confederation. *Federation* in its broad
> sense includes any union under the terms of a league

or covenant; but specifically it designates a sovereign
state, especially one formed by the union of other states,
with a central general government and several local
governments; . . . in the strictest sense the United States
of America constitutes a federation.

This indicates how dictionaries reflect the existing loose
usage, and contribute to the resulting confusion.

Study of the sense in which each of the various terms
used today for interstate groupings is generally meant shows
that they readily fall into two types. These two can be most
simply and surely distinguished by the supreme or sovereign
unit of, by and for which the combination is formed. In last
analysis (see *Union Now,* Chapter VI) there are only two
possible units: Man taken as an *individual person* or sovereign,
and man taken as a *collective person* or sovereign—a man-
made body politic taken as supreme instead of a God-made,
flesh-blood-and-soul human body . . . John Bull instead of a
John Q. Citizen.

If the citizen is the sovereign, and power is divided between the representatives he elects to his state and his inter-
state government, then the combination is variously called a
union, organic union, federal union, federal republic, federation. I see no significant difference between these terms and
use them all interchangeably. As regards the outside world,
each creates a "sovereign" state in the sense of diplomacy.
From the domestic standpoint, however, its "sovereignty" is
limited by that which the member states retain. Each is
"sovereign" in relation to the other as regards the powers
assigned it by the constitution. But the supreme sovereignty
is equally divided among the citizens, who have merely delegated a portion of their sovereignty to their representatives
in their state and interstate governments, and retain the
power to re-delegate this.

If, to the contrary, some body politic—tribe, city, kingdom,
state, nation—is taken as the supreme sovereign unit, the
resulting combination is variously called a bloc, coalition,
alliance, league, confederation, confederacy, or—when used
in the modern international sense—community. None of
these forms a new "sovereign" state or government in the
usual sense of the terms; however close some types may
come to this, they remain in last analysis an association of
sovereign states. The different names indicate different de-
grees of association, though one finds many exceptions to
whatever distinguishing rules one seeks to apply. I lump all
these terms together when seeking to distinguish the category
to which they all belong from the other basic category. But

when using them in contra-distinction to others in their own category, I would define them broadly and briefly as follows:

A *bloc* or *coalition* is the loosest and most temporary form; neither usually involves a treaty, and the former indicates more common interests than the latter, which implies association despite conflicting interests. Both imply a number of members.

An *alliance* may have two or a number of members; it implies a treaty and a longer period of duration, with some definite commitments, presumably military, though possibly political.

League now implies a treaty associating a still larger number of states for a longer time and for more purposes, with some common institutions, such as a secretariat and council, and a headquarters city.

Confederation and *confederacy* I use interchangeably to mean a league that usually has fewer members but should have closer ties, stronger commitments and more developed institutions—the system in which member states may (but rarely do) join together as closely as is possible while still remaining the supreme sovereign units in it.

All the above terms involve a political association, though alliances may and leagues and confederations do involve more than political and military affairs.

Community has entered the international field since World War II from Western Europe where it is used with reference to associations which are highly confederal in character except that they have thus far been non-political and limited each to one field, as the European Economic Community or Common Market of the Six Nations, and the projected European Defense Community. Though the term began as part of the "functional" approach to union, it has recently taken on broader scope, but vaguer meaning. Thus 1957 brought the Bruges "Conference on Atlantic Community" which conspicuously omitted the article *the* before Atlantic to make clearer that it meant "community" in the older and widest sense. Then the London Atlantic Congress sponsored by the NATO Parliamentarians Association in 1959 repeatedly used the term, "the Atlantic Community," in the sense of something existing. Yet at the same time its Declaration also said: "The time is ripe for these nations to build an Atlantic Community with responsibilities extending to military, political, economic, social and scientific fields."

The term, *community,* in short, seems to be moving in the international sense from the functional and specific to the political and general, and from the confederal to the federal type of structure. But the degree depends so much on the user of the word, or the listener, that its growing popularity increases the existing confusion considerably.

Unfortunately for clarity, many organizations of states or nations fall between these—or other—definitions, or their own choice of terms causes confusion. The Articles of Confederation established a most advanced type of confederacy; Article II gave it that name—but Article III called it a "league of friendship," and the other Articles usually referred to it as "the united states in congress assembled" (without the capital letters used today). The Charter of the United Nations calls that body an "organization"; I would call it a league, leaning toward a confederation. The North Atlantic Treaty gave no name whatever to the grouping it formed; the parties to it later styled it the "North Atlantic Treaty Organization" (NATO). It is universally termed an alliance and is, in fact, an exceptionally developed "grand alliance." It might well be called a league, were it not so predominantly military in its development thus far. It has far to go before it could be rightly called a confederation.

THE U. S. CONFEDERATION WAS STRONGER THAN NATO

Since the Nixon-Rockefeller agreement calls for a North Atlantic Confederation, let us now compare the existing structure of the North Atlantic alliance with that of the Articles of Confederation. However hazily the two authors of that agreement may have had the latter in mind, this comparison will serve to show how greatly NATO can be strengthened while remaining an association of sovereign states—without crossing the Rubicon that separates confederation from a federal union of sovereign citizens.

The NATO Council, like the United States Congress under the Confederation, is composed of delegates named, paid and instructed by each member nation's government, with each state having one vote, regardless of the number of people in it. NATO, like the United States then, has no executive organ but simply a figurehead president. He serves one year and his name is as forgotten a year or so later as are the names of all the "Presidents of the United States" who preceded George Washington. But though the United States Congress was then only a "diplomatic assembly," as John Adams contemptuously called it, the Confederation it represented was far stronger than NATO structurally at every significant point of comparison. Consider these nine points:

1. The Congress of the Confederation could act; the NATO Council can only make recommendations to the member nations.

2.   To make even these recommendations, NATO requires unanimity; the Congress of the Confederation could act in a number of fields, by a majority of seven of the Thirteen States, and in others, by a vote of nine states.

3.   The North Atlantic Treaty provides no judicial machinery whatever; the Confederation not only established machinery for settling disputes between states but authorized Congress to act as a court of "last resort" by a majority of seven of the Thirteen States.

4.   With the assent of only seven states Congress had the power of fixing the standards of weights and measures throughout the Confederation, regulating trade between the states, establishing and regulating postal service "throughout all the United States," appointing "all officers of the land forces, in the service of the United States, excepting regimental officers" and commissioning all naval officers. NATO not only has none of these powers but has never dared even to make recommendations in any of these fields.

5.   With the assent of only nine states, the Confederation could and did make war and peace, enter into treaties and alliances, coin money and regulate its value, fix the expenses "for the defense and welfare of the United States," emit bills, borrow on the credit of the Confederation, appropriate money, decide on the land and naval forces to be raised, and the quota to be furnished by each state, and appoint the commander-in-chief of the army and navy. NATO has no such powers, nor has its Council dared to make recommendations in any of these fields except as regards the total military forces to be assigned to NATO, and the contributions to joint defense to be made by member nations. It is not free to choose its commander-in-chief, but must accept, in practice, an American nominated by Washington.

6.   Congress could not only formulate foreign policy for the Confederation but name diplomatic envoys to other states—as Franklin and Jefferson to France and Adams to London. NATO has never dreamed of sending even its Secretary General—although Paul Henri Spaak has often been Premier and Foreign Minister of his own country—to speak for it in Moscow . . . let alone think of naming an envoy to represent it in any country, or formulating a NATO foreign policy toward the world.

7.   No state without the consent of Congress could send or receive any diplomatic envoy, or enter into any treaty, alliance or confederation, or engage in war unless invaded. In NATO no nations—not even the Six Nations who

have established such "communities" as the Common Market, Coal and Steel Authority and Euratom—dream of such a commitment.

8.   In 1783, Virginia, the largest state in the Confederation, followed the example of Connecticut and New York, and turned over to the Confederation its much larger and stronger claims to the Northwest Territory. The Confederation thereafter governed this huge area. In 1784 it decided that one square mile in each township of thirty-six in this Territory should be reserved for the maintenance of public schools; and by the Northwest Ordnance of 1787 it provided for the government of the Territory and for its eventual division into states and their entry into the Confederation on an equal basis with the Original Thirteen. Out of this territory came the states of Ohio, Indiana, Illinois, Michigan and Wisconsin—after the Confederation had been transformed into the present Federal Union.

None of the NATO nations has ever offered to turn over any of its territory in Africa or elsewhere to the alliance; the latter has no important joint possession of any kind to hold it together and make it less dependent on its member nations. There has been increasing talk in NATO of the need of a common policy for the building up of the under-developed countries, but—despite the fear of Communist expansion there— nothing has been done to meet this need. Even the talk is timid, compared to the bold solution of this problem by the Thirteen Confederated States.

9.   Finally, the Confederation allowed the citizens of each state to move freely in and out of all the others, and enjoy in each all the privileges of its own citizens. This was done "the better to secure and perpetuate mutual friendship and intercourse among the people of the different states." NATO faces the same need, only more acutely, but it has made no such provisions, nor has its Council yet recommended any important step in this direction.

This may suffice to show what confederation meant from the start in United States history, how primitive by comparison is the NATO structure, and how far one can go in developing it into a confederation, while still keeping it an association of sovereign states.

THE "SUPERSTATE" BOGY

Governor Rockefeller said that the confederations he had in mind involved no "superstates." Yet if he proposed concretely to bring NATO up to the level of the Articles of

Confederation in even one or two of the above nine respects, the cry of "superstate" would doubtless be raised. It was raised in the Senate against the League of Nations, although that League, like NATO today, had none of these powers our early "League of Friendship" enjoyed. But even the most benighted Member of Congress would not think of calling that Confederation of ours with all its powers a "superstate." He would be laughed out of Congress, for that Confederation is indelibly associated in the American mind with wretched weakness, not with strength.

This bogy, however, still has power to frighten American politicians. They do not blanch at the ghosts of all the myriads who were slaughtered in World War II because the League of Nations proved too weak. Nor do they blanch at the certainty that far more millions will be slaughtered sooner or later if NATO is not made strong enough to keep the peace. But they do blanch at the word "superstate."

The Nixon-Rockefeller compact, happily, calls for a North Atlantic Confederation "strong enough to meet modern problems and challenges." No candidate for President, or for Senator or Congressman, and certainly no statesman, could dare propose anything less—openly call for some solution which he admitted was "too weak" to do the job.

Both presidential candidates in 1960, and both parties agreed that NATO is too weak, that it must be strengthened. The candidate who won the White House—and all those who won seats in the Senate and the House—thus have a strong moral commitment to the American people to unite the North Atlantic peoples strongly enough to meet "modern problems and challenges"—to win for freedom without another world war or depression.

The basic question, therefore, is this: Can this obligation be met by converting NATO into a confederation—or "community" or "partnership"—that is no stronger structurally than the Articles of Confederation (to say nothing of something weaker)?

The answer is flatly but demonstrably, *No*. The proof is easy: Since so strong a "superstate" as the American Confederation failed to meet the problems and challenges of oxcart, sailing ship years, what American in his senses can hope that a North Atlantic Confederation can meet those of our rocket-atomic age? The highly advanced confederation of the Thirteen States did not face Red Russia and Red China; it faced only small tribes of Redskins, who were as divided among themselves as the NATO "tribes" are today. The Thirteen American States were relatively self-sufficing, with simple economies. Yet the fact is undeniable that their super-superstate failed to meet even the problems of that day, and has left its name as a symbol of feeble futility.

All of us Americans rightly honor our forefathers for scrapping that Confederation promptly—not in any gradual, evolutionary way—before it delivered them to anarchy, tyranny, war. We honor them for not waiting long, as we have waited with NATO, before replacing it with a revolutionary experiment. We revere Washington for calling on them at the Federal Convention, to "raise a standard to which the wise and the honest" could repair—for leading them to take the "con" out of confederation and create a system that was truly strong enough to meet the challenge. We rightly honor him and them, because their answer—federation of the free—met the challenges of 1789, 1803, 1832 and 1861, and then of 1917, 1933, 1941, and offers now the one reasonable hope of meeting today's and tomorrow's challenges.

The common sense conclusion is that we should waste no more billions of taxpayer money and still more precious time on answers which failed to meet even lesser tests; that we should try next the federal union solution that has succeeded wherever it has been tested; that we should skip the confederation stage now, as we should have skipped the alliance stage in 1949. But when one draws this conclusion he is met by a perennial argument, though it is put forward a little less dogmatically now than formerly.

We heard this argument from 1939 to 1949 when we cited the example of American history as a warning against wasting time, money and lives trying to secure peace and freedom through a league system, unsupplemented by an Atlantic Federal Union. After the United Nations had to be supplemented with NATO, we heard the same objection when we cited the American example as a warning that alliance would also fail, and urged the Atlantic democracies to call a convention, as the Thirteen did in 1787, to explore the possibilities offered by the federal alternative. Now that NATO has proved inadequate, and confederation is proposed in its place, the same objection is raised when we propose that Atlantica skip making a costly experiment with this system that failed the Thirteen States, and try now the method that worked so well for them—and all the other peoples who since have tried it.

This hardy perennial argument is that the comparison is not valid, that conditions are too different for there to be any analogy; and especially that it was much easier for the

Thirteen to federate than it is for the Atlantic nations to do so now.*

And so we are told that the nations around the North Atlantic are separated by history, language, different political and economic institutions and customs, the ocean and other barriers. The people of the Thirteen States, the argument continues, had much more in common—the same historical background, the same language, the same political system, the same basic "New World" problems and psychology, the same relatively simple economy, and they were all on the same continent, and had never been in war with each other.

CONFEDERATION FAILED THEN—IN THE BEST CONDITIONS

There is much that is obviously true in all this, and much that will not stand investigation, either because it simply isn't so or omits the other side of the picture.† Let us pause for a smile while we hear one contemporary witness, the English traveller, Burnaby, who wrote after visiting the colonies in 1760:

> Fire and water are not more heterogeneous than the different colonies in North America. Nothing can exceed the jealousy which they possess in regard to each other. The inhabitants of Pennsylvania and New York have an inexhaustible source of animosity in their jealousy for the Jerseys. Massachusetts Bay and Rhode Island are not less interested in that of Connecticut. Even the limits and boundaries of each colony are a constant source of litigation. In short, such is the difference of the character, of manners, of religion, of interest in the different colonies, that I think, if I am not wholly ignorant of the human mind, were they left to themselves there would soon be a civil war from one end of the continent to the other; while the Indians and negroes would, with

---

* As if the question were one only of relative ease, and not primarily one of relative necessity and advantage—whether they required federation to preserve their liberties and lives then in America more or less than we do now in Atlantica.

† See the description of the Thirteen States during their Confederation by Tom Paine and Josiah Tucker in Chapter I of *Union Now*. See also the powerful case that Prime Minister Michel Debré and Emanuel Monick, former Governor of the Banque de France, make that "Oceans Unite Men—Land Divides Them," in the November 1959 *Freedom & Union*, and their book, *Peace by Oceanic Union* (*Demain La Paix*, Plon, Paris), from which this article was drawn. Land formed so much more of a barrier in 1787 than water that the delegates of South Carolina to the Federal Convention found it easier, safer and faster to come to Philadelphia by ship.

better reason, impatiently watch the opportunity of exterminating them altogether.

The widespread belief that it was easy to federate the Thirteen States is more plausible than informed. It remains true that they did have certain advantages, but it is also true that they faced difficulties we do not have today, and that we have advantages they lacked. When the balance is struck, some may still conclude that it was less difficult to federate America then than Atlantica now. But this leaves their argument confronted with this self-evident, unanswerable fact:

All the advantages that made federal union a workable solution for the Thirteen States were equally enjoyed by the Confederation. Since their highly developed type of confederation failed to work in these most advantageous conditions, how can any practical statesman hope that NATO will prove adequate if only we convert it into a similar confederation—let alone a far weaker one?

Whether or not the difficulties facing federation then were less than now, there can be no doubt that we now face far more formidable dangers. It is no less certain that we live in a world that requires much swifter political and economic adaptation to changing conditions as the price of life, liberty and happiness, than did the people of the American Confederation.

How then can any reasonable man believe that the practical and prudent policy is to risk seeking salvation now in the confederation solution that failed in more advantageous and safer conditions?

How can you agree that Washington was right in rejecting half-way measures and in boldly raising "a standard to which the wise and the honest" could repair, and then conclude that in our rocket-atomic day we can wisely spare the time to try the experiment in confederation that failed in more hopeful conditions, and at the slow-rising dawn of the steam-electric world?

CHAPTER 4

The U.S. Experiments with Confederation and Federation

Example is of the first importance in politics, because political calculations are so complex that we cannot trust theory, if we cannot support it by experience. Now the experience of the Americans is necessarily an impressive lesson to England.—*Lord Acton, The Civil War in America, January 18, 1866.*

Certainly the experience of the United States has been one of the most exciting and thrilling in the history of the world.—*Governor Nelson A. Rockefeller, April 22, 1960.*

On May 17, 1957, Secretary Dulles told P. F. Brundage, then Director of the Budget Bureau, and me: "I have long been in favor of the federal principle" for the North Atlantic democracies, and added that the United States experience with the Articles of Confederation proved that the effort of the United States and other NATO nations to make the alliance system work was an attempt "to do the undo-able." But while Secretary of State he always found some reason for putting off a little longer the calling of the Convention to work out a "do-able" system . . . some reason that looked important then but already has lost significance. Before Secretary Dulles got round to doing what he meant for years to do, his time on earth ran out.— *The author in the December, 1959, Freedom & Union.*

Reasoning from analogy is, of course, beset with pitfalls. Many, therefore, dismiss the thought that American history can give us guidance on which remedy to try for freedom's ills today: Federal union—or confederation, community, alliance. They forget that there is no other way to profit from experience, and that alternative lines of reasoning, which they themselves follow, have worse traps in them, and are often pure speculation or theory. They forget, too, that in the complex political field, example is, as Lord Acton pointed out, of prime importance.

Others, who are not so foolish as to brush aside reasoning from analogy, argue—as we have noted—that no sound resemblance can be drawn between the Thirteen States in 1787 and the North Atlantic peoples today. Granted, the differences between the two are indeed great and obvious, but they are not so great, or so obvious, as those between guinea pigs and men. Perhaps the least obvious and most significant difference between the latter two is this: The guinea pig can see no analogy between himself and man, whereas man can see enough such resemblances to save many human lives by drawing conclusions by analogy from experiments made on guinea pigs.

The experience of the Americans which Lord Acton held to be "necessarily an impressive lesson to England," certainly should be even more impressive to Americans. Had we but studied our own history with half Lord Acton's insight, followed its teachings and tried its remedy before trusting the lives of our children to pure theory, and to Old World methods that have always led to disaster, how far ahead we would be today!

Before we Americans expose our families further as guinea pigs in the trial and error laboratory of witch-doctor statesmanship, let us study more closely what we can learn from the experiments our forefathers made, first with confederation and then with federal union. There is no better way to understand the difference between *confederation* and *federation,* and how vital it is.

Our forefathers began, as we have seen, by making the mistake our own generation has made. They, too, assumed that the only way to secure their own individual freedom was to make sure that their states would be free not only from foreign autocracy but from their fellow democracies. To this end their Articles of Confederation guaranteed the sovereignty of each of the Thirteen States, but included nothing else to assure the sovereignty of their citizens. By the same line of thought our generation set up for the same purpose first, the League of Nations, and, when it failed, next the United Nations and, when it proved insufficient, the North Atlantic alliance. And now that NATO also has proved inadequate, it is proposed that we seek to assure our freedom as citizens by trying next still another type of organization based on the sovereign state—confederation.

We have already noted how much stronger than NATO the Confederation of the Thirteen was, not only in structure but in linguistic, historical and other community ties. Yet these confederated states, even when they had their common war for independence to help keep them united, suffered such chronic disunion as to make General Washington almost despair. Confederation was so feeble that, as Madison pointed out in the Federal Convention, even tiny "Delaware during the late war opposed and defeated an embargo to which twelve states had agreed, and continued to supply the enemy with provisions in time of war."

HIS EXCELLENCY, GEORGE C, AND HIS MAJESTY, GEORGE III

Once the war was won, disunion degenerated into chaos. Although the Confederacy had the power to issue and borrow money, the failure of its member states to back it up soon made its "Continental" currency an enduring byword for worthlessness—"not worth a Continental"—and ruined its credit at home and abroad; it could not borrow even at usurious interest rates. Each of the Thirteen States had retained the right to issue its own currency; their money, with few exceptions, fared worse or little better. These currencies, together with the tariffs by which the Thirteen sought to protect themselves from each other, proved too much for even the relatively simple business and agriculture of those days. Soon galloping inflation and depression (not so deep as we experienced in 1929-33) ravaged the states of the Confederation. This led some of them to centralize power in their state government (though far less dangerously than in the Nazi dictatorship which depression brought to the German democracy—or than the centralization that another depression would now cause in Washington, London, Paris and the other allied sovereign capitals of Atlantica.)

By turning to Chapter I of *Union Now* one can get perhaps enough other details to see the situation in the Thirteen States in those days when the chief executive of a sovereign state styled himself "His Excellency George Clinton, Esquire, Governor of the State of New York, General and Commander-in-Chief of all the Militia and Admiral of the Navy of the same." Incidentally, His Excellency was one of those who bitterly opposed "sacrificing" state sovereignty to transform the Confederation into a federal union.

In our misguided day, the majority seem to regard the Declaration of Independence as His Excellency did, as if the memorable thing it accomplished was to separate us from Britain and as if the independence it declared was for the state rather than the citizen. But to other leaders of that day, whom we remember better than we do His Excellency, the separation from Britain and the establishment of Thirteen "Free and Independent States" were not ends in themselves, but merely means to establish the principles of free government and of equal individual liberty for "all men" which the Declaration began by declaring.

The Confederation's failure to serve these ends reminded these leaders that the Declaration had also asserted that "whenever any Form of Government becomes destructive of these aims it is the Right of the People to alter or to abolish it, and to institute new Government, laying its foundations on such principles and organizing its powers in such form, as to them shall seem most likely to effect their Safety and Happiness." The language was clear, but many of their fellow American could not believe that the unlimited sovereignty of their own state could become as destructive to life and liberty as George III's had been. They were as confused as was His Excellency, George C. There was then no threat of attack by any powerful autocrat to unite them; instead there was a depression to keep them divided. Even so, they sent their delegates in 1787 to Philadelphia and there—in the same room in Independence Hall where they had signed their revolutionary Declaration—their Convention devised the federal union way . . . of "life, liberty and the pursuit of happiness" . . . for citizens, not states.

CREATING FEDERAL "GOVERNMENT OF, BY AND FOR THE PEOPLE"

We can see now more clearly than was possible then the essential thing they did in changing from confederation to federal union. They simply made their inter-state government a representative democracy like each democracy in it. They changed from a government of, by and for states to a "government of the people, by the people, for the people"— thus establishing the basic difference between all federal unions and all confederations, leagues, alliances. We have become so used to Lincoln's famous phrase that we now glide over its deep meaning. That meaning had to be written in his time in blood before enough men could see it. We cannot ponder Lincoln's words too thoughtfully now.

Government of the people: All government must govern something, operate on something, maintain itself and enforce its laws against some sort of lawbreaker. Inter-state government has only two choices: It must either be a government of states as units, or a government of the people individually as units. Whereas the Confederation sought to govern sovereign armed states, the new Federal Union was organized to govern only the citizen in each state.

The framers of the Federal Constitution had learned from personal experience that a government could not effectively operate on states—that a government of governments was, as Hamilton said, a "political monster." In their state governments they had not followed the absurd principle of trying to coerce and govern towns and counties as units; they governed instead the citizens in them individually. Thanks largely to George Mason, they decided to follow the same common-sense way in their inter-state government. It seems simple enough, but, as Tocqueville pointed out, this had never been done before in all the world's various attempts to organize inter-state government. He ranked it "as a great discovery in modern political science."

Government by the people: Some unit must govern in

any government—and inter-state government must be a government either by the states or by the people in them individually. We have noted that the state governments governed the Confederation through their appointees, with each state accorded equal weight regardless of the number of people in it. The new Federal Union was organized to be governed on the principle of majority rule by the citizens in each state, weighed roughly as equals.

Here again the framers of the Constitution did the common-sense thing. They had tried to run none of their state governments by the grotesque confederation system, with one vote for each county, and unanimity necessary for serious action. They merely transferred to their inter-state government the system they used in their state governments, after adding safeguards against the small states being dominated by the larger ones, and against centralization.

It was this change that has allowed the Federal Union government to escape the remoteness from the people that has been the curse of all confederations, leagues and alliances, and to respond to public opinion as quickly and effectively as any democratic government must. This innovation, too, seems simple enough. Yet nothing in the Constitution threatened more to disrupt the Federal Convention than this shift in the basis of power from equal states to equal citizens. And nothing in American history was more completely forgotten by the drafters of the Geneva Covenant, the United Nations Charter and the North Atlantic Treaty Organization.

Government for the people: Government is always made for some primary purpose, and inter-state government must either be made for the states in it or for the people, the citizens. The Articles of Confederation began, "We, the undersigned delegates of the states affixed to our names," and set out to safeguard each state's "sovereignty, freedom and independence." The framers of the Constitution made Federal Union—as George Mason put it—"a government for men and not for societies of men or States." They made this clear in the very first words of the Preamble:

> We the People of the United States, in Order to form a more perfect Union, establish Justice, insure domestic Tranquility, provide for the common Defence, promote the general Welfare, and secure the Blessings of Liberty to ourselves and our Posterity, do ordain and establish this Constitution for the United States of America.

Here, once more, they did the common-sense thing. They made their inter-state government clearly for themselves, like their state governments. None of these was organized for the preposterous purpose of keeping the town or county governments absolutely independent. Yet here, too, the framers of the Constitution were doing something new in inter-state government, correcting a fatal error and making another fertile contribution to political science.

Uniting the People and Dividing their Governments, the Better to Rule Them

They made Federal Union a government for the people not only in their clear-cut words, but in a most substantial way. Their American forefathers had learned this way to greater freedom one hundred and fifty years before—in the Fundamental Orders of Connecticut of 1639.

They had proved by experience that men can secure more freedom by (a) uniting instead of dividing themselves and (b) dividing instead of uniting their governors. They had learned to divide the powers of government according to whether the majority of citizens would gain more by having them local or by making them general, and to keep all who exercised these powers equally dependent on the people. Just as they employed one set of men to run their house for them, another set to run their farm, and another to run their looms, they employed one set of men to govern their town, another set to govern their country, and a third to govern their state. They kept each set as directly dependent on them as are spokes on the hub of a wheel.

But, until 1787, they had not only stopped this system at the state line, but reversed it there as we still do. They had let the men elected to govern their relations inside the state govern their relations with other states, too.

In setting up our present Constitution they arranged to govern those relations also by men they chose themselves for this particular job. They returned again to the way of common sense. They centered this fourth spoke, too, on themselves as the hub, instead of on the rim of their wheel, as in the Confederation.

Then they divided the powers of government between the new Union government and the Thirteen State governments according to which would serve the people better. Wherever they agreed that they would all gain freedom by transferring a power from each state government to the Union government they transferred it—and forbade their state representatives to meddle henceforth in their inter-state affairs. Wherever they agreed that the people would be freer if the powers of government were left where they were, they kept them there, and forbade their Union representatives to meddle in such affairs. They required the Union to guarantee that all rights not specifically given it would remain in the hands of the state governments, respectively, or in the hands of the people.*

The makers of the Constitution ended by shifting only five major powers from the state governments to the Union government. But by this shift they gained for the people these five tremendous advantages:

First, they abolished those Thirteen independent armies that were threatening to embroil them in war, and they secured a far more effective power for peace and for defense.

Second, they abolished those Thirteen fluttering currencies and gained a common, stable means of doing business.

Third, they removed Thirteen tariff walls at one blow, and gained the rich free-trade market the world envies.

Fourth, they brushed aside Thirteen barriers to communications. They already enjoyed under the Confederation the freedom that a common postal service brings; they gained a cheaper, freer inter-state river and coastal service—while clearing the way for steamship, railway, telegraph, telephone, automobile, airplane, wireless, and television.

Fifth, they avoided the many restrictions and dangers of being divided into Pennsylvanians, New Yorkers, Rhode Islanders, and so on, and secured the vast freedom of American citizenship, without losing their state citizenship.

They gained all these advantages for all the 3,000,000 freemen of the Thirteen States equally—and far more for us, their posterity, 180,000,000 strong, who now enjoy Federal Union in fifty states. I call this making "government for the people" in a great way, both in principle and in practice. This was another of the innovations that distinguish federal union from confederations, leagues, alliances and all other systems of inter-state organization. It helped make the Constitution, as one of its critics, Luther Martin, told the Federal Convention, "a perfect medley of confederated and national government, without example and without precedent."

The "Astonishing, Unexampled Success" that Followed

Such was the revolutionary experiment our forefathers made when they replaced confederation with the world's first

---

* For clarity and brevity I am including in the Constitution the first ten amendments. I consider them, moreover, as being practically part of the original Constitution since it could not have been ratified had there not been a tacit understanding to add them.

federal union. We shall see in Chapter 7 the confusion in which this change—which seems so simple now—was made. But first, consider the result.

The result, as Lord Acton has said, was an "astonishing and unexampled success." The inventors of federal union had thus "solved," he said, "two problems which had hitherto baffled the capacity of the most enlightened nations: they had contrived a system of federal government which prodigiously increased the national power and yet respected local liberties and authorities; and they had founded it on the principle of equality, without surrendering the securities for property and freedom." *

Can you name three of those eleven territorial disputes that were dividing the Thirteen States in 1787? Speaking on the lecture platform, I have put that question to many thousands of Americans all over the Union. I have never found a single one who could name even three. That shows how thoroughly federal union makes for peace. It settled these disputes so well they are forgotten.

Of course, there was one Civil War. We shall consider it in Chapter 8. Meanwhile we need but to note that all governments (centralized republics, monarchies, aristocracies, what not) have also suffered civil war, while leagues, alliances and confederations have had no end of wars between members. I recall no federal union that has ever been threatened with war between two member states.

So much for peace. Consider human equality and freedom. When the first federal union was established no country on earth could be rated democratic by present standards. The Thirteen States were the most advanced, but though they declared "all men are created equal," they restricted the vote to men of property, and they permitted slavery. Almost no one in them then even suggested giving women any rights. *The history of our Federal Union has been the history of the elimination of the exceptions to the great principle of equal liberty which, as Lincoln said, "the great Republic . . . lives by and keeps alive."*

First, our Union was extended to include all white men by the establishment of manhood suffrage. Next we extended it to the slaves—though these new citizens still, to our shame, do not enjoy equal rights in some states. And then we admitted even our mothers, sweethearts, wives and daughters to the Union's full citizenship. Meanwhile public schools were spreading out more than ever before in history, as were other opportunities equally open to all. We are still far from the ideal, but no form of government has ever brought nearly

* *Historical Essays and Studies*, Macmillan, London, p. 124.

so much liberty and equal dignity to so many millions as our Federal Union has already done.

Turn to the economic side. In the first ten years of Federal Union those Thirteen poverty-stricken States quadrupled their foreign trade. The Union began with a debt load of $75,000,000 inherited from the Confederation. Then it purchased Louisiana for $15,000,000, bought Florida for $5,000,000 and borrowed $98,000,000 during the War of 1812. But instead of accumulating debt, the Federal Union was able to pay off the debt so rapidly that, by 1835, it distributed a surplus of $28,000,000.

THE ONE GREAT CHANGE THAT CAUSED
THE GREAT SUCCESS

How are you going to account for this astounding change from war alarms to peace, from depression to prosperity, from failure to success?

Some say it was all due to economic factors, to the frontier, free land, rich natural resources. But when the Confederation possessed all that vast wilderness to the Mississippi River, it could not even borrow a dollar.

Others attribute the success to great leaders we had then —but Washington, Hamilton, Jefferson, Madison, Franklin, were all alive under the Confederation; yet even they could not make that system work.

Nor did success result from any change in human nature. The same Americans were alive in 1786 and in 1790. But in 1786 they were getting into more and more depression and disputes, and in 1790 they were getting out.

How can you account for that astonishing transformation from failure to success, except by attributing it to the one great change that had occurred—to the change in the basis of government from the sovereign states to the sovereign citizens, to this "more perfect" application of the principles of the Declaration of Independence?

And so we Americans who call ourselves Federal Unionists or Atlantic Unionists today say to you now: How much longer are we going to waste precious time, and treasure, and lives, fiddling along with the diplomatic system's leagues, alliances, confederations, which have already brought us two World Wars and a great depression, and now threaten us with worse war, depression, dictatorship?

Why is it, we ask you, that this great American invention is the one answer to the problem of peace which we Americans have neglected most? Why is it that even now the boldest among our statesmen are rated bold because they propose confederation—a system which, though better than an alliance or league—has failed in the best conditions? Why have we done so little to apply beyond our shores the 100 per cent American principles which our fathers carried steadily on, from the Atlantic to the Pacific?

True we have now—at long last—carried them beyond our Pacific shore by admitting Alaska and Hawaii as states in the Union. We have ended the long rule of two assumptions that never had any basis in the Constitution—that states of the Union must be connected by land, and dominated by the white race. This is a most encouraging sign. But why then should any Americans still shy at Atlantic Union? Since we can federate with Alaska, a state that is only a few miles from Soviet territory, why can we not federate with Norway and the German Federal Republic which also adjoin the Soviet empire, to say nothing of such nations as France, which are far from Moscow's frontiers? Since we can federate with the multi-racial Hawaiian Islands, why should we first go through a confederate stage with the British Isles which are much closer to Washington?

Why not at least attempt once to form an Atlantic federation before saying that we can't—or that we must try confederation first? Why not try instead to transfer from our national democracies to a new Atlantic Union democracy those same basic powers which the Thirteen States transferred to the American Union—since we have proved ever since 1789 that this makes astoundingly for peace, prosperity and freedom for everyone?

Why not have the Atlantic Union guarantee, as does our own Union, that all powers, not specifically given to the Federal Government, shall remain in the hands of each state in it? Why not try to organize an Atlantic Union government broadly on the same basis as our own federation and all others—with Legislature, Court and Executive? Why not put representation in it on the same population basis as in our Union, with the same safeguards that its Senate gives the smaller states?

We run no risk in attempting this at the Atlantic Convention, we sign no check in blank. No one can tell in advance what the details of such a Constitution would provide. They could and should be worked out in the Convention. We are committed to nothing the Convention does until we have not only seen and studied the text of any Constitution it produces, but ratified it after full discussion. If we think anything in it is too risky, we can reject it then. We run no risk whatever in this process. The only real risk we run lies in delaying further to try our hands at federal union.

We, the free people of Atlantica, still possess the power to make the world immensely safer for democracy simply by changing our minds, simply by having the courage, the common sense, the vision, to do for our children what the Virginians and the Pennsylvanians and the New Yorkers had the courage, the common sense, the vision to do in 1787-1789—unite behind a common Bill of Rights in a Federal Union. Why should not the Americans, Britons, French, Dutch, Canadians, and other Atlanticans at least try to do this too . . . today?

CHAPTER 5

British Riddle, French *Mystère*, American Enigma

> It is a riddle wrapped in a mystery inside an enigma.
> —*Sir Winston Churchill, October 1, 1939.*

> Every American knows one must sacrifice part of one's selfish interests in order to save the rest. We French seek to keep all, and thus often lose everything.—*Tocqueville*, Democracy in America, *Vol. IV, Chapter 8, 1835 (my translation).*

Perhaps we should ask first, not why shouldn't we try to federate Atlantica, but why haven't we tried already? Why is it that we the people of the Disunited States of Atlantica have delayed so long to attempt this? Here is indeed "a riddle wrapped in a mystery inside an enigma"—as Churchill said of Russian policy. Why have the British, the French and, above all, the Americans—to mention no more—shied away so long from even exploring the possibility of Atlantic Union?

THE BRITISH RIDDLE

Consider first what a triple-wrapped riddle this is as regards the British. These pioneers invented representative government. Their Parliamentary system has been copied all round the world. Their Union of England and Scotland in 1707 was a very helpful precedent for the drafters of the Federal Constitution at Philadelphia. The fact that the federal union system was not invented by them but by their "colonials"—worse still, by colonials who had won the only war the British have lost in centuries—this would explain why any people, except the British, might scorn to explore Atlantic federal union. The British rightly pride themselves on being not petty but practical in political affairs, on not nursing grudges and on adapting themselves to changed conditions.

British history has long been one of turning peacefully from systems that were no longer giving results, and trying in time other systems that promised to work better. And so it is not surprising that they were the first Europeans to recognize in an official report the practicability of the federal system, and to recommend—as did Lord Durham's farsighted report in 1838 proposing the Union of the English and French in Canada—that they try it in their own territory. With this encouragement from London, and the statesmanship of such Canadians as Sir John A. MacDonald, Canada in 1867 became a federal union. Since then the British have done far more to spread federal union around the world than we Americans have (except by the power of successful example). With London's encouragement, the Australian federation, for which the Australian statesman, Sir Henry Parkes, had worked so long, came into being in 1901. In 1910, thanks to the vision of such British apostles of *The Federalist* as Lionel Curtis and Lord Lothian, the victor and the vanquished of the Boer War federated in the Union of South Africa.*

FEDERATION FOR SHEIKDOMS— NOT FOR ATLANTIC DEMOCRACIES

Since then federal union has increasingly become Britain's ready remedy for many kinds of political problems, whether in the densely populated multilingual sub-continent of India, the Malayan peninsula or the far-scattered islands of the British West Indies. The British Empire has spawned ten federal unions thus far; in the Commonwealth that has replaced it, seven of the eleven members are federations.

London's willingness to try to solve almost any problem by

* Both Lionel Curtis and Lord Lothian gained, by study of American constitutional history, an understanding of and a devotion to federal principles, and a willingness to try to solve the toughest problems by them, which I have rarely seen equalled by my compatriots. I cannot recommend too strongly *World Order* (*Civitas Dei*) by Lionel Curtis (Oxford Press, 1939). As for Lord Lothian, my own belief is that, had it not been for his untimely death in 1941, while he was ambassador in Washington, the great opportunity to build an Atlantic Union which we had during the war would not have been lost.

federal union was perhaps never carried to a greater extreme than when *The Economist* on May 24, 1958, described the dangers that Britain faced in the ten tiny sheikdoms on the Persian Gulf and Arabian coast, and asked:

> Is there any choice but federation, or else ultimate absorption by Saudi Arabia? And if the British preference is for the former, how many British interests would be jettisoned if encouragement were given to federation under multi-national auspices instead of on purely British responsibility?

To gain the full flavor of *The Economist*'s belief in federalism, one must add that it described these sheikdoms as feudal "fiefs" with undefined frontiers, "poor, quarrelsome, living on little beyond hope of oil, disinclined to be harnessed in unfamiliar traces, entailing federations, frontiers, courts or police," and inhabited by "ragged, hungry and unlettered" people. I confess that *The Economist*'s faith that federal union would work even in these conditions far surpasses mine, although some in London have found my faith in a federal Atlantic Union "extravagant." Be it noted that *The Economist*, in proposing to federate the Arab sheikdoms, suggested that this be done under the "multi-national" auspices of the British, American, French and Dutch governments—but not that the latter nations federate themselves. This brings us to the conundrum:

Why has this great British journal not led in getting the Atlantic problem tackled federally? Why has it not shown here half the faith it has shown in federation elsewhere? I would not single it out for criticism—its attitude, in this regard has been all too common in London since the war: *The Economist*, in fact, has been relatively advanced on the subject of Atlantic Union—though, like most other British opinion-makers, its receptivity toward Atlantic Union was much greater in 1939 than since 1945. Why is it that British policy-framers, who found *Union Now* worthy of such serious consideration in 1939 when they faced the Nazi dictatorship, have been so silent or negative as regards Atlantic federation since the still more formidable Communist dictatorship replaced Hitler as the danger?

THE CHURCHILL PUZZLE

The puzzlement grows when one turns to Sir Winston Churchill. His gifts of leadership are magnificent, his prestige vast throughout Atlantica, and particularly in America.

Why has he not urged that the United Kingdom and the United States lead in uniting the Atlantic community by the federal principles that had united so successfully the British and the French in Canada? In 1936 he had the vision to write in *While England Slept:*

> I have watched this famous island descending incontinently, fecklessly the stairway that leads to a dark gulf. It is a fine broad stairway at the beginning, but after a bit the carpet ends. A little farther on there are only flagstones, and a little farther on still these break beneath your feet.

Ten years later, he spoke in Fulton, Missouri—after events had proved his prophetic powers. Why did he not make his island still more famous then by leading boldly toward Atlantic Union? Did he think that Britain must await American leadership? Such considerations never kept him during the war from standing up stoutly for his ideas, however much they differed from President Roosevelt's. After the latter's death left Sir Winston the one towering statesman and hero of Atlantica, he did not hesitate to give a lead to America in his Fulton speech of March 5, 1946 on "The Sinews of Peace." But the lead was toward Anglo-American alliance—to base peace on the sinews that had failed the Thirteen States in the Articles of Confederation and that Washington in his Farewell Address had warned against, as bound always to fail. Sir Winston had offered Union to a falling France when alliance failed Britain in 1940; why did he not propose Union to America in the speech that first drove home the danger behind "the Iron Curtain" it made famous? This leader's parents had united in him both Britain and America; yet he never suggested that we even explore the possibilities for peace that lie in an Atlantic-wide development of the federal sinews that made his motherland no less famous than his father's isle. Why?

To the Land of Locke, Can the Lands of Lincoln and of Lenin be Equal?

Why have his successors in London continued to shy away from any proposal—whether on an Atlantic or a European scale—that applied to the United Kingdom the same federal principles that London was then encouraging the people of the Empire, from India to the West Indies, to apply in more difficult circumstances? Did these Prime Ministers feel that, lacking the Churchillian prestige, they must follow

Washington's lead? But they, too, did not hesitate to differ from Washington. They recognized Red China. They opposed General MacArthur's strategy in Korea. They landed at Suez. They led a skeptical President Eisenhower to seek peace through the Summit meeting . . . that blew up in Paris.

Some Britons say the reason is that federal union and written constitutions are foreign and distasteful to the British spirit, which prefers the "functionalist," "gradualist" approach. But none of this has deterred the British from recommending written federal constitutions for Britons from Canada to Australia—and proposing one even for illiterate sheikdoms. Certainly no one would say that the United Kingdom has never proposed trying to solve its own Atlantic problem by this method because the British feel themselves to be less politically mature than the Americans, Australians, Burmese, Canadians, Hindus, Nigerians, South Africans, West Indians—(not to mention again these sheikdoms).

Who can explain the postwar attitude of the British—parent of Parliaments, godfather of Federal Unions, nurse of John Stuart Mill, tutor of Lord Acton,—situated on their famous island, the natural bridge between Western Europe and North America . . . this practical people, this magnanimous people, whom Churchill called "unique in this respect: They are the only people who like to be told how bad things are, who like to be told the worst" (of course, about themselves, too)? Here is this people, of all peoples, helping divide Europe in Sixes and Sevens, helping balance the Earth between Communism (Chinese and Russian) and Freedom (American and British) and preaching federal union to everyone, but themselves. They talk as if it were practical to base disarmament on the assumption that equality in weapons counts more than inequality in the will to kill . . . that if only they can get the Russian or Chinese Communist believer in violence, and the American believer in the ideals of freedom and peace (which the finest spirits of Britain itself have always held high) both to agree to outlaw or limit atomic weapons, all will be well—that gunmen are no more likely to attack than pacifists . . . if only both are armed equally with .22 caliber pistols.

Here are the people who produced and who cherish Locke (and the Labour Party), seeking to prevent war by putting the Power that produced and cherishes Lenin on a par, as regards peace, with the Power that produced and cherishes Lincoln. Here are the great British people, through whom I, like so many others, have learned so much, and come to expect so much . . . putting their trust now in the antitheses of all that made them great—not in trying themselves to practise on an Atlantic scale the federal principles they have spread to all the races of mankind . . . not in working with bulldog tenacity to create the oceanic nucleus of Tennyson's Parliament of Man . . . Is this not "a riddle wrapped in a mystery inside an enigma"?

THE *Mystère* OF DE GAULLE'S FRANCE

When we turn to President de Gaulle's France, the riddle is no less baffling, if we have some of the understanding of the French (and of what they have done for freedom and union) that we have of the British and Americans.

No other people has in their blood the spirit of individual freedom through union of sovereign states so much as have the Americans—*except the French.* The very name of *France* stands, indeed, for the political ideal of all the Atlantic Community—as the names, *America, Britain, Germany* and that of other nations do not in their derivation. *France* and *French* come from the Franks; that Teutonic tribe left their name even in English as an adjective, *frank,* originally meaning "free—not in bondage," and now meaning in a positive way, "free in uttering one's real sentiments"—the same as *franc* means in French. And *francais* meant *freeman*—what we all aspire to be—long before nationalism reduced its meaning to the present one, a citizen of one nation.

Before nationalism became a disuniting foe of freedom, it was a force for union. I would agree with Bernard Shaw that it began among the French, with Jeanne d'Arc, to unite people of the same language in an ever-wider community and government. The French were not only the first great people on the European Continent to be united under a common government; as Tocqueville pointed out in his *Ancien Regime,* they had, long before the French Revolution, gone much further than any other nation there in breaking down feudalism's multitudinous barriers.

The French Revolution has some striking things in common with the American Revolution that immediately preceded it. It wiped out the customs barriers among the provinces of France as the Federal Constitution removed those among the Thirteen States. Both peoples established free trade over an immensely greater area than it had known before, and both did it by peaceful agreement, and at one stroke—not gradually over a long period, as elsewhere. What is more important, both achieved this miracle by tying economic union to free political union.

Most strikingly similar of all, both the American and the French Revolutions began their work of union of the free in the same way. They both began by declaring in writing fundamentally the same principles of individual freedom and equality as the basis and the purpose of government. Practically no other peoples on earth accepted these principles then; now practically no people on earth does not at least pretend to practice, or aim at some of them. Having thus agreed on their aims, both the Americans and French proceeded to set up written constitutions to provide institutions by which to attain them.

As the United States led in the New World in uniting states by its federal example, so France has led in the Old. First, it set the example of uniting people of the same language, divided by feudal sovereignties, in the modern nation-state—an example that Italy and Germany followed in the 19th century. Then France led in trying to unite nation states by federation.

Blind to the fact that nationalism could be a balkanizing as well as a uniting force, the United States raised Woodrow Wilson's banner of the "self-determination of nations," and the ideal of a League of all nations rather than a Union of any. It was France that then raised the federal banner. As *The New York Times* correspondent at the League in Geneva, I had the ironic experience of reporting the efforts of Aristide Briand to unite Europe as early as 1929 on principles more American (though not fully federal) than those of Wilson's League.

When National Socialism seemed on the verge of victory, it was again a Frenchman, Jean Monnet, who led with the proposal for an Anglo-French Union. And it was General de Gaulle—as his *Memoirs** relate—who urged Churchill to make this offer then. It was again from France (after an ephemeral Churchillian gesture) that came the leadership which produced the Schuman Plan, Euratom, the Common Market.

PRIME MINISTER DEBRÉ FOR ATLANTIC UNION

President de Gaulle himself picked for his Prime Minister, Michel Debré, who in the book, *Peace by Oceanic Union†*, which he co-authored in 1945 with Emmanuel

---

* See "De Gaulle Urged Federal Union on Churchill in 1940," July 1958 FREEDOM & UNION. A reprint is available from it for 10¢.

† This book was published serially under this title by *Freedom & Union*, starting in July 1959, from the original French book entitled, *Demain La Paix* (Plon, Paris). These reprints of chapters in it may be had from the magazine: "National Sovereignty—an Obsolete Dogma" (30¢), "Let the Atlantic Peoples Unite" (20¢), and "Oceans Unite Men" (20¢).

Monick, eloquently called for Atlantic Union in such words as these:

> Let the Atlantic Peoples unite in the same union that brings together the inhabitants of a great city when threatened, and there will then immediately be an opportunity for peace.

How then to explain the Atlantic policy that President de Gaulle has pursued? Does it result, as so many say, from an "obsession" with the "grandeur" of France? In an "Open Letter" to him, entitled " 'Grandeur' or Greatness?" which I wrote in the April, 1959, *Freedom & Union* on the eve of his visit to the United States, I explained at length why I believed that this explanation was not valid. To quote it:

> Why am I so bold as to differ so completely on these basic matters with the multitude? Partly because I believe that France means to you basically what America means to me. It does not mean primarily the land or even the people (though we love the land we were born in and have a sublime faith in its people). It means certain ideals for which our country stands and which to you are the soul of France as they are to me the soul of America.
>
> If this intangible, immortal spirit were not France to you, if the land and the people came first, then you would have agreed with Pétain that all was lost when the latter two were occupied and surrendered. Instead, from another country and all alone, you broadcast, "France is not lost!" You held that the true France was not then on the Continent but on an island, and that its true spokesman was not its government, but a lone Frenchman in London. You proved that your concept of France was the latent concept of your countrymen.
>
> Another reason why I am so bold as to differ with the multitude about you is that even you can not be more passionately devoted to your concept of France than I to my concept of America. Nor can even you— with all respect—have more faith in your fellow-citizens than I in mine, nor be surer that what we love above all in our countries is not only latent in our compatriots, but the thing they will sacrifice most for in the end.

GREATNESS NEEDS NO PASSPORT

The basic question, I added, was this: Shall France, America, Britain, continue to seek greatness in nationalistic terms that convince no one of their greatness, least of all Mr. K— who boasts that Communist dictatorship will soon "bury" even the greatest of the three by this definition? Or shall we all seek the kind of greatness that we all know at heart is truly great—that History will confirm and that will meanwhile bury dictatorship? Shall we seek it together, in union— and thereby, incidentally, put behind our common free ideals far more of the armed and industrial power we now prize so much than any of our nations can possibly gain alone or in mere alliance? I then appealed to President de Gaulle personally to lead:

> To change our present concept of national greatness to the one by which we ourselves judge the past, and by which the future will judge us in turn, some statesman with a deep sense of History must point the way. You have that sense of History, Mr. President, to a rare degree. You have also the courage and the Atlantic-wide personal authority that are needed too, for this is no little change. And so I turn to you.
>
> I suggest no sacrifice of the true greatness of France, nor of America, Britain or any other people. I firmly believe that France's greatness is beneficial and essential to us Americans as ours is to the French. I know the inspiration, courage, faith that I myself have drawn from Jeanne d'Arc, from Valmy, from Verdun, and, if you will pardon me, from you. I have seen plenty of proof that the virtues of those who incarnate the greatness of America, as do Washington and Lincoln, help make Frenchmen and France greater, too. Greatness needs no passport. The quality that permits this transfusion of spirit across national boundaries, oceans, ages, is to me a precious asset of human nature and it is found throughout our species. It is no less human—but no asset—that we all see the faults in other men and nations much more easily than our own.

My appeal to President de Gaulle to lead in bridging the Atlantic concluded with these words:

> A bridge so wide cannot be built from either shore alone. It must be built simultaneously from both, and from solid bases. What firmer bases does History offer for bridging the Atlantic by political union than France and the U.S.A.? The momentous enterprise seems about to begin on the American shore. It depends now on you, Mr. President, in France. Shall France not continue to lead in the Old World as America in the New, in this, the great line of their history? In this greatest

venture toward Union of the Free, it rests now with
you whether they shall lead together.

Is it not another "riddle wrapped in a mystery inside an
enigma" that so great a man, with so great a love for France,
should not yet have given this honor to the land of Lafayette,
Tocqueville and Victor Hugo—to the people from whose
Congrès, Parlement, Constitution and *Union Fédérale*
the English-speaking world drew the words for our most cherished free institutions?

The American Enigma

The enigma of America's long failure even to explore Atlantic Union is the greatest of all—but it is so obvious as to
need the fewest words. We Americans created federal union
—or the Federal Constitution created the American people,
as a body politic—whichever way you prefer. We have more
experience with federation than has any other people, or
than we have with diplomacy, alliance, league, confederation
or any other system of inter-state relations.

No people has ever been so immensely rewarded by any
political system as we have been by federal union. Nor has
any people ever been warned so strongly against the other
inter-state systems as we by rightly revered statesmen. In his
Farewell Address, Washington stressed that alliance would
never work even among our own Thirteen States. He said:

> To the efficiency and permanency of your Union, a
> government for the whole is indispensable. No alliance,
> however strict, between the parts can be an adequate
> substitute; they must inevitably experience the infrac-
> tions and interruptions which all alliances at all times
> have experienced.

Both Washington and Jefferson warned against entering
into entangling alliances with the nations of Europe—never
against our federating with other democracies. Yet we have
risked Atlantic alliance rather than attempt Atlantic Union.

How can it be that in our federated "home of the brave,"
presidential candidates, party platforms and Congressional
resolutions do not dare even breathe aloud such honored
American words as "Union" and "Federal," when they refer
to the Atlantic democracies? Why is it that, however much
they may stress the "imperative" need to unite effectively,
they speak instead of "unity," "community," "cooperation"?
Those who would be tomorrow's leaders call on the Ameri-

can people to open "new frontiers" . . . and never recall the
means by which we have always pushed the frontier forward—Federal Union. Or they call on us to "have the courage
and the confidence that inspired our forebears" . . . but
would have us show this by moving "toward confederation"
in Atlantica—not toward the goal of "a more perfect Union"
in which our forebears put their trust, and to which they ded-
icated us, in the Preamble of the Federal Constitution.
Why? Why? *Why?* Is this not the greatest "riddle wrapped in
a mystery inside an enigma" that any Atlantic people presents? Here even the Kremlin must concede we lead.

If any one thing is the answer to this British riddle, this
French *mystère,* this American enigma, is it not the confusion over sovereignty that afflicts all the free people of Atlantica? Let us seek again to clear it away.

CHAPTER 6

Cancer Cell No. 1 in the Free Body Politic

To thine own self be true,
And it must follow as the night the day,
Thou canst not then be false to any man.
—*Shakespeare,* Hamlet.

The Soviet leaders have also appeared in the role of
the most uncompromising defenders of national sovereignty known to modern times ** The defense of national sovereignty, far from contradicting the goal of a
Soviet world state, has actually become one of the most
formidable weapons in the struggle for its attainment.
**Soviet pre-occupation with construction and indefi-
nite expansion of an all-powerful, all-embracing state
authority, while originally justified as a necessary,
transitory means, has instead become the indestructible,
unwithering end of Soviet society.—*Elliot R. Goodman,*
The Soviet Design for a World State.*

A far greater danger to freedom than the Russian and Chinese dictatorships lies here at home. It is as invisible as cancer cell No. 1, and as virulent. Yet it remains as protected

* The three citations are from pages 114, 125 and 471. I warmly
recommend this entire volume (published by Columbia Press in 1960)
as a timely and fully documented reminder that Communism has a

by tabu, as worshipped as any Baal or Moloch ever was—
and capable of causing, and even inspiring, much more human
sacrifice. What is it? A concept of national sovereignty that
is demonstrably false to the fundamental nature of all the
free peoples whom it now confuses, deceives and betrays. It
is true only to the nature of dictatorship, whether Communist,
National Socialist or Fascist, which alone it serves.

What is evil in one body politic may be good in another,
much as what is poison to one species feeds another. To
Communism our current concept of national sovereignty is
natural and nourishing—as vital as is venom to a viper.
Only to the free is it fatal.

THE CURRENT CONCEPT OF NATIONAL SOVEREIGNTY

This concept, which the free now share with the dictatorships, makes the nation supreme, above all law. It holds the
nation's absolute independence to be the highest good. It calls
on the people to sacrifice their individual liberties and lives
to maintain their nation's freedom to do as it pleases, insofar
as other nations are concerned. In the Congress of the United
States, as in Cuba and the Congo, this concept inflames fiery
opposition to the "surrender" of an iota of the nation's
"right" to be a law unto itself, even where this "sacrifice"
would clearly extend the rights of the citizen, or secure him
against needless sacrifice of his or her liberty and life.

This concept of national sovereignty is, of course, part and
parcel of the ancient dogma that man is made for the State.
We have seen how it was once embodied in "divine right"
sovereigns. Since they claimed absolute power over their own
people, these autocrats naturally had to be, in their relations
with each other, no less sovereign, no less a law each unto
himself. And since the Communist dictatorships are much
more totalitarian than the Czars in their enslavement of their
people to the authority of the State, it is all too natural that
they should continue to uphold between nations the same
concept of sovereignty as did the Czars. They are true to
themselves, inside and out, in their adherence to it.

Not so the other nations, which have overthrown this concept of sovereignty at home, yet still permit it to rule all their
foreign relations. It is most alien to the peoples who have led
the revolution against such absolutism, reversed at home the
dogma that man is made for the State and replaced their unlimited Kings with themselves as the sovereign people. To

thoroughly worked out and never neglected plan for a completely
centralized world government—the antithesis of Atlantic Federal
Union, and the real alternative to it.

these peoples, the concept of national sovereignty which they apply to one another is as unnatural a growth in the body politic as is cancer in the human body. It is a disease as malignant and fatal . . . a far more widespread cause of suffering and grief to their citizens than cancer . . . a more massive killer even than the H-bomb, which is but one of the myriad ways of destroying men that it now commands.

THE TRUE DEMOCRATIC CONCEPT OF SOVEREIGNTY

One cannot too often repeat that the concept of national sovereignty that is true to the nature of a free people holds that: (1) The State is made of, by and for man; (2) the nation's sovereignty resides in its citizens equally; (3) they delegate a part of their sovereignty to the national government, and other parts to their state, county and municipal governments; (4) they reserve to themselves the remainder, including the right to re-delegate any of it (except the right to delegate and re-delegate) when and as they please, provided this is done by Law that they have consented to; (5) the purpose for which they delegate any of it to any government is always and only to preserve and advance equally the individual sovereignty of the citizens—his or her life, liberty and power to pursue happiness as he or she pleases (always under the Rule of Law which these sovereigns have freely constituted).

This democratic concept of sovereignty is opposed to the totalitarian concept no less completely in other respects. It admits of no absolute, unlimited sovereignty even in its sovereigns—to say nothing of the bodies politic they together create. It leaves no sovereign citizen a law unto himself; holds no man or institution above the Law. Although its sovereign citizens never alienate their sovereignty, they always agree to limit even their own exercise of it. Such limitation is inherent in their acceptance of the establishment of their constitution by some degree of majority vote, and in their elimination, practically, of the right of veto that is theoretically inherent in sovereignty.

Kings who maintained an absolute veto over their own people could reason that such sovereignty required them to insist on an unlimited veto in their affairs with other kings who claimed equal sovereignty. Such sovereigns could fancy it to be practical, or possible, to get this claim admitted. The great are subject, as Descartes said, to great aberrations.

Common men have more common sense. Enough at any rate to realize that there is a vital difference between their sovereignty and that of autocrats.

Such kings could hope to survive amid the anarchy their sovereign claims created. For they could send their subjects to get killed for them—"for King and Country"—in the wars to which their concept of sovereignty inevitably led, and leads. But when each citizen is sovereign, none can hope thus to escape. Each sovereign then has his own life directly at stake. In such circumstances most men readily understand that life is not possible if each citizen sovereign claims that his sovereignty must be as unlimited in relation to his fellow sovereigns as is his rule over his own body.

And so men, in making themselves each sovereign in their own nation, never lay claim to such attributes of sovereignty as having a veto, and being above the law. They readily accept the Rule of Law as made by a freely formed majority of them, so long as the law and the majority are also limited by enough individual liberty to keep each citizen reasonably sovereign. For the democratic concept of sovereignty, which always makes all citizens subject to the Law, also makes the Law always subject to the will of the citizens. Its Law is not absolute, as was the law of the Medes and the Persians "which altereth not"—even at the instance of Darius, as he found when, against his own will, his own law forced him to throw Daniel into the den of lions.

The democratic concept of sovereignty also keeps the citizen reasonably sovereign in other ways. For example, by having the principal representatives to whom he delegates part of his sovereignty elected by equal vote of the citizens and periodically responsible to them, and by establishing a Bill of Rights and judicial machinery, to assure that the sovereign powers which the citizens reserve to themselves are not infringed by their representatives, or by their fellow citizens.

Perhaps the most significant proof of the sovereignty of the citizens in any nation is the degree to which it leaves the individual free to follow his conscience—where conscience is not a subterfuge—as in refusing to obey draft laws that require him to kill other men, or otherwise violate what to his conscience is a moral Law, superior to any law made by men. In last analysis, the sovereignty of the citizen, as we have seen, is founded on the idea that the most sacred thing in every man is the spark of God within him. The absolutist concept holds the state sacred, deifies the nation, and denies —today—even the soul's existence. Freedom's concept of sovereignty holds nothing human sacred except the life, liberty and dignity of the individual, and recognizes in him no unlimited divine right—except that of his conscience. There could be no sharper, deeper, soul-revealing contrast than that between the concept of sovereignty we uphold at home and the one we uphold abroad.

THE CANCEROUS CONCEPT THAT ENDANGERS FREEDOM

Would you not agree that the concept of sovereignty set forth in the preceding section is the true democratic one? Must you not also agree that in our foreign relations we reverse this concept—even when we deal with other peoples whose bodies politic were created by it, too? Must you not further agree that the principle of national sovereignty we and they apply to one another is part and parcel of the absolutist dogma from which we and they recoil with instinctive horror when embodied in a Hitler, a Stalin? Why do we not recoil at its presence in ourselves? The reason is that we have not yet seen it there. And so this cancer has become the deadliest danger we now face, and the hardest one to extirpate.

To take half a loaf is usually better than to take none, but to take out only half a cancer is better only if one seeks to kill the victim in the cruellest way.

To understand how much more dangerous this invisible cancer in us is than the dictatorships whose massive arms we see so well, let us suppose that we remove their armaments, and even them, but not the cancer in us. To thwart thus their aim of "burying us" would be far more dangerous now than this operation proved to be in World War I and II. But let us assume that it succeeds once again (in the sense of removing the dictatorship)—and that we survive. Even so, past experience proves it only too probable that we would soon thereafter face the totalitarian threat in even more fearful form.

World War I removed the Kaiser type of autocrat completely; none of the deeply-rooted hereditary despots of Europe remained. The Romanoff, Hapsburg, Hohenzollern and Ottoman dynasties went down for good. The world lay as never before in the hands of the most democratic powers. But the war left their relations with one another governed by the concept of unlimited national sovereignty. Soon absolutism, in the more virulent form of Hitler's National Socialism, regained control of Germany.

To remove the Nazis proved much more dangerous than to remove Kaiser, Czar and Sultan. Again the only thing removed was the monstrous visible growth, not the hidden cancerous concept in the free bodies politic. Result: Now again we face a still more formidable form of dictatorship. Communism is more aggressively armed than were the Kaiser and the Fuehrer; it holds a stronger defensive position, and it can win by other means than war,—by economic warfare, by depression, by subversion . . . and by the cancerous concept of national sovereignty that still devours our vitals.

How and Why Communism Champions National Sovereignty

The Russian dictatorship has been the most ardent and extreme champion of national sovereignty since World War II. As E. A. Korovin pointed out, as early as 1924, in page 43 of the textbook on international law he published then in Moscow:

"At a time when the general development of European international law moves in the direction of draining sovereignty of its content in the name of contemporary interdependence of states . . . the Soviet government is recognized as the champion of the doctrine of 'classical' sovereignty."

Moscow champions it not to keep the world divided forever into many sovereign nations, but to advance its ultimate goal—the universal Communist State that Marx and Lenin dreamed of. In that world there would be only one sovereign nation in today's diplomatic sense, nor would there be, within that Communist State, any sovereign states in the sense in which they are called "sovereign" in such federal unions as the United States and Switzerland. The world state that Marx and Lenin envisioned is fantastically centralized, not federalized. Lenin especially attacked federalism. True, the problem of nationalities in Russia forced a little federation on him, and the present Soviet Constitution states that "the Union of Soviet Socialist Republics is a federal state." But when these concessions were first made, Lenin himself explained on March 28, 1918 that: "Federation is only a transitional step . . . The federation we are now introducing and which will develop in future, will serve as the surest step to the most solid unification of the different nationalities of Russia into a unitary, democratic, centralized Soviet state."

This policy has continued.* As it has evolved in Russia, Communism has not only discarded the eventual "withering

* Professor Goodman points out on page 262 of *Soviet Design for a World State*:

"Soviet leaders have contrived elaborate federalist-appearing devices that have attempted to take advantage of and to give minimal play to national sentiment not only for the nations under their control, but also for those nations that they seek to attach to their self-proclaimed embryo of a world federation. But using the vocabulary of federalism has never touched the core of their political philosophy, which is thoroughly centralist, nor would it seem to have altered their ultimate aim of a unitary world state." This is the conclusion of his Chapter 7, a 73-page discussion of "The Issue of Centralism versus Federalism in the Leninist Era."

away" of the state into a "stateless" world, envisioned in its
early theory, but has developed to an incredible degree
Marx's highly centralized idea of the final world state. It
plans a world dictatorship in which all power on the planet
would be centered. Such is the appalling apotheosis of the
principle from which our current doctrine of national
sovereignty springs. To bring it about, the Soviet leaders
have become—to quote Dr. Goodman again—"the most uncompromising defenders of national sovereignty in modern
times." He continues:

> There are three basic reasons which would seem to
> account for this urgent Soviet defense of national sover-
> eignty. The first is to perpetuate the anarchy of the
> nation-state system in the non-Soviet world. The Soviet
> leaders are aware of the fact that they would have
> much to lose and the non-Soviet world much to gain if
> that anarchic system were overhauled and strengthened
> . . . Since the second World War, the Soviet regime has
> tried to separate the United States from its allies by
> posing as the defenders of the national sovereignty of
> America's allies against the encroachments of "Ameri-
> can imperialism." *

The other reasons for which Moscow exploits national
sovereignty are 1) to speed the breaking up of the empires
of the West, 2) to keep the new nations formed from them
suspicious of Western offers of help in developing themselves,
and therefore weak and subject to Communist influences,
and above all, 3) to guarantee to the Soviet Union its independence † until it can become strong enough to destroy

---

* *Ibid*, p. 114.

† When the United States offered to place atomic power, of which
it then had a monopoly, under international control, Mr. Gromyko
rejected this on March 5, 1947 as an intolerable threat to the "internal affairs and internal life of states." Replying to Albert Einstein's plea of Sept. 22, 1947 for "a world society based on law and
order," four distinguished Soviet scientists answered that the Soviet
Union was a radical break from the capitalist system, "and now the
proponents of a 'world super-state' are asking us voluntarily to surrender this independence." Einstein replied: "You are such passionate opponents of anarchy in the economic sphere, and yet equally
passionate advocates of anarchy, e.g. unlimited national sovereignty,
in the sphere of international politics." This letter went unanswered.
When the United States proposed veto-free international control,
Vyshinsky on Oct. 18, 1954 denounced this as a "world government"
and emphasized that the United Nations "is an assembly of sovereign states in which the will, interests, desires and views of each
must be respected."

On some earlier occasions—as when Litvinoff sought collective security at the League of Nations against Hitler—Moscow has also
belittled national sovereignty, but only to preserve itself and thus
advance its own scheme for world government.

the independence of all other nations, and men. Just as it invokes the democratic rights of free speech, free press, free assembly to protect its efforts to destroy them, it invokes the rights of nations to preserve and promote* its campaign to merge all nations into the faceless, nation-less, single world sovereignty of the Communist World Dictatorship.

THE COMMUNIST CONCEPT WE ACCEPT—AND NURSE

Nonetheless, of all the false ideas Communism spreads, only its concept of national sovereignty is widely accepted by Atlanticans in general, and by Americans most of all. Moscow cannot take credit for this. This concept is a home-grown fallacy in each Atlantic people. That is one reason why it is so hard for them to rid themselves of it, and so easy for Communism to exploit it. No deception is so persuasive and tenacious as self-deception. Evil is most evil, and hardest to dislodge, when men deem it good.

The current concept of national sovereignty, instead of being recognized by its democratic victims as cancer, is tenderly nursed and carefully protected by these people as vital to health. Most of the political doctors they trust to cure their body politic of the resulting ills seem no wiser. Their remedies are as wrong as those which physicians prescribed prior to Pasteur. And in their attitude toward those who do trace these ills to their true source, they also remind one of the doctors who denounced the French chemist for daring to attack as false the assumption that underlay their therapy.

True, I find an increasing number of political leaders who now agree, in private, that the prevailing concept of national sovereignty endangers the free peoples. Yet most of them still pay lip service to it in public and thus help to maintain Baal's grip on the hearts of men. Few actively attack it; still fewer, openly, or head on.

The braver political doctors tell the patient the cancer is a tumor, or just a little cyst whose removal will involve the sacrifice of no vital organ. Others say that the only "safe" way to remove it is not to let the people know what the doctor is doing; their strategy is the "gradualist" one: They seek to cut the cancer out in a long series of operations, and so little at a time, that the patient will not realize

---

* Even Moscow's brutal suppression of the Hungarian revolutionary government was defended by *Izvestia* on March 9, 1957, as based on the Soviet principle guaranteeing "the strengthening of the sovereignty of each socialist state."

he is losing what he fondly believes to be his heart.* This strategy is safe, but only for the surgeon.

Among the political leaders who are widely trusted, very few indeed dare to question, when seeking election to office of trust, the validity of the prevailing concept of national sovereignty. I can recall no nominee for President of the United States in my time who has ever denounced this concept as false to freedom or sought openly to rid the people of it. Nor have any American Presidents—with a few truly great (and distant) exceptions. . . . Washington, Jefferson, Madison, Jackson, Lincoln.

This concept is indeed a fearfully difficult fallacy to overcome. That is one reason why I am devoting so much attention to it now. Another reason is that there is no other way to cure the ills it causes. From this concept of sovereignty surges the opposition that has already killed so many moves, however slight, to advance freedom's law and order between nations, and has nipped in the bud so many others . . . while it goes blindly on producing policies that advance Communism by further dividing the free. It arms not only those who oppose Atlantic Union, but those who would protect this or that barrier to trade, or who defend the Connally amendment against efforts to breathe a little life into the World Court, or who seek to unite the scientific resources of Atlantica—to mention no more.

Hydra-headed, the prevailing concept of national sovereignty guards like Cerberus the gates of Hell against all attack—none too minor or too wily to elude it. But Cerberus was once overcome: Hercules, unarmed, seized and dragged him up to daylight, by greater strength, applied directly. And to overcome our "monster"—as Herculean George Washington dared to call the current concept of sovereignty —I find no way as sure as this: Frontal attack with the superior power of truth.

A final and greater reason to continue this attack is that Washington proved that by so doing we can hope not only to overcome the monster, but achieve thereby good beyond measure. We can make the Communist threat no more dangerous than Nazi-ism is now—and do this without world war, and much sooner than seems possible today. We can do far more—we can create the high civilization that physical

---

* These are the political doctors who keep telling us that we must resign ourselves to "thirty years of tension" such as we have now —or prepare to live with it even longer, indefinitely. This is considered "realistic"—as if we could keep our freedom healthy by staying in the hospital forever, being treated by defeatists whose diagnosis is wrong and whose advice is dispiriting.

science now puts within the reach of free men, when effectively united and reinspired by their most vital principles. Fear of catastrophe has now reduced hope to talk of mere survival. Once we dreamed of the marvellous life our great grand-children would know. Our own children, and even we ourselves, can enjoy the advantages and challenges of that life—*if* we renounce our false concept of national sovereignty for the one that is true to freedom's nature. No struggle is so worthy of another effort. Let us make it now.

CHAPTER 7

Two American Revolutions Made You Sovereign

A thirst for power, and *the bantling, I had liked to have said monster* [his emphasis] for sovereignty, which have taken such fast hold of the states individually will . . . form a strong phalanx against it [the proposed Federal Government] . . . Yet I would fain try what the wisdom of the proposed Convention will suggest . . . It may be the last peaceable mode.— *George Washington of Virginia, March 10, 1787.*

Col. Mason, [of Virginia, asked]: Is it to be thought that the people of America, so watchful over their interest, so jealous of their liberties, will give up their all, will surrender both the sword and the purse, to the same body, and that too not chosen directly by themselves? . . . Why is it hoped that they will part with it to a National Legislature? The proper answer is that in this case they do not part with power: They only transfer it from one set of immediate representatives to another set . . . He took this occasion to repeat, that notwithstanding his solicitude to establish a national Government . . . "I never will consent to destroying the State governments, and will ever be as careful to preserve the one as the other . . . That the one government will be productive of disputes and jealousies against the other, I believe; but it will produce mutual safety." *Madison's Journal of the Federal Convention, June 20, 1787.**

The question turns, sir, on . . . the expression "We,

* Except that the two sentences quoted at the end are from the notes taken by Robert Yates.

the *people"* instead of the *States* of America. [His emphasis] I need not take much pains to show that the principles of this system are extremely pernicious, impolitic and dangerous . . . Here is a solution as radical as that which separated us from Great Britain . . . Our rights and privileges are endangered, and the sovereignty of the States will be relinquished."—*Patrick Henry, opposing ratification of the Federal Constitution by Virginia, June 5, 1788.*

Confusion has run rife over sovereignty ever since the American Revolution founded the United States on a revolutionary concept of it. There was no such confusion before because there was no such challenge to the hoary dogma that held the State supreme, with man its subject, made to serve it. That dogma then governed not only the external affairs of all of them but, as we have noted, their internal affairs, too. Even in such rare exceptions as the Swiss cantons, it was not challenged clearly, dramatically, as it was in the American Revolution.

True, it had been challenged in the English Revolution of the seventeenth century, and the drama there was personal to a point it never reached in the American Revolution. The latter cut off, politically, the sovereign King and Parliament who sought to tax British subjects without the consent of their representatives, whereas in the English Revolution Parliament physically cut off the head of the sovereign who had governed England unlimited by Parliament.* But though such stark personification of the issue undoubtedly deepens drama, it confuses thought with emotion. Even without this troubling factor, the English Revolution was far from being as clear on principle as was the American Revolution it helped inspire.

Moreover "about the year 1770," as Lord Acton pointed out in his *History of Freedom,* "things had been brought back . . . nearly to the condition which the [English] Revolution had been designed to remedy forever. Europe seemed incapable of becoming the home of free States. It was from America that the . . . ideas long locked in the breast of solitary thinkers, and hidden among Latin folios—burst forth like a conqueror upon the world they were destined to transform, under the title of the Rights of Man. . . . The general presumption was immense on the side of authority; and the

---

* At his trial in 1647, Charles I contended that he was upholding "the freedom and the liberties of the people" . . . as do those Americans and Britons today who oppose limiting by any Atlantic Parliament the sovereignty of their nation in its relations with others.

world believed that the will of the constituted ruler ought
to be supreme, and not the will of the subject people. Very
few bold writers went so far as to say that lawful power may
be resisted in cases of extreme necessity. But the colonizers
of America . . . who had gone forth not in search of gain,
but to escape from laws under which other Englishmen were
content to live were . . . sensitive even to appearances."*
Lord Acton added later:

> American independence was the beginning of a new
> era, not merely as a revival of Revolution, but because
> no other Revolution ever proceeded from so slight a
> cause, or was ever conducted with so much moderation.
> . . . It established . . . democracy in its highest perfec-
> tion, armed and vigilant, less against aristocracy and
> monarchy than against its own weakness and excess.
> Whilst England was admired for the safeguards with
> which, in the course of many centuries, it had fortified
> liberty against the power of the crown, America ap-
> peared still more worthy of admiration for the safe-
> guards which, by the deliberations of a single mem-
> orable year [1787], it had set up against the power of
> its own sovereign people.†

THE TWO AMERICAN REVOLUTIONS

The American Revolution was, in fact, two successive
Revolutions. The First one, which has pre-empted the title,
proclaimed in 1776 a revolutionary concept of sovereignty
within the state; the Second established in 1787-89 this concept *between* states. This Double Revolution challenged and
overthrew in America, inside and out, the dogma of sovereignty which then ruled all nations both ways, since time
immemorial. Both Revolutions were one in this sense:
Each was made for precisely the same principle—that the
citizen is sovereign. Yet to establish this concept between
states was so immense an achievement as to be a Revolution in itself. It was, indeed, a greater revolution than the
First American Revolution for at least three reasons.

Colonies had often won their independence from the
motherland in the past. The principle that the citizens were
equally the sovereigns had already been practised in Athens
and other city republics of ancient Greece and Medieval

* Acton, *Essays on Freedom and Power*, Beacon Press, Boston,
pp. 81-82. The whole of that chapter and the preceding one com-
prise his "History of Freedom"; they deserve to be read and re-read
by all who seek light on liberty.
    † *Ibid,* page 150.

Europe, and in the Six Nations of the Iroquois Indians of America. But never before had men carried this concept of their own sovereignty to the point of freely uniting across state lines to create a new state composed of them all. The city democracies of Greece had perished because they were unable to unite on the basis of the free principle they shared, even to defend it. They did not go beyond leagues of sovereign states, nor as far toward federation as the Iroquois Confederacy, which helped inspire Franklin's original plan for a Union of the Colonies in 1754. This profound Revolution in human affairs was accomplished for the first time in history by the Thirteen States in their Federal Constitution.

It was the greater of their two revolutionary achievements, secondly, because, without it, the first revolution would have come to naught and the Thirteen Sovereign States would have gone the way of the Sovereign Cities of Greece. Before they reached that dismal end, the lustre which the First Revolution gave to the names of Washington and Franklin would have been lost in wars between Virginia and Pennsylvania. Such wars must have followed inevitably, had not these statesmen, by their leadership in the Second American Revolution, saved the American states from governing their common affairs by the same rule by which King George III and Czarina Catherine II governed theirs. The Second Revolution saved the First, and did far more: It led to an immeasurably greater success—a triumph of democratic principle much vaster, proportionately, than the United States is today in size when compared to Virginia or Pennsylvania.

Finally, the Second American Revolution was the greater because it was achieved more rapidly, and without violence or bloodshed, through free and full debate. In less than two years it wrought its enduring reversal of the age-old, universal concept of sovereignty that has afflicted mankind with—in last analysis—all the wars it has suffered. The fact that this was achieved without war—despite the emotions which its war of words aroused*—was rightly judged by Acton to be a revolution in itself.

Ironically, this triumph of reason over force has kept even Americans from recognizing that the establishment of their Federal Union was a Revolution. They give all the

---

* Both Patrick Henry and Governor Edmund Randolph feared the debate in Virginia over ratification of the Federal Constitution would "kindle a civil war"—especially if Virginia ratified it, as it did, 89 to 79. See the June 1955 *Freedom & Union*, p. 12, for excerpts from their speeches on June 24, 1788. That issue includes a digest of all that debate which ran from June 4 to 25 with Patrick Henry leading the opposition. A reprint is available from *Freedom & Union* for 20¢.

honor to the Revolution that was made by war. Forgetting September 17, the day when the Federal Constitution was signed, and March 4, the day when their Federal Union began, they celebrate as the birthday of their country July 4—the day when the Thirteen Colonies declared themselves united in upholding the sovereignty of their citizens, but divided henceforth into Thirteen "free and independent" countries.

Thus, the confusion over sovereignty began, paradoxically, with the very two American Revolutions which reversed the old concept, in both its senses, and thereby faced all men thereafter with two successive choices. Starting among the people of the Thirteen States themselves, it inevitably spread as the peoples around the North Atlantic gradually established themselves as the true sovereigns of their own nations. For that left them, and the American Republic, facing the same choice the Thirteen had faced—whether to follow this revolutionary concept all the way through, or reverse it in their relations with one another.

THE TRUTH IN THE FALSE CONCEPT OF SOVEREIGNTY

Another cause for the confusion that followed is that the concept of national sovereignty by which the Atlantican peoples still choose to govern their mutual relations contains, as does all error, some truth—and more emotion.

To begin with, there is the truth to which *Union Now* had pointed,* that men must limit their individual sovereignty and delegate some of it to their state in order to secure the rest. But this seems contradicted by another truth, that the sovereignty of the nation, in the sense of its independence from outside sovereigns, has served in many ways to secure the sovereignty of the citizen, still does and always will.

We each learn this latter truth at a time and in a way that impresses it on us the more. We learn it as children, when the mind is least trained and experienced in distinguishing truth from error, most totalitarian in its tendencies, and most capable of forming habits and impressions that are deep and lasting. We learn it in school-book histories from which we get the little that most of us ever know about our nation's history—together with the modicum we know about the history of other peoples, even those nearest us. These histories over-simplify and heighten all that the nation's independence has done for the lives and liberties of its citizens. They also emphasize all that neighboring nations have done to imperil them by war or otherwise; and they minimize,

* See especially Chapter VII.

or ignore, all that these neighbors have contributed to freedom—to ours and to their own. They do this to the point where children in the most enlightened countries gain the same lasting impression which they gain in the Congo tribes, namely, that danger lies in all other nations, and safety only in one's own.

Then there is the natural love we all feel for the nation from which we sprang and the country where we grew up; and our desire to "belong" that is no less natural. These two emotions suffice to make men die defending their country, even though they enjoy no more liberty in it than the Russians do today in theirs.

Add all this together and it becomes too easy to understand why confusion over national sovereignty should be so rampant . . . and hard to remove.

Yet if our reasoning is clear enough, even a child of twelve will see not only the truth, the good, there is in the current concept of national sovereignty but the error, the evil, that outweighs the truth and makes this concept false, on balance. And any child of twelve already knows the advantage of holding on to the good in anything, while discarding the bad.

We easily see the monstrous error the Communists make in reasoning that since it is necessary for men to delegate to the state some of their sovereignty, it is necessary for them to delegate to it all the rest; that since they gain by renouncing some of their liberty in order to form and maintain their state, it follows that they must gain still more if they renounce all their liberty and make the state all-powerful, inside as well as out.

The Trap Free Men Fall in from Opposite Sides

It is, of course, much harder to see the monstrous error in our own thinking on the subject in its international aspect. Quite opposite errors are made about it by two opposing schools of thought. One school, which is very small in each free people, seems to reason that because national sovereignty is obviously dangerous to peace and individual freedom in some ways it must therefore be dangerous in all; they denounce it indiscriminately as if it were wrong at all times, with all nations and in all fields. Although the harm it does blinds them to the services it performs, they tolerate it, in most fields, for practical reasons. They center their attack on what they deem to be its most dangerous aspects, but do not positively uphold it as good in any respect. They fall, in short, into the same pitfall the Communist totalitarians do, though only as regards sovereignty between nations.

The reasoning of the other school falls into the same totalitarian fallacy, but from the opposite approach. This school includes the great majority of the people in most of the Atlantic democracies. They see nothing but good in national sovereignty; any limitation of it seems a "sacrifice". They may tolerate such "surrender" as slight, or temporary or direly needed, to avoid a greater evil—but they never urge or defend it as a positive good.

Ironically, the most ardent spokesmen of this school, which insists that the sovereignty of their national government be unlimited even as regards the freest peoples, are also nearly always almost equally ardent in seeking to limit their government's sovereignty over themselves as citizens. In the United States they include the Republican conservatives who oppose any extension of the Federal government's power over them individually, and the Southern conservatives who seek to limit also Washington's power as regards their own states.

They want the national government to exercise the least sovereignty over them—but the most as regards their closest counterparts—the conservatives in the other free countries, who share this paradoxical desire. Those loudest in demanding that their government retain and exercise its sovereign right to raise barriers that interfere with business by making it impossible for a foreign firm to compete with them in their national market, oppose no less vehemently any exercise of its sovereignty that would limit their freedom to compete at home—let alone any policy that would favor producers in one section against those in other sections.

Clearly these champions of unlimited national sovereignty are not moved, as are "total" totalitarians, by any love of the state for the state's sake. Apart from the selfish interests that enter into all human calculations, their motivation is the same as that of the opposite school in their nation—they seek to save individual life and liberty. But whereas the former aim to save these ends by sacrificing all national sovereignty, the latter see any loss of it as a sacrifice of life and liberty.

They see what the other group is blind to—that unlimited national sovereignty undoubtedly was essential to these ends in the past, and still is as regards many nations and many fields of government. But they themselves are blind to the exceptions to this rule which the opposite school sees so well. Yet they need but stop to think, to see that it is wrong to reason, as they do, that the unlimited sovereignty of the nation must remain essential to individual life and liberty,

a) *now,* because it obviously has been in the past;

b) *with the peoples most advanced in free government,* because it obviously still is as regards those least developed in freedom, or totally submerged by dictatorship, and

c) *in every field of government,* because it obviously is essential in many fields still, even between the freest peoples.

No one would think it common sense to reason that he must live only on milk forever because this was essential at one time in his life, use sign language with his brothers because he must so converse with a savage, or refuse to agree with his brothers on anything because there are certain personal matters that he must decide for himself. Yet such totalitarian "logic," when applied to the subject of national sovereignty, passes for reason so widely that relatively few even question it.

THE WAY OF REASON AND EXPERIENCE

Sound reasoning runs, of course, between the totalitarian type of thinking that afflicts both these extreme schools. If we start with the premise that the state is made for man, we lose our base if we turn totalitarian in reasoning about the nation. We can conclude neither that because it brings some evil to us it can bring no good and should be abolished, nor that because it works some good it can do us no evil and should be maintained 100 per cent.

We know this is contrary to experience as well as to reason. We know that the state was once the caveman family, and later a tribe of kindred families, and later a city state or kingdom of neighboring tribes, and later a nation of kindred or neighboring cities and kingdoms. We know that total sovereignty was once lodged in each of these forms of the state, and that each not only did serve man at some time but still does today. We know that the good each of these forms of the state did for man, when it was supreme, never kept him from moving to a higher form, and we also know that, even though this change was nearly always made by violence rather than reason, enough reason remained in men never to destroy completely the previous "state", but always to keep it where it still best served their purposes.

And so today, every state includes within it the family, and local government in various forms. We all agree that none of these suffices, but that each continues to serve us better in some respects than do any of the other forms of the state.

It is only when the issue lies between our highest existing

form, and a still higher one, that we cease this process of discarding the bad while retaining the good, and fall into the totalitarian all-or-nothing trap. It has caught man precisely at this point at each stage of this long development, as it still does, even where, as in the United States, we have already passed beyond the nation state and achieved a federal state. Yet we know that reason requires us—especially those of us who most believe that the state, from the family on up, is made for the individual—to remain always ready to withdraw some of our sovereignty which we have invested in any form of the state and re-invest it in a still higher form, wherever and whenever we find that we are endangering our capital by the present investment, or would gain greater returns elsewhere. In other words, common sense requires us to continue to eliminate the bad and retain the good in the highest as well as the lowest forms of the bodies politic we create.

THE ELEMENTARY TRUTH *Union Now* BEGAN WITH

This seems elementary, and because it *is* elementary *Union Now* began with this truth. In its fifth paragraph it explained that the proposed "Union would be designed (a) to provide effective common government in our democratic world in those fields where such democratic government will clearly serve man's freedom better than separate government, (b) to maintain independent national governments in all other fields where such government will best serve man's freedom." I then listed under point (a) five fields which I found the peoples of the North Atlantic democracies could govern better through a Union government than through their nations, and added: "By (b) I mean the Union government shall guarantee against all enemies, foreign and domestic, not only those rights of man that are common to all democracies but every existing national or local right that is not clearly incompatible with effective union government in the five named fields."

Later in that chapter (and elsewhere) I sought to make it still clearer that although I believed it in our interest to transfer our sovereignty in a few fields from our nation to an Atlantic Union, I favored guaranteeing the national independence of each people in all other fields as an asset. For the reader's convenience let me quote from Chapter I:

> This does not mean eliminating all national rights. It
> means eliminating them only where elimination clearly
> serves the individuals concerned, and maintaining them

in all other repects—not simply where maintenance clearly serves the general individual interest but also in all doubtful cases . . .

Our Union could afford to encourage the existing diversity among its members as a powerful safeguard against the domestic dangers to individual freedom. Just as the citizen could count on The Union to protect his nation from either invasion or dictatorship rising from within, he could count on his nation's autonomy to protect him from a majority in The Union becoming locally oppressive. The existence of so many national autonomies in The Union would guarantee each of them freedom to experiment politically, economically, socially . . .

I thought I had made amply clear in *Union Now* that, far from seeking to abolish the independence of any nation, I sought to preserve it and make it legal—*de jure* and not just *de facto* as at present *—in all the fields where it served individual life and liberty better than any Union could; that I regarded it not as a necessary evil to be tolerated but as a positive good to be maintained in all but a few fields.

Experience has proved that I did not make this nearly clear enough. *Union Now* has been and is attacked as a proposal to "destroy" national sovereignty, "abolish" the United States, "tear up the Declaration of Independence."

WHERE THE FOUNDING FATHERS GROPED

The elementary truth with which *Union Now* began was stated in that Declaration itself, which it cited on page 6. Though it was set forth in the Declaration of Independence more lucidly than ever before, men fell into precisely the same totalitarian traps to thought then as now when they faced the question of applying it between their states.

The Founding Fathers began by rebelling against the over-centralization of the British colonial system—and by swinging immediately to the other extreme. They made their Thirteen States independent not only of the Crown but of each other, united only in a Confederation whose highest aim, as we have seen, was to preserve the sovereignty of each state. By this excessive decentralization they saved individual liberty from the excessive sovereignty of George III—only to expose it to anarchy among the Thirteen. With no central

---

* I would refer the reader also to Chapter X, particularly the section entitled, "The Great Federal Problem."

sovereignty to limit the sovereignty of the states, political disputes developed among them, while economic difficulties led
even the most democratic of these states, Rhode Island,
to assert more and more coercive power over its sovereign
citizens. In guarding against their Confederacy becoming
despotic, the people of the Thirteen States had opened the
door to tyranny in their home state.

Their experience with both extremes led them, as we have
seen, to work out the golden mean between the two that
federal union is. But it is highly important (as well as con-
soling) to note that even these exceptionally wise men *
worked out this happy balance by groping their way through
confusion—by making mutually reluctant compromises
rather than by reasoning clearly. One side thought that the
people should transfer all sovereignty from their states to
the Union; the other contended no less totally that they
should transfer none. Mainly because neither could persuade
the other, they settled on the federal union system. It
gave half a loaf to each side, by having the people transfer
some sovereignty to the Union while leaving some in their
respective states. It combined, in other words, a Union government with a confederation of governments. Precious
few of the Founding Fathers, however, saw at the time the
great merits of this division of sovereignty that we can see
today. The result was to give the sovereign citizen, not half
a loaf but the whole loaf in two halves. They did not see
this—so deeply did these Framers of the Constitution fall
from opposite approaches, into the same totalitarian fallacy
that befuddles us now.

GEORGE WASHINGTON, TOO, FELL IN THIS TRAP

Even the Father of his Country fell into it—and he
stumbled into the pitfall on the side from which the fewest citizens do today. Valley Forge and all the war had
given General Washington a much more acute understanding of the vices than the virtues of state sovereignty. We
find him denouncing this "monster," and speaking with
scorn of the "darling sovereignties" of the states—without a qualifying phrase to concede that the people needed
to keep part of the sovereignty delegated to their states.
Even in his Farewell Address as President, eight years after

* Lord Acton paid this tribute to them, with which I fully agree:
"The convention which sat in Philadelphia 1787 . . . included the most
eminent men of America. It is astounding to observe the political
wisdom, and still more the political foresight, which their delibera-
tions exhibit." *Essays on Freedom & Power*, Beacon, Boston, p. 200.

the Federal Constitution was established, Washington put his accent on the central government. He did this to the point of discussing the country in terms of regions—"the North," "the South," "the East," "the West"—omitting even to mention the states, dismissing them as "subdivisions" of the Union. In all the sound advice he gave the people in that Address, there was none enjoining them to maintain the sovereignty of their states to the degree which the federal balance requires for it to work most in favor of the sovereign citizens.

Alexander Hamilton not only shared Washington's view; in his main speech at the Federal Convention, on June 18, 1787, he flatly declared that it would be wiser if the state governments "were extinguished." True, he quickly added that he did not "mean to shock the public opinion by proposing such a measure." Yet the plan he offered effectively stripped the states of their sovereignty; their governors were to be appointed by the central government and to exercise a general veto on all state laws. *"Cui bono"*—what good was there in leaving any sovereignty to the states, he asked, and obviously saw none.

At the Convention, James Madison was readier than Hamilton to tolerate the state governments, but like him did so merely as a lesser evil. Lord Acton found that "a note preserved in Washington's handwriting records: 'Mr. Madison thinks an individual independence of the states utterly irreconcilable with their aggregate sovereignty, and that consolidation of the whole into a simple republic would be as inexpedient as it is unattainable.'" Speaking in the Convention on June 21, Madison agreed that "the great objection made against the abolition of the state Governments was that the General Government could not extend its care to all the minute objects which fall under cognizance of the local jurisdictions." He went on to contend, however, that "were it practicable for the General Government to extend its care to every requisite object without the cooperation of the state Governments, the people would not be less free as members of one great Republic than as members of thirteen smaller ones. . . . Supposing therefore a tendency in the General Government to absorb the state Governments, no fatal consequence could result."

Washington, Hamilton and Madison were the three who took and kept the lead in changing the Confederation into an organic Union, but if they had achieved their heart's desire they would have jumped from that association of Sovereign States to the opposite extreme, and united the sovereign people in a single unitary nation, as centralized as

Britain or France. They and their friends sought to do this, in fact, at the start of the Convention, and went far in this direction in the Plan Virginia proposed May 29, on which all the discussion centered at first.

By June 13 the Convention had accepted the basic features of this Plan. This included its grant of sweeping powers to a "National Legislature"—in which it gave no control to the state governments—(a) to act in all "cases to which the states are not competent," and (b) "to negative all State laws contravening in the opinion of the National Legislature, the articles of union." After very brief discussion, on May 31, point (a) was approved by nine state delegations, none opposing, but with the only other state represented—Connecticut—evenly divided.

In the next breath the Convention approved, "without debate or dissent," the absolute veto which (b) gave the national government. It is instructive to note that a little later, on June 8, Madison sought to make this veto all-embracing. He said he "could not but regard an indefinite power to negative legislative acts of the states as absolutely necessary." Young Charles Pinckney of South Carolina went further and held that "the states must be kept in due submission to the nation." By this time, however, fear of such concentration of power led to the defeat of their motion, seven states voting against it and three in favor.

Through the first five weeks of the Convention's debate, this school showed little understanding of the danger of centralization, or of the advantages that individual liberty gains from the citizen leaving enough of his sovereignty in his state to prevent centralization. This danger helped arouse such opposition that on this basic point the Virginia Plan's victory of June 13 was lost by July 2. Thereafter this school accepted limitations of the central government's power, but against their will, and only as a necessary evil.

PATRICK HENRY FELL IN THE TRAP FROM THE OTHER SIDE

The opposition which forced this compromise on them was led by other Founding Fathers who fell into the same fallacy from the opposite approach—which is so thronged today. This group saw dangers only in the citizens transferring any of their sovereignty from their states to the Union, and only good in keeping it totally there. Neither school spoke then in these terms of citizen sovereignty; instead, this group called this transfer "sacrificing" the sovereignty or independence of their state, as many do now. In the Convention their leading spokesmen were from the small states, notably William Patterson of New Jersey and Luther Martin of Maryland. The "New Jersey Plan" they offered in opposition to the Virginia Plan would have strengthened the Confederation considerably, but kept it still an association of sovereign states, in no sense a Union of sovereign Citizens.

Like their opponents, they accepted compromise in the end, not because they saw the wisdom in it, but as a lesser evil.

Though the leaders of the New Jersey group lacked the prestige of Washington, and the talent of Hamilton and Madison, they held out stubbornly, because they felt that the majority of the people in the various states would never consent to "surrender their state's sovereignty." They were encouraged, too, by the fact that, even in Virginia, so famous a patriot as Patrick Henry was convinced that individual liberty required Virginia to retain its full sovereignty—so much so that he refused to attend the Convention, though named as a delegate.

EXAMPLES OF HOW SOVEREIGNTY
SPLIT THE FOUNDING FATHERS

These extracts from Madison's *Journal* may show better how sharply these two opposing views on Sovereignty clashed in the convention:

> A confederacy supposes sovereignty in the members composing it and sovereignty supposes equality. If we are to be considered as a nation, all state distinctions must be abolished . . . New Jersey . . . would be swallowed up. We had rather submit to a monarch, to a despot, than to such a fate.—*William Patterson, June 9, 1787.*

> Distinct states would be a perpetual source of discord. There can be no cure for this evil but in doing away with states altogether and uniting them all in one great Society.—*George Read of Delaware, June 11.*

> Had the legislature of the state of New York apprehended that their powers [those of the delegates] would have been construed to extend to the formation of a national government, to the extinguishment of their independency, no delegates would have appeared on the part of that state.—*John Lansing, Jr. of New York, June 16.*

> I cannot support the General Government at the expense of the state Governments, but will contend for

the Safety and Happiness of the particular states at the expense of the U. S. —*Luther Martin, June 18.*

At the separation from the British Empire, the people of America preferred the establishment of themselves into 13 separate sovereignties instead of incorporating themselves into one . . . They are afraid of granting powers unnecessarily . . . lest the powers should prove dangerous to the sovereignties of the particular states. —*Luther Martin, June 20.*

As states are a collection of individual men, which ought we to respect the most, the rights of the people composing them, or of the artificial beings resulting from the composition? Nothing could be more preposterous or absurd than the sacrifice of the former to the latter. It has been said that if the smaller states renounce their *equality,* they renounce at the same time their *liberty.* The truth is it is a contest for power, not for liberty. Will the men composing the small states be less free than those composing the larger? The state of Delaware having 40,000 souls will *lose power,* if she has 1/10 only of the votes allowed to Pennsylvania, having 400,000: but will the people of Delaware *be less* free, if each citizen has an equal vote with each citizen of Pennsylvania?—*Alexander Hamilton, June 19. (His emphasis.)*

The states and the advocates for them were intoxicated with the idea of their *sovereignty.*—*Elbridge Gerry of Massachusetts, June 19. (His emphasis.)*

Can we forget for whom we are forming a Government? Is it for *men,* or for the imaginary beings called states?—*James Wilson of Pennsylvania, June 30. (His emphasis.)*

Each extreme agreed to give the other half a loaf only after the Convention had reached a deadlock, five states against five, (with the other, Georgia, split in two itself) in the decisive vote that came on one phase of the issue on July 2. But the compromise (which also had several phases, with votes on each) was agreed to in the final test only five to four (with New York absent and Massachusetts split in two).

THE PRECIOUS TRUTH THAT PRECIOUS FEW SAW THEN

In between the two extreme schools there stood a few

Founding Fathers who had contributed considerably to bringing about the deadlock, working out the basic compromise, and getting both sides to accept it. These were indeed a "precious few"—for they were the only ones in the Convention who showed a good grasp then of what has since become accepted, at least within the United States, as the true democratic concept of sovereignty in a federal union. They alone saw clearly the simple truth that individual liberty required the people both to transfer some of their sovereignty to a Union they themselves composed, and to continue keeping their states independent of each other and of the Union government in other respects. To these few, the only total evil lay in the people giving total power to either the Union or the states in respect to each other, and the only total good lay in keeping these two agencies balanced in the way that served their sovereign citizens best. The first delegate to express this view at the Convention was John Dickinson of the smallest state, Delaware, famed throughout the Confederation for his "Farmer's Letters." George Mason of Virginia, author of its Bill of Rights, was perhaps an even more influential advocate of this concept. Dickinson put this case before the convention first on June 2 in these words, as summarized by Madison in his *Journal*:

> One source of stability is the double branch of the Legislature. The division of the country into distinct states formed the other principal source of stability. The division ought therefore to be maintained, and considerable powers left with the states . . . Without this, and in the case of a consolidation of the states into one great Republic, we might read its fate in the history of smaller ones . . . If ancient republics have been found to flourish for a moment only and then vanish forever, it only proves that they were badly constituted; and that we ought to seek for every remedy for their diseases. One of these remedies he conceived to be the accidental lucky division of this Country into distinct states, a division which some seemed desirous to abolish altogether.

One may see the degree to which this issue divided the Founding Fathers (and also the degree to which delegates from each state spoke freely as individuals in the Convention) in Madison's report of this clash on June 6 between Dickinson and his fellow delegate from Delaware, George Read, who spoke immediately after him:

> *Mr. Dickinson* considered it as essential that one

branch of the legislature should be drawn immediately from the people, and as expedient that the other should be chosen from the Legislatures of the states . . . He was for a strong National Government but for leaving the states a considerable agency in the System.

Mr. Read. Too much attachment is betrayed to the state Governments. We must look beyond their continuance. A national Government must soon of necessity swallow all of them up . . .

The next day Dickinson returned to the charge with the support of Mason. To quote from Madison's *Journal*:

Mr. Dickinson. The preservation of the states in a certain degree of agency is indispensable. It will produce that collision between the different authorities which should be wished for in order to check each other. To attempt to abolish the states altogether would degrade the Councils of our Country, would be impracticable, would be ruinous. He compared the proposed National System to the Solar System, in which the states were the planets and ought to be left to move freely in their proper orbits. The Gentleman from Pennsylvania [James Wilson] wished, he said, to extinguish these planets.

If the state Governments were excluded from all agency in the national one, and all power drawn from the people at large, the consequences would be that the national Government would move in the same direction as the state Governments now, and would run into all the same mischiefs. The reform would only unite the 13 small streams into one great current pursuing the same course without any opposition whatever.

Col. Mason. Whatever power may be necessary for the National Government a certain portion must necessarily be left in the states. It is impossible for one power to pervade the extreme parts of the U. S. so as to carry equal justice to them. The state Legislatures also ought to have some means of defending themselves against encroachments of the National Government . . . And what better means can we provide than giving them some share in, or rather to make them a constituent part of the National Establishment? There is a danger on both sides no doubt; but we have only seen the evils arising on the side of the state Governments. Those on the other side remain to be displayed.

No one during the Convention showed so good an understanding of the whole thorny problem as Mason did in his speech of June 20, 1787, quoted at the head of this chapter —and his grasp of it was far from perfect.

PEACEFUL REVOLUTION THROUGH CONFUSION

Looking back, with not only experience but such men as Marshall, Jackson, Webster, Calhoun, Tocqueville, Emerson, Whitman and Lincoln to teach us, we can see what was not at all clear in 1787-89. The Constitution which emerged from the collision of the three conflicting concepts of sovereignty was animated throughout by the basic democratic one—that the state is made for men, and of and by them, too, as individual citizens. That this should have resulted from so much confusion seems astonishing. And yet it was but natural. The upholders of each of the conflicting concepts, represented by the three great men of Virginia cited at the head of this chapter, were all permeated by this basic principle that sovereignty lies in the citizen. Though they talked in terms of the sovereignty or independence of the state, not of the citizens, they all agreed that the former was but power delegated to the latter.

Whether they favored transferring practically all this power from their state to the new Union, as Washington did, or practically none, as Patrick Henry urged, or dividing it between the two as Mason advised, they all sought thereby to preserve and advance the individual's liberty and life. Since the same basic concept of citizen sovereignty animated each, this principle understandably reached so high and comprehensive an embodiment in the resulting Federal Constitution as to be truly revolutionary.

If Washington, Hamilton and Madison seemed more confused than Mason and Dickinson at the time, their contribution to this result was still by far the greater. Had they not seem so well that individual life and liberty required an organic Union of all the American people, they would not have led so tenaciously toward this end; and without their leadership there would have been no such Constitution, no such issue in the Convention and no such Convention. If they were more confused than Mason early in the Convention, they were much less confused about its result than he was in the end. George Mason was one of the prime inventors of the federal solution in more ways than the one I have touched on, but he failed to see that he had won the battle in the Convention. He refused to sign the Constitution and joined Patrick Henry in actively opposing its ratification. That is perhaps why his immense contributions to Federal Union are so little recognized. Washington, Madison and Hamilton had conceded far more than he, but they were wise enough to see that their basic principle had won, on balance. They not only signed the Constitution but fought for its ratification as if it embodied all their dreams—and none fought for it so hard as did Hamilton who had conceded the most. In nothing did their greatness shine forth so truly as in this.

WHAT'S IN A NAME? NO END OF CONFUSION

To achieve the second American Revolution peacefully, its leaders added to the confusion enduringly. They did this partly by disguising the new system's revolutionary character by giving it the name of the one it replaced. The terms, *federal, federal union* and *union*, which we now use to distinguish this system from both a unitary nation and a confederacy of nations, were then commonly used to describe the existing Confederation. The Virginia Plan had aimed openly to replace this with a "national" government, and *national* studded the first draft of the Constitution until June 20. On that day the nationalists, in their battle with the defenders of confederation, agreed to have *national* stricken out entirely, so as to save the substance of the change they sought. By tacit agreement the opposite adjective, *federal*, was also omitted from the Constitution.

That instrument carefully avoids specifically giving any name to the unprecedented federal-national system it created. Apart from casual references to it as the "Union," the Constitution always refers to the government it set up as "the United States," the name of the Confederation it replaced. This was ambiguous, and—we shall see in the next chapter—dangerously confusing. To use that name implies that the United States still *are*; whereas to say, as we do now, that the United States *is* reflects the revolution that had taken place. The vital difference between states united in a confederation and states united in a union of their citizens comes out, of course, in syntax. The verb, or pronoun, for the former is plural, the latter singular. So careful were the drafters of the Constitution to keep this point ambiguous that the term "United States" is used throughout the Constitution in ways that avoid using either *are* or *is, them* or *it*. There is only one exception, and it, ironically, is in this clause: "Treason against the United States shall consist only

of levying war against them, or in adhering to their enemies . . ."

Nor did the semantic confusion end there. Although *federal* was the banner under which their opponents fought in
the Convention, the most extreme of the nationalists, Hamilton, took it over in the ensuing battle to get the Constitution ratified. To the classic papers that he edited, and co-
authored with Madison and Jay, to expound its principles, he
gave the title of *The Federalist*—pouring the new wine into
a bottle bearing the old familiar label of the Confederation.
Thus the nationalists of 1787 became the Federalist party,
while the Federalists of 1787 became known as the Anti-
Federalists in 1788. This dizzy confusion helped keep many
Americans from recognizing the revolutionary nature of the
new Constitution—but not Patrick Henry: "Here is a solution
as radical as that which separated us from Great Britain," he
rightly called it. But this time he was against the revolution
he had led in 1775.

THE "GREAT DISCOVERY IN MODERN POLITICAL SCIENCE"

As time went on, the world began to see this revolution,
too—with the help of Tocqueville who pointed out in 1835
in his *Democracy in America*; "This Constitution, which may
be confused with federal constitutions that have preceded it,
rests, in fact, on a theory that is entirely new, and which
stands as a great discovery in modern political science." Tocqueville saw, too, that its newness lay in combining, through
the citizens, a unitary nation (in some respects) with a confederacy (in other respects) and thus making a "form of government that was not precisely either national or federal"
(meaning *federal* in the old, confederate sense). In his aware-
ness of, and enthusiasm for the full play America thus gave
to sovereignty of the citizen, he wrote:

> Whenever the political laws of the United States are
> to be discussed, it is with the doctrine of the sover-
> eignty of the citizen that we must begin. The principle
> of the sovereignty of the people, which is always to be
> found, more or less, at the bottom of almost all human
> institutions, generally remains there concealed from
> view. It is obeyed without being recognized, or if for a
> moment it is brought to light, it is hastily cast back into
> the gloom of the sanctuary.

> "The will of the nation" is one of those phrases that
> have been most largely abused by the wily and the
> despotic of every age. Some . . . have even discovered

it in the silence of a people, on the supposition that the fact of submission established the right to command.

In America the principle of the sovereignty of the people is neither barren nor concealed, as it is with some other nations; it is recognized by the customs and proclaimed by the laws; it spreads freely, and arrives without impediment at its most remote consequences. . .

At the present day the principle of the sovereignty of the people has acquired in the United States all the practical development that the imagination can conceive.*

True though this was in 1835, it is also true that Americans can now conceive of a further practical development of their sovereignty by the constitution of an Atlantic Union. And it was true even in 1835 that confusion over sovereignty had already raised its head enough again to cause a dangerous crisis in 1832, when South Carolina asserted its "sovereign" right as a state to nullify federal laws and secede from the Union. This was not carried out, thanks to President Jackson's vigorous reply. The Constitution not only "forms a *government,* not a league," he replied, but sets up a government "in which all the people are represented, which operates on the people individually, not upon the states"; therefore such "disunion" as South Carolina threatened, if upheld by "armed force is *treason,*" and any citizen guilty of it would be punished accordingly. Nonetheless, the confusion and conflict between the two concepts of the sovereignty of the people spread, and led to the Civil War in 1861.

CHAPTER 8

How the Civil War Kept You Sovereign

Plainly, the central idea of secession is the essence of anarchy. A majority held in restraint by constitutional checks and limitations, and always changing easily with deliberate changes of public opinions and sentiments, is the only true sovereign of a free people. Whoever rejects it does, of necessity, fly to anarchy or to

* *Democracy in America,* Vol. I, Chap. 4 (my translation).

despotism. Unanimity is impossible; the rule of a minority, as a permanent arrangement, is wholly inadmissible; so that, rejecting the majority principle, anarchy or despotism in some form is all that is left.— *Abraham Lincoln,* First Inaugural, *March 4, 1861.*

The dispute between absolute and limited power, between centralization and self-government, has been, like that between privilege [of Parliament] and prerogative [of the Crown] in England, the substance of the constitutional history of the United States. This is the argument which confers on the whole period that intervenes between the convention of 1787 and the election of Mr. Davis in 1861 an almost epic unity. It is this problem that has supplied the impulse to the political progress of the United States, that underlies all the great questions that have agitated the Union.— *Lord Acton, in* The Rambler, *May 1861.**

The North and the South were in greater agreement on sovereignty, through all their dispute about it, than were the Founding Fathers. The truth in their conflicting concepts was expounded by statesmen of the calibre of Webster and Calhoun, and defended in the end by leaders of the nobility of Lincoln and Lee. The people everywhere had grown meanwhile in devotion to basic democratic principle, in understanding of and belief in the federal balance, and in love of their Union. Repeated efforts—beginning with the Missouri Compromise of 1821—were made by such master moderates as Clay and Douglas to resolve the difference peacefully by compromise, rather than clear thought and timely action. Even so, confusion in this period gained such strength (from compromise and other factors) that it led to the bloodiest war of the Nineteenth century. Nothing can show more than this the immensity of the danger to democratic peoples that lies in even relatively slight deviation from their true concept of sovereignty.

The present issue in Atlantica—whether to transform an alliance of sovereign nations into a federal union of sovereign citizens—resembles the American one of 1787-89 rather than the one that was resolved by Civil War. And so I would only touch upon it now (much as I have long wanted to write a book about it.) I think it is essential, however, to pinpoint here the difference between the two concepts of sovereignty that went to war in 1861—if only to see better how

* Acton, *Essays on Freedom & Power,* Beacon Press, Boston, pp. 198-99.

imperative is our need today to clarify completely our far worse confusion on this subject.

The difference came down to this: The Southern States insisted that the United States was, in last analysis, what its name implied—a Union of States. To their leaders the Constitution was a compact made by the people of sovereign states, who therefore retained the right to secede from it. This right of the State, its upholders contended, was essential to maintain the federal balance and protect the liberty of the people from the danger of centralizing power in the Union government. The champions of the Union maintained that the Constitution had formed, fundamentally, the united people of America, that it was a compact among sovereign citizens rather than states, and that therefore the states had no right to secede, though the citizens could. Writing to Speed on August 24, 1855, Lincoln made the latter point clear. In homely terms whose timeliness is startling today, he thus declared his own right to secede.

> We began by declaring that *all men are created equal*. We now practically read it, *all men are created equal except negroes*. When the Know-nothings get control, it will read, *all men are created equal except negroes* and foreigners and Catholics. When it comes to this, I shall prefer emigrating to some country where they make no pretence of loving liberty—to Russia, for instance, where despotism can be taken pure, without the base alloy of hypocrisy. [His emphasis]

When the Southern States exercised their "right to secede," they formed what they officially styled "The Confederate States of America." Dictionaries, as we have seen, still cite this government, along with the Articles of Confederation of 1781, as an example of a confederacy. The fact is that the Southern Confederacy differed from the earlier one almost as much as the Federal Constitution did. The Confederate Constitution copied much of the Federal Constitution verbatim, and most of the rest in substance. It operated on, by and for the people individually just as did the Federal Constitution. It made substantially the same division of power between the central and the state governments, and among the executive, legislative and judicial branches.

THE DIFFERENCE BETWEEN CONFEDERACY AND FEDERAL UNION IN 1861

Many believe—and understandably—that the great difference between the Constitution of the Southern Confederacy and the Federal Constitution was that the former recognized the right of each state to secede. But though each of its members had asserted this right against the Union, the final Constitution which the Confederacy signed on March 11—nearly a month before hostilities began—included no explicit provision authorizing a state to secede. Its drafters discussed this vital point, but left it out of their Constitution. Their President, Jefferson Davis, interpreted their Constitution to mean that it "admits of no coerced association," but this remained so doubtful that "there were frequent demands that the right to secede be put into the Constitution." *

The Constitution of the Southern "Confederation" differed from that of the Federal Union only in two important respects: It openly, defiantly, recognized slavery—an institution which the Southerners of 1787, even though they continued it, found so impossible to reconcile with freedom that they carefully avoided mentioning the word in the Federal Constitution. They recognized that slavery was a moral issue and not merely an economic interest, and that to recognize it explicitly in their Constitution would be in explosive contradiction to the concept of sovereignty they had set forth in the Declaration of 1776 that "all men are created equal, that they are endowed by their Creator with certain unalienable rights, that among them are life, liberty and the pursuit of happiness. . . ." The other important difference between the two Constitutions was that the President of the Confederacy held office for six (instead of four) years, and was limited to one term.†

These are not, however, differences in federal structure. The only important difference from that standpoint, between the two Constitutions, lies in their Preambles. The one of 1861 made clear that in making their government the people were acting through their states, whereas the Preamble of 1787-89 expressed, as clearly as language can, the opposite concept, that they were acting directly as its citizens. Here are the two Preambles:

Federal Constitution, 1787-89
We the People of the United States, in order to
form a more perfect Union, establish Justice, insure

---

* E. Merton Coulter, *The Confederate States of America*, 1861-1865, Louisiana State University Press, p. 30.

† Other differences include these: The first ten amendments to the Federal Constitution (its "Bill of Rights") were incorporated in the body of the Confederate Constitution; the latter also required a two-thirds (instead of a simple) majority in both Houses for the admission of a new state.

domestic Tranquility, provide for the common Defence, promote the general Welfare, and secure the Blessings of Liberty to ourselves and our Posterity, do ordain and establish this Constitution for the United States of America.

Confederate Constitution, 1861

We the People of the Confederate States, each state acting in its sovereign and independent character, in order to form a permanent federal government, establish justice, insure domestic tranquility, and secure the blessings of liberty to ourselves and our posterity—invoking the favor and the guidance of Almighty God—do ordain and establish this Constitution for the Confederate States of America.

One is tempted to say that, on the difference between the concepts of sovereignty in these two preambles, the worst war of the Nineteenth century was fought. But though the Southern States, when drafting a constitution to unite themselves, narrowed the difference to this fine point by omitting to assert the right to secede, the fact remained that by seceding from the Union they had already acted on the concept that it was composed primarily of sovereign states. If the Union conceded this to them, the same right must be conceded to each remaining state whenever it saw fit to secede: This would destroy the federal balance between it and the states, and in the end sacrifice to the sovereignty of the states all the liberty the citizens had gained by their Union.

Lincoln saw that the act of secession made the issue for the Union a vital one: Whether it was a Union of sovereign citizens that could continue to live, or an association of sovereign states that must fall prey either to "anarchy or despotism."

Much as he abhorred slavery, Lincoln was always willing to concede to each "slave state" the right to decide independently whether to continue or end it. Though his election was interpreted by many Southerners as the forerunner of a dangerous shift in the federal balance in favor of the Union, Lincoln himself proposed no such change in the rights the Constitution gave the states. After the war began, he long refused to permit emancipation of the slaves by Union action even in the Border States that stayed with the Union. He issued his Emancipation Proclamation only when he felt that necessity left him no other way to save the Union.* In

* See his letter to Horace Greeley, August 22, 1862, and his letter to James Conkling, August 26, 1863.

his Message of December 2, 1862, he put his purpose and his policy in these words—which I would call the Lincoln Law of Liberty-and-Union: *"In giving freedom to the slave, we assure freedom to the free."*

What Lincoln could not concede was that the states rather than the people were sovereign in the Union. He fought to the end to preserve it as a "government of the people, by the people, for the people."

THE TRUTH ON EACH SIDE WON IN THE CIVIL WAR

The fact that the Americans who upheld the sovereignty of their states did this in order to keep many of their people more securely in slavery—the antithesis of individual liberty—made the conflict the grimmer, and the greater. Out of this ordeal the citizen emerged, in the South as in the North, as America's true sovereign, in "a new birth of freedom," as Lincoln promised. But before this came about, 214,938 Americans had given their lives in battle for the two concepts of the sovereign rights of men and of states.

On their decisive battlefield Lincoln did not distinguish between them when he paid tribute to the "brave men, living and dead, who fought here." He understood that both sides were at fault, and he reached the height of saying so explicitly in his Second Inaugural.

To my knowledge, Lincoln remains the only Head of State and Commander-in-Chief who, while fighting a fearful war whose issue was in doubt, proved man enough to say this publicly—to give his foe the benefit of the fact that in all human truth there is some error, and in all our error, some truth. So great a man could not but understand, too, that the thing that moves men to sacrifice their lives is not the error of their thought, which their opponents see and attack, but the truth which the latter do not see—any more than they see the error which mars the truth they themselves defend.

It is much less difficult now than in Lincoln's day to see that on both sides sovereign Americans had given their lives in the Civil War to maintain the balance between the powers they had delegated to their States and to their Union. They differed in the balance they believed essential to the sovereignty of the citizen—but the supreme sacrifice each made served to maintain a still more fundamental truth: That individual life, liberty and happiness depend on a right balance between the two—and on the limitation of sovereignty, in all its aspects, which this involves. The 140,414 Americans who gave "the last full measure of devotion" to prevent disunion, preserved individual freedom in the United States from the dangers of anarchy, inherent in confederations, which throughout history have proved fatal in the end to all associations composed primarily of sovereign states, and to the liberties of their people. But the fact that 70,524 other Americans gave the same measure of devotion to an opposing concept served Liberty-and-Union in other essential ways.

Their appeal from ballots to bullets at Fort Sumter ended by costing the Southerners their right to have slaves—a right that was even less compatible with the sovereignty of man. The very fact that they came so near to winning by the wrong method, war, led directly to their losing both the war and the wrong thing they fought for, since it forced Lincoln to free their slaves as a military measure. There was a divine justice in one wrong thus undoing another. There was also a lesson, one that has served ever since to keep Americans, in their conflicts with one another, from turning from the ballot to the bullet. Yet though the Southern States lost the worst errors in their case, they did not lose the truth they fought for. The lives so many of them gave, to forestall what they believed would be a fatal encroachment by the Union on the powers reserved to their states have continued ever since to safeguard all Americans against freedom's other foe. The South remains today our surest brake against the trend toward over-centralization that inheres in central power, and that leads inevitably to despotism—as Lincoln saw—when men fail to guard against it vigilantly and vigorously.

The basic federal balance, formed by the rights delegated by the citizens to their Union and to their states, continues to check this danger. True, power has gravitated in recent years increasingly from all the states to the Federal Government, but no states have maintained their rights so much in practice and in principle as have the Southern ones; the current conflict over integration testifies to this.

The Continuing Issue in American History

What Lord Acton expressed in English terms in 1861 in the quotation at the head of this chapter, continues to be true of the United States.

In other terms, the history of the United States has always centered on the revolutionary concept of sovereignty that gave it birth—"the principle it lives by and keeps alive," as Lincoln put it. Twice already this concept has moved the American people as it has moved no other people, and as nothing else has ever moved Americans. Here is the kernel of our history: To give this concept life we first took thirty-five years—from Franklin's proposal of Union in 1754 to the Federal Constitution he lived to see go into effect in 1789. In that period we created states of sovereign citizens by eight years of Revolutionary War, and then by a bloodless, shorter, bolder Revolution united these states in a grander Union of Sovereign Citizens. The next struggle was to preserve the sovereignty of the citizens in both the Union and their states—a forty-four-year struggle, if dated from the Missouri Compromise in 1821 to the Union victory. It included only four years of war, but fifty times more lives were sacrificed than in the First Revolution.

Both times the American people, when their leaders and friends almost despaired of them, ended by drawing from the confusion and the conflict an astonishing extension of their freedom-and-union concept. Here lies their genius as a people. Here is the reason why they honor as their highest heroes those who have done the most to clarify this concept, and to establish, preserve, extend it. These heroes of theirs are the Americans whom all the world, too, most esteems—Franklin, Washington, Hamilton, Jefferson, Lincoln. That each of these is honored everywhere reflects how profoundly true, and universally appealing in the end, is the democratic federal concept of the sovereignty of Man. It would not be the world's, or ours, today without each of these heroes . . . or without the myriads of unknown men who gave volume to their voices, and proved their concept true.

Since the creation of the American Union, and even more since its preservation a century ago, this revolutionary concept of sovereignty has gone marching on—and nowhere have its victories been so early and enduring as around the North Atlantic. And so its success has led us into a third period of confusion and conflict. Oceanic in scope, the current period also centers in the true concept of sovereignty and the primal issue with which we began: Can citizens remain sovereign only within their nation? Must they not establish their sovereignty over their common interests with other democratic nations, too, if they are to stay sovereign at home? We living Americans have been in this struggle now for more than forty years—ever since we set out in 1917 under Woodrow Wilson to make the world "safe for democracy."

THE CURRENT AMERICAN CONFUSION

Through the same confusion as in 1776, we began in 1917 by seeking to make the world safe for the sovereignty of man by centering our attention totally on the sovereignty of his nation. This notion, which identified self-government only with the independence of nation-states from empires, has in forty years won the whole world. It has destroyed all the empires save the Russian and the Chinese; it has produced scores of new independent states that, from the Congo back to Cuba, all call themselves democracies. If this notion could make the world safe for democracy, Earth should be a Heaven now, for the planet is today completely papered with democracies—even the Communists describe their tyrannies as "people's democracies." Instead of Heaven, we find Hell on Earth. We find we have but balkanized Europe, the Mideast, Southern Asia, and all Africa. From the Balkans we have spread all over the world the cancerous concept of sovereignty with which World War I began. And so we have inevitably brought our concept of the sovereignty of man into direr danger than it was when we set out in 1917.

The first products of this misconception—the free and independent states of Eastern Europe which rose from the ruins of empire there—lacked the experience to federate freely. These new Balkanlands among which World War II began, have been the first nations to fall back under empire. That empire is the most totalitarian type of imperialism. Its Czech subjects have formed its foremost tools of penetration from Cairo on to the Congo. Our confusion over sovereignty has already punished us with two World Wars and one in Korea—nine years in all—and a Hitler-breeding Depression. It has allowed the totalitarian concept of national sovereignty to capture the Russian and Chinese peoples inside-out and arm itself until it now faces our true concept with by far the most formidable challenge in our history.

Yet, like the alcoholic who seeks strength in what has already stupefied him, we have kept our trust only in the bottle that betrayed us. We have persisted for more than forty years in the nihilistic notion that individual liberty lies in the unlimited sovereignty of the nation, and neglected our own idea that it lies in the supreme but limited sovereignty of our individual selves. In these forty years a number of American leaders have enjoyed even more military or political prestige at home, and throughout Atlantica, than did Washington in Virginia and America. Yet none of them has thus far shown Washington's degree of understanding of the revolutionary American concept of sovereignty; still less has any shown his devotion to it, his determination to advance it. This concept then sent into orbit a galaxy of great men drawn from some 3,000,000 American sovereigns. It has yet to bring forth any man of their heroic stature from the 180,000,000 sovereign Americans who now profit, materially, from their wisdom, vision, courage—and timely action. And we wonder that the immense faith which the world, and even more the Atlantic community, and most of all we Americans, have had so long in the American people—in this people each of whom, as Tocqueville saw, was so openly and truly the sovereign that every man on earth dreams he himself should be . . . we wonder that this faith everywhere is famishing, despite all the billions we now spend to send into orbit . . . mice and monkeys.

The Founding Fathers took but eleven years to see that they had started wrong and to meet in the Convention where they made the revolutionary change from confederation to Federal Union. The best that we have thus far done has been to recognize that our problem lies in the community which the experienced democracies around the North Atlantic form, and to unite with them in a grand alliance. But there is cause for hope in this mouse of wisdom that a mountain of disaster has brought forth. There is still greater hope in the fact that we now have political leaders daring enough to propose changing the alliance into a confederation. Most hopeful of all is the fact that leadership by the Congress of the United States—as by the legislature of Virginia in 1786 —has made it possible at last for leading citizens from the free states of Atlantica to meet in a Convention, patterned on the Federal one, to explore afresh the problem of uniting their peoples both democratically and effectively.

Let us not despair of the American people—nor of the other free peoples of Atlantica whom we despair of so readily, as they do of us, and of each other. All these nations are composed of more than sovereign citizens. Each has within it all the potential heroes, small and great, the hour demands. Many are potentially so great that even the certainty of remaining individually unknown forever will not keep them from responding to the revolutionary concept of their own sovereignty, with the heroic wisdom they showed when the first Federal Union was submitted to them . . . and with the heroic self-sacrifice, on many a less known battlefield than Gettysburg, by which they have, in the end, not only maintained but advanced the Union of the Free ever since.

Let us not despair, but renew our faith in ourselves. That, after all, is the soul of our concept of sovereignty.

One way to renew our faith is to note the rewards in sovereignty that resulted for the citizens who established the first Federal Union on this concept—and compare this gain with the senseless sacrifices of our sovereignty that we

citizens are each personally making today . . . on the altar of
the false totalitarian concept of the sovereign nation. Let us
strike this balance now.

CHAPTER 9

The Sovereignty You Gain by Atlantic Union

The American Way of Life has become the religion
of the masses in five continents: as with so many other
religions, the nature of its Deity remains a mystery.
. . . The greatest achievement of American civilization
is not the opulent standard of living, nor even the
economic machine that created it: It is the political
system that made both of them possible. The U. S., it is
often said, is a young country, immature and even
adolescent. Culturally, it may be. Politically, it is the
oldest and most mature democracy, in the modern
world. Americans like to think of themselves as practical people with a genius for gadgets. In fact, they
are idealists with a genius for politics almost unequalled
in history. But why?—*David Marquand, reviewing
W. R. Brock's* The Character of American History
in Manchester Guardian Weekly, *March 17, 1960.*

If there is a country in the world where the doctrine
of the sovereignty of the people can be fairly appreciated, where it can be studied in its applications
to the affairs of society, and where its dangers and its
advantages may be judged, that country is assuredly
America . . . It is unencumbered by those fictions that
are thrown over it in other countries, and it appears in
every possible form, according to the exigencies of the
occasion . . . The people reign in the American political world as the Deity does in the universe. They are
the cause and the aim of all things; everything comes
from them, and everything is absorbed in them.—
Tocqueville, Democracy in America *(1835)*

When the signers of the Federal Constitution posed to
their fellow citizens the simple, revolutionary idea that the
way to secure and to advance their lives and liberties was to
unite themselves, and divide their governments, the better to
rule them, the cry that this meant "sacrificing" their sovereignty was raised even more loudly than in the Convention—

though perhaps not more than now by opponents of an Atlantic Union. Mercifully for Patrick Henry—but unfortunately for themselves—most Americans have forgotten how confused this great Virginian patriot was on this issue. He warned that by ratification of the Constitution not merely "the sovereignty of the States will be relinquished" but "the rights of conscience, trial by jury, liberty of the press, all your immunities and franchises, all pretensions to human rights and privileges, are rendered insecure, if not lost, by this change." He commiserated his fellow Virginians "who, by the operation of this blessed system, are to be transformed from respectable, independent citizens to abject, dependent subjects or slaves." He continued down this line, day after day, from June 4 through June 25, 1787, when the convention which the people of Virginia had elected to ratify or reject the Federal Constitution, voted down the country's most famous orator 88 to 80, and voted in the Union, 89 to 79.

How Both Virginians and Delawareans Gained Sovereignty

The majority in every state was wise enough to see that it was not the citizens who sacrificed sovereignty when they shifted certain powers of government from their state government to other men they elected to represent them in the Federal Government. Each of Virginia's sovereigns had one vote in electing the members of the state government, and each enjoyed the same equal power with all the sovereigns of all the Thirteen States in electing representatives to the Federal government.

Since there were many more Virginians than Delawareans, the people of Virginia thus gained ten times the votes they had enjoyed in the old Confederation which, we have seen, gave each sovereign state the same single vote. The change, however advantageous to Virginia, seems at first glance to the disadvantage of the sovereign citizens of Delaware—but they saw, even sooner than the Virginians, that in reality they had lost nothing. In fact, they had gained, if anything, even more than the Virginians.

Although little Delaware alone had sent delegates to the Federal Convention who were explicitly instructed to reject any surrender of the state's equal vote in the Confederation, it was the first to ratify the abolition of this principle—and it ratified the Federal Constitution unanimously. Yet the latter also deprived the state governments of their right to be the sole representative of their people in the Confederation. They could no longer name their delegates to its Congress, instruct them on how to cast the state's vote, and recall them at will. In their federal union—as in all federations—the state governments as bodies politic had no voice whatever in the affairs of the Union; it was independent of them, and they were no less independent of it. The citizens of Delaware saw, however, that the new Union guaranteed them as complete an independence in their purely state affairs as did the Confederation—but did this much more effectively. To them Virginia seemed big enough to maintain its independence amid the Confederation's anarchy, but Delaware was much too small to survive in such conditions.

The Delawareans saw, too, that the Federal Union also gave them equality of representation with Virginia in the Senate where each had two votes, but on a different basis— one which strengthened them. For one thing, Federal Union gave the Senate the sole voice in ratifying treaties and important executive appointments. Moreover, whereas it gave the House a veto over all *other* legislation passed by the Senate, it gave the Senate a veto over *all* bills passed by the House.* Since there were more small than large states in the Union, the people of the smaller states could be sure that they would always command a majority in the Senate, and could thus veto any move the large states might make through the House to upset this balance between the states.

CITIZEN SOVEREIGNTY IN A FEDERAL SENATE AND HOUSE

It should be noted that the Senators were then to be elected by their state legislatures—not directly by the people as the Members of the House have always been. But since even then the two Senators were elected separately, at intervals of two years, for a term of six years (not subject to recall), and were paid by the Federal Treasury, not by their state government, the latter, as a body politic, lost all control over them in practice.† Moreover, the Federal Constitu-

---

* The veto of each House over the other results from the fact that our Constitution requires the concurrence of a majority of both Houses for any bill to become law. This veto, significantly, is the only absolute veto in the federal union system; not only does no citizen or state have a veto, but the "veto" which the Constitution gives the President is limited, since a two-thirds majority in both Houses can over-ride it.

† The state government's complete loss of control over the state's Senators has been made clear to all since 1913 when the 17th Amendment to the Constitution deprived the Legislatures of their right to elect them and gave this directly to the citizens.

tion authorized each Senator to cast his vote independently of the other. Since the two may be from opposing political parties, and necessarily always differ on many measures, their two votes often cancel each other out.

None of this works, however, to keep the Senate, whenever the essential federal balance is involved, from being an effective upholder of it and a strong brake against overcentralization. It does work instead to give more citizens of each state a vote they could not otherwise have, on all the multitude of inter-state measures on which they differ. For example, if the citizens of a state are divided about equally between two parties, those in each party can, by federal union, have their own Senator. Again, if many citizens in a state favor a given treaty whose ratification many others in it oppose, both the pro and con may have a spokesman and an equal vote in a Federal Senate. In NATO, or in a confederation, only the party in power in each nation can speak or vote.

These gains for the citizens are, of course, even greater in the Federal House. The citizens elect their Representatives in it from the district in which they live. The populations of these districts are differently composed, and may have quite opposing interests—as, for example, city districts and rural ones do. It results that small groups of sovereign citizens in Virginia, who had no spokesman and no vote in the Confederation, gained representation on interstate affairs through Federal Union. In like manner, the huge groups and interests in the United States, Britain, France, and all the other NATO nations who have none now in it, would gain representation on Atlantic affairs through an Atlantic Union. What the citizens of the larger states thus gain from federalism is obvious—but it is also an asset to those of the smaller states.

Certainly, the people of Delaware understood this, even though their smaller number allowed its citizens only one representative in the House. In the Convention the Delaware delegates had pleaded that "it would not be safe for Delaware to allow Virginia" so many votes. They found, however, that even this was in the end an improvement over the Confederation. For the fact that the representatives from the larger states were elected in different districts guaranteed that the ten votes from Virginia would rarely if ever *all* be cast against the interests of Delaware—as was inevitable in any conflict of interest in the Confederation, where the state government put *all* of Virginia's weight behind its one vote. By the federal system, it became possible that, whenever the interests of the people of Delaware happened to be the same as that of the people in various districts in Virginia, the votes of those Representatives would be cast on the same side as Delaware's lone vote. There was the possibility too that the party that commanded a majority in Delaware might also elect a majority of the Representatives from Virginia, Pennsylvania and other large states.

This may suffice to show why Federal Union's transfer of voting power on interstate affairs from the state government back to the citizens proved so attractive to the people, and most of all in the small states. It is significant that New Jersey, whose delegation led the opposition in the Federal Convention to any "surrender of state sovereignty," was the third state to ratify the Federal Constitution—and New Jersey, like Delaware, ratified it unanimously. All the major battles against ratification and all the close votes for it came in the larger states: Pennsylvania, 46 to 23; Massachusetts, 187 to 168; Virginia, 89 to 79; and New York, 30 to 27.

THOSE WHO LOSE AND THOSE WHO WIN BY UNION

The truth was, and is—and it can hardly be stressed too often—that whether or not the change from alliance or confederation to federal union results in loss of sovereignty depends entirely on whether one considers as supreme the "sovereignty" of the state or that of the citizen. If one shares the Communist idea that the state is supreme, then one is right in concluding that federal union involves a sacrifice of sovereignty by the states included in it. But if one shares the American concept that the citizen is the true sovereign, then federal union involves no sacrifice whatever of his sovereignty, and brings only gain.

Before the Federal Convention met, George Washington wrote a letter to Henry Knox on February 3, 1787; in explaining his grave doubts that it could possibly succeed, he put his finger on the only persons who actually lose power in such a change:

> I believe that the political machine will yet be much tumbled and tossed, and possibly be wrecked altogether, before such a system as you have defined will be adopted. The darling Sovereignties of the States individually, the Governors elected and elect, the Legislators, with a long train of *et cetera* whose political consequence will be lessened, if not annihilated, would give their weight of opposition to such a revolution.

Though some of the state executives and legislators

helped instead to bring about the change, others did seek, as Washington foresaw, to prevent the change to Federal Union by representing their loss of power as a sacrifice by the people of their own sovereignty. But the people were not fooled—not the majority of them. They grasped the basic truth which James Wilson of Pennsylvania had hammered home in the Federal Convention. Speaking on June 16, "he could not persuade himself," Madison noted, "that the State Governments and Sovereignties were so much the idol of the people, nor a National government so obnoxious to them, as some supposed. . . . Will each Citizen enjoy under it less liberty or protection? Will a Citizen of *Delaware* be degraded by becoming a Citizen of the *United States*?" (His emphasis.)

Again, on June 20 Wilson argued: "A private Citizen of a State is indifferent whether power be exercised by the general or State Legislatures—provided it be exercised most for his happiness." And Hamilton chimed in on June 29: "The state of Delaware, having 40,000 souls, will lose power, if she has 1/10 only of the votes allowed to Pennsylvania, having 400,000 [people]; but will the people of Delaware be *less free,* if each citizen has an equal vote with each citizen of Pennsylvania?" (His emphasis.)

The sovereign citizens proved Wilson and Hamilton right by ratifying the Constitution—and so did Federal Union by its results. Under it no citizen lost his citizenship in his own state, but each gained citizenship in the United States. Each remained sovereign in his state, but won a sovereignty he had never had, for he became an American sovereign, too. This gave him far greater dignity and power than even the citizens of the largest states enjoyed before. Nor was this all. The citizens also gained in sovereignty by each of the transfers of power they made from their state governments to their Union.

FIVE POWERS CITIZENS GAIN BY FEDERAL UNION

Consider how much the people have gained in all the fifty states by having a common United States force to defend their individual liberties and their state rights. What if each state had to uphold the liberty and state rights of its citizens all by itself, be prepared to fight not only Old World dictators but neighboring states? Before the Thirteen federated, troops of New York and of Massachusetts were moving to their frontier, threatening war over Vermont. What taxes, military service and war we would suffer now if each of our fifty states had to defend its rights alone!

Consider the gain to all the citizens of all the fifty states from having a common foreign policy. Let any American ask himself: What if my state could have a tough policy toward Soviet Russia, while neighboring states could appease Moscow? Before the Thirteen federated, when Massachusetts closed its ports to British ships, Connecticut welcomed them, made the most of this chance to get business—much as the British recognized Red China when the United States refused to . . . while the master of the Kremlin chuckled scornfully, and attacked the divided democracies, first in Korea, then in Indo-China, and has since advanced through their division, in Suez as in science.

Consider the gain to all the citizens of the Thirteen States when federation freed them from the vexation and cost of doing business with thirteen currencies. Think of the enormous advantages we Americans now have from having one currency throughout the fifty states. . . .

Consider how much American citizens everywhere gained when federation removed the tariffs between their states, and allowed every American to sell whatever he had to sell in the highest market in the United States and buy whatever he needed in its cheapest market—without any state government interfering with his trade. How our American standard of living would be cut down if our states regained the "sovereign right" to vex the citizens with trade barriers as do the states of Africa, Latin America and Europe's Seven and Six. . . .

Consider, finally, how much even the Texans admit they gain by being citizens of the United States as well as of their own state, with no passports or visas to impede their travel, business, study or change of residence anywhere in the Union . . .

By every one of the United States transfers of power from the state to the Federal Government, the citizens in every state gained immensely, became much stronger, freer sovereigns.

In achieving for each of us all these—and other—gains in sovereign equality, dignity, freedom, power, the citizens of the Thirteen States sacrificed not only none of theirs, but no iota of the revolutionary American concept of national sovereignty. It is only our generation that has been sacrificing this concept. Like Cinderella confined to the kitchen by her ugly sisters who monopolize all relations with the neighbors, our revolutionary concept of sovereignty is now confined to purely domestic duties while we let the theory of sovereignty which Communism stands for—in the Congo and in Cuba as in the Soviet kitchen—govern our relations even with our closest friends.

Such has been and is our confusion that some organizations of American veterans have led in demanding that the United States "surrender none" of . . . this brand of national sovereignty on which Communism feeds. Their confusion is understandable, since most living veterans were drafted to fight for that concept in the two World Wars it has caused, whereas the veterans of the American Revolution fought to overthrow it.

One might expect that the descendants of these first veterans, who with filial piety and pride call themselves Daughters of the American Revolution, or Sons of it, would be the first to set our living veterans right on this vital point. Instead, these organizations have themselves been even more insistent champions of the same counter-revolutionary concept. They long opposed even calling an Atlantic Convention, patterned on the Philadelphia one, to explore how far the federal principles of their Fathers might be applied now to unite the Atlantic peoples in upholding the revolutionary American concept which all these nations now share.

THE CONTINUING NEEDLESS SACRIFICE OF U. S. SOVEREIGNS

Our generation has been sacrificing American sovereignty not merely in principle but concretely in practice—increasingly, tragically. If you agree that the American people are equally the sovereigns of the United States, then every limitation on the citizen's life and liberty that he suffers to maintain merely certain powers he has delegated to the nation-state, is a needless sacrifice of his sovereignty.

Consider how much freer each of our lives would be if we did not have to pay the heavy taxes we pay now. P. F. Brundage, who retired in 1958 as Director of the Budget Bureau of the United States, testified before the House Foreign Affairs Committee on May 17, 1960 that at least $10 billion dollars could be saved each year by effective Atlantic Union as regards defense alone. There you have an example of *needless* sacrifice of each citizen's sovereign right to spend his hard-earned income as he pleases—a sacrifice made to maintain not his own sovereignty but merely that of his national government. In his testimony, Mr. Brundage said:

> In my work on the Federal Budget for four years, I was deeply concerned by the amount of duplication within the NATO group and the lack of uniformity

in our Atlantic policies, in our equipment, in our training procedures and in our defense plans. I became convinced that a closer cooperation or coordination, even
to the extent of a limited union of our NATO countries,
would greatly reduce our over-all expenditures and
greatly increase the effectiveness of our defense
measures.

My own experience has indicated how difficult it is
to put a dollar mark on any expected savings. I have
estimated that the over-all saving, if we were to accomplish a real effective coordination to the extent of
unified forces, common bases, common weapons and a
common master plan, could amount to more than $10
billion a year. I still believe that this is a very moderate estimate of the potential savings.

This $10 billion economy was Mr. Brundage's estimate
of the saving for American taxpayers alone. This would be
about one-fourth of the present American expenditure on defense. A similar saving by the other NATO nations would
make the economy for all fifteen of them total $12.8 billion
a year. British and French taxpayers would also save the
huge expenditures their governments are now making to
catch up with the United States in atomic weapons. The
French at this writing are planning to spend $2.4 billion
more on their five-year atomic program—or about one-fifth
of the total of their previous general budget. Apart from the
waste of money which results from the example of atomic
nationalism which we Americans were the first to set, there is
the even worse waste of scientific and technical knowhow
which goes with it.

It should be noted, too, that Mr. Brundage's estimate was
based on NATO merely achieving "effective coordination to
the extent of unified forces, common bases, common weapons
and a common master plan." Full federal union would permit
even greater strength at still greater saving for the Atlantic
community.

Every citizen who is drafted into the armed services is
sacrificing another big portion of his share of our "national
sovereignty." As with taxes, some such sacrifice is necessary
—so necessary that it is rather an investment than a sacrifice,
as *Union Now* pointed out in Chapter VII. The only portion
that is truly a sacrifice is the needless part. The power that
lies in union is proverbially great and, being inherent in the
principle, involves relatively no burden. The defensive power
we fail to get thus by Atlantic Union, we now try to get
from our citizens, not only in taxes but by drafting men.
All the power thus gained which could be gained by Union

at less cost in money and men represents a needless sacrifice of the citizen's share of the nation's sovereignty.

Every citizen who is slain in war that could have been prevented by Atlantic Union is sacrificing, of course, all the rest of his sovereignty as a citizen.

Consider how much these sacrifices of the citizen's sovereignty on the altar of the state have been mounting:

In 1938 the bill for United States defense amounted to only $16 a citizen. Now it is $253 for every man, woman and child —sixteen times as much as it was before the worst war in history. In 1938 no American citizen was subject to draft. Now millions are drafted and subject to draft. In World War I, the United States called into the services 4,609,190 men, of whom 53,403 were killed in battle. In World War II, 15,-513,657 United States citizens were called into the armed services, and 293,105 sacrificed in battle their entire share of the nation's sovereignty. All this adds up to an appalling sacrifice of sovereignty by American citizens.

How much more will be sacrificed in military service before World War III, with so many drafted now?

How many, many more Americans will sacrifice all their share of the national sovereignty in the third World War toward which we are moving, despite all this taxing and drafting—a war in which millions can be killed by a single H-bomb?

We Atlantic Federal Unionists are anxious to prevent more of this fearful, flesh-and-blood sacrifice of sovereignty which the citizens of our nation have already suffered. We want to save the real sovereigns of this republic, and of every democratic nation, from *unnecessary* sacrifice and make them stronger sovereigns. We believe this can be done only by extending America's federal principles around the North Atlantic.

ATLANTIC UNION GUARANTEES YOUR LANGUAGE, CULTURE AND NATIONAL GOVERNMENT

Whether you are an American or a Belgian, a Briton or a Dane, a Canadian or a Dutchman, a Frenchman or a German—whatever the people of which you are now an equal sovereign, you would lose no sovereignty by federating your nation with others in an Atlantic Union; you would gain instead. You would gain even more than the people of the Thirteen States did by Union because this Union—like the dangers now facing us—would be a hundred times greater than theirs.

The creation of this greater Federation would involve no change whatever in the languages, customs, institutions that diversify Atlantica. The laws of the Union would operate in Danish in Denmark, in Dutch in The Netherlands, in French in France and Belgium, in English in Britain, Canada and the United States, just as the national laws do now. No one, whether Icelander, German or other, would be under any more compulsion to learn any new language than he is now. True, debates of the Union Congress or Parliament would no doubt be conducted, for convenience sake, officially in only two of the major languages—probably English for the Germanic ones and French for the Latin ones. But representatives who spoke neither of these would remain free to address the Congress in their native tongue and have their words translated, as in the United Nations. The Union would, of course, give much greater incentive to people in every one of its nations, large and small, to enrich their individual culture by learning to speak other languages.

Each nation would continue to educate its children as it saw fit, and regulate relations between church and state, and worship in the ways its own people wished.

The Union's creation would bring no change whatever in the existing municipal, county, state or other local governments within the member nations, nor any change in the structure of their national governments. Except for the few powers that would be transferred from each of them to the Union government, they would continue to operate under their existing constitutions as they do now. The American people would still elect their President and he would still be their President only. The British would still have their Queen, but she would reign only where she reigns now. The same, of course, would be true of the Presidents of France and of Germany, the King of the Belgians and the Queen of the Netherlands, and so on. The British would still govern their national affairs through their Parliamentary system, the Americans by their Presidential system of divided powers, the French through their intermediate system. The national governments of Britain, France, Italy, would remain unitary, while those of the United States, Canada and Germany would continue to be federations within the Atlantic Union

You would, in short, continue to belong to your nation and it to you, just as now. You would retain all your sovereign right to govern your national affairs as you please, free from interference by the governments or people of any other nation, inside or outside the Union. But now you are able at the showdown to count only on the combined strength of your fellow Dutchmen (or your fellow Norwegians, or Frenchmen, or Americans) to uphold all this independence. By forming part of an Atlantic Union you can count on the united power of its 471,000,000 citizens to guarantee this. And they would guarantee it not merely against the British, French, Germans, or other nations in the Union whom your nation has had to fight for independence in the past, but —far more important—against any attack, or threat, or pressure, from the Communist empires.

SOVEREIGNTY—WHERE NATIONS DEPRIVE YOU OF IT NOW

While thus strengthening immensely your sovereign right to govern directly and independently all the purely national affairs of your nation, you would gain similar citizen sovereignty in a much greater country in which you already live, but in which the tyranny of unlimited national sovereignty now gives you no citizenship and no sovereign rights whatever—the Atlantic Community. All the 471,000,000 persons who form this community share in common certain affairs— notably the defence and advance of their common concept of citizen sovereignty. To defend and advance it, what should be the common policy toward the Communist dictatorship? What should be our "foreign policy" toward all the nations of Latin America, Africa and Asia who are seeking to govern themselves in freedom—and therefore offer so vast and promising a field for the growth of our revolutionary democratic concept of citizen sovereignty? What policy will best serve this, as regards both foes and friends, in military, economic, monetary, scientific and other fields of common Atlantic concern? And what policies and institutions for governing the intense relations of the Atlantic peoples with each other—the inter-state trade, travel, communications of these 450,000,000 free Atlanticans with one another—will best serve their lives, liberties and pursuit of happiness as individual men and women?

These fields are not national but Atlantic-wide. On them depend peace or war, the freedom or the slavery of each of us Atlanticans, the life and death of millions of us—and of our concept of citizen sovereignty. Here is the area of government that most vitally concerns each of us Atlanticans—yet it is precisely here that none of us sovereign citizens now enjoys any of the sovereign rights our forefathers won for us within our own nation. We each would gain all this sovereignty on an Atlantic scale by Federal Union. Only by being its Founding Fathers ourselves can we and our children enjoy the equal and direct voice in Atlantic affairs that we have in our national and local affairs—*plus* (if we follow the American example) the extension throughout Atlantica of our sovereign right to work, play, trade, travel, study and live where and when we please. Only by Atlantic Union can we each gain this sovereignty to the degree we now possess it within our national fraction of the Land—or perhaps we should say, the Ocean—of the Free.

Wherever You Live in Atlantica—You Gain by Union

Our gains in citizen sovereignty would vary, of course, with our nations. For example, in an Atlantic Union of 471,000,000 citizens, the 144,000 Icelanders would gain 3,000 times more strength, in manpower alone, to defend their freedom, both as individuals and as a nation than they now have. The 4,448,000 Danes would gain 100 times more strength by this one measure, the 44,500,000 Frenchmen ten times and the 180,000,000 Americans only 2.5 times. But *all* of us would gain.

The reverse ratio would be true by another measure: By shifting from the Atlantic Alliance's one vote for Iceland, Denmark, France and the United States to federation's one equal vote on Atlantic affairs for every Icelander, Dane, Frenchman and American, 3,000 Americans would gain a vote for every Icelander who did. In other words, each Icelander would no longer have the weight of 3,000 Americans. But, again, *every one* would gain a direct voting on Atlantic affairs, a power he does not have today—without the Americans gaining any voice in purely Icelandic affairs, or vice versa. And since one vote could make a majority, in the Atlantic Union as in Iceland, each Icelander would gain as much from this standpoint as each American.*

One can measure the relative gains in other ways; the results vary even more than in the two opposite examples just given. For example, the gain the Union would bring each of our peoples, and each of us, by enlarging our domestic market could be measured in terms of wealth or productive power or knowhow as well as of population. On the population basis, Atlantic Union would increase the domestic market of the French from 44.5 millions to 471 millions, or more than ten times; it would increase that of the United States from 180 to 471 millions, or 2.6 times. But if the French gained four times more in domestic market by Atlantic Union than the Americans did on a population basis, the latter would gain more on another basis. Their greater financial power and experience in doing business in a vast market would give

* See *Union Now,* Chapter VII for more on this matter.

them a compensating advantage. Whatever the degree of gain in any respect, and whatever the varying totals might be if all the factors that enter into life, liberty, happiness and citizen sovereignty could possibly be measured, the important fact remains that each of us would gain in some degree in some way. And the total gain for us all would be incalculable.

CHAPTER 10

Union Now, the U.N. and World Government

The world must be made safe for democracy.—
Woodrow Wilson, April 2, 1917.

What of the United Nations? The establishment of this successor to the League of Nations since *Union Now* appeared raises several questions. Many assume that they must choose between the U. N. and Atlantic Union, and some devotees of the former fear the establishment of the latter must injure or destroy it. Ever since President Roosevelt first used the term, United Nations, I have urged the establishment of *both* a Union of the Free and a universal United Nations league in which the Union would be a member. I have given priority to the former, as more important to freedom and peace, but I have always seen the two supplementing each other. As early as 1944 I said to the Resolutions Committee of the Republican and Democratic national conventions:

> I would readily grant that, as far as universal international organization is concerned, the best we can hope for at this stage of human development is the league system. So valuable do I hold such an international organization, that from my experience at Geneva, I would recommend a league with every nation in it rather than a more limited league with "teeth," for its "teeth" would be illusory. But to have all the national governments meeting regularly together would be a very real blessing indeed.
>
> There is no sense in not getting the good there is in such a league simply because it is not good enough; but I see no reason, either, in putting all our hopes for peace in so weak a basket.

The mistaken idea that the U. N. and the proposed Atlantic Union are in conflict is unfortunately held much more widely than the true view, that they complete and strengthen each other. The belief that they are competitive arises partly from the fact that they are based on opposite principles though aiming at the same general objective.

The two are so different that it is easy to conclude they can no more mix than can water and gasoline. But though an automobile would not work if water were mixed with the gasoline, one can use the two together in it very effectively by keeping each to its proper function, and being careful never to pour gasoline in the radiator or water in the fuel tank. Water would never give the motor the power it needs to run, nor would gasoline keep it from over-heating. Similarly, the principles of the U.N. can not provide the power that peace requires, but they can provide a climate in which that power can function most effectively for peace in present conditions.

THE U.N. CHARTER PERMITS ATLANTIC UNION

In so dangerous a world situation as the present one, surely only the fanatical supporter of the U.N. would over-estimate its role in Korea, Suez and the Congo to the point where he would want the Atlantic Pact dissolved and all trust placed in the U.N. flag. More reasonable men must concede that the great bulk of the power on which the U.N. must depend to protect its members from aggression is centered in the North Atlantic community, that it will be hard and slow enough to organize this ungoverned community's power, and that it will be impossible to organize a more effective force in time.

The reasonable must also agree that nothing could so endanger the U.N. and its individual members from Latin America through Africa, the Mideast, and Southern Asia than military defeat of the Atlantic Alliance, or its economic collapse, or its moral and political disintegration. The more the Atlantic community can unite its power, the less it will be faced with inflation and the more others can obtain from it the means they lack to raise their living standards, and the greater will be the protection the new, under-developed nations will enjoy against both the military and the economic threats of Communism. This would seem to reduce the issue to this: Is there anything in the Charter to prevent these Atlantic peoples from transforming their alliance into a federal government? The answer is, No. Nothing in the Charter prevents any members from peacefully federating. There are not even the restrictions on this that the Charter places on non-federal regional associations or alliances. It does not so much as mention federal unions. Supporters of the U. N. have generally hailed the steps toward union taken by the Western European nations as helpful to it.

Unlike proposals to change the U. N. into a world government, Atlantic Union would require no amendment of the Charter, nor involve any action by the U.N. This proposal could not be vetoed by the Kremlin.

Formation of the Union need not affect the voting power of its members in the U.N., except that the Union government would decide how all these votes would be cast. The Union could follow the precedent that gave three votes and plural representation to the Soviet Union. Since the United States, the United Kingdom and France are specifically named in the Charter as permanent members of the Security Council, this solution would avoid the need of making even this change in the Charter. If the Atlantic Union should prefer to follow instead the precedent of the American Union which has but one representative and one vote, the Soviet Union would no doubt quickly agree to this Charter amendment.

With nothing in the Charter to prevent Atlantic Union, is there danger that its creation would cause other members of the U.N. to feel offended or "excluded?" The formation of a union involves no more threat to non-members than does an alliance, and no worse "exclusion." There are a number of groupings of nations already, and none has seriously offended those excluded.

The issue then boils finally down to this: Is an Atlantic Union incompatible in any way with the Purposes and Principles of the Charter.* Would it weaken them? The answer is again, No. Atlantic Union is in harmony with them and would greatly strengthen them.

THE VETO AND U.N. POLICE FORCE

What of the veto, and a U. N. police force? The intrinsic importance of the U.N. veto is much over-rated, as are also the votes in it. What really counts in any league is not so much the way their delegates vote as what the governments behind them do to carry out these votes. A delegate's vote is even less binding than his signature to a treaty. Americans should remember from President Wilson's experi-

* See *Atlantic Union and the United Nations* by the author. This reprint, available from *Freedom & Union* for 20¢, compares in parallel columns the effect of Atlantic Union on each of the "Purposes and Principles" of the Charter.

ence that even a Chief Executive's signature does not necessarily mean a treaty will be ratified.

Even if every Great Power agreed to abolish the veto entirely in U.N. proceedings, this "delayed veto" power—which every sovereign nation, large and small, still retains (in NATO as in the U.N.)—would remain to frustrate action, particularly when the Security Council sought to enforce peace. As Geneva's experience in applying sanctions to Italy indicated, it is easier to get sanctions voted than to get them applied. There is no way to abolish the "delayed veto" short of full federation, for the veto is inherent in national sovereignty.

"Suppose the United States should follow the short-sighted theorists who would have it lead in pushing abolition of the U.N. veto to a showdown." I wrote in 1948 in the Postwar edition of this book. "Suppose all the non-Communist nations should stand with it when the break came. What would be the result? The United States would be morally bound to organize its non-Communist league on a non-veto basis where the United States would have to supply most of the men, money and material for the war with Russia that this would hasten—but would have no legal control over them. It might well find itself in a small minority. Control over diplomatic and war policy would have passed not only out of its hands but out of those of the experienced democracies, and into the hands of the immature democracies who would form the majority. This chaotic coalition would have to face the most centralized of dictatorships. If the United States held to this policy, and did not resort to the 'delayed veto,' it would simply be delivering itself, and all the free, and all the world, to dictatorship."

Since 1948 all this has been made only the more valid by the number of new members added to the U.N. and by other developments.

While the "delayed veto" remains, let alone the present U.N. veto, the hopes placed in the establishment of an international police force or disarmament must also be vain. And even if the veto difficulty could be overcome, there would be the difficulty of actually forming from sovereign nations a force effectively controlled by them all, yet capable of overawing and overcoming any of their own national forces, or any combination of these. If the international force were not capable of this, what Great Power would trust it enough to disband its own means of defense?

True, it is easy for any one to work out on paper a "quota force" or a "weighted representation" that is satisfactory to its author. But to get sovereign nations to accept it means getting each to accept a fixed ratio of its own power in relation to that of every other nation's. There lies the rub, not only for the international police question but for disarmament. To solve it proved much too tough a job for the Geneva Disarmament Conference in 1932—and for all the meetings that have followed. Apart from the problems of national pride and suspicion that vex it, it requires bafflingly intricate calculations of the relative importance, now and in future, of land power, sea power, air power, atomic power, rocket power, industrial power and raw material power. The nations are differently equipped with these various elements of power; some are in course of rapid development and others in course of decline. It is significant that the only example of a quota or ratio in power that was actually agreed on by sovereign nations was confined to the simplest arm to measure and control, the navy. Even there it could not be extended to all types of warships, and proved at Pearl Harbor to be anything but a contribution to peace.

Grant that those who hope to make the U.N. work by equipping it with an international force, or limiting national armaments, find some way to overcome all these obstacles. They would still face the basic obstacles to league coercion of sovereign states set forth in Chapter IV and section 3 of Chapter VII of *Union Now*. The patchers still are with us, but patching still won't do.

UNION NOW AND WORLD GOVERNMENT

Union Now devoted to world government only one chapter —but it was entitled, "Public Problem No. 1." Many have jumped to the utterly wrong conclusion that I believe, or believed, that a universal world government could or should be formed at once. I meant that the problem as a whole was urgent—not that it could be solved in one stroke, or that a universal organization should be the first step.

My reasoning was simply this: The development of machines and science is driving the world relentlessly closer and closer together. This increasingly requires us to solve the problem of organizing the world for freedom and peace.

It was obvious to me that current solutions in the 1930s must inevitably plunge mankind into a worse World War. To avert this imminent danger, a sound plan for governing our world had to be devised at once. It was in this sense that I meant that world government was "Public Problem No. 1." I still believe it is—but only in this sense.

The war *Union Now* sought to avert did prove to be far worse than World War I—but happily did not throw us back into Dark Ages, as it might have done. Instead, it resulted in accelerating the development of science, technology and the speed of change. One must pause in awe at the astounding vitality of man and of the civilization which freedom has developed. Despite the devastation, production and standards of living almost everywhere are higher now than before the war—even in England, Japan, Italy, France, Germany and Russia which suffered the worst destruction. And despite the millions killed, the world's population has increased so fast—thanks again to science and technology—and is rising so rapidly that it is likened to an "explosion" and feared now by many more than war itself.

The problem of governing the world that was No. 1 in 1939 remains only more urgently No. 1 in our dawning rocket atomic age. This is not yet evident to some Congressmen who vote billions for the exploration of Space, while forgetting that they cannot bring the moon within reach without developing machines that must also bring Europe and the rest of the world far closer than they already are. But this fact has impressed others so much that they not only rate this problem as No. 1 but center their attention on the universalist approach to it. Even in 1939 the prevailing logic was that since the problem was world-wide the solution must embrace all, or nearly all, the nations from the start.

The more practical members of this school have always recognized that the greater the number of nations organized, the lesser must be the ties that bind them, and therefore a solution that begins with a world-wide organization must necessarily be very rudimentary, much too weak to cope either with war or depression. It can at best contain only the germ of a world government. The hope is that this germ gradually will grow strong enough to do the job. That was the hope behind the first such solution, the League of Nations. It is the hope behind the United Nations now. And the same approach animates most of those who would transform it into a "world government" in some one respect, as by abolishing the veto, or giving it an "international police force," or control of weapons of mass destruction.

The *Union Now* solution has always been just the opposite. It recognized world government only as an eventual, ultimate goal. It proposed to solve the problem by (a) rejecting universality at the start and beginning with only the few Atlantic democracies that could be united in a full, free federal union, and (b) counting on this nucleus to grow in numbers by gradually extending its federal relationship to others. Though few in numbers, these Atlantic peoples had—and still have—together so great a share of the world's moral, material and military power that by federating it fully they could—and can—avert current dangers of war, depression and dictatorship from the start—a hope that no universalist solution can give—and gain enough time and experience for the nucleus to grow peacefully in numbers.

FREEDOM'S ANSWER TO THE WORLD PROBLEM

Union Now was, and is, proposed as freedom's answer to this world problem. Dictatorship already in 1939 had its plans for world government; the universalists who put peace first had theirs in the League of Nations; but those who put freedom first had no world plan in 1939. The Nazi plan was then the most aggressive, but the Communist blueprint was already much more carefully worked out, and much wider in its actual and potential appeal. Since the destruction of its Nazi rival, the Communist plan for a world government has grown far more formidable than Hitler's ever was. The *Union Now* plan differs diametrically from both not only in seeking to make sure that the world shall be governed by the principles of individual freedom, but in two other important respects. Whereas dictatorship seeks to advance its plan by exploiting hate, prejudice, the mob mind, *Union Now* has directed its appeal to reason, common sense,—to the open mind of the individual and to such emotions as may sway him when alone with his conscience. And whereas dictatorship seeks to build its world government by subversion, violence and war, the *Union Now* program has always confined itself to the democratic methods of full, free and open discussion and agreement at every stage in the long process, from beginning to end.

The *Union Now* approach to world government is so centered on freedom and its Atlantic nucleus that believers in the universalist approach have long criticized it as "exclusive," "dividing the world into two camps," and so on. It has been attacked as a universalist "world government scheme" only by American isolationists or nationalists (few of whom could have read it) and by Communists, here and abroad.

Within the Federal Union organization I long had to battle continually with those who sought to change its accent from Union of the Free to world government or the United Nations. By 1945* practically all these universalists had

---

* Since 1945 there has been no controversy on this issue within the Federal Union association, which has steadily and increasingly kept its accent on Atlantic Union.

withdrawn either to the United Nations Association or to the United World Federalists.

When the atomic bomb added "nuclear physics" to the jargon of science, it ironically blew many nuclear scientists —and a surprising number of nuclear unionists and "practical" politicians—into the camp of the universal "world governmenters." In the days of the Acheson Plan and the Baruch offers to Soviet Russia, when there was far stronger support of the United World Federalists than now, I re-examined the universalist approach carefully. I gave my reasons for rejecting it in the 1949 Postwar Edition of *Union Now*, listing "ten fallacies in the universalist approach" to world government which confirmed me in the view that it was untenable. Events since then have made this so clear to the great majority that there seems no need to make the case again here.*

CHAPTER 11

We Must—Like William Tell—Aim High

O my son Absalom, my son, my son Absalom!
  would God I had died for thee,
O Absalom, my son, my son!—II Samuel 18:33

This feat of Tell, the archer, will be told
While yonder mountains stand upon their base.
By Heaven! the apple's cleft right through the core.
    —Schiller, *William Tell,* Act III, Scene 3

Two chronic blunders have contributed heavily to past failures to unite the Atlantic community effectively enough. One is that its leaders have either failed to keep their eye on the target, or have expected to hit it while manifestly aiming under it. The other is that they have persistently tackled the problem piecemeal, never as the whole it is. Few Atlanticans would deny that their true target is:

> To unite the Atlantic community soon enough, ef-
> fectively enough and economically enough to save
> freedom—for once in our time—without another
> World War or another Depression . . . and lead the

---

* I would refer those who are still in doubt to pages 259-262 of the Postwar Edition. A reprint of these pages is available free from *Freedom & Union.*

world to the new era which scientific, industrial,
political and moral development make possible now.

Would you not agree that this is the target the people want
their leaders to hit, and that they are not likely to hit it
unless they keep aiming clearly at it?

For years they have undershot the target with tragic
consequences, and constancy. But still we do not yet even
make sure that those who fill our front pages with their
proposals and policies are so much as looking at the bull's-
eye. Nor do we yet ask them the commonsense question:
Have you raised your sights enough to correct the previous
miss?

The disconcerting fact is that our leaders have never
really aimed at hitting our true Atlantic target. They have
aimed instead at not disturbing the habits and prejudices
of those who depend on leadership to keep them from war
and depression—and not keep them forever on some brink,
or facing "long years of tension." When failures have dis-
turbed the people, leadership has lured them back to a
fool's paradise by piping that old, old tune—the shot was
aimed "in the right direction."

THE APPLE—OR OUR SONS?

The fallacy that it suffices to aim in the right direction
did not fool William Tell. He aimed straight enough and
high enough to hit the apple, not the son—and he hit it,
even with bow and arrow.

If we are to save our own sons (instead of the apple of
Atlantic discord we seem often to treasure more), it can not
be said too often that we must raise our sights. True, this
involves doing something that no Madison Avenue flannel-
suiter would dare risk: Aiming over the head of a boy.
Even so, wise citizens will henceforth subject every proposal
to this practical test: Is it likely to hit the apple? Or is
it just another of those shots "in the right direction" that
have been killing our sons? The Atlantic Convention is a
good occasion to begin applying this test.

Contrast the present spirit with that of the Founding
Fathers when they tackled the problem of uniting Thirteen
States effectively. If the United States is freedom's citadel
today, it is because a few leading citizens had the vision
at the dawn of the steam age to aim explicitly at giving
the people what they really wanted, a free "government intended to last for ages" (to quote James Madison at the 1787
Convention), and to build it on lines great enough to permit

their infant federal union to grow in 170 years to one of fifty states and 180,000,000 citizens, drawn from all races and nations of men.

Is it realistic and practical, after all, for the Atlantic Convention to allow its vision to be limited to half-measures now, when men in other fields are preparing to circumnavigate the moon as boldly as Magellan prepared more than 400 years ago to girdle the Earth?

THE TREES, NOT THE FOREST

Had William Tell been able to use a shotgun instead of an arrow, there would have been less doubt of his hitting the apple—but his son would have faced another danger our sons do, as does also the Atlantic Convention. The fashion in such meetings today is to center attention on the trees, not the forest. They divide the delegates into a number of committees and subcommittees, each of which will discuss some pine, oak, thorn, apple or nut tree. That was what happened at the Atlantic Congress in London in 1958. It made no provision for any discussion of the Atlantic problem as a whole. True, it had a "Declaration Committee," but it was composed of committee officers rather than delegates and its duty was to nail together their separate findings. This amounts to building a house of lumber sawed from pine, oak and other trees—doing a useful thing but hardly providing the view that sees the living forest despite the trees.

The Atlantic Congress set-up was, of course, the one that has been followed for fifty years. It seems a very practical approach to a complex problem. . . . Until one recalls how often it has failed, how illusory its successes have been.

The Atlantic Convention will be under heavy pressure to devote its attention to current problems; it needs to keep in mind that its true task is not to tackle such problems, but to work out machinery that will tackle them effectively.

If we liken current affairs to rocks and agree that we need something better than the hammer we are now using to break them with, then the function of this Convention should be, not to hammer at any rocks nor bother the diplomats who are hammering at them, but to confine itself strictly to devising a better implement—a rock-crusher that will break rocks with less effort and cost, and crush even those that our hammers now are unable to break.

Put in other terms, the task is to find how to make the Atlantic body politic healthy enough to meet growing demands, dangers, opportunities. As I pointed out in testifying in favor of calling this Convention at the hearing which the House Committee in Foreign Affairs held on this proposal on May 17, 1960:

.   NATO is filled with specialists on the muscular, or military, side of the Atlantic problem. Recent plans for organization of Atlantic economic cooperation show that the specialists on its digestive ills are not idle. There is obvious need for these and other specialists—but it is no less obvious that the military, economic, monetary and political parts of the Atlantic community are as intricately inter-related as are the muscles, stomach, heart and brain of each of us. Good health requires us to keep always in mind the body they together form. But we have been so concerned with the various parts of the Atlantic man that we have neglected completely to provide him with a family doctor—or even a college to educate some general practitioners to treat this body politic as a living whole.

As *The New York Times* correspondent covering the League of Nations from 1929 to 1939, I had to report all kinds of conferences that tackled its problem piecemeal—none that tackled it as a whole. This piecemeal approach gave the illusion then, as it still does, that it simplified the problem, was more "practical." In reality, this illusion gave a false sense of security, wasted the time in which realistic remedial action was still possible, led to World War II.

The ten-year course I had in this school of experience led me to appreciate what I fear is still very little understood in our country today—the superiority of the Convention method by which our Founding Fathers tackled the problem of getting their thirteen nation-states to work together effectively yet democratically. Their Convention set up no committee of military specialists, no political committee, no economic committee. It had only *one* committee (apart from drafting committees)—a Committee of the Whole through which it wrestled from beginning to end with the problem as a whole.

Compare the common sense of their approach with the complications of the "functional" approach. When you look at where the Atlantic community stands today after eleven years of this piecemeal approach and think of the enduring contribution to freedom our Founding Fathers made in only three months with their

Convention approach—do you wonder that I feel that
any patriot should support this resolution which would
at least tackle the problem now by a method that makes
sense? Certainly I do not wonder that two [of the
Committee] sponsors of this wise approach are experienced family doctors, general practitioners—Dr. Morgan and Dr. Judd.*

WHY THE FEDERAL PACKAGE IS PRACTICAL

The overall approach is, of course, a federal unionist one.
But most non-federalists would agree that the political,
moral, cultural, military, economic and other questions before the Atlantic Convention are, in fact, closely inter-related
—so much so that to tackle them as a whole is at least as
practical—if not more so—than the piecemeal method.

The federal union approach is concerned with each of the
major problems facing the Atlantic Convention—and Community—but with each *as a part of the whole*, not as something to be considered without relation to the rest. It offers
an answer to them all together, which is also an answer to
them each. Nor is this a theoretical approach, or solution.
Ever since the 1787 Convention stumbled onto the overall
approach and answer, every one of the federations now
existing in the world has been created by this same basic
technique: Delegates who centered on the overall problem
put together in one package, called a constitution, a political,
economic, monetary, military, cultural and moral union,
combined with free federal legislative, executive and judicial
machinery to handle what remained of these problems in
future.
Some fear that this method endangers progress that might
be made on a small scale—that it risks the bird in hand for
two in the bush. But the Convention has no bird in hand;
at most it risks losing only a few feathers. And history makes
the risk seem even less. The fact is that Thirteen States which
were never able to agree even on a mild treaty to regulate
trade between them, did accept not only this regulation but
full economic union when it was wrapped up inseparably
with an effective federal government and an organic political,
military, monetary, moral and citizens union. No single item
in this impressive package would probably have been ac-

* Dr. Thomas E. Morgan (Democrat, Pennsylvania), Chairman of
the Foreign Affairs Committee and Dr. Walter Judd (Republican,
Minnesota).

cepted had it been offered separately. Certainly none ever has been.

TRUTH IS STRANGER—AND STRONGER

That the greater overall answer should be accepted where the smaller step failed may seem paradoxical, even incredible. But truth is proverbially stranger—and stronger—than fiction; and to succeed, the Atlantic Convention needs to hear and follow truth.

To affect reality, the Convention must reflect it, at least to the point of adequately confronting the piecemeal with the overall approach, the functionalist with the federalist answer, "gradualism" with "do-it-in-time." If it confronts these opposites strongly enough, it may not merely blow away the cobwebs that now entrap Atlantic thinking, but generate the power and vision that peace requires and that full and free debate of great issues gives.

WHY UNION WINS APPROVAL
WHERE HALF-MEASURES LOSE

How can the same people who have rejected this or that piecemeal proposal paradoxically accept the full federal answer? Because it faces them with down-to-earth reality, yet high inspiration. A tariff is part-and-parcel of the depression-dictatorship-war complex, but when the only thing in this complex that the people are called on to decide is a tariff question, they tend to think of it only in terms of dollars, cents and their most selfish economic interests; they become very narrow-minded and short-sighted indeed. When the federal answer is submitted to them, they have to face their problem as a whole. Instead of thinking that they live by bread alone, they see that life requires much more than that. The broader picture broadens their thinking, improves their vision, develops their judgment, inspires their souls. So many elements in it are important to them that they have to decide which are the more important.

Instead of calculating only in dollars, they have to weigh intangibles, too. Where the trade issue directly interests only a part of the people, federal union presents an issue with something in it to interest deeply every citizen, the politically-minded as well as the economic-minded, the intellectual, the churchman, the parent. the student, the scientist—all manner of minds and men. Instead of a picture that seems all loss to these, all gain to those, and a matter of indifference to the rest, Atlantic Union has something to interest each directly. It presents so many possibilities as both to defy and invigorate the imagination; no one can feel that he is a total loser, everyone sees some gain in it to compensate for whatever loss he may fear it will cause him. Each has to decide which are his higher values.

What happens in such circumstances? True values assert themselves with most men. And so, when the people of the Thirteen States, who had refused to enter into even a mild degree of economic union, had to decide on the Federal Constitution, the fact that it created a full economic and monetary union played a very minor role in the discussion that followed. The great debate—and it was a great debate indeed in Virginia and New York*—centered on the moral and political issues that the Constitution raised.

Despite Shays's Rebellion, resulting from the fact that economic depression and monetary depreciation had led a reluctant Congress to call the Federal Convention, the debate on ratifying the Constitution gave scant attention to the subjects that engrossed the United States in the days of the New Deal. The classic book which it produced, *The Federalist,* is no treatise on trade, economics, finance, or military defense. Although its editor and chief author, Alexander Hamilton, prided himself on his war record, and was a genius in the economic and financial field, it is concerned almost exclusively with political and moral questions.

This will surprise many today—so widely have we unconsciously accepted the Marxist view that man lives by bread alone. (This at a time when no people on earth devotes so small a fraction of their daily work to satisfying the body's needs, and so much to the moral—or immoral—business of "keeping up with the Joneses," as do we Americans, and Atlanticans.) Yet I feel sure that, if we put people to the test, we shall find that they still have today the same values as the generation that centered attention on the political and moral issues that the Federal Constitution raised. To think otherwise is to believe that all the sacrifices made since then to preserve and advance the moral and political principles of liberty-and-union were made in vain.

After all, when men (and now also women, who then had no vote) face an Atlantic Federal Constitution and have to consider not merely what its effect will be on the price of wool, automobiles, chemical products, perfume or cheese, but

* See "When Patrick Henry Fought the Federal Constitution," by Jonathan Elliot, "How Virginia Came to Vote for Federal Union," by Albert J. Beveridge, and "How Hamilton Won New York for Federal Union," by Bower Aly, 20¢ each, Freedom & Union Press, Washington 9, D. C.

which is more important to them: The value of this or that alias for bread, or the value of their own dignity, liberty and life—and that of their sons, daughters, grandchildren. When they have to face this issue, there can be but one answer.

When the issue is full federation, the great moral as well as material and military advantages that its economic and monetary side would bring will shine forth—not be hidden by the smoke-screens of selfishness which economic union would face if presented alone. Only by presenting to the people of Atlantica a full Federal Constitution for them to ratify, or reject, can one put before them this realistic yet idealistic choice—and give them a chance to show their mettle.

"Everyone knows that we would make this Atlantic Union if we got into another World War—and still could—and so it seems common sense to me to try to make it in time to prevent such war." A Southern United States Senator once said this to me. and it set me thinking:

The Founding Fathers sacrificed 4,435 sons in the Revolutionary War before the Thirteen States "would sacrifice their sovereignty" enough to ratify the Articles of Confederation. Thanks to the fact that the William Tells at the Philadelphia Convention courageously aimed high enough to hit the target which the Declaration of Independence had set up, the people took the still more revolutionary step from confederation to Federal Union without a single family sacrificing a single son.

It took the sacrifice of 53,403 sons to bring the League of Nations Covenant before the Senate, but this was not enough to get it ratified.

When 293,986 more sons of American families had been sacrificed, the Senate ratified the United Nations Charter, 89 to 2.

There is no question that we must, sooner or later, take the step from Atlantic alliance to Atlantic Federal Union. The only question is: How much sacrifice of life will it cost?

Shall we continue to aim so low as to sacrifice millions of sons before we take this step? Or shall Atlantic Union come without the killing of a single boy—because the members of the Atlantic Convention prove to be a composite William Tell? It is for them to answer—and for you.

CHAPTER 12

Fourfold Fulfillment

If thou doest well, shalt thou not be accepted? and if
thou doest not well, sin lies at the door.—*Genesis 4:7.*

Some village Hampden that with dauntless breast
The little tyrant of his fields withstood.
Some mute inglorious Milton here may rest.* * *
—*Thomas Gray,* Elegy in a Country Churchyard.

We have more than danger to spur us on; we have the certainty of high fulfillment in all four of our embodiments—as
part of mankind, as part of Atlantica, as part of the nation we
love, and as ourselves, individually rather than compositely.

As part of mankind, we fulfill ourselves through Atlantic
Union by doing the highest service we can do for Man; we
do our part—which only we can do—in assuring that today's
lurid atomic-electronic light is the sunrise of man's vast future, not the sunset. We meet the responsibility we must meet
if we are to merit the name which Paine rightly called man's
"high and only title"—"Man."

We must expect much of mankind to mistrust us and our
motives at the start of our Union of the Free. Our past faults
now outweigh our virtues among all those who have suffered
from them. We must expect this to continue to color their
judgments of us for some time to come, and keep them more
inclined to have fear than faith. After all, we ourselves fear
rather than trust the rest of mankind; the obvious faults in
the other nations, old and new, make us more skeptical than
confident of their future and its effects on us. But whatever
doubts and fears about them we may express, or have, we
do know that it is in the interest of our freedom that they
should succeed in their efforts to advance in liberty-and-
union themselves. We *do* wish them well, and we do *not*
mean to do anything to interfere with their efforts, however
misguided they may seem to us—unless they lose their fight
against dictatorship and directly aid its efforts to destroy
liberty-and-union among us, too.

We know that no matter which of these nations—whether
as great as India or as small as Lebanon, as new as Ghana
and Nigeria or as old as Japan and Thailand, as far West
as Brazil or as far East as Burma, whether Afghan, Arabian,

or Argentine, Iranian, Iraqi or Israeli, Mexican or Moroccan, Pakistani or Peruvian, Spanish or Sudanese; whether Animist, Buddhist, Christian, Confucian, Jewish, or Islamic; whether heir of the ruins of Ankar-vat, Assyria, the Aztecs, Babylon, Baghdad, Egypt, the Incas, Persia—no matter which of these peoples, we know that we shall warmly welcome every proof they bring in the coming years that they are winning in their sector of Man's struggle to free himself, and work peacefully with his neighbors.

We can therefore trust that, no matter how fearful and suspicious they may be of Atlantic Union at the outset, they will each in their hearts hope that our Union's policies toward them will remove their fears. As our deeds destroy their doubts, and our Union proves, as did that of the Thirteen States, that its success is in their interest, too, we can have faith that Atlantica will attract them to it more and more. If America has lost some of that appeal in the last decade, is it not because it ceased to lead forward with the principle of freedom-and-union, and turned instead toward the Old World's system of power politics, alliances and arms racing? For America to return to its true tradition, by leading the way to a "more perfect Union," should suffice both to win back its lost friends and to assure them that no such error would mar the Atlantic Union's appeal to mankind.

Our Union of the Free should start with greater attracting power than the United States, for the latter began with the stain of slavery on it, and without the experience in freedom and federation we now have. But suppose that the Atlantic Union should merely equal the American Union in rousing and fulfilling the hopes of mankind. Even so, it would draw to it the new nations—and those still suffering oppression— by the same magnetic power that America has so long possessed, as Lord Acton attested in 1866:

> Historians affirm that the French Revolution was partly caused by the successful revolution which founded the United States. If that could be at a time when nothing had been achieved but independence, and their Constitution was only beginning the career it has so grandly run, it is easy to estimate how much their influence would be increased by the permanence of their success. Accordingly America exercised a power of attraction over Europe of which the great migration is only a subordinate sign. Beyond the millions who have crossed the ocean, who shall reckon the millions whose hearts and hopes are in the United States, to whom the rising sun is in the West, and

whose movements are controlled by the distant mag-
net, though it has not drawn them away?*

RE-ASSURANCE TO THE NEW NATIONS

Some fear to federate Atlantica lest the new nations should
interpret this as a "ganging up of the imperialists against
them" and troop into the Kremlin's arms. Moscow undoubtedly will try to make them do this. Three facts, however
should re-assure the fearful:

First, whatever the leaders of the under-developed nations
may fear or say, most of them are realists enough (a) to
know that such a policy would sacrifice all the advantages
they hope to gain from neutrality, and all the material aid
which they can get only from Atlantica, and (b) to refrain
from jumping thus from the devil into the deep sea before
they have taken time to see the Union in action, and test
whether its policies are in fact so dangerous in their regard
as to justify so desperate a jump. Those of their leaders who
are not this realistic are bound to come to grief, from so
great a defect in their judgment, and be replaced by wiser
compatriots.

Secondly, there is no reason whatever to expect or fear
that an Atlantic Union would follow any policy that would
cause many, or any, of these nations to become satellites,
protectorates or colonies of the Communist empires. If the
Union's leaders were that unwise—and that untrue to the
very principles that led them to found it—and if the people
of Atlantica did not replace them at the next election with
better men, the Union would deserve to lose.

Thirdly, there are at least three strong reasons—military,
material and moral—to expect this Union to pursue a far
wiser and more liberal policy toward the under-developed
nations than any country now follows, or is likely to follow
without Atlantic federation. The military reason is that the
Union's much stronger defensive power would make it need
allies less than does the United States, and therefore it should
be more willing to help neutrals, with no strings attached to
its aid. At the same time the huge economies on defense,
which only federation permits, would make much greater public and private funds available. As we noted in Chapter 9,
the former United States Budget Director, P. F. Brundage,
has estimated that Atlantic unification, even in moderate degree, would save the United States at least $10 billion a
year on defense. On this basis we estimated the saving for

* Acton, *Historical Essays and Studies*, Macmillan, 1908, p. 127.

all the NATO nations would be nearly $13 billion annually. Part of this would no doubt go back to the citizens in tax reductions—but that would increase the funds available for private investments. The other part might well go into the aid projects that are better handled on a public basis. Nor would these $13 billion a year be the only fresh resources that Union would bring to the solution of this problem.

Turn now to the material side of the question. The establishment of this Union would improve the economy of Atlantica to an incalculable degree by cutting costs and spurring action in industrial production, trade, agriculture, mining, transportation, finance, invention, science and education. It would do this (a) by eliminating the multitudinous barriers, waste efforts, uncertainties and vexations with which unlimited national sovereignty now hobbles all these activities in Atlantica, and (b) by replacing them with the greater efficiency, the sounder currency, the stronger confidence, the vaster and more economic mass production, and the immense stimulus to private enterprise—and to thinking and acting on a grand scale—which the achievement of political and economic Union would bring in every nation and in every economic sector.

We saw in Chapter 4 how immediate and immeasurable was the improvement in the economy of the Thirteen States, once they changed from confederation to Federal Union. But their economic assets were of a kind that could not benefit from Union half so much, or half so fast, as can those of Atlantica today. Not only would the Gross Union Product of Atlantica be much greater at the start than the sum total of the Gross National Products of the Atlantic nations now; it would grow at a faster rate thereafter. But this very growth would mean a better market for the other nations, both as regards the sale of their products and the purchase of goods from the Union. So astonishing is the prospective economic growth that union would bring Atlantica that Professor Maurice Allais, the noted French political economist whose book, *L'Europe Unie*, won in 1960 the Grand Prize of the Atlantic Community in Paris, went so far as to assert in it:

> The economic advantages the free nations would derive from this policy would far surpass those which they derive from the peaceful uses of atomic energy.
> Moreover, the powerful attraction such a community of the free Atlantic countries would exercise by its very existence, its exceptional prosperity and the immense hope it would raise among men everywhere,

would result in slow dissolution of the totalitarian world.*

The combination of stronger defense and greater production, both attained at much less cost than is possible otherwise, would provide the huge material means needed if the problems of the under-developed nations are to be tackled with any hope of success. By no other policy than Atlantic Union, in fact, can these nations, or we, find the vast means needed in the fast time required. Self-interest on both sides would suffice to assure that Union would result in much greater development of these countries. Such development through mutually advantageous trade would be much healthier than any help on a charity basis—or on the political pressure basis that is inevitable where the economy is monopolized by the state, as it is in the Communist empires. The Atlantic Union could not realize its potentials in higher standards of production and living for its citizens without buying much more raw materials from Latin America, Africa and Asia than they can now supply—and so it would have to help them develop themselves. Nor—as we have already noted —can they sell enough of their products in the Communist market, or in any other market except the Atlantic one, to finance themselves in this self-respecting way.

Now for the moral reason why one can be sure that an Atlantic Union would be vastly to the advantage of the under-developed countries. Consider its moral effects. Before a federation could be made by the people of the Atlantic nations in peacetime, there would have to be a profound moral revolution among them, particularly in the stronger ones. They must not merely overthrow the principle of unlimited national sovereignty, which now has such a stranglehold on them, but replace it with the opposite principle of citizen sovereignty. They must discard the notion that their nation is a law unto itself in its dealings with other peoples. They must begin to practice in some fields, with some nations, the democratic Rule of Law which they now practice only within their own boundaries. By that Rule, even the Sovereign Citizens do not claim to be above the Law. Union means they have put the Rights of Man above the Rights of Nations, that they seek to increase their own power over their government, and lessen its power to interfere with their individual lives, liberties, happiness. Union means they have shifted from fear of foreigners to faith in foreigners, and that they have begun to "love thy neighbor as thyself" in a far greater way

* From a chapter of his book published in the September, 1960, *Freedom & Union.*

than they, or any other nations, ever have done before. To achieve Union they must be moved by the deepest desire to live in peace that any people can have.

They must, in short, have attained broader understanding, deeper virtue and high spiritual standards than they have now—or they will not peacefully agree to form an Atlantic Federal Union. It does not make sense to assume that a Union thus established is going to follow policies toward the under-developed nations that are not imbued with the same understanding, virtue and spirit that brought the Union into being—let alone "gang up" against these peoples whom its Member Nations have already liberated peacefully. One can be sure that once the people of Atlantica cross the Rubicon separating unlimited national sovereignty from the citizen sovereignty of freedom-and-union, all their actions thereaftei will be favorably affected by this moral revolution.

The moral effect on the under-developed nations, which the achievement of Atlantic Union will have, will be no less beneficial. The prestige that goes with strength and unexpected success made them look with more respect on Communism, once Moscow led with Sputnik. To achieve Atlantic Union in peace in the near future will be no less impressive a success, no less unexpected—and the strength it will give to freedom will be much more immediate and down-to-earth. When the under-developed nations find that their fears, and Communism's propaganda, about the Union were unfounded, and realize what a boon its creation is to them, this pleasant surprise will attract them to it all the more. The example the Atlantic peoples have set in the past, in putting national sovereignty above all, has been followed in the Balkans, Central Europe, Asia, Africa. The example we Atlanticans will set, in putting the rights of men above the rights of nations when we form an Atlantic Union of the Free, should work a moral revolution, too. in all these other nations. So, too, should the fact that Union brings far greater strength to freedom than national sovereignty ever has. All this should also speed the evolution of these nations from unlimited national sovereignty to the realization of the dream of Latin American federation, African federation. Mideast federation and Southern Asian federation which the wisest leaders in these areas have cherished since the time of Bolivar—thus far in vain.

YEAST IN THE EMPIRES OF THE EAST

What of the yeast effect that Atlantic Union will have on the many peoples who are now held in the cruelest oppression by the Russian and Chinese empires—many for centuries, some only for fifteen years or less? Certainly Moscow will have reason to fear the effect the mere creation of the Union of the Free will have on its Achilles heel—the peoples of Eastern Europe. Unlike the rest of the Russian Empire, they have known in their lifetimes something better than Czarist and Communist despotism. Who are these peoples? They include the Poles whose extreme democratic instincts led them to the anarchy that was the source of their undoing when Kosziusko fell and who remain the most dauntless, romantic fighters for freedom (with one exception). . . . And the East Germans, who only a few years ago stood up—though armed only with stones—against Russian tanks. . . . And the Balts who have kept alive their dream of renewed independence even longer. . . . And the Czechs and Slovaks who revere John Huss, and knew Mazaryk and Benes in the flesh. . . . And the Hungarians who in 1956 wrested from the Poles the title for incredible gallantry for freedom, . . . And the stalwart peoples of the Balkans . . . the Albanians who gave great heroes both to the Roman and Turkish empires . . . the Serbs, Croats, Slovenes who, typically, led in defying the thunders of Moscow . . . the Rumanians who cannot forget their name which recalls the frontiers of Rome . . . and the Bulgarians who, I am sure, respect their assassinated Stambouliski even more than I do still, although my acquaintance with him in the early 1920's as a foreign correspondent was all too short.

No empire has ever found these peoples of Eastern Europe easy to digest—and when the achievement of Atlantic Union revives their hopes, they will give Moscow worse than ulcers. Nowhere will Atlantic Union, by its mere existence, have so strong a magnetic power so soon as in these peoples, so many of whom cherish student memories of Paris and London, or family ties with the United States. It needs but exist to make them hope that they could become members of it, once they freed themselves. Hope can work wonders— and we can not devise a greater wonder-worker than this Union would be to the oppressed in Eastern Europe . . . and in the Russian and the Chinese empires.

It will exert a far greater attraction on them than European Union. They—and especially the Poles and Czechs—have cause to fear Germany. They dread that the Germans would soon dominate a European Union and lead it into adventures eastward. But there would be no possibility of the Germans dominating an Atlantic Union. The addition of the Americans, British, Canadians and Scandinavians to their friends in France and Benelux would make this Union of the Free the most positive attraction to them that is conceivable.

To Bring Dictatorship Down from Within

Atlantic Union would also bring new hope, only to a less degree, to the Ukrainians, Georgians, Armenians and the many other peoples whom the Czars conquered. Those who have suffered oppression longest are, of course, the Russian and the Chinese peoples themselves. I would not count on their throwing off their present oppressors soon—but I would not be surprised if this followed the creation of the Union of the Free much sooner than others would expect. Certainly I would not lose faith in the future freedom of peoples who have shown the courage and resourcefulness of the Russians, and who have behind them so long and great a civilization as the Chinese—and so many close ties with the people of Atlantica. The very intensity and persistence of the anti-American campaign in Communist China is to me strong proof that it is hard to kill the warm feeling that so many living Chinese have had so long for America as the land of freedom and their surest friend.

So long as the dictatorships in Russia and China fear to let their subjects hear two sides of basic questions with equal freedom, or freely choose between two parties, I shall conclude that they themselves have no confidence in the solidity of their regimes. There is much talk today of the difference in viewpoint on Communist doctrine between dictators Khrushchev and Mao Tse-tung. This reminder that believers in anything are certain to divide on some things if they are free to do so, serves to point up the lack of confidence each dictator has in his own country. There are known to be Russian Communists who agree with Peiping's interpretation of Communism, and no doubt there are many Chinese Communists who still follow Moscow. But neither Moscow nor Peiping permits its domestic Communist opposition (let alone a Capitalist or Socialist opposition) to organize itself as a right wing or left wing Communist party and put its case freely before the people. While both Moscow and Peiping are afraid to let their people choose even between two brands of Communism, it would seem to me that their "monolithic unity" is built on sand, and that one need only await the right climate conditions to witness its inevitable fall.

By this, I do not mean war or any tough policy on our part. Every system has its inherent weakness which can bring it down from within. The basic weakness in our free system is the tendency to carry freedom to the point of anarchy. Communism does all it can to exploit this weakness and to help create the conditions in which the free peoples are most

likely to divide against themselves to their mutual destruction. The corresponding inherent weakness in the Communist
system is that it carries unity to the extreme degree of tyranny, which exposes it to the dangers of rigidity and corrosive,
all-pervading suspicion. Its leaders do not trust their people,
or even the rank-and-file in the Communist party; they distrust still more each other. This distrust is bound to be even
greater between Moscow and Peiping, and between Moscow
and Warsaw, and between Moscow and its viceroys in the
other satellites. The restiveness and hope which the creation
of an Atlantic Union would cause in Eastern Europe by giving new life to the American, English and French revolutions, would make both Moscow and its Kadars far more dis-
trustful of the people they rule, and of each other. It would
thus, willy-nilly, create the kind of "climate" in which mutual suspicion behind the Iron Curtain would be undermin-
ing most effectively the foundations of the rigid Communist
structure.

Atlantic Union would also face Moscow with this dilemma:
To hold its satellites then, it would have to make its rule
either more oppressive or more liberal. The former course
would cost it heavily in the outside world, serve to unite
the Atlantic peoples more strongly, and increase the revolutionary pressure in Eastern Europe. The latter course would
make it hard for Moscow to keep control of the satellites—
or to keep from liberalizing its rule in Russia, too. These
examples may suffice to suggest the domestic dangers and
difficulties which the mere creation of the Union of the Free
would bring to the "monolithic" Empires of the East.

OUR FULFILLMENT AS ATLANTIC CITIZENS

Atlantic Union would enable us to fulfill ourselves as Atlanticans. This is perhaps the part of our personality that we
have starved the most. We all do belong to the free community of Atlantica—and in "we" and it I would include
for present purposes such non—NATO peoples as the Australians, Austrians, Irish, New Zealanders, Swedes and Swiss—
but we do not yet acknowledge our love for it and our belonging to it, as we do for our nation. We show in many
ways, however, that we *are* Atlanticans.

Most people in this community, when they travel or study
abroad, do so in the other nations of Atlantica. Most of the
"foreign" books, plays, works of art we like the most in each
of our nations come from the other Atlantic nations. We do
our "foreign" business mainly with the rest of Atlantica, and
most easily. The "foreign" history we know best is their his-

tory—and our own (no matter which our nation) closely interlocks with that of other Atlantic peoples. Most of our heroes and heroines lived in Atlantica. Our nations—especially the English-speaking ones, but also the French, Belgians, Dutch, Italians—are a mixture of Atlantic peoples. Inter-marriage is still greatest, most successful and most rewarding within our Atlantic community.

Each of our peoples thinks its own way of life is peculiar to it—but the nearest approach to it each finds in other Atlantic nations. And so, whatever our nation may be, when we go abroad we feel most at home in other parts of Atlantica. We share more concepts and customs with each other than with others. When in Asia or Africa we find we Atlanticans naturally gravitate toward each other—and Asians and Africans tend to lump us all together, whether favorably or unfavorably. When the freedom each of our peoples holds dearest is endangered in any of our nations, we turn most hopefully to each other for help, or for refuge. More than once most of us have fought together the battle of freedom. Actions, we all say, speak louder than words, and our actions say we all belong at heart to Atlantica. Why not say it then in words? And in votes—hallmark of the citizen?

ATLANTICA—THE COUNTRY WITHOUT A MAN

Why not fulfill the dreams of our Victor Hugos, our Goethes, our John Stuart Mills? Why not begin to answer by Atlantic Union the prayer that our Benjamin Franklin sent to a fellow Atlantican on the other side of the ocean on December 4, 1789—a few months after his thirty-five-year dream of uniting the Thirteen Colonies under a common free government had been achieved:

> God grant that not only the Love of Liberty, but a thorough knowledge of the Rights of Man may pervade all the nations of the Earth so that a Philosopher may set his Foot anywhere on its Surface and say, "This is my Country."

Since then liberty has won all the peoples around the North Atlantic which Franklin crossed so often in its service. Yet still Americans, Britons, Frenchmen, and the other free peoples of Atlantica remain alien to each other in one respect—politically. When they set foot on each other's soil they feel at home—but do not say, as the dying philosopher prayed they would—"This is *my* Country!" We have heard the story of the "Man without a Country," and we would wish no worse fate for anyone. Yet there can be something perhaps worse—a country filled with millions of sovereign citizens of various nations, who act as if it belonged to them, but do not yet dare say they belong to it. There is only one such country now, and it is Atlantica.

This is the embodiment of ourselves which we Atlanticans still keep as Cinderella in the cellar—and which Atlantic Union would bring to the ball and to Prince Charming. And what a true fairy tale of fulfillment that would be!

Consider how the different peoples of Atlantica supplement each other—the French and the Germans, or the French and the British, or the British and the Italians or Germans, or the Dutch and Belgians, or the Greeks and Turks—to mention no more examples in Europe. Consider, too, how the people of North America and those of Western Europe complement one another, as man and woman do. Consider how much they need each other to be their true selves.

Consider the marriage of Western Europe and North America, of the old in culture with the old in free self-goverment, of the new in so many arts and ideas with the new in so many practical things, of the lands where the outstanding building in town is a medieval church with the lands where the finest building in town is a public school . . . Consider the interchange of teachers and students which now goes on among the fifty states of the United States, and project this on an Atlantic scale. How many more European young men and women will be studying in American colleges, and how many more Americans and Canadians will be having part of their education in Europe . . . once they are all citizens of the Ocean of the Free!

Think of the cross-fertilization that would result in education, art, science, invention, business, philosophy, religion —in being, in doing, in living, in loving . . .

Think of the basic cross-fertilization, the inter-marriage of the young people of the European nations with each other, and of the Europeans with North Americans that would result from the political welding of their nations. Think of their children, who would have the advantage of starting life with two national heritages instead of one to draw on, and perhaps with two languages—with keys to two great literatures acquired the easiest way . . .

Children of Franco-German or Italo-American or of other such marriages are handicapped now with the conflict in loyalties that results from their having to subordinate one parent's national heritage to the other's. But the children of

such marriages in an Atlantic Union would be hurt by no
such inner conflict in their formative years. Instead, they
would have the advantage of three loyalties and loves—for
the land of their father, for the land of their mother, and
for the Union of the Free that their parents themselves had
made, as fellow citizens, and added to their children's
heritage.

WHY MOVE FROM FEAR WHEN FAITH OFFERS US SO MUCH?

When one thinks creatively even a little of these and other
effects that flow from our embodiment of ourselves as sovereign citizens of Atlantica, one can not help but believe that
from this Union would soon rise a far higher civilization
than Man has yet attained, anywhere, any time. Our machines have already outdone the seven-league boots, Alad-
din's Lamp, and other wonders of our fairy tales. In like
manner the civilization that would follow our constitution of
this new Atlantis would far surpass from every standpoint
—moral, material, artistic, scientific, spiritual humane—that
of the fabled Atlantis which Plato dreamed of, as a world
swallowed up long before by the Atlantic—not a world that
could ever be.

Here is something now in our grasp that should spur us
on much more than the fears and dangers that too long have
been our major motive power. If fear has made many men
outdo themselves, faith and hope in something better has
led to much more prodigious feats. Not fear, but reasoned
hope led Columbus to brave the Atlantic. Not fear, but faith
in Mohammed's Paradise led the Arabs to make their obscure
Mecca the Mecca of mankind from Afghanistan to Spain
in less than eighty years.

No people ever had such cause for faith and hope as have
we Atlanticans today—or such means to turn them soon into
reality. Let Mr. K get what strength he can from his hope of
"burying" us, from his faith that our grandchildren will be
Communists. We have far sounder reason to know that we
need but fulfill ourselves now, as citizens of the Union
of the Free, to assure our grandchildren—and his—the greatest blessings that Freedom-and-Union have ever brought to
men.

OUR FULFILLMENT AS NATIONS

Atlantic Union would also mean the highest fulfillment of
the nation we belong to, whichever one it may be. Here

would be the peaceful reunion of most of the Hellenic and Roman worlds, and of that of Charlemagne. Here would come together again the Celts, Romans, Danes, Angles, Saxons and Normans who mixed to make the English people. This would reunite the Italians and French, the French and British, the British and Americans, the Americans and Canadians.

With Atlantic Union, the British invention of representative government would climb the highest political Everest in the range of Freedom. How that would please Burke, Mill, Bryce! The French would win for their Revolution's trinity —*Liberté, Egalité, Fraternité*—more than Napoleon dreamed of winning, and win it without a battle, with no retreat from Moscow, no Waterloo. How this would make Jeanne d'Arc rejoice, Voltaire and Lafayette! The Vikings would venture on their ocean as never before. The glories of the Dutch Republic—and the ideals of Grotius—would blossom anew, as would those of the Belgians to whom Caesar paid such tribute. Here the eternal dream of the Germans would be realized in the way that Goethe, Heine, Schiller would applaud. Here would be restored the Rule of Law that Italy first gave the West; here would be far more than Columbus dreamed of in Genoa. Here too would be the apogee of ancient Athens and of modern Ankara. By Atlantic Union, Canada would bring its British fatherland and French motherland to live in Union as their children do in Ottawa. And here the greatest of American inventions—Federal Union—would come to its finest flower . . . in the peaceful, reasoned way the seed was created by Franklin, Washington, Hamilton, Madison, Mason.

Every nation has developed a certain character, personality and genius of its own. Would not those of every Atlantic people be best fulfilled by a Federation of the Free that guaranteed to each nation its own independence in everything that was purely national, and yet gave it a better means of spreading its virtues to other nations, and replacing its vices with the virtues it could gain from them? Federation would give each nation possibilities it could not otherwise have to make experiments in the political, economic, social and other fields that interest it most, and by the success of its pilot plant lead the rest of the Union to follow it. The world's first experiment with woman suffrage was made in the sparsely peopled frontier state of Wyoming. From there it spread from state to state through the American Union, and also from nation to nation, around the world. This is but a hint of the innovations whose inauguration and whose spread (if successful) would both be fostered in all the nations an Atlantic Union federated. Their greater diversity would assure an even wider range of fruitful experiment than the fifty pilot plants have already provided the fifty United States.

OUR FULFILLMENT AS PERSONS

Above all we are each individuals. In all our other embodiments we are individual. Unions and nations and tribes can divide. Even the closest "plural" person—marriage based on mutual love—can be divided by death, or divorce. But though each of us feels often of two minds, of two hearts, none of us can divide himself and live. Each remains individual, the basic and supreme flesh-blood-and-soul reality in human life. No man can escape himself, each woman must always live with herself. And only you can fulfill yourself.

Consider for a moment how Atlantic Union would help its citizens to fulfill themselves better than they can now. One illustration may serve to stimulate the reader to paint more of this picture for himself.

In every field of life, Atlantic Union would open a much higher possibility of fulfillment to every citizen who is specially gifted or deeply interested in that particular field. Take statesmanship, as a typical example. In any Atlantic democracy now, any citizen, however small the town or humble the family he was born in, can hope to rise to the higher levels of government in his nation—but no higher.

A Norwegian may be much more gifted as a statesman than the occupant of Downing Street or the White House, but the highest development of his gifts that he can hope for now is to be Prime Minister of some three million Norwegians. In an Atlantic Union he could become the Chief Executive of 471 million people. Such a Union would permit a gifted Senator from Greece to gain by sheer ability the influential role as regards Atlantic policy that young Senator Frank Church has already won in the United States Senate, although he represents one of the least populous states, Idaho. Through an Atlantic Union a gifted Dutchman can gain the decisive power over Atlantic foreign policy that another Senator from Idaho, William Borah, once wielded over Washington's. Through Atlantic Union the gifted son of an obscure family in a forgotten trading post on Hudson Bay can have an even vaster opportunity than the American Union gave to a rail-splitter in a frontier village in Illinois— and, if he has the stuff in him, he can serve freedom everywhere as nobly as did Lincoln.

FROM "VILLAGE HAMPDENS" TO
ATLANTIC CHURCHILLS

Now look at the other side of this picture. All the citizens of New Salem, and of Illinois, and of the United States, and all men everywhere who prize liberty-and-union, gained immensely from the fact that Lincoln was not limited to a sovereign city but could use his great gifts on a vaster stage. Atlantic Union gives us a still greater possibility of freeing the "man in a hundred million"—the Lincoln of tomorrow —to fulfill himself by serving individual liberty on the scale his gifts require, meeting the higher challenge that he was born to meet . . . and cannot possibly meet in any Republic smaller than the Union of the Free.

Had Churchill or de Gaulle been born in an earlier century, their great potentialities would have limited them to some petty kingdom, long since forgotten. They could have been those "village Hampdens" whom Gray lamented in his *Elegy*:

> Th' applause of list'ning senates to command,
>   The threats of pain and ruin to despise,
> To scatter plenty o'er a smiling land . . .
> Their lot forbade . . .

Because village kingdoms had already been painfully united into the British and French nations when Churchill and de Gaulle were born, they had a greater state to inspire them, a greater stage on which to develop their gifts, a greater service they could perform for a greater number of fellow citizens. If we—and they—now make the most of the opportunity they helped preserve for the free, England's next Churchill and France's next de Gaulle will be born citizens of Atlantica, too. They will start with a greater country to inspire and enable them to reach a higher plane of patriotism, and a deeper philosophy of freedom-and-union . . . and widen further man's vast future.

Consider the possibilities of self-fulfillment resulting from the billions of dollars that Union would save on defense and the even huger amounts it would add to income by the economies of mass production on a scale nearly three times greater than that of the United States, unhampered by nationalism's costly barriers to business. Part of the saving on defense would go to the citizen in lower taxes, and he would reap nearly all the benefit from the increased prosperity.

The taxpayers in each nation could spend those billions then on educating better their children—and themselves—and on health, travel, the arts . . . and on helping their fellow man.

Nearly every citizen has at least one or two ideas for improving life that are dear to him or her. It may be a mechanical invention, one of the arts, a new process in manufacturing, a teaching program, a scientific theory, a spiritual or philosophic concept, or something else whose possibilities appeal to him. It may be one of the innumerable "good causes" that lead free people to join this or that private association, whose purpose somehow attracts them personally, so much more than others do, that they lie awake at night thinking how to help it get the funds, and members, and attention it needs.

There are innumerable foxholes in the fight against ignorance, poverty and disease and for the ever greater growth of body, mind and spirit. Freedom permits, and expects, every sovereign citizen to volunteer to fill whatever foxhole is most important to him. Since human beings are so richly diversified, the more freedom they have to choose the way they would fulfill themselves, the surer we can be that those myriad foxholes will be filled always by all the men and women who can best be depended on to hold and advance that sector. To increase the private income each of them has at his or her disposal is to permit each to develop his personality the more. Atlantic Union would help in this way, too.

It would also help by providing greater private funds on which colleges, churches, and private associations could draw in their efforts to raise funds to fight cancer or juvenile delinquency, to finance scholarships or missionaries, to exchange students or art exhibits, to help the blind child overcome his handicap and the budding genius to develop his potentialities, to advance peace, knowledge, wisdom, virtue, freedom. There are countless things that need doing, and that are struggling now for funds and volunteer workers. But the achievement of none of them would do half as much as would the achievement of Atlantic Union to help advance all the other causes that deserve support. Atlantic Union would free more money, more volunteers and more time, and would distribute these more effectively among all the foxholes of civilization, than would any other single change that is within the reach of the people of Atlantica today.

CHAPTER 13

Time for an Heroic Step Ahead

Courage grows
As a rose.
Thorn on thorn
It is born.
—*C. K. S.*

I will lift up mine eyes—*Psalms 121:1*

Now, risking a little repetition for its unique advantages, let us try to compress the essence of this book into something as small as a cherry, compared to its tree—yet containing all the tree, and something more, something fresh and nourishing, a thing in itself.

Many find the human race never so divided as today. Yet never before has all our planet been governed by so many ideas, ideals and institutions held in common, not by force, but by free acceptance—by the power of proved virtue. Nearly all of them originated in the relatively free peoples living round the North Atlantic. Here they were first advanced in modern times. Here they were first put to the test of experience—always at painful sacrifice. When they proved their merit here, they spread round the globe.

The glory that was Greece and the grandeur that was Rome rose, like their successor now, not on a single continent but around that ancient and modern means of communication, a common sea. The ideas, ideals and institutions of individual liberty, equality and fraternal union have made the North Atlantic ocean the modern Mediterranean. Together, the people dwelling on its eastern and western shores have created a civilization which, with all its shortcomings, has given more freedom, greater dignity and a higher standard of life, both moral and material, to more myriads of men through more generations than any men ever enjoyed before.

Growing out of the higher reaches of the mind and spirit that were attained by the civilizations of the ancient Mediterranean, our new Atlantis has risen where sank the fabled Republic. From it, be it repeated, have come practically all the basic ideas—sound, unsound, and in between—that rule the world today.

From it have spread around the world the concepts and institutions of national sovereignty (in the diplomatic sense) and of the sovereignty of the people (or "citizen sovereignty" in the domestic sense), federal union, universal suffrage, liberty of conscience, speech, press, and all the other Rights of Man, the Rule of Law, equality before the Law, international law, and world-wide organization for peace, justice, disarmament, social improvement and better living standards. True, interpretations differ, and lip service only is paid to some of these in some major countries. The point is that they are now recognized, at least, as ideals almost everywhere.

So, too, have risen and spread the emancipation of woman, protective measures for women and children, compulsory free education, the abolition of slavery, labor unions, Red Cross. "Mass production" is but the most striking of the economic concepts of Atlantica that have circled the globe, as have also its basic approach to science and technology. From it have come every one of the ever more prodigious new sources of power that the human race has gained in the past 200 years—steam, electricity, petroleum, atomic energy. Here originated the "miracle" fabrics that have captivated mankind, all its means of swift communication—telegraph, cable, telephone, wireless, radio, television, railway, steamship, automobile, airplane, rocket—and how many conquests of disease . . .

All along this vast front the people of the North Atlantic have led in the world-wide war against the true enemies of man—ignorance, poverty, disease, premature death.

They gained this leadership by leading first in certain moral and spiritual principles. At least one of these is now universally accepted (in principle though not in practice)—the principle of the equal importance and dignity of each human being. But this is only part of the banner under which the Atlanticans have gained their victories for all mankind against so many of its enemies. That banner is formed, too, of the common Atlantic concept of man as being above all a moral being with a God-given right to equal freedom and equal opportunity, and a God-given duty to recognize this right in all other men, to love his neighbors as himself and unite with them for the common good. With this concept goes the ideal of the fatherhood of God and the brotherhood of man; with it also goes the idea that the State is made for Man, not Man for the State.

These concepts and ideals are not yet universal, though they are world-wide. Nor did they originate in the Atlantic community. They are older than it. They had to be—for the new Atlantis was created by them, and by the common devotion of its people to them.

Even the ideas that now divide humanity most—Communism vs. capitalism, economic determinism vs. moral determinism, trade barriers vs. free trade, nationalism vs. federation—all these conflicting concepts originated in our Atlantic civilization. The fact that they are now struggling to govern the minds of men as fully as do the ideas of representative government, equal rights for women, mass production, Cartesian reasoning and the scientific method—this should not blind us to the fact that this struggle is itself but further proof that Atlantica is the leading creator of the modern world.

I say this in no vainglorious spirit. Nor do I mean to imply that only the Atlantic people are capable of such leadership. Earlier civilizations have made immense contributions. People everywhere and of every race and color are contributing increasingly today. Some have already surpassed us in their applications of our scientific principles and technical methods. We Atlanticans claim no superiority in the people of the Atlantic community. We must assert, however, the superiority of our basic principles, since they are so widely acclaimed by mankind now as the key to the future, the way to a better life for every man, woman and child, living and to be born.

The leadership that Atlantica has been privileged to give faces us with two tremendous responsibilities today. One is negative: To lead now in saving mankind from the economic disaster and atomic war which threaten to result from the conflicting concepts that came out of Atlantica and are now struggling for world acceptance. The other responsibility is positive: To lead in making now the heroic step ahead which our other concepts, already world-accepted, make possible today—and imperative, if man's war against ignorance, poverty, disease and premature death is to be won. These two responsibilities, preservative and creative, are closely interrelated. Both require Atlantica to choose rightly between its own conflicting ideas—and to provide once more the pilot plant which alone can prove to all the world that the concepts we choose are indeed right.

Too often the conflicts between the ideological children of Atlantica have led in the past to wars within the Atlantic community itself. In our time these wars have twice engulfed all the world. The devastation already suffered must not be repeated now in a war to determine whether free government or dictatorship, individual initiative or Communism, shall rule the future. This time Atlantica, which fathered these ideological Cains and Abels, must make sure

that their struggle for the mind of man will be determined—
as was the struggle between the scientific vs. the authoritarian
method—by the proofs that peace alone can safely give.

There is this sharp difference between the present conflict
and the previous ones: This time the struggle is not within the
Atlantic community itself, but between it and the Communist empire, whose armed and industrial power lies entirely
outside the Atlantic world. This is both a great difficulty
and a great advantage. A difficulty, because the armed power
of one camp is for the first time in our era controlled outside the Atlantic area—controlled by men whose people have
never learned the language of liberty and in all their history
have never known any regime save tyranny. An advantage,
because—also for the first time—the people of Atlantica are
not themselves divided on the basic issue. All their power is
on the side of freedom; Communist dictatorship rules none
of them.

True, the Atlantic democracies are still divided by another
of their children—the prevailing theory and practice of national sovereignty. It originated among them as a liberating
and uniting principle. It brought smaller states together in
such nations as Italy and Germany, removing barriers to
trade and consolidating currencies. But in our century when
the airplane, mass production and atomic power demanded
still broader governments and markets, unlimited national
sovereignty turned into a divisive force, creating several
currencies where one served before, criss-crossing common
markets with trade barriers, "balkanizing" the world ever
more dangerously.

Thus national sovereignty, in its unlimited, diplomatic
sense, has outlived its usefulness as a uniting force for
peace, and turned against the individual liberty that inspired it. And so the time has come when the safety of all
mankind, and its hopes of being benefited, instead of buried,
by the prodigious power now at its disposal, depend on our
making a truly heroic step forward—uniting nations today
as nationalism united smaller principalities, and doing this by
peaceful, free agreement.

Happily, as this need arose there also rose a better way
to unite states peacefully. It safeguarded each of them from
domination, preserved their diversity in culture, language
and liberty, but removed their barriers to the free movement
of goods, money and men—and proved that what leads nations to war for a better market is not free enterprise, as
Communists assert, but unlimited national sovereignty. This
federal way has already proved its merits on both sides of
the Atlantic, and on every continent. But it still remains to

be shown that historic nations on opposite shores of an ocean can unite peacefully by federal union, or any other common government.

Mankind awaits the establishment of this new pilot plant. If we the nations of the new Atlantis do not provide it, who can? If we dare not pioneer in this human venture, who will? With the courage of our fathers and the faith in God's help their triumphs justify, let us now take this heroic step in man's millenary march ahead.

A DECLARATION OF LIBERTY-AND-UNION

Let us conclude—and begin—with a fresh Declaration of the principle of Liberty-and-Union that we of Atlantica live by and keep alive:

Liberty is man's high goal, and Federal Union of the Free is his best means to advance it.

Liberty without Union is no longer Liberty but anarchy, just as Union without Liberty turns Union into tyranny.

Without Union, Liberty is an end with no means to secure it in human society; without Liberty, Union is a means turned against its rightful end.

Too long Liberty and Union have been seen separately, and as irreconcilables; these two vital truths must be always seen and always kept together, as forming a creative unit; to bear their finest fruit we must unite them lovingly, realistically, enduringly, dynamically.

Man's password to a better world can not be Liberty alone or Union alone—neither the individual nor the collectivity alone—but Liberty-and-Union as "one and inseparable, now and forever."

Words without action are a mockery. The preservation and advancement of life depend on keeping Liberty-and-Union not merely together but in dynamic balance. This is a practical problem which every generation in our rapidly widening world must ponder and solve afresh. Ours has too long neglected it.

And so we now solemnly affirm that:

Our common supreme unit of government is the individual free person.

Our common supreme purpose of government is the life, liberty, happiness and advancement, in the broadest sense of these words, of each person equally.

Our common means to our common purpose is the Union of free persons as equals under a commonly instituted and accepted Rule of Law, guaranteeing the liberties of each minority, even of one, as well as the means of assuring timely practical action on common affairs by the whole community through a freely and lawfully formed majority of it.

Our common sense tells us that the time has come when we must begin to apply this means to this purpose between our democracies, and no longer merely within our own.

To be able to continue practising within our individual countries our common principle that the state is made for man, we must henceforth cease practising between our democracies the opposite, absolutist, Communist principle, that man is made for the state. We betray our own principle for that of dictatorship if we say that the nation's sovereignty must not be sacrificed even when this would advance the sovereignty of the citizen—or even when, as now, this lessening in the rights of our state is the only way to preserve not only our own rights as citizens but our very lives.

Like our forefathers—Americans, British or Canadians, French, Germans, Italians, Dutch, Scandinavians, Greeks and Turks—we must now choose between the sovereignty of the State and the sovereignty of the Citizens. Shall we sacrifice the citizen needlessly—worse than needlessly—merely to preserve unaltered a form of Union of free men (the democratic nation) which, like the city-state and tribe before it, has now outlived itself in some respects and thus has put in jeopardy the lives and liberties it served so long? Or shall we preserve and advance our nation's citizens by transferring to a broader Union of the Free whichever powers they delegated to the nation that they now agree would serve their purpose better if re-delegated to this new Union? There can be no doubt whatever of our choice. We can not to ourselves be false, and still be true to others.

The only doubt is whether we shall choose Union of the Free in time to save the liberties and lives of countless millions, or only after it is too late to prevent catastrophe.

Since we would make this choice once disaster fell, let us make it now. Let us run no risk of acting too late to prevent another catastrophe and—God forbid—the complete triumph of the ancient dogma that makes man bow down to the state and that would utterly destroy our way of life. Delay has cost us appallingly already; let us not risk acting so late that all the sacrifices we thereafter make will prove to be vain.

The difficulties and dangers that now seem so certain—to dictatorship and to many of us—to keep us divided against ourselves: Will they not seem to the next generation as small as those our fathers faced seem now to us? What are these difficulties and dangers compared to those we face by any other course? As Lincoln nobly said: "The occasion is piled high with difficulty, and we must rise with the occasion."

All that we hold true and sacred requires us, the people of the Atlantic community, to begin now, with no further delay, to work out a practical way of governing our common affairs by the same democratic Rule of Law that already governs our national, local and city affairs, through the constitution of a still greater Federal Union of the Free.

Our most imperative and noblest task today is to unite all our people in a Union so constituted that it will govern our common affairs democratically and effectively, while guaranteeing not only our Bill of Rights as individuals, but the rights of each of our nations to continue to govern independently its purely national affairs.

We must form this Union not as anything exclusive but in such fashion that it will spread by example's peaceful and prodigious power. We must create it as a nucleus destined by its nature to grow with gentle gradualness. We must so constitute it as to hasten the distant day when liberty-and-union will gain universal acceptance by its success in our pilot plant, as have already representative government, nationalism, universal suffrage, mass production, scientific objectivity, and many other Atlantic concepts.

How to create the seed of this giant tree of Liberty-and-Union presents many problems—spiritual, cultural, political, military, economic. They form a whole as intricately related as the organs of a living body, and we must see and solve them as a whole.

We can, and must, declare that there are some fields in which an Atlantic government would serve our liberties and lives better than can our national governments—even though we differ on which fields they are. And though we may differ on the form this government should have, we can and must declare that the time has come for the people of the Atlantic community to form an effective democratic federal government in those fields which they agree they share in common, with adequate guarantees for national independence in all other fields, and for individual liberty, justice and peaceful growth.

We can, and do, declare our faith that we the people of the Atlantic community possess the vision, courage, maturity and resourcefulness to work out and agree on a constitution for such a government. The sooner we set about it, the sounder will be our Federal Union of the Free, the safer world peace, the surer man's vast future.

In this mighty undertaking we invite all our fellow Atlanticans to share. To it we each solemnly pledge ourselves, personally.

*   *   *   *   *

Such is the Declaration that we are still privileged to make, individually and through the Atlantic Convention. It needs to be made not merely by leaders but by followers. In our free society, we each must be both to some degree, on some level. Any citizen who feels—or wants to feel—himself to be a sovereign can make this declaration. To be turned into reality, many must make it now.

Last Word

The Bishop: Do you believe that you are not bound to submit your acts and your statements to the Church militant—to anyone but God?

Jeanne d'Arc: I will maintain what I have always said during the trial . . . If I were condemned, and saw the torches lighted and the executioner ready to set fire to the pyre, and if I were in the fire, still I would not speak other than I have spoken and I would maintain until death what I have said at the trial.—*Official Record, Trial of Jeanne d'Arc, May 23, 1431.*

To myself I seem to have been only like a boy playing on the seashore, and diverting myself in now and then finding a smoother pebble or a prettier shell than ordinary, whilst the great ocean of truth lay all undiscovered before me.—*Sir Isaac Newton (1642-1727.)*

We—even we here—hold the power and bear the responsibility . . . We shall nobly save or meanly lose the last best hope of earth . . . The way is plain, peaceful, generous, just—a way which, if followed, the world will forever applaud, and God must forever bless. —*Abraham Lincoln, December 1, 1862.*

Let us cease saying to ourselves: "We can't . . . I can't . . . It's too big for me . . . My bit is too little to be missed, or count . . . Besides, the others will never agree . . . It can't be done." The voice saying this to us is not the still small Voice that asked: "What doest thou here, Elijah?" It is time to stop saying we can not do . . . what our Fathers did long ago. Let us remember that the Russians have gained so much respect in the past twenty years because they have done more than the world, or they themselves, expected. Their sputnik achievement brought them the prestige and confidence it did because it came as a surprise to them, and all the world.

If we need to take the foe by surprise to win a war, we need even more to surprise the world if we are to win for freedom without war. To surprise the world, we must begin by surprising ourselves. To surprise ourselves, we must outdo ourselves—and our Fathers. Nothing lower will hit the apple, trembling now upon our grandchild's head.

From illiterate peasants came Jeanne d'Arc. From a yeoman's widow came the tiny infant known as Sir Isaac Newton. From a log cabin's dirt floor rose Abraham Lincoln. And none of the three could have done what makes them remembered by all mankind had it not been for a host of unremembered men and women . . . the unknown "knight, equerry and four servants" who escorted Jeanne safely through the long and dangerous journey from Vaucouleurs to the King at Chateau Chinon . . . the two nameless neighbor women who on Christmas Day, 1642, went to the village for medicine to save the newborn Newton—so tiny that his mother said she could have put him at birth in a quart pot . . . "the brave men, living and dead, who struggled here," whom Lincoln remembered at Gettysburg—and without whom he could not be revered as he is . . .

If those who put their trust in material things can do so much today, what can *we* not do—we who, like Jeanne, have put our faith in "the angel" in each man and woman? What can we not do . . . if only we free that faith from fear, and let the angel in us act?

"This is the true joy in life," as Bernard Shaw wrote in *Man and Superman*, "the being used for a purpose recognized by yourself as a mighty one; the being thoroughly worn out before you are thrown on the scrap heap; the being a force of Nature."

Do you want to taste the joy of knowing that you are devoting the best you are endowed with, the best you can, for the best of purposes? Are you as sure as I am that the best part of you—and of all the rest of us—is that inner angel? Do you agree that the best way to free the light, which these sparks of the divine together give, is to help unite them? Then all you need, to taste that joy now, is to start today to work for Atlantic Federal Union of the Free.

BOOK II

UNION NOW

A Proposal for an Atlantic
Federal Union of the Free

*For the Great Republic, For the Principle It Lives By and
Keeps Alive, For Man's Vast Future. Lincoln*

The Basic Parts
of the 1940 Concise Edition
By Arrangement with
Harper & Brothers, Publishers
New York

To the Memory of Emma Kirshman, My Mother

And to all those for whom she spoke when with two sons away in the war she wrote:

Surely some great good will come out of so much suffering... Our home is broken and empty, but I am not without hope. Some day you will return improved by this awful experience, for by experiences we grow bigger and get a deeper insight in life and its mysteries.

Introduction

I. To This Edition

This book deserves to be read by those who have not done so, and read again now by those who read it years ago. Although one does not have to agree with every detail, it has proved too right too long to be neglected now.

Many books on world affairs are dated in a year or two. That *Union Now* has remained alive now for twenty-one years speaks volumes. At twenty-one it has the strength and maturity of manhood, and yet has kept the fresh vigor of youth. Twelve years ago I wrote in the Introduction to its Postwar Edition:

"The truths and principles set forth in *Union Now* are fundamental—they will never grow old or dated. Time and experience add to this book's undeniable logic."

Reviewers agreed. "If this book was important in 1939, it is more so today," Orville Prescott declared in *The New York Times*. August Heckscher wrote in *The New York Herald-Tribune*: "With realism, faith, audacity and prudence . . . the postwar edition of *Union Now* comes with earmarks of a classic. A book with a life of its own, one of the very few in any generation that rise above the influence which gave them birth to shape and direct the future."

The Minneapolis *Tribune* found "Streit's case was a formidable one when he first made it in 1939. It is even more formidable in this postwar edition which ought to be read by every citizen concerned with the survival of free institutions." And in my own State of Tennessee, the Memphis *Commercial-Appeal,* said: "It was a Book-of-the-Month then (1941), and time, the ultimate test of a classic, has only enhanced its prospects of becoming the Book-of-the-Century."

These were strong statements, but the past twelve years have made them stronger. Meanwhile history has moved relentlessly if painfully in *Union Now's* direction. Consider:

When *Union Now* was first published in March 1939, our people believed that neutrality would keep us out of war.

War converted us to wholehearted acceptance of the United Nations in 1945. Within three years we learned that this too was not enough. By 1949 the United States led in establishing the North Atlantic Treaty.

In proposing that the democracies unite, *Union Now* launched a frontal assault on the assumption that regions could only be continental. In 1939 when people took for

187

granted that oceans divided and land united nations, this
book saw "the enormous advantage of being . . . grouped . . .
around that cheap and excellent means of communication, a
common body of water," which the Atlantic nations enjoyed.

Written before transatlantic commercial flights became
commonplace, before jet planes were known or the sound
barrier broken, Chapter V told of the many bonds that already united these peoples. No one before, to my knowledge,
had recognized that they formed what we now commonly
call "the Atlantic community."

In 1949 the prevailing view was that the NATO alliance
would be enough. A goodly number in both Houses of Congress, however, had already been impressed by *Union Now's*
warning that alliance would no more suffice than did the
United Nations which it supplemented. They joined me in introducing in that year a resolution asking the United States
to call a convention of delegates to explore how we might
unite the democracies more strongly, federally or otherwise.

By 1955 an annual Conference of Members of Parliament
of NATO nations was established. In 1957 I was a delegate to
the Conference they held the month after sputnik went into
orbit. It unanimously endorsed the Convention idea. In
Book I, Clarence Streit has dealt with the approval
of it by the Atlantic Congress in 1959, the authorization of
the Convention by the United States Congress in 1960, the
pledge of a "broader partnership" which the Democratic Platform gave the Atlantic Community and the Nixon-Rockefeller proposal of Atlantic Confederation. All this makes
the chapters of *Union Now* which follow timely indeed.
A book that has so consistently proved so right through so
many years of upheaval *is* worth reading now—or re-
reading by previous readers.

"Clarence Streit," I wrote in my previous Introduction, "is
a great American. He has faced many obstacles in securing
consideration for *Union Now*, but with vision and determination he has persisted."

In my campaign for renomination this Summer, my opponent spoke disparagingly of my friendship with Clarence
Streit. My answer was:

"I am proud to be counted among Mr. Streit's friends, and
I have a deep respect for his dedication to an ideal which
seeks to find a real answer to the problem of peace in
a world which can blow itself to cinders at the touch of a
button. We need more Clarence Streits today."

And he deserves to be read, and re-read, today.

ESTES KEFAUVER
Nov. 19, 1960   U.S. SENATOR FROM TENNESSEE

Union Now is remarkable because it was born out of the kind of circumstances which produced the few great books of the world's political literature. Our matter-of-fact era commits a great mistake in believing that the really significant accomplishments of political literature are simply the result of long and dispassionate research, which the investigator carries on from sheer curiosity or—what is worse—from the exigencies of professorial competition. This is manifestly not enough. Those few works that constitute landmarks in our political history were creations of men who on the one hand were keenly suffering under the burdens of unsolved problems which threatened to crush their own lives and who on the other hand grasped those problems with the greatest sincerity and the most universal human outlook possible.

And when these two conditions of creative activity are present, works appear like the *Republic,* the *De Monarchia,* the *Defensor Pacis,* the *Prince,* the *Vindiciae,* the *Six Books of the Republic,* the *Two Treatises of Civil Government,* the *Spirit of the Laws,* the *Social Contract,* the *Wealth of Nations,* the *Essay on Liberty, Das Kapital*—to mention only the most portentous for the future. Accomplished scholarship, sophisticated terminology are not necessary attributes of these works. Many of them appeared to contemporary scholars as dilettante attacks against their professional monopoly.

I do not hesitate to class Mr. Streit's *Union Now* among these great works of human emancipation. One might say that it combines the acute, realistic analysis of a Hamilton with the exuberant vision of a Walt Whitman. As a matter of fact, his book is the new *Federalist,* a carefully and minutely elaborated plan for a federal union of democracies, which may serve as a stepping stone to broader and more universal union. In writing this book, he has practically written his own personal history, from the moment when the World War snatched him from his own home, through his experiences as war correspondent, and through his sad disillusionment with the League of Nations. [See Annex, "My Own Road to Union," p. 296; some prefer to begin the book by reading this first.] From that time he realized keenly that the present anarchy of the world, with all its disasters, was and *is* primarily not a problem of the states but a problem of the individual; that the League of Nations was doomed to failure because it was not a union of free men but a league of jealous and egotistic governments; that our present misfortunes were due not to narrow-minded and wicked statesmen but to a system which must necessarily and inevitably sacrifice the individual to the Moloch of national sovereignty.

And here appears the great eighteenth century animus of the book, by which it became a successor to the spirit of the American and French Revolutions. It shows magnificently how a system in which the individual abandons his moral sovereignty will make of him a tool or slave of the state [Chaps. VI, IX]. It shows no less forcefully that a truly individualistic conception of society leads unavoidably to the highest amount of human cooperation, both inside and outside of the state, until it reaches the ultimate possibilities.

These are not *all* new ideas. On the contrary, there is nothing in the author's argument which would not be understandable to the Stoics, the philosophers of Christian universality, the founders of international law, and the fighters for English, French and American democracy. But his new and creative vision is the sober and at the same time inspired elaboration of the remedy. He demonstrates that the task for the union of the democracies is *not* essentially different from the task which the United States has accomplished, and that this union would not only be a protection against war but the most spectacular step ever taken to solve our social problems while maintaining individual liberty and human dignity.

I venture to say that from no textbook or series of textbooks will you understand the essence of the political process and the dynamics of international relations so clearly as from the study of *Union Now*. At the same time, it makes you conscious participants in a supreme moral task. It will convince you that the future does not lie in the hands of the dictators or of the bankrupt democratic statesmen of Europe but rather in the determination of courageous individuals conscious of their own power. Or, as Mr. Streit puts it: "For man's freedom and vast future, man most depend on man. It is ours together or no one's, and it shall be ours."

OSCAR JASZI

P.S. I gave the preceding introduction first as a review of *Union Now* on April 13, 1939, at Oberlin College Chapel. The eventful years since then have confirmed, not changed my opinion of it—O. J., PROFESSOR OF POLITICAL SCIENCE, OBERLIN COLLEGE, *August 16, 1948*. [He died in 1957.]

PROPOSAL

CHAPTER I

What This Book Is About

> Now it is proposed to form a Government for men
> and not for Societies of men or States.—*George Mason
> in the American Union's Constitutional Convention.*
> I am convinced that this is the safest course for your
> liberty, your dignity and your happiness. . . . I frankly
> acknowledge to you my convictions, and I will freely
> lay before you the reasons on which they are founded.
> . . . My arguments will be open to all, and may be
> judged of by all. They shall at least be offered in a
> spirit which will not disgrace the cause of truth.—
> *Alexander Hamilton, opening* The Federalist.

Now when man's future seems so vast, catastrophe threat-
ens to cut us from it. The dangers with which depression,
dictatorship, false recovery and war are hemming us in
have become so grave and imminent that we no longer need
concern ourselves with proving how grave and near they
are. We need concern ourselves instead with the problem
of escaping them and the cruel dilemma we face: Whether
to risk peace or freedom? That is the problem with which
this book is concerned. I believe there is a way through these
dangers, and out of the dilemma, a way to do what we all
want, to secure both peace and freedom securely, and be
done with this nightmare. It promises not only escape, but
life such as I, too, never hoped could be lived in my time.

It is not an easy way—who expects one?—and to many
it will seem at first too hard to be practical. But this is because its difficulties and dangers are greatest at the start;
other ways that seem easier and safer to begin with, grow
increasingly hard and dangerous, and lead nowhere. How
could we feel hemmed in if the way through were so easy to
take, or even see at first? For my part, to find it I had to
stumble on it. Once found it soon opened so widely that I
wondered how I had failed so long to see it. I shall not be
surprised, then, if you begin by being skeptical or discour-

aged. But I ask you to remember that the essential question is: Which way will really lead us through?

Since 1933 when I stumbled on this way I have been exploring it all I could and trying, in the writing of this book, to clear away the things hiding it. By all the tests of common sense and experience I find it to be our safest, surest way. It proves in fact to be nothing new but a forgotten way which our fathers opened up and tried out successfully long ago when they were hemmed in as we are now.

The way through is Union now of the democracies that the North Atlantic and a thousand other things already unite—Union of these few peoples in a great federal republic built on and for the thing they share most, their common democratic principle of government for the sake of individual freedom.

This Union would be designed (a) to provide effective common government in our democratic world in those fields where such common government will clearly serve man's freedom better than separate governments, (b) to maintain independent national governments in all other fields where such government will best serve man's freedom, and (c) to create by its constitution a nucleus world government capable of growing into universal world government peacefully and as rapidly as such growth will best serve man's freedom.

By (a) I mean the Union of the North Atlantic democracies in these five fields:

a union government and citizenship

a union defense force

a union customs-free economy

a union money

a union postal and communications system.

By (b) I mean the Union government shall guarantee against all enemies, foreign and domestic, not only those rights of man that are common to all democracies, but every existing national or local right that is not clearly incompatible with effective union government in the five named fields. The Union would guarantee the right of each democracy in it to govern independently all its home affairs and practise democracy at home in its own tongue, according to its own customs and in its own way, whether by republic or kingdom, presidential, cabinet or other form of government, capitalist, socialist or other economic system.

By (c) I mean the founder democracies shall so constitute The Union as to encourage the nations outside it and the colonies inside it to seek to unite with it instead of against it. Admission to The Union and to all its tremendous advantages for the individual man and woman would from the outset be open equally to every democracy, now or to come, that guarantees its citizens The Union's minimum Bill of Rights.

The Great Republic would be organized with a view to its spreading peacefully round the earth as nations grow ripe for it. Its Constitution would aim clearly at achieving eventually by this peaceful, ripening, natural method the goal millions have dreamed of individually, but never sought to get by deliberately planning and patiently working together to achieve it. That goal would be achieved by The Union when every individual of our species would be a citizen of it, a citizen of a disarmed world enjoying world free trade, a world money and a world communications system. Then Man's vast future would begin.

This goal will seem so remote now as to discourage all but the strong from setting out for it, or even acknowledging that they stand for it. It is not now so remote, it does not now need men so strong as it did when Lincoln preserved the American Union "for the great republic, for the principle it lives by and keeps alive, for man's vast future." It will no longer be visionary once the Alantic democracies unite. Their Union is not so remote, and their Union is all that concerns us here and now.

THE AMERICAN WAY THROUGH

These proceedings may at first appear strange and difficult; but, like other steps which we have already passed over, will in a little time become familiar and agreeable.—*Thomas Paine in Common Sense.*

One hundred and fifty years ago a few American democracies opened this Union way through. The dangers of depression, dictatorship and war, and the persuasiveness of clear thinking and courageous leadership, led them then to abandon the heresy into which they had fallen. That heresy converted the sovereignty of the state from a means to individual freedom into the supreme end itself, and produced the wretched "League of Friendship" of the Articles of Confederation. Abandoning all this the Americans turned back to their Declaration of Independence—of the independence of Man from the State and of the dependence of free men on each other for their freedom—the Declaration:

That all men are created equal, that they are endowed by their creator with certain unalienable rights, that among these are life, liberty and the pursuit of happiness, that to secure these rights governments are instituted among men, deriving their just powers from the consent of the governed, that whenever any form of government becomes destructive of these ends it is the right of the people to alter or to abolish it, and to institute new government, laying its foundations on such principles and organizing its powers in such form as to them shall seem most likely to effect their safety and happiness.

Finding they had wrongly applied this philosophy to establish Thirteen "free and independent States" and organize them as the League of Friendship so that "each State retains its sovereignty, freedom and independence," they applied it next as "We the people of the United States" to "secure the blessings of liberty to ourselves and our posterity." To do this they invented and set up a new kind of interstate government. It has worked ever since as the other, league, type has never worked. It has proved to be an "astonishing and unexampled success," as Lord Acton said, not only in America but wherever democracies have tried it regardless of conditions,—among the Germans, French and Italians of Switzerland, the English and French of Canada, the Dutch and English of the Union of South Africa. It is the kind of interstate government that Lincoln, to distinguish it from the opposing type of government of, by and for states, called "government of the people, by the people, for the people." It is the way that I call Union.

To follow this way through now our Atlantic democracies —and first of all the American Union—have only to abandon in their turn the same heresy into which they have fallen, the heresy of absolute national sovereignty and its vain alternatives, neutrality, balance of power, alliance or League of Nations. We the people of the Atlantic have only to cease sacrificing needlessly our individual freedom to the freedom of our nations, be true to our democratic philosophy and establish that "more perfect Union" toward which all our existing unions explicitly or implicitly aim.

Can we hope to find a safer, surer, more successful way than this? What democrat among us does not hope that this Union will be made some day? What practical man believes it will ever be made by mere dreaming, or that the longer we delay starting to make it the sooner we shall have it? All it will take to make this Union—whether in a thousand years or now, whether long after castastrophe or just in time to prevent it,—is agreement by a majority to do it. Union is one of those things which to do we need but agree to do, and which we can not possibly ever do except by agreeing to do it. Why, then, can we not do it now in time for us to benefit by it and save millions of lives? Are we so much feebler than our fathers and our children that we can not do what our fathers did and what we expect our children to do? Why can not we agree on Union now?

Are not liberty and Union, now and forever, one and inseparable as in Webster's day? We can not be for liberty and against Union. We can not be both for and against liberty and Union now. We must choose.

DEFINITIONS

Democracy I would define more closely than the dictionary that defines it as "government by the people," (though I would not attempt needless precision and would indicate an ideal rather than an average). I would add with Lincoln, and I would stress, that democracy is also government for the people and of the people—the people being composed of individuals all given equal weight, in principle.

Democracy to me is the way to individual freedom formed by men organizing themselves on the principle of the equality of man. That is, they organize government of themselves, in the sense that their laws operate on them individually as equals. They organize government by themselves, each having an equal vote in making law. They organize government for themselves, to secure equally the freedom, in the broadest sense of the term, of each of them.

By democracy I mean government of the totality by the majority for the sake equally of each minority of one, particularly as regards securing him such rights as freedom of speech, press and association. (If merely these three rights are really secured to all individuals they have the key, I believe, to all the other rights in all the other fields, political, juridical, economic, etc., that form part of individual freedom.)

Union to me is a democracy composed of democracies— an interstate government organized on the same basic principle, by the same basic method, and for the same basic purpose as the democracies in it, and with the powers of government divided between the union and the states the better to advance this common purpose, individual freedom.

Union and *league* I use as opposite terms. I divide all organization of interstate relations into two types, according to whether man or the state is the unit, and the equality of man or the equality of the state is "the principle it lives by and keeps alive." I restrict the term *union* to the former, and the term *league* to the latter. To make clearer this distinction and what I mean by unit, these three points may help:

First, a *league* is a government of governments: It governs each people in its territory as a unit through that unit's government. Its laws can be broken only by a people acting through its government, and enforced only by the league coercing that people as a unit, regardless of whether individuals in it opposed or favored the violation. A *union* is a government of the people: It governs each individual in its territory directly as a unit. Its laws apply equally to each individual instead of to each government or people, can be broken only by individuals, and can be enforced only by coercing individuals.

Second, a *league* is a government by governments: Its laws are made by the peoples in it acting each through its government as a unit of equal voting power regardless of the number of individuals in it. A *union* is a government by the people: Its laws are made by the individuals in it acting, each through his representatives, as a unit of equal voting power in choosing and changing them, each state's voting power in the union government being ordinarily in close proportion to its population. A union may allow in one house of its legislature (as in the American Senate) equal weight to the people of each state regardless of population. But it provides that such representatives shall not, as in a league, represent the state as a unit and be under the instructions of, and subject to, recall by its government, but shall represent instead the people of the state and be answerable to them.

Third, a *league* is a government for governments or states: It is made to secure the freedom of each of the states in it, taken as units equally. A *union* is a government for the people: It is made for the purpose of securing the freedom of each of the individuals in it taken as units equally. To secure the sovereignty of the state a league sacrifices the rights of men to justice (as in the first point) and to equal voting power (as in the second point), whereas a union sacrifices the sovereignty of the state to secure the rights of men: A *league* is made for the state, a *union* is made for man.

This may suffice to explain the sense in which the terms *democracy, union* and *league* are meant in this book.*

FIFTEEN FOUNDER DEMOCRACIES

In the North Atlantic or founder democracies I would in-

---

* All that has been said here about leagues applies with still greater force to alliances and cooperative associations of states, for these, too, take the state as unit.

clude at least these Fifteen (or Ten): The American Union, the British Commonwealth (specifically the United Kingdom, the Federal Dominion of Canada, the Commonwealth of Australia, New Zealand, the Union of South Africa, Ireland), the French Republic, Belgium, the Netherlands, the Swiss Confederation, Denmark, Norway, Sweden and Finland.

These few include the world's greatest, oldest, most homogeneous and closely linked democracies, the peoples most experienced and successful in solving the problem at hand —the peaceful, reasonable establishment of effective interstate democratic world government. Language divides them into only five big groups and, for all practical political purposes, into only two, English and French. Their combined citizenry of nearly 300,000,000 is well balanced, half in Europe and half overseas. *None of these democracies has been at war with any of the others since more than 100 years.*

These few democracies suffice to provide the nucleus of world government with the financial, monetary, economic and political power necessary both to assure peace to its members peacefully from the outset by sheer overwhelming preponderance and invulnerability, and practically to end the monetary insecurity and economic warfare now ravaging the whole world. These few divide among them such wealth and power that the so-called world political, economic and monetary anarchy is at bottom nothing but their own anarchy—since they can end it by uniting to establish law and order among themselves.

Together these fifteen own almost half the earth, rule all its oceans, govern nearly half mankind. They do two-thirds of the world's trade, and most of this would be called their domestic trade once they united, for it is among themselves. They have more than 50 per cent control of nearly every essential material. They have more than 60 per cent of such war essentials as oil, copper, lead, steel, iron, coal, tin, cotton, wool, wood pulp, shipping tonnage. They have almost complete control of such keys as nickel, rubber and automobile production. They possess practically all the world's gold and banked wealth. Their existing armed strength is such that, once they united it, they could reduce their armaments and yet gain a two-power standard of security.

The Union's existing and potential power from the outset would be so gigantic, its bulk so vast, its vital centers so scattered, that all the autocracies even put together could not dream of defeating it. Once established the Union's superiority in power would be constantly increasing simply through the admission to it of outside nations. A number would no doubt be admitted immediately. By this process the absolutist powers would constantly become weaker and more isolated.

When the really powerful members of a community refuse to organize effective government in it, when each insists on remaining a law unto himself to the degree the democracies, and especially the United States, have done since the war, then anarchy is bound to result, and the first to feel the effects of the chaos are bound to be the weaker members of the community. When the pinch comes the last to be hired are the first to be laid off, and the firms working on the narrowest margin are the first to be driven to the wall or to desperate expedients. That makes the pinch worse for the more powerful and faces them with new dangers, with threats of violence. It is human for them to blame those they have unwittingly driven to desperation, but that does not change the source of the evil.

So it has been in the world. The younger democracies have been the first to go. The first of the great powers driven to desperate and violent measures have been those with the smallest margin. There is no doubt that their methods have since made matters worse and that there is no hope in following their lead. Their autocratic governments are adding to the world's ills but they are not the real cause of them. They are instead an effect of the anarchy among the powerful democracies.

The dictators are right when they blame the democracies for the world's condition, but they are wrong when they blame it on democracy. The anarchy comes from the refusal of the democracies to renounce enough of their national sovereignty to let effective world law and order be set up. But their refusal to do this, their maintenance of the state for its own sake, their readiness to sacrifice the lives and liberties of the citizens rather than the independence of the state,—this we know is not democracy. It is the core of absolutism. Democracy has been waning and autocracy waxing, the rights of men lessening and the rights of the state growing everywhere because the leading democracies have themselves led in practicing, *beyond* their frontiers, autocracy instead of democracy.

The rising power of autocracy increases the need for Union just as the spread of a contagious disease increases the need for quarantine and for organizing the healthy. But it is essential to remember that though the victims carry the disease they did not cause it, and that quarantine of the victims and organization of the healthy are aimed not against the victims but against the epidemic, the purpose being to end it both by restricting its spread and by curing its victims.

It is wrong, all wrong, to conceive of Union as aimed against the nations under autocracy. There is a world of difference between the motives behind Union and those behind either the present policy in each democracy of arming for itself or the proposals for alliance among the democracies. For such armament and such alliance are meant to maintain the one thing Union does attack in the one place Union does attack it—the autocratic principle of absolute national sovereignty in the democracies. Unlike armament and alliance policies, Union leads to no crusade against autocracy abroad, to no attempt to end war by war or make the world safe for democracy by conquering foreign dictatorship. Union is no religion for tearing out the mote from a brother's eye—and the eye, too—while guarding nothing so jealously, savagely, as the beam in one's own eye.

Union calls on each democracy to remove itself the absolutism governing its relations with the other democracies, and to leave it to the people of each dictatorship to decide for themselves whether they will maintain or overthrow the absolutism governing them not only externally but internally. Union provides equally for the protection of the democracies against attack by foreign autocracy while it remains, and for the admission of each autocratic country into The Union once it becomes a democracy in the only possible way—by the will and effort of its own people.

The attraction membership in The Union would have for outsiders would be so powerful, and the possibility of conquering The Union would be so hopeless that, once The Union was formed, the problem the absolutist powers now present could be safely left to solve itself. As their citizens turned these governments into democracies and entered The Union, the arms burden on everyone would dwindle until it soon disappeared.

Thus, by the simple act of uniting on the basis of their own principle, the democracies could immediately attain practical security, and could proceed steadily to absolute security and disarmament.

They could also increase enormously their trade and prosperity, reduce unemployment, raise their standard of living while lowering its cost. The imagination even of the economic expert can not grasp all the saving and profit democrats would realize by merely uniting their democracies in one free trade area.

They need only establish one common money to solve most if not all of today's more insoluble monetary problems, and save their citizens the tremendous loss inherent not only in depreciation, uncertainty, danger of currency upset from foreign causes, but also in the ordinary day-to-day monetary exchange among the democracies.

Merely by the elimination of excessive government, needless bureaucracy, and unnecessary duplication which Union would automatically effect, the democracies could easily balance budgets while reducing taxation and debt. To an appalling degree taxes and government in the democracies today are devoted only to the maintenance of their separate sovereignties as regards citizenship, defense, trade, money and communications. To a still more appalling degree they are quite unnecessary and thwart instead of serve the purpose for which we established those governments and voted those taxes, namely, the maintenance of our own freedom and sovereignty as individual men and women.

By uniting, the democracies can serve this purpose also by greatly facilitating the distribution of goods, travel and the dissemination of knowledge and entertainment. With one move, the simple act of Union, the democrats can make half the earth equally the workshop and the playground of each of them.

Creation of The Union involves difficulties, of course, but the difficulties are transitional, not permanent ones. All other proposals in this field, even if realizable, could solve only temporarily this or that problem in war, peace, armaments, monetary stabilization. These proposals would be as hard to achieve as Union, yet all together they could not do what the one act of Union would—permanently eliminate all these problems. These are problems for which the present dogma of nationalism is to blame. We can not keep it and solve them. We can not eliminate them until we first eliminate it.

WHICH WAY ADVANCES FREEDOM MORE?

This does not mean eliminating all national rights. It means eliminating them only where elimination clearly serves the individuals concerned, and maintaining them in all other respects,—not simply where maintenance clearly serves the general individual interest but also in all doubtful cases. The object of Union being to advance the freedom and individuality of the individual, it can include no thought of standardizing or regimenting him, nor admit the kind of centralizing that increases governmental power over him. These are evils of nationalism, and Union would end them. Union comes to put individuality back on the throne that nationality has usurped.

Everywhere nationalism, in its zeal to make our nation, instead of ourselves, self-sufficing and independent, is centralizing government, giving it more and more power over the citizen's business and life, putting more and more of that power in one man's hands, freeing the government from its dependence on the citizen while making him more and more dependent on it—on the pretext of keeping him independent of other governments. Everywhere the national state has tended to become a super-state in its power to dispose of the citizen, his money, job, and life. Everywhere nationalism has been impoverishing the citizen with taxes, unemployment, depression; and it is poverty—the desert, not the jungle,—that stunts variety, that standardizes. Everywhere nationalism is casting the citizen increasingly in war's uniform robot mold.

Union would let us live more individual lives. Its test for deciding whether in a given field government should remain national or become union is this: Which would *clearly* give the individual more freedom? Clearly the individual freedom of Americans or Frenchmen would gain nothing from making Union depend on the British converting the United Kingdom into a republic. Nor would the British be freer for making Union depend on the Americans and French changing to a monarchy. There are many fields where it is clear that home rule remains necessary for individual freedom, where the maintenance of the existing variety among the democracies helps instead of harms the object of Union.

It is clear too that a Union so secure from foreign aggression as this one would not need that homogeneity in population that the much weaker American Union feels obliged to seek. Our Union could afford to encourage the existing diversity among its members as a powerful safeguard against the domestic dangers to individual freedom. Just as the citizen could count on The Union to protect his nation from either invasion or dictatorship rising from within, he could count on his nation's autonomy to protect him from a majority in The Union becoming locally oppressive. The existence of so many national autonomies in The Union would guarantee each of them freedom to experiment politically, economically, socially, and would save this Union from the danger of hysteria and stampede to which more homogeneous unions are exposed.

Clearly, individual freedom requires us to maintain national autonomy in most things, but no less clearly it requires us to abolish that autonomy in a few things. There is no need to argue that you and I have nothing to lose and much to gain by becoming equal citizens in The Union while retaining our national citizenship. Clearly you and I would be freer had we this Great Republic's guarantee of our rights as men, its security against the armaments burden, military servitude, war. It is self-evident that you and I would live an easier and a richer life if through half the world we could do business with one money and postage, if through half the world we were free to buy in the cheapest market what we need to buy, and free to sell in the dearest market what we have to sell.

In five fields—citizenship, defense, trade, money, and communications—we are sacrificing now the individual freedom we could safely, easily have. On what democratic ground can we defend this great sacrifice? We make it simply to keep our democracies independent of each other. We can not say that we must maintain the state's autonomy in these few fields in order to maintain it in the many fields where it serves our freedom, for we know how to keep it in the latter without keeping it in the former. We have proved that in the American Union, the Swiss Union, and elsewhere.

What then can we say to justify our needless sacrifice of man to the state in these five fields, a sacrifice made only to maintain the nation for the nation's sake? How can we who believe the state is made for man escape the charge that in these five fields we are following the autocratic principle that man is made for the state? How can we plead not guilty of treason to democracy? Are we not betraying our principles, our interests, our freedom, ourselves and our children? We are betraying, too, our fathers. They overthrew the divine right of kings and founded our democracies not for the divine right of nations but for the rights of Man.

Clearly absolute national sovereignty has now brought us to the stage where this form of government has become destructive of the ends for which we form government, where democrats to remain democrats must use their right "to abolish it, and to institute new government."

Clearly prudence dictates that we should lay our new government's foundations on such principles and organize its powers in such form as have stood the test of experience. Clearly democracy bids us now unite our unions of free men and women in The Union of the Free.

THE ALTERNATIVES TO UNION

Fantastic? Visionary? What are the alternatives? There are only these: Either the democracies must try to stand separately. or they must try to stand together on some other basis than Union; that is, they must organize themselves as a league or an alliance.

Suppose we try to organize as a league. That means seeking salvation from what Alexander Hamilton called "the political monster of an *imperium in imperio.*" We adopt a method which has just failed in the League of Nations, which before that led the original thirteen American democracies to a similar failure, and failed the Swiss democracies, the Dutch democracies, and the democracies of ancient Greece. We adopt a method which has been tried time and again in history and has never worked, whether limited to few members or extended to many; a method which, we shall see, when we analyze it later, is thoroughly undemocratic, untrustworthy, unsound, unable either to make or to enforce its law in time. Is it not fantastic to expect to get the American people, after 150 years of successful experience with union and after their rejection of the League of Nations, to enter any league?

Suppose we try to organize instead an alliance of the democracies. But an alliance is simply a looser, more primitive form of league, one that operates secretly through diplomatic tunnels rather than openly through regular assemblies. It is based on the same unit as a league,—the state,—and on the same principle,—that the maintenance of the freedom of the state is the be-all and the end-all of political and economic policy. It is at most an association (instead of a government) of governments, by governments, for governments. It has all the faults of a league with most of them intensified and with some more of its own added.

The lack of machinery for reaching and executing international agreement in the economic, financial and monetary fields in time to be effective did much to cause the depression that led us through Manchuria and Hitler and Ethiopia to where we are today. What could be more fantastic than the hope that any conceivable alliance could provide this machinery, or that without this machinery we can long avoid depression and war?

Only one thing could be more visionary and fantastic, and that is the third possible alternative to Union, the one that would seek salvation in rejecting every type of interstate organization and in pursuing a policy of pure nationalism,— the policy of isolationism, neutrality, of each trusting to his own armaments, military and economic. For if the democracies are not to try to stand together by union or league or alliance, the only thing left for them is to try to stand alone.

The experience of the United States shows that even the most powerful nations can not get what they want by isolationism. The United States sought through the nineteen twenties to preserve its peace and prosperity by isolationism. The United States has never armed in peace time as it has since it adopted this policy. And the end is not near.

The balance of power theory that prepared catastrophe now as then—there is no more sterile, illusory, fantastic, exploded and explosive peace policy than the balance of power. Look at it. Take it apart. What does it mean in common words? It means seeking to get stability by seeking to equalize the weight on both sides of the balance. One can conceive of reaching stability this way—but for how long and at the cost of what violent ups and downs before? And when the scales do hang in perfect balance it takes but a breath, only the wind that goes with a word spoken or shrieked in the Hitlerian manner, to end at once the stability, the peace that was achieved. Stability can never be more in danger, more at the mercy of the slightest mistake, accident or act of ill will than at the very moment when the ideal of the balance of power is finally achieved.

We do not and can not get peace by balance of power; we can and do get it by *unbalance* of power. We get it by putting so much weight surely on the side of law that the strongest law-breaker can not possibly offset it and is bound to be overwhelmed. We get lasting stability by having one side of the balance safely on the ground and the other side high in the air.

Even the moment's stability which the balance of power may theoretically attain is a delusion since each side knows it can not last. Therefore neither can believe in it and the nearer they come to it the harder both must struggle to prevent it by adding more weight on their side so as to enjoy the lasting peace that unbalance of power secures,—and the race is to the strongest.

The race is to the strongest, and the democracies to win need only scrap this balance of power and neutrality nonsense and directly seek peace in the unbalance of power that Union alone can quickly and securely give them.

THE TEST OF COMMON SENSE

Because Union is a fresh solution of the world problem it appears to be something new. The deeper one goes into it, however, the better one may see that there is in it nothing new, strange, untried, nothing utopian, mystic. The fact is that we democrats have already strayed away from the road of reason and realism into the desert of make-believe and mysticism. We strayed away seeking the mirage utopia of a world where each nation is itself a self-sufficing world, where each gains security and peace by fearing and preparing war, where law and order no longer require government but magically result from keeping each nation a law unto itself, where the individual's freedom is saved by abandoning at the national frontier the principle that the state is made for man and adopting there the dogma that man is made for the nation. It is proposed here that we have done with these dangerous delusions, that we return to the road of reason and seek salvation by tested methods, by doing again what we know from experience we can do. I ask nothing better than that we stick to the common interests of us individual men and women and to the simpler teachings of common sense.

Common sense tells us that it is in our individual interest to make the world safe for our individual selves, and that we can not do this while we lack effective means of governing our world.

It tells us that the wealthier, the more advanced in machinery, the more civilized a people is and the more liberties its citizens enjoy, the greater the stake they have in preventing depression, dictatorship, war. The more one has, the more one has to lose.

Common sense tells us that some of the causes of depression, dictatorship, war, lie inside the nation and that others lie outside it. It tells us that our existing political machinery has let us govern strongly the conditions of life within the nation but not outside it; and that all each people has done to overcome the dangers inside it has been blighted by its failure to reach the dangers outside it, or remains at the mercy of these ungoverned forces.

Common sense reminds us Americans that we are part of the world and not a world apart, that the more we keep our lead in the development of machines the more important to us we make the rest of the world, that we can not, without catastrophe, continue, through good times and bad, improving these machines while refusing to develop political machinery to govern the world we are thus creating. It tells us that the principles of this Union of the Free are the principles that America was born to champion, that Americans can not deny them and still remain Americans. For the loyalty of the American is not to soil or race. The oath he takes when he enters the service of the American Union, is altogether to the principles of Union, "to support and defend the Constitution." That Constitution is already universal in its scope. It allows for the admission to its Union of any state on earth. It never even mentions territory or language. It mentions race and color only to provide that freedom shall never on that account be denied to any man.

American opinion has always been remarkable for seeing from afar danger to democracy and quickly adopting the common sense solution, however remote and radical and difficult and dangerous it seemed to be. What other people ever revolted at less oppression? Independence was so remote from American thought at the start of 1776 that it was not even proposed seriously until Jan. 10, when Paine came out for it. Yet his *Common Sense* then so swept the country that within six months the Declaration of Independence was adopted.

To understand how difficult and remote the Union of the Thirteen States really was when 1787 began, and how encouragingly the example they set applies to our democracies today, common sense suggests that we turn back and see the situation then as contemporaries saw it.

"If there is a country in the world where concord, according to common calculation, would be least expected, it is America," wrote Paine himself. "Made up as it is of people from different nations, accustomed to different forms and habits of Government, speaking different languages, and more different in their modes of worship, it would appear that the union of such a people was impracticable."

Conditions among the American democracies of the League of Friendship were such that John Fiske wrote, "By 1786, under the universal depression and want of confidence, all trade had well-nigh stopped, and political quackery, with its cheap and dirty remedies, had full control of the field." Trade disputes threatened war among New York, Connecticut and New Jersey. Territorial disputes led to bloodshed and threat of war among New York, New Hampshire and Vermont, and between Connecticut and Pennsylvania.

War with Spain threatened to break the League of Friendship in two camps. The League could not coerce its members. Threats of withdrawal from it were common. Its Congress rarely had money in the treasury, could no longer borrow.

The total membership of Congress under the League of Friendship was ninety-one, but the average attendance in the six years preceding Union was only about twenty-five. Often Congress could not sit because no quorum came. Things reached the point where little Delaware, though it had the same voting power in Congress as the largest state and though it was not thirty miles from Philadelphia, where Conress met, decided it was no longer worth the expense to send a delegate.

The states issued worthless currency, misery was rife, and courts were broken up by armed mobs. When these troubles culminated early in 1787 with the attempt of Shays's rebels to capture the League arsenal in Massachusetts, so strong was state sovereignty and so feeble the League that Massachusetts would not allow League troops to enter its territory even to guard the League's own arsenal. Jay had already written to Washington in 1786, "I am uneasy and apprehensive, more so than during the war."

Everything seemed to justify the words of the contemporary liberal philosopher, Josiah Tucker, Dean of Gloucester:

> As to the future grandeur of America, and its being a rising empire under one head, whether republican or monarchical, it is one of the idlest and most visionary notions that ever was conceived even by writers of romance. The mutual antipathies and clashing interests of the Americans, their differences of governments, habitudes, and manners, indicate that they will have no centre of union and no common interest. They never can be united into one compact empire under any species of government whatever; a disunited people till the end of time, suspicious and distrustful of each other, they will be divided and sub-divided into little commonwealths or principalities, according to natural boundaries, by great bays of the sea, and by vast rivers, lakes, and ridges of mountains.

The idea of turning from league to union was so remote in 1787 that it was not even seriously proposed until the end of May when the Federal Convention opened. And the opening of the Convention had to wait ten days in order to have even the bare majority of the Thirteen States needed for a quorum. The Convention itself had been called by Congress merely to reform the League—"for the sole and express purpose of revising the Articles of Confederation." It was not deflected away from patching and into building anew until the eve of its session,—and then thanks only to George Washington's personal intervention. Even then the Union as we know it now was more than remote: It was unknown, it still had to be invented.

Yet, once the Convention decided to build anew, it completed this revolutionary political invention within 100 working days. Within two years—two years of close votes and vehement debate in which Hamilton, Madison and others, now called "men of vision," were derided as "visionary young men" even by Richard Henry Lee, the revolutionist who had moved the Declaration of Independence in 1776,— within two years the anarchy-ridden, freedom-loving American democracies agreed to try out this invention on themselves. Twenty months after they read its text the American people established the Constitution that still governs them,— but now governs four times as many democracies and forty times as many free men and women.

Can it be hard-headed reason that holds it easier for the American democracies to invent and agree to try out Union in the infancy of self-government than it is for our more mature democracies to adopt it now?

It does seem practical to ask first how all the difficulties in changing from national sovereignty to Union are to be met. Yet the makers of the first Union were not delayed by such considerations. They abolished each State's rights to levy tariffs, issue money, make treaties, and keep an army, and they gave these rights to the Union without waiting for a plan to meet the difficulties of changing from protection to free trade, etc. They did not even bother trying to work out plans to meet all these difficulties of transition.

Yet they lived in a time when New York was protecting its fuel interests by a tariff on Connecticut wood, and its farmers by duties on New Jersey butter, when Massachusetts closed while Connecticut opened its ports to British shipping, when Boston was boycotting Rhode Island grain and Philadelphia was refusing to accept New Jersey money, when the money of most of the States was depreciated and that of Rhode Island and Georgia was so worthless that their governments sought to coerce the citizens into accepting it. In those days New York was massing troops on its Vermont frontier while the army of Pennsylvania was committing atrocities in the Wyoming valley against settlers from Connecticut.

Some factors, of course, made Union easier for the American democracies than for us; others made it harder. It can be urged that they were all contiguous states that had been colonies of the same country. Their peoples, though much more divided than we now assume, did have a common language, a predominantly British background and nationality, the same pioneering traditions and problems. It can be urged on the other hand that they lacked some tremendous advantages our fifteen democracies now enjoy. One of them is political experience, another is speed of communications.

They lived in the infancy of modern democracy, when it was a bold experiment to let men vote even with a property qualification. They had to invent federal union. We have behind us now 150 years of experience with democracy and federal union which they lacked. It took a month then for a message to go by the fastest means from Philadelphia to the most remote state; a delegate took still longer. A delegate can now reach Philadelphia in one-fourth that time from the most distant of the fifteen democracies; a message can be broadcast to them all in a flash.

Although it does seem to me, on balance, that Union is easier now than then, I would grant that it is hard to strike this balance. But we can not have it both ways. Those who say that I am wrong, that conditions were so much more favorable to Union of the American democracies then than they are for Union in our day, are also saying implicitly that conditions then were also much more favorable than now to all the alternative solutions—league, alliance, or isolationism. If a common language, a common mother country, a common continent and all the other things the American democracies had in common, made Union easier for them than us, they also made it easier for them to make a league succeed. If even they could not make a league work, then how in the name of common sense can we expect to do better with a league than they did? Even if Union is harder now than then, we know we can succeed with it.

Common sense leads to this conclusion: If we the people of the American Union, the British Commonwealth, the French Republic, the Lowlands, Scandinavia and the Swiss Confederation can not unite, the world can not. If we will not do this little for man's freedom and vast future, we can not hope that Europe will; catastrophe must come, and there is no one to blame but ourselves. But the burden is ours because the power is ours, too. If we *will* Union we can achieve The Union, and the time we take to do it depends only on ourselves.

CHAPTER VI

How to Organize the Democracies

All men are created equal.—*Declaration of Independence.*

A frequent recurrence to fundamental principles . . . (is) absolutely necessary to preserve the blessings of liberty, and keep a government free.—*Pennsylvania's Declaration of the Rights of Man, 1776.*

How shall world government be organized among the few democracies with which it must begin? Basically there are only two ways of organizing inter-state government—the league way and the union way—and we must choose between them.

Every science has its units, though political science seems to neglect them. One rarely finds political organization analyzed according to its unit or hears the term, *unit*, used in constitutional discussions. Yet government, whether state or inter-state, has to be government of some unit, by some unit, for some unit. Since in all human organization, whether political, economic, or other, men must be taken either singly or plurally, that is, as individuals or as subordinate parts or cells of an organized body, there would seem to be, in the constitutional field that concerns us, only two basic units, Man and the State.

In organizing themselves as a body politic, men raise the problem: What shall be the relation between each of them and the whole of them, between the individual and the collective or "plural man" of which he forms a part and helps create? This question has the importance for political organization that a continental divide has on the course a raindrop will take on reaching earth. However imperceptible it may be, the point where a continent divides into two opposing slopes suffices, though two raindrops fall only an inch apart on either side, to send each inevitably to oceans worlds apart. So it is with our political problem. Just as the divide has only two basic slopes, and these are hidden amid those running every direction in the labyrinth of mountains around it, there are basically only two answers to this question of the relations between man and the state.

Either one must consider man as a cell in the body politic, a means to an end, the state supreme and the individual subordinate to it. Or one must consider man as himself the entity and the state as his tool, a means to his ends, the individual as supreme and the state as subordinate. Compromises between the two extremes are, of course, possible, but in the last analysis men in organizing government must either allow themselves to be taken plurally as parts of something greater and organized with the organization as unit and end, or they must take themselves singly and organize on the basis that they themselves constitute the equal units and the equal ends of their organization.

The solution that relegates the individual to the role of cell is a mystic one. Its indivisible unit. the body politic, is, as Hobbes admitted. an imaginary body. Unlike individuals it has no flesh. no blood, and can neither live nor die in the common sense of the words. Men can pretend to endow the state with their own attributes, they can work themselves into believing their own make-believe. They can not change themselves from an organic whole into an organic cell, least of all into the cell of so abstract a body as the body politic. The individual remains indivisible, individual, and the body politic is always dividual.

The solution that would create the state in the image of man out of men tends to carry its false and mystic analogy to the point of reducing men as far as possible to cells with specialized hereditary functions. It leads to governing power over all the people being given to a special class or person as absolutely as power over the body is given to the head. It reaches its ultimate expression when some one man, whether Louis XIV or Adolph Hitler, declares, "I am the State." This is the absolutist conception.

The opposite conception has nothing mystic about it. It centers in the tangible fact that individual man is a living, indivisible, independent entity, that he has blood, not ink, in his veins, that he can enjoy life and suffer death, that he has deep within him a longing to be more independent, to be freer from everything that hems him in and holds him down, and to live his own life, and that his most vital interest and dearest possession is himself. This conception gives majesty not to the state but to Man. It treats the state as only an instrument made by man for his own benefit as he has made houses, weapons, tools,—a great instrument, but still an instrument. It sees nothing intrinsically more sacred in a method of government than in a method of transportation. It judges each according to the service it renders the living individual, —and that depends on the conditions in which he must live, for as the automobile is better for men than the horse where there are roads, the horse is better where no roads exist.

Men of this second conception do not refuse, simply because a mechanism is a political one, to scrap it in favor of a better one. Their attitude toward the existing form of the state is at bottom the attitude of men toward the existing form of any instrument for doing what they want, one determined less by gratitude for past service to them than by their present and future needs and desires. They dismiss as contrary to observed fact and common sense the theory that men of one family or class are born to rule and others to obey. They delegate, but never alienate, their governing power; they carefully safeguard their right to re-delegate it; they employ men to serve them in politics as in anything else. This conception of politics, in short, begins with the plainest facts, proceeds by reason, sticks to the ground; it keeps its emotion and its awe for Man. It is the democratic conception.

The question, which shall be the unit, man or the state, is

then a basic question in political organization. That becomes clearer when we pass from the general to the particular field that concerns us, inter-state government among democracies.

In a union by our definition each man counts for one; it follows that in a union the states with more men count for more than the less populous ones: Union is based on the principle of equality for men rather than for states. In a league each state counts for one; therefore the citizen of the least populated state counts for more than the citizen of the most populated one: There is equality for states but not for men. A union organizes inter-state government of, by and for the people of each state as individual men and women; a league organizes government of, by and for the states as states, as individual bodies politic made up of men and women as cells.

When we take the state as unit we are led into taking the state as sacrosanct. When we organize a government of states we are bound to have its laws bear on them as units, for if they bear directly on the citizen regardless of his state government the state is not the unit and the citizen is. Our government must therefore govern state governments, not individual men. Our choice of the state as unit obliges us also to provide that our inter-state government shall be by these state governments, for if we provide inter-state government directly by the people in the states then the states can not be equals, for the more populous will have more representatives than the less populous. In order to have this government of and by states, we are bound to provide government for the sake of these states, to preserve their integrity, equality, independence, sovereignty. That is precisely what we were led to do in the League of Nations by our choice of unit, and we have not been making the world safer for democracy.

Our choice of unit has led us instead into trying to make it safer for national sovereignty first of all, and we have succeeded only in making it safer for absolutism. Instead of making government for men we have organized men for the sake of government. And so each of the democracies has been driven into strengthening the state against its citizens in order to strengthen it against other states, into centralizing more and more power in each national government. By confusion and frustration we have been led to the rampant nationalism we are suffering and to the dogma of the divine right of the nation which Hitler preaches.

Much of our confusion now roots in our two-faced use of *nation* to' mean both people and state, and in the tendency to use the former to mean race, too. The way democracy has developed has contributed heavily to this ambiguity. Democracy grew first in one existing state and then in another. By replacing royal sovereignty in an existing state with popular or national sovereignty it seemed to make nation and state one. According to democratic theory the nation (in the sense of a people) made the nation (in the sense of a state) to preserve the freedom of the nation (in the sense of a people). The nation seemed thus both means and end, though in reality the nation-state or nation-unit was the means and the nation-people, the individuals in it, was the end.

In his far-sighted essay, *Nationality*, that great liberator of the mind, Lord Acton, pointed out in 1862 that the theory of nationalism had already come to cover two opposing ideas which he called the theory of unity and the theory of liberty. The latter is our democratic or individualist conception of the nation, the former the Fascist or Nazi or absolutist conception of it. To distinguish between the great good and the great evil that the nation can do us and our individual liberty, and to keep the good while avoiding the evil, we can not do better than re-read what Acton wrote prophetically of nationalism. Here is his conclusion, taken from his illuminating *History of Freedom*: *

> Nationality does not aim either at liberty or prosperity, both of which it sacrifices to the imperative necessity of making the nation the mould and measure of the State. Its course will be marked with material as well as moral ruin, in order that a new invention may prevail over the works of God and the interests of mankind. There is no principle of change, no phase of political speculation conceivable, more comprehensive, more subversive, or more arbitrary than this. It is a confutation of democracy, because it sets limits to the exercise of the popular will, and substitutes for it a higher principle. It prevents not only the division, but the extension of the State, and forbids to terminate war by conquest, and to obtain a security for peace. Thus, after surrendering the individual to the collective will, the revolutionary system makes the collective will subject to conditions that are independent of it, and rejects all law, only to be controlled by an accident.

Mussolini and Hitler, by carrying the theory of nationalism to its logical absurdities, have made clearer now how right Acton was and is.

It was not this that Mazzini and Cavour saw in nationalism;

* *History of Freedom*, p. 288 ff., Macmillan, London.

they preached national unity in the interest of individual free-dom, the rights of nations as a means to the Rights of Man. So, too, did the French, British, and Americans from whom they drew their theory. But, as we have seen so strikingly in Czechoslovakia,—where the democratic theory of the rights of nations has been used to strengthen the declared foe of democracy—the liberal fathers of nationalism were un-wittingly fathering, too, the absolutism of Hitler and Musso-lini. Thinking of domestic affairs, they used *nation* to mean ten million heads working freely together to make each one freer, and then, thinking of external affairs, they used *nation* in the next breath as if these individuals had melted or should melt into one composite head ten million times greater,—and as usual the conception in the greater or su-preme field grew supreme. With this tendency to personify, there slipped in the inevitable tendency to glorify, and then deify, this giant champion of individual freedom and com-plete the myth. Mysticism, too, abhors a vacuum.

Considering how far the most advanced democracies have gone in this direction it is not surprising that the peoples who had no long background of sturdy, rational individualism to brake the centralizing tendency and who had only recently thrown off divine-right rulers, should fall a prey to the mystical absolute nationalism of the Mussolinis and Hitlers.

But the great danger now to our freedom and theirs does not lie in their mistakes, it lies in the confusion among the older democracies. It is only our own nationalism, not theirs, that can prevent our union. Indeed, the nationalism of Hitler and Mussolini is doing much to drive the democracies back to their senses, and to force them to apply to each other their own democratic principles.

It is for us of the older democracies, first of all, to remem-ber that *nation* and *state* are bloodless words, and that the millions of us men and women they represent are living in-dividuals—not mystic symbols, legalistic abstractions, com-posite photographs. We know our millions form together a unit only in desiring the freedom to have our own individual opinions about everything, be our different selves and live our own lives. We know we made the nation only as a step toward making the world safe for the enjoyment of these individual liberties and individual differences. We know now that the next step we need to make toward this end is to unite our-selves in a world democracy. It is for us who know better to do better, and cease blaming others for our ills.

CHAPTER VII

League or Union? Three Tests

Man is not the enemy of man but through the medium of a false system of Government.—*Paine.*

The fatal tendency of mankind to leave off thinking about a thing when it is no longer doubtful is the cause of half their errors.—*Mill.*

We may now turn from these general considerations to more particular reasons why we must organize our democracies as a union instead of a league, to the reasons why leagues are undemocratic and unions democratic, why leagues can not work and unions can, why leagues can not be trusted to enforce law and unions can. In other words, we shall now submit our choice to the super-state test, the practical test and the acid test.

1. The Super-State Test

Why Leagues Are Undemocratic

Suppose we organize our democracies as a league. This league would have obvious advantages over the League of Nations. Yet because it was a league this organization of democracies would be a perversion of democracy. Its equality would still be the equality of states. It would accord one vote each to 4,000,000 Swiss, 40,000,000 French, 130,000,000 Americans,—flouting the most elementary democratic principle to this extreme degree for the sake of the state. It would require for any important action unanimous agreement among its state members; democracy proceeds by majority agreement among men.

Even were all our democracies equal in population, to organize them as a league would still be to encourage dictatorship among them. A league by giving an equal vote to the government of each nation in it allows the government least responsible and responsive to its people to manœuvre best.

The more democratic a people is the more it respects the minority and requires a government to explain policies to the people before committing them, and the more important the issue the more vigilant is its public opinion. But the more these conditions obtain the more handicapped the government is in defending the interests of its citizen in a league. The league system thus places a premium on whatever strengthens the government as regards its own people and a penalty on whatever strengthens the citizen's power to restrain his government.

In a democracy patriotism calls on all good citizens to defend the inalienable rights of the individual. In a league it calls on them to sacrifice their own rights in order to strengthen the government and preserve the state. National solidarity thus replaces respect of the minority or individual as the ideal. The idea spreads that the salvation of the nation depends on a party, having once gained power, maintaining its power by suppressing all other parties and all freedom of speech and press so that the government may be stable and strong in its dealing with the rest of mankind; and the race is on toward the totalitarian state. Those who want the proof of experience need only look about them.

WHY UNIONS ARE DEMOCRATIC

It is not on these grounds, however, that the League of Nations has usually been attacked as undemocratic. The great cry against it has been that membership involves sacrificing a democracy's independence, that it forms a super-state. This cry is invariably raised against every proposal for inter-state government, whether league or union.

Where Senator Borah urged against the League of Nations that it would sacrifice the national sovereignty of the American Union, Patrick Henry opposed the Constitution of the American Union as sacrificing the state rights of Virginia. Both meant that inter-state government sacrifices the citizen's individual freedom. Even the backers of inter-state organization usually seem to accept this view; they concede the sacrifice but plead that it is needed for the general good.

This reflects profound confusion over what occurs when democratic government, whether national or inter-state, is formed. We have already noted how this confusion rises partly from the assumption that the freedom of the state and the freedom of its citizens are necessarily identical. It also rises from the assumption that the organization of democratic government involves "sacrifice" of rights by the citizens.

"Sacrifice" is a most misleading word for what we do with our rights when we organize democratic government; the operation is really one of safeguarding or investing these individual rights.

When we hand over money to a bank to have it keep an

heirloom in safe deposit for us we do not say we are sacrificing the money and the heirloom for the good of the bank. We say we are safeguarding our heirloom and paying for the service. When we hand over money to a corporation in order to gain more money through ownership of its stock we do not say we are sacrificing our money for the good of the corporation. We say we are investing it for ourselves. Even if we lose we do not call the operation a sacrifice; we call it a bad investment. We sacrifice our money only when we hand it over with no intention of gain.

No more in politics than in business can we get something for nothing. To keep our freedom and to get more of it we must give freedom. It would not seem to need proving that individuals have always needed to give some of their liberty to the state in order to secure the rest of it; every free people has always admitted this.

Nor would it seem to need proving that united action by men, such as the organization or maintenance of government, involves some loss of freedom or power by each individual unit in it, and yet may result in a net gain in freedom or power by each. Where a government is made of, by and for the people every citizen, as Lincoln was fond of saying, is an equal sovereign, and national sovereignty would seem to be composed of the sovereignty its citizens have given it to secure better the rest of their individual sovereignty. *In a democracy a state's rights can only be the rights its citizens have individually invested in it.*

All this is so evident that when men form a democratic government they say that they make the government for the sake of their own freedom. It is, in fact, because this is so clear that they tend to identify their individual freedom with the freedom of their state, and are thus led into the great mistake of assuming that any loss of the nation's sovereignty is necessarily a loss to them.

They forget that, for the individual citizen to gain rights, the state must lose rights, just as a bank must reduce its charges if the heirloom is to be guarded more cheaply, or a corporation must not merely pile up power in the form of surplus if stockholders are to get dividends on their investment in it. If, for example, the citizen is to gain the right to buy and sell freely in a larger market, his state must lose the right to levy a tariff.

The object of democratic government is to provide increasing return in individual freedom to the citizens in return for decreasing investment of their freedom,—for example, more individual security for less taxation and military servitude. Consequently, loss of rights by a government, far from being a thing necessarily to be avoided or deplored, is a thing to be sought whenever the rights of the citizens are thereby really increased.

Investing in Union

When democracies form a union what really happens is this: The citizens of each withdraw certain powers they had invested in their national state and reinvest them, or part of them, in the union state. The operation involves loss of power by their national states but no loss of power by the citizens. They give the union state no more rights than they gave the national state. They simply shift certain rights from one to another.

The reason why there is no loss but merely a shift is that the citizens base their union government on the same unit that each of their national governments is based on, namely, individual man. Each man consequently remains in precisely the same relation to the new government as to the old. When 10 men unite on this basis each equals 1. When 10 men thus unite with 90, or with nine groups of 10, each of the 100 men still equals 1 for all political purposes. If a democracy of 100,000,000 men thus unites with others of, say, 5,000,000 and 10,000,000 and 50,000,000, each of the 165,000,000 citizens of the union still equals what he did before, 1.

It is different when democracies league together. When 100,000,000 men league with 50,000,000 they lose power as regards the field of government they transfer to the league, for whereas each formerly had the power of 1 over policy in this field they now have only the power of one-half, since the league weights 50,000,000 and 100,000,000 alike. Because it thus shifts the unit in shifting the field of government, a league entails loss of power to the citizens of all but the least populous of the democracies in it.

As for the common illusion that citizens also lose when democracies unite, two things contribute to it: (A) One of the possible relations of 1 unit to 10 units is 1/10th, and of 1 to 100,000,000 units, 1/100,000,000th, and so the greater the number the less important each man appears to be. (B) Since 100,000,000 is more than 10, and 10 is more than 1, the greater the number of citizens the more important the state appears to become. But the action of a democracy, whatever its population, is determined in final test by 1, any 1 of the citizens, for it is determined by a majority, and 1 can make a majority. If 10 men are divided 5 to 5 and 1 changes sides he carries with him the power of all 10, for he makes a majority of 6 to 4. Raise the number of voters to

100,000,000 and the majority that determines action is not 60,000,000 to 40,000,000 but 50,000,001 to 49,999,999. No matter what the population of a democratic state or union, the citizen's relation to the government and his power to decide its action remain precisely the same.

Far from losing, the citizen gains power by union. While his power to decide action remains unchanged, the power of the union whose action he decides becomes much greater as the population increases. If a man must depend on himself alone for his security he must be on guard 24 hours daily. When he unites with five other men democratically for mutual security he needs stand guard only four hours. He gets 24 hours security for an investment of four hours. He gets six times more freedom, six times more defensive power. The more men with whom he unites the more freedom and power he has for less investment of them. In union therefore the progression from 1 to 1/10th to 1/100,000,000th is a progression downward, not in power and freedom for the citizen, but in the amount of it he needs to invest in government; and the progression from 1 to 10 to 100,000,000 is a progression upward, not in the absolute power of the state over the citizens, but in the power it places at the service of each.

When the citizens of several democracies form a union they create a new state but, as we have said, this creates no new rights or powers for the state as State. If they have invested a total of, say, 15 rights in each national government, and they shift five of these rights to the union and leave the others untouched, the total rights of Government remain precisely what they were, 15. The citizens divide them between two governments, instead of centering them in one, but lose none of their own power over Government.

On the contrary they gain power and Government loses power as regards the citizen. By dividing the rights of Government between two governments the citizen leaves each of them incomplete. The national state loses supreme right to the union state, but the latter is not the complete State the former was, for the union's supreme right is limited by all the rights that remain reserved entirely to its member states. By this division and by the fact that both governments equally and independently originate in him, the citizen gains the power of balancing two governments to his own advantage, of shifting rights or appealing from one to the other as circumstances may suggest. The citizen of a complete national state has no such check-and-balance power over Government. He is in the exposed position of one with all his eggs in one basket, all his investments in one company.

How a union extends the individual's effective freedom

from the State,—whether the national, the union, or the foreign state,—may be seen by considering the state rights that he completely transfers to the union. These usually are:

1. The right to grant citizenship.
2. The right to make war and peace, to deal by force or treaty with foreign states.
3. The right to regulate inter-state and foreign trade.
4. The right to control the value of money.
5. The right to control postal and other means of communication.

(The union also has the right to tax individuals and enforce its laws on individuals, but these rights are not transferred to it from the national state, for the latter retains these rights equally. These are really enabling rights required by both governments to govern effectively in their fields. They are inherent in democracy's choice of individual man as the unit.)

When the citizens of, say, fifteen democracies withdraw from each of the above five rights and reinvest these in a union they create within the much larger area of their common state the conditions which had prevailed in each of its component parts, namely, one citizenship, one defense force, one free trade area, one money, one stamp. While leaving each citizen legally where he was as regards the outside world in these five respects, they greatly reduce the area of that outside world by removing from it fourteen sovereign states. In reducing fifteen state sovereignties to one in these fields they reduce enormously the amount of actual interference from the State suffered by the inhabitants of this whole area—and, it is worth noting, by the outside world, too. Without taking any right from any citizen of any state anywhere on earth they thus free each citizen to exercise his existing rights on a far greater scale—in fourteen states which before gave these rights to their citizens, but not to him.

TODAY'S SUPER-STATE: THE NATION

The term *super-state* must be read in terms of power of the state, and since this can be understood in several ways *super-state* can easily be misunderstood. This term can really have terror for democrats only when it means greater power for the State over the citizens. When it merely means greater power for the democratic state over their foes, whether Nature, chaos, or aggressive absolutist states, they must welcome the super-state, for then it means more power for each democrat.

Yet many shy at any inter-state organization simply because it must be greater in size than any member. They assume this means greater governmental power over themselves, as if territory meant tyranny. Tyranny is tyranny, whatever the geographic scale on which it is practised, but the wider this scale the less intolerable men generally seem to find the same degree of tyranny. The states that gave us the word *tyrant* were among the smallest, not the largest, in antiquity. The tyranny that seems to irritate men most is petty personal tyranny. Though tyranny in a great state may sometimes be petty, the tyranny of a small state must be petty.

It is not size that the individual really fears in the state, but power over himself, interference with his liberties, meddling in his life. He resents his travel being vexed by more and more frontiers and frontier restrictions, his savings wiped out by monetary magic, his market cut off by a tariff, his source of supply ended by a quota. He resents having higher taxes to pay, being forced to depend increasingly on the state, having to turn to its soup-line to live, being exposed to more military service. He resents, in short, being afflicted with more and more government. It is the snooper state, the trooper state, that men really fear when they shy at the epithet, *super-state,* and that super-state today is the nation-state.

Nationalism has shown that it can even eliminate many of the normal advantages of size and, by pitting such great democracies as the American, British and French against each other, raise governmental meddling to monumental proportions and armaments to appalling figures. Nationalism has proved in Germany how far it can outdo the absolutism of the past. And the nation-state has only begun in recent years to show itself, we have only hints of what it has in store.*

Bureaucracy and centralization and taxes growing, growing, growing; the state's power over the citizen reaching out, reaching in, reaching all round him, taking livelihood first, money next and freedom all the time until it troops him off to war,—if the nation-state everywhere today is not the super-state, what super-state then need be feared?

The dustbins clogged with superfluous government and unnecessary generals, the war clouds gone, tariffs down and taxes trifling, the individual freed to roam and trade in half the world, needing neither to carry passport or change money, the security and freedom of each extended in every

* This entire section was written in 1934.

way and magnified a hundredfold, and the same equal opportunity assured each whether born in the largest or smallest nation in the union—it is union of the free that ends the snooper trooper super-state.

2. THE PRACTICAL TEST

It may perhaps be asked, what need there is of reasoning or proof to illustrate a position which is not either controverted or doubted; to which the understandings and feelings of all classes of men assent, and which in substance is admitted by the opponents as well as by the friends of the new Constitution? . . . But the usefulness of the concession . . . is destroyed by a strenuous opposition to a remedy, upon the only principles that can give it a chance of success. . . . This renders a full display of the principal defects of the confederation necessary, in order to show, that the evils we experience do not proceed from minute or partial imperfections, but from fundamental errors in the structure of the building, which cannot be amended; otherwise than by an alteration in the first principles and main pillars of the fabric.
—*Hamilton* in *The Federalist, XV.*

WHY LEAGUES CAN NOT WORK

We come to the practical test of everything: Will it work, can it work? Men have shown time and again that they prefer undemocratic, even tyrannical government to ineffective, futile government; indeed, it is to escape this latter that they turn to dictatorship. There would seem no need to prove, after all the evidence of history (of which Geneva's record is only the last chapter), that leagues do not work, can not work. Yet though there is widespread agreement that leagues have not worked, there is still widespread faith that the league system can work.

Our civilization, we have seen, requires constant and rapid political adjustment to be made to meet change. The league system does not allow this adjusting to be done in time. Because each state must act in a league through its state government, public opinion must be strong enough in each state to move the whole government before important league action is possible. Because public opinion can not act directly on league delegates but only indirectly through the governments that name them, and because the delegates do not depend directly on the voters, much more pressure is needed to get action in a league than in a union.

Moreover, public opinion in a union can exert pressure directly over the whole union area, and a majority leader always risks seeing the minority leader carry the fight into his own district and defeat him. But a league divides its public opinion into state compartments, and the delegate of one sovereign government can not go campaigning in another state to have its sovereign government thrown out or its delegate changed.

Again, since a league holds the state sacrosanct and is formed to preserve the state, the first concern of each state government in it must be state, not league affairs.

Even could a league avoid the difficulty of having to act through government delegates, its action would remain slow and doubtful because of the unanimity rule. At best it is extremely hard to get unanimous agreement on any important matter. It requires a technique, and a degree of tact, understanding, and persuasive power that Geneva experience shows is extremely rare even among the world's ablest and most experienced politicians and statesmen.

The worse the emergency the more swiftly there must be action, but the more a league then requires unanimity for action and the harder it is to get unanimity.

The units of a league, unlike those of a union, are not mobile but rigidly fixed to earth. Voters in a union being men can move from one region to another if political controversy gets too dangerous for them, but the voters in a league being states can not change neighbors. Consequently the men who decide how the state's vote is to be cast must not only consider the issue on its general merits but ponder even more how their vote is liable to affect their relations with a neighbor, especially a more powerful neighbor. All this makes for hesitation, vacillation, inaction.

There seems no escaping the unanimity rule in important matters so long as the unit of organization is the state. The choice of this unit means that the supreme object of government is the preservation of the state's sovereignty. One must then admit that each state government is more competent than any outside government to decide what is essential for its own sovereignty.

An organization that gives each state one vote and lets the majority of states rule the minority is repugnant both to democracies and autocracies. It lets a minority of men over-ride the majority. That defeats democracy even more than does the unanimity rule, for though the latter allows a minority to block the majority, it does let any minority take positive control. As for the absolutists, majority rule in a league puts other states or the league above their state, and that is incompatible with the absolutist principle that nothing can be higher than the state.

The unanimity rule may save the absolutist, but not the democrat. Absolutism thrives on disorder and chaos, whether caused by action or inaction. Democracy needs law and order to survive, it can not get them without practical governmental means of timely action, and the unanimity rule allows it no such means. For it saves individual freedom from bad law only to expose it to the danger of no law, or law so weak and ambiguous that it can not be relied on, or law made too late to do any good.

Then there is the difficulty of ratification. In a league one must persuade not only all the delegates but the governments behind them. After one has persuaded a delegate his government may drop him, or after he has persuaded his government it may be overthrown—perhaps on this very issue, perhaps on something quite unrelated to it. Even if the delegate remains at the league he may be unable to persuade the new government. While the league statesman is bringing one government in line another may break loose—for time is passing and conditions changing. When all sorts of delicate adjustments have made agreement finally seem possible, conditions may have changed so that this delicate balance has to be readjusted to meet new facts: One must start this heartbreaking work again. If the treaty does reach signature it must then be ratified by all the governments whose unanimity was practically required in negotiating it, and this may take years. The failure of only one or a few states to ratify their delegate's signature has crippled or killed many a treaty.

None of this is theory, it is all the history of the League of Nations, of the League of Friendship among the Thirteen American States, of the international conference method.

WHY UNIONS CAN ACT SWIFTLY

Because it takes man for unit a union can put any important proposal directly before all its principals simultaneously, as in an election or plebiscite. Even if a league could assemble in conference the whole executive and legislative branches of each government instead of a small delegation, it would not be equalling the direct action possible in a union. It would still be dealing with agents, not with the sources of power, the men and women, the citizens, who elect the state executives and legislatures.

When a union proceeds indirectly, through agents or representatives of its units, it can still act more rapidly and easily than a league. In a league no agent ever represents more than one unit. In a union every agent must represent many units. His power is always delegated to him by several hundred or thousand of the union's units. A league inevitably makes the delegate a puppet depending on the instructions of his government; a union inevitably keeps its representatives from being rigidly tied to instructions and makes them freer to respond quickly to new facts or arguments.

The representative in a union may be advised by different units in his district to do this or that on a given issue; the advice may be contradictory; he must use his own judgment and strike a balance between the conflicting instructions he thus gets—and guess what all the silent units in his district want him to do. Presumably he will try to follow the wishes of the majority of units in his district, but he is free to decide (under penalty of being defeated at the next election) what these wishes are. He is free, too, to vote against the wishes of the articulate majority in his district, presumably in the belief that the inarticulate are with him, or that time will justify him, or that he can persuade a majority at the next election that he was right. The delegate to a league can not possibly do this; he would be recalled at once by his government. Because a union acts by majority it can act much more quickly than a league.

Once there is agreement in a union to act, action can follow at once. There is no need in it to wait for its units to ratify the decision of their agents; the vote of these representatives suffices for law to take effect. Here again union has a tremendous advantage over a league.

Finally, the greater the emergency in a union the greater is the popular pressure for action—that is, the greater is the pressure of the units on their agents—and the faster the union machinery moves. The difficulty and danger in a union are that it can and may act too swiftly. Where the problem in a league is to get up enough steam to turn the wheels, in a union it is to control the speed, to arrange safety valves, governors, brakes, such as the American Union has in the powers reserved to the people and the states, the two-house Congress, the presidential veto, the Supreme Court, and the time required to amend the Constitution.

3. THE ACID TEST

> The important truth . . . is that a sovereignty over
> sovereigns, a government over governments, a legisla-
> tion for communities, as contradistinguished from in-
> dividuals, as it is a solecism in theory so in practice it

is subversive of the order and the ends of civil polity, by substituting violence in place of law, or the destructive coercion of the sword in place of the mild and salutary coercion of the magistracy.—*Hamilton* in *The Federalist, XX.*

WHY LEAGUES CAN NOT ENFORCE LAW

It is not enough for a government to be able to make laws in time, it must also be able to insure their effective execution. This brings us to the core of the problem of political organization, whether state or inter-state, the acid test of any government. Law depends on confidence that it will be executed. No system of political law has yet gained that confidence without providing for execution of law by force against those who refuse to accept it.

To be sound any government or system of law must be built to meet the danger of an attempt being made to upset it, and to meet it in a way inspiring confidence that its law-enforcing machinery can and will overwhelm the lawbreaker. To do this the system must be designed to give the greatest possible guarantees that, the more dangerous the violation is, the stronger the position of the law-enforcer will be, and the weaker the position of the lawbreaker.

Nowhere is the question of the unit in government more important than here. If the unit is the state, then the law can be enforced only by states against states; if the unit is man, the law can be enforced only by men against individual men. To quote Hamilton, the "penalty, whatever it may be, can only be inflicted in two ways—by the agency of the courts and ministers of justice or by military force; by the coercion of the magistracy or by the coercion of arms. The first kind can evidently apply only to men; the last kind must of necessity be employed against bodies politic or communities or States." The effect of taking the state as unit is to weaken the law-enforcing machinery and strengthen the position of the lawbreaker. Here are some of the reasons why:

Suppose we form a league of democracies and one of them, say with a population of 20,000,000, elects by 60 per cent majority a government that proceeds to violate its league obligations. If the league law is to be enforced, it must be enforced against a group so powerful and well organized as to give the enforcer pause. This group is not simply 12,000,000 strong, as it may seem at first glance, but 20,000,000 strong, because its government has control of the state's whole war power and because the league law must be enforced against the state as a unit. Whether the coercion is by war, blockade, or non-military sanctions, it can not possibly be restricted to the 12,000,000, it must punish just as much the 8,000,000 who presumably sought to prevent the violation. This fact, on top of the patriotic ideology responsible for the democracies having organized a league instead of a union, must encourage the 8,000,000 to join the 12,000,000 in resisting the law.

Here we have the essential unsoundness of the enforcement machinery of a league. This system begins by making sure that its weakest lawbreaker will be far stronger than any gang or mob of men—the strongest lawbreaker that a union faces—for a league lawbreaker must be, at least, an organized nation of men. Then the league system proceeds to strengthen its lawbreaker by itself outraging justice. Worse, it is incapable of sparing the innocent when it would punish the guilty. Still worse, it is bound to punish the innocent common people more than the responsible leaders. Its blockade strikes the ruler only by starving the half-starved into revolt, its bullets kill few statesmen. While it is putting the whole nation behind the offending government, this stupidity and injustice is demoralizing and weakening those upon whom it must depend to coerce the offender. To remember the Ethiopian experience is to see how serious is this defect in a league.

WHEN LAWBREAKERS ARE IMMORTAL

Again, the league system requires enforcement by immortals against immortals. Its unit is the nation, and nations are immortal, compared to individual men. Because of this a league in coercing a state of 20,000,000 population must really coerce a state that is more than 20,000,000 strong, for the state disposes of all the power past generations have stored in it and is fortified by its generations to come, by its aspirations for and obligations to them.

To enforce law one must find the offender guilty. It is one thing for the immortal state to brand as a criminal one of its millions of mortals, and quite another for a few mortal statesmen to attach the stigma of guilt to an immortal nation. It is an appalling blunder, a monstrous thing.

"I do not know the method of drawing up an indictment against a whole people," Burke declared in his plea for conciliation with America.

All this would be true even were a nation mortal, and the fact that a people does not die makes Burke's statement only truer. What could be worse folly than to encourage men (as a league does by its subordination of individuals to their state) to put their pride in their nation, to identify their individual self-respect with their nation's status in the world —and to condemn then their nation as criminal? This system, which visits on the children the sins of the fathers, seems designed to rouse and maintain a spirit of bitter resistance to league law both among the fathers and the children; it strikes at what every self-respecting individual must hold dear, the name he inherits, has made for himself, and would pass on. The effect of Geneva's verdict against the Italian government in uniting Italians behind that government, stimulating them to sacrifice and invent, spurring them in the field and at home to much greater effort than most people expected, should suffice to show how any system that would enforce law against immortal nations tends to defeat itself.

There remain the after-effects. Whether a league fails or succeeds in coercing its guilty nation, the condemned people is not likely to rest until it has forced its judges to recant, to absolve even the guilty among it in order to save their innocent compatriots, dead, living and unborn. One can not better organize enduring bad blood, feud on a colossal scale, than by trying to establish peace and justice, law and order, through the coercive machinery of a league.

To make matters worse, a league's unit is not only immortal but immobile. An individual man who has been found guilty can hope to escape the disgrace by moving elsewhere, changing his name, beginning anew, or his family can. Not so the nation. It is fixed. The individual Englishman can change from one condition of life to another and another, but the English as a unit must face the world forever as an island people. The Italians as a nation cannot escape from the problem Gibraltar and Suez pose, though the farmer whose gates to the highway are similarly held by another can always, at worst, move away. The immobility of a league's units breeds and nourishes unnecessary conflict and makes its enforcement machinery stiff and rigid. It also makes it harder for the nations that must adjoin forever the accused nation to condemn it, or for it to accept such disgrace from its neighbors.*

The neighboring nations must remember, too, that condemning the accused endangers them more than other league members; on the neighbors falls the main burden of coercion in a league, their trade suffers most from economic sanctions, and they are the most exposed to the acts of desperation or vengeance of the condemned. These neighbors may be as weak

* This was written four years before the Scandinavian countries and China abstained from voting when the League of Nations "dropped" Russia in 1939 for aggression against Finland.

compared to the lawbreaker as Switzerland and Austria compared to Italy, may have no material interest in enforcing the law against this particular offense, may hope to profit considerably from not enforcing it. Their failure to enforce the law may strengthen the offender as greatly as did the action of Switzerland and Austria in keeping open Italy's communications with Germany. This shows how the immobility of a league's units undermines its power to enforce law.

WHERE TRIAL PRECEDES ARREST

People often talk as if the League of Nations could enforce the law in about the same way their own government does. The difference in unit, however, makes the procedure of the two radically and inevitably different. One can lock up a man pending trial, but not a nation—one can not imprison a nation at all. When a policeman sees a man, knife in hand, creeping up behind another man he doesn't stop to consider whether perhaps no crime but only a practical joke is intended. He doesn't wait till the blow falls, the blood spurts, the victim appeals to him. He jumps in at once and arrests the man on suspicion. When the Italian government openly prepared for nine months to invade Ethiopia and the League of Nations did nothing to stop it except try to reconcile the two, many criticized the League for not acting like a policeman. But one can not arrest a nation on suspicion.

Even had a league the force to do this it would lack the will. Coercion in a league means war or risk of war. One can get few if any members of a league to agree to risk war on mere suspicion of aggression. To move public opinion to that degree one must arrange that the crime, if committed, will seem as flagrant and black as possible. To do this one must first convince the public that all means of peacefully preventing the crime have been exhausted.

If, as in the case of Italy, the suspected government not only protests its peaceful intentions but agrees to arbitrate, what can a league do but take it at its word? If the league does not, it itself spoils the possibility of conciliation, assures the suspected government stronger support at home and sacrifices the league's chances of rousing public opinion among its members to support coercion. It thus strengthens the potential offender while weakening the enforcer.

If the league takes the supected government at its word, shows the utmost trust in its good faith, leans backward to be just and patient, then the crime, if committed, appears more heinous and may rouse enough indignation to make effective coercion possible. But this means waiting till the crime has

been committed. It also means making eventual reconciliation and peace among these immortal immobile nations all
the harder, for it makes the crime and stigma worse. It
means that the league is really a partner in the crimes it
would repress, responsible for their being worse than they
would have been otherwise. What must one say of a system
of law whose possibility of repressing crime depends on its
success in making crime worse?

Moreover, what law and order would any nation enjoy if
the police could not arrest even a flagrant offender before
they had convicted him in court? Yet this is just what any
league must do.

After the Italian government had invaded Ethiopia the
League's Council and Assembly met, heard Italy's defense,
and decided that the Italian government had resorted to war.
Only then could the League begin action. Yet how can any
organization of sovereign states allow even its highest-
ranking official to act against an aggressor as the lowest-
ranking policeman does? How can Sovereign States let him
use their armed force against a state before they have
formally agreed in each given case to such grave and dangerous action? In a league the trial must come *before*, not
after, the arrest.

THE FALLACY OF BLOODLESS SANCTIONS

All this forces a league to begin enforcement gently and
slowly, to turn then to stronger measures, and to encourage
the aggressor thereby to commit worse crimes.

At best every nation is very strongly and naturally reluctant
to participate in the bloodshed which decision to apply military sanctions risks involving. This reluctance is made all the
stronger by the hopes of success that non-military measures
seem to hold. On paper one can make an attractive case for
such measures. One can argue—as was argued in the Italian
test—that sufficient agreement can be obtained on economic
sanctions to make sure that the aggressor will be brought
down eventually without the coercers themselves shedding
any blood. It was also argued in the Italian test that the aggressor, seeing that such wide agreement against him is bound
to ruin him in the end, will not wait till his ruin is consum-
mated but will give up long before.

This, however, is never likely to work out in a league better or differently than in the Italian test. A case can be made
not only for gradually increasing pressure, but also for stak-
ing all on a bold policy.—and the merits of this aggressive
policy are bound to appeal most to the aggressive-minded,

and therefore to the aggressor, just as the merits of passive action appeal most to the pacific. Where desire to win by economic sanctions leads the coercers to see the possibilities of victory through the aggressor reading the handwriting on the wall, the same process of wishful thinking leads the aggressor to concentrate on the possibilities of nullifying these sanctions by economies, inventions, quick military triumph. He becomes too engrossed in this to see the handwriting on the wall. And so the war continues week in, week out, the league appears to be doing nothing effective even to stop the crime or aid the victim, public opinion is outraged by the spectacle, it demands that the killing be stopped and refuses to keep coolly and patiently content with slow-moving sanctions in the face of continued slaughter. The cry for something more effective is bound to rise, just as the demand for the oil sanction rose soon after the other sanctions were applied to Italy.

But what is the effect of this threat of stronger measures? It encourages the victim to continue an otherwise hopeless war. It encourages the aggressor to redouble his attack and resort to more frightful warfare—just as Italy turned to poison gas as Geneva turned toward the oil embargo—in the hope of winning the war before the sanction takes effect.

JUDGE, SHERIFF, CRIMINAL—ALL IN ONE

These examples by no means exhaust the difficulties and absurdities into which a league falls through having the state as its unit. Another result is that each member is at once judge, juryman, and sheriff. Worse, as I helped point out when the Italian government, while undergoing sanctions, took part in the League's hearing on Germany's violation of the Locarno treaty, the league system "allows a nation to fill simultaneously the roles of condemned lawbreaker in one case and judge and sheriff in another." This weakness, the dispatch continued, was "exemplified by the first international meeting to be held in the new League palace, that of the Locarno powers on the afternoon of April 10, 1936. In it the Foreign Ministers of Britain and France, who that very morning had debated before the Committee of Thirteen in the old League building what to do about Italy, whom the Council found guilty of committing the worst crime in the League's calendar, debated with Italy what to do about Germany, whom the Council, with Italy as one of the judges, found guilty of committing its next worst crime."*

This may help make clear why a league can have no effective

* *The New York Times,* Apr. 19, 1936.

central or executive authority. There can be no sheriff in a community where every man is equally sheriff. The example should make clearer, too, why projects to endow a league with a permanent league police force for the coercion of members are doomed to failure. It is not the international character of such a force that makes it impossible—look at the French Foreign Legion—but the fact that a league army's real unit is not man but the nation.

When a league does decide to enforce its law it must then improvise its instrument, whether non-military or military. It "must at the last minute organize an army out of a mob of armies of sovereigns so jealous of their sovereignty that they are unable to organize a league force beforehand."* We have already noted why a league can not provide even the advance military planning needed for confidence in its enforcement machinery. For similar reasons it can not make concrete advance plans to enforce its law by non-military means.

The result is that a league can not inspire confidence among its law-abiding members nor respect and fear among the aggressively inclined. This encourages its members to arm, and whether they arm for defence or aggression they make matters worse by putting the enforcement problem on a still more enormous scale.

Since no league, no matter how strong its paper guarantees to enforce its laws, can possibly remove the fatal defects inherent in itself, it can not possibly succeed in getting its members to trust it enough to disarm and avoid chaos. As long as the state must depend, in a vital emergency, on its own arms it must also protect strategic industries and prepare against blockade by artificially maintaining its agricultural production. So long as it must do this it can not afford to renounce control over such essential weapons as its currency and trade. Practically, there is no more possibility of monetary stability or free trade than there is of disarmament, security, or peace in any inter-state government requiring coercion of states. Through and through the league system is untrustworthy.

WHY UNIONS CAN ENFORCE LAW

To be sound, a system of law, we have said, must be built to meet the danger of some attempt being made to upset it, and to meet it in a way inspiring confidence that its law-enforcing machinery will overwhelm the lawbreaker. To do this it must be so devised that, the more dangerous the vio-

* *The New York Times,* Dec. 29, 1935.

lation, the stronger the position of the law-enforcer will be and the weaker that of the lawbreaker.

A union pins any violation of its law on the weakest possible political unit, a single mortal, and arrays against him the organized centralized power of millions of these units—the union state. Suppose we have fifteen democracies of 20,-000,000 population each. If they league together the theoretical ratio of law-enforcing power to law-defying power is at best 280,000,000 to 20,000,000, or 14 to 1. If they unite the ratio is 299,999,999 to 1. This shows how overwhelmingly the change of unit from state to man weakens the lawbreaker and strengthens the law-enforcer.

For law (whether treaty or statute) to be broken some individual man has to break it. A union by pinning the responsibility for the violation on this individual and on him alone tends to deprive him of all support. Members of his family or gang may help him, but they are not to be compared in power with a government which controls the force of an organized nation and can appeal to patriotic sentiments to justify its treaty violation. Union law does not by its very operation drive the innocent to support the lawbreaker as does league law; instead it tends to isolate him even from those most likely to support him. His family seldom resists his arrest.

No group, not even the family, is stigmatized legally in a union by the guilt of one member, let alone punished simply because of relation to him. The criminal's family may suffer some social disgrace, but the family can move away, change its name, begin afresh. Or it may find protection in the fact that many other unrelated men have the same family name. The name of each nation in a league is unique, and so there is no escape from that name and any blot on it stands out more, lasts longer, and is harder to bear.

There have been many celebrated murderers, but how often is one of their descendants identified as one—as, say, the grandson of Dr. So-and-so who was executed for poisoning a patient? The children of criminals often attract attention during trials, but how long does it last? They are soon mercifully lost or forgotten among the millions of men.

In a union there is, then, no enduring disgrace attached to the group to which a lawbreaker belongs, nothing to entangle all its members willy-nilly in the crime and turn them, as in a league, against the law in order to right this injustice or save their self-respect. By its condemnation a union, unlike a league, does not inevitably turn against it even the condemned criminal, for, unlike an "aggressor nation," he can hope to live down the stain on his name, change it if it is uncommon, move away.

The union system, moreover, gives those it arrests much stronger guarantees of justice and much greater hope for acquittal than does a league. It is therefore easier for the innocent to accept arrest unresistingly. As for the guilty, it is noteworthy that a union's guarantees to each individual that its overwhelming power will not be used unjustly against him helps to weaken him at the critical time when he is about to break the law or is breaking it. The Bill of Rights serves to isolate the criminal and deprive him of misplaced sympathy by assuring all other men that their combined power will not be used wrongly against the weakest man, that the innocent individual will not be punished, that punishment will fall on the guilty or on no one.

These guarantees to the individual, together with the individual's inherent weakness, mortality and mobility, allow a union to act against offenders much more quickly than can a league. They allow it to stop crime in the bud, to arrest on *prima facie* evidence of criminal intent. The number and weakness of its units not only permit a union to have the powerful central authority a league can not possibly have— and to maintain law and order normally with a tiny fraction of the power at its disposal. It can have, say, one policeman to 1,000 potential lawbreakers and yet be able in an emergency quickly to outnumber or outpower the lawbreaker. The nature of a union's unit, moreover, permits and requires specialized functions for the enforcement of law—this union unit being a soldier. that union unit a policeman. another a judge, another a juryman, still another a prosecutor. It thereby escapes the grotesque absurdity into which a league is led by its unit; in a union no condemned criminal can judge for it the crimes of others while continuing his own.

The union system of law enforcement does not work perfectly. Sometimes the guilty escape, sometimes the innocent are punished, sometimes the union may even suffer revolt, civil war. But its principle is sound and the system does work well: it insures general respect for and enforcement of law by insuring that at the critical moment—the moment when the law is flagrantly broken—the enforcer will be at his strongest and the violator will be at his weakest. And it does this in direct ratio to the importance of the violation. It does insure the citizen more security against burglary than petty theft, and still greater security against murder than against burglary, and still greater security against war than against murder.

HOW UNION ELIMINATES INTER-STATE WAR

It may be objected that the enforcement of law against thieves and murderers is normally left to each state in a union, that such examples do not apply to conflicts between states in the union, or between one or more states and the union itself. The examples were used, however, to illustrate the idea of varying degree of crime and security.

It is true that in a union, as in a league, conflicts may rise between member states in their corporate capacity, and between them and the union. A union may refer such disputes to its supreme court, but refusal to accept the court's decision faces it with a league's problem of enforcing law against a state. There remain, however, great differences in favor of union.

In a league such conflicts and problems are the only ones possible; in a union they are abnormal. The state's position in a union differs radically, as we have seen, from its position in a league. The transfer to the union of some of the state's most important rights (which it most jealously retains in a league) tends to remove many of the worst sources of dispute and war among states. It leaves the state no longer an economic entity, the regulation of its trade with other states inside and outside the union is transferred to the union government, which enforces its inter-state commerce laws not against the states but against individuals in them. Above all, the fact that its citizens have transferred from state to union the power to make war and peace eliminates the chief danger of inter-state disputes resulting in war. The state government, loses not only its motives for war, but also the means of waging it successfully.

The knife edge is removed from disputes between states in a union because the citizens of each state are also citizens of the union, have the same control over both, and inevitably rate higher the citizenship that opens the wider field to them, lets them move freely from state to state, and gives them their standing in the world. When a man is equally sovereign in two governments as he is in a union, disputes between these two agents of his tend to make him an arbiter instead of a partisan.

History is even more reassuring than reason in these regards. For example, there were many disputes—including eleven territorial ones—among the Thirteen American States during their league period. War threatened to result from some of these disputes, and this danger was one of the reasons that led them to shift from league to union. All these disputes lost in explosiveness after union, none of them threatened war thereafter. Supreme Court decisions settled them without the theoretical danger of a state defying the Court ever actually arising.

There is no example in the history of the American Union of a state refusing to accept the Court's decision in an interstate dispute, of seriously threatening to use force against another state. A state that contemplated such action in the American Union could not gamble on being left to fight it out with the other state as could Italy with Ethiopia, and Japan with China in the League of Nations. Each state government knows that, should it resort to force, it would change its conflict from one with another state to one with the government of the United States, which is required by the Constitution to "protect each of them against invasion" and "domestic violence," which has enough armed power at hand to overwhelm at once the strongest single state and which can draw immediately, directly and without limit on the Union's whole potential power. The Union, moreover, can aim its coercive power at the Governor and other responsible members of such a state government as individual offenders. It can act against them personally on the ground that they, and not the people, are to blame, and that as American citizens who are waging war against the Union they are committing treason.

The only memorable conflicts in American Union history in which states figured as parties were both, significantly, conflicts not with other states, as in the American league period, but with the Union government. There was South Carolina's nullification of the Tariff Act; President Jackson's blunt warning that he would uphold the Union law with force against such treason* sufficed to maintain the law. Then there was the attempt of the eleven Southern States to secede which the Union overcame by force in the Civil War.

This last, however, was not, strictly speaking, a test of the Union's ability to enforce its laws but a test of its ability to maintain itself. The fact that the American Union has suffered one civil war in 150 years can not be held against the union system, for secession and civil war can occur and have more often occurred in other systems of government. The American Civil War must be cited, if at all, in favor of the union system. It shows what tremendous resistance

---

* See Jackson's *Proclamation to the People of South Carolina,* "The dictates of a high duty oblige me solemnly to announce that you can not succeed. The laws of the United States must be executed. . . . Disunion by armed force is *treason.* Are you ready to incur its guilt?"

that system can successfully overcome. What is more important, it shows too how swiftly, completely and solidly a union can make peace, even in the exceptional case where it must use its coercive power against a state.

Theory and practice, which alike condemn a league, alike attest that a union works. Both testify that this system is trustworthy, sound. We can not go right if we organize our democracies as a league. If we go wrong in organizing them as a union of ourselves we shall be the first to fail with union.

CHAPTER IX

Isolation of the Germ

I have no other purpose than to place truth before my eyes . . . and to draw the world away from its old heathenish superstitions.—*Leeuwenhoek,* discoverer of the microbe world.

It is only when a man or beast has tuberculosis that I can find these bacilli. In healthy animals I never find them.—*Robert Koch.*

Science has shown that the only sure way to overcome disease is to isolate the germ. It has shown, too, that what seems to be a complicated condition of the body, or separate ills in it, can be cured by the simple act of removing a microscopic germ. Though political science does not have guinea pigs to experiment with, those with remedies for ills of the body politic need to give what proof they can that they have really isolated the germ.

We hold that the major ills of the world today originate in the assumption by democrats that their individual freedom requires them to organize the relations among the democracies on the absolutist principle of nationalism instead of the democratic principle of federal unionism. For clarity we can name the germ, *absolute nationalism,* and the serum that eliminates it, *unionism.* We may now prove isolation of the germ by showing that injection of absolute nationalism in healthy political organisms will give them the disease the democracies now suffer, and that injection of unionism will cure it.

There are two democracies which are themselves composed of many states: The United States with forty-eight and Switzerland with twenty-two. Neither of these groups of democracies has the ills of our world group of fifteen. Switzerland, that is, is afflicted with such things as quotas only in its relations with other states; the Swiss cantons are not afflicted with quotas in their relations with each other. The citizens of each American state suffer as citizens of the United States from the armaments disease ravaging the fifteen democracies, but they are free from it in their relations with the citizens of the other forty-seven American states. *If all the world should sink except the area occupied either by the forty-eight states or by the twenty-two cantons their citizens would no longer suffer from ineffective government, armaments racing, war, trade barriers, monetary instability; all mankind would then be free of these ills.*

One may therefore consider the states within the American and the Swiss areas to be healthy organism, and consider as diseased organism the fifteen democracies.

Inject now into the people of each of these forty-eight states and twenty-two cantons the virus, *absolute nationalism.* Let the people of New York and of New Jersey, or of Zurich and of Geneva, think and act toward each other in terms of the state instead of the citizen precisely as Americans and Swiss now do toward each other or toward the British or French. Let their relations be infected with the same confusion that makes anarchy of those of the fifteen.

Let them too identify the freedom of the citizen with his state's freedom, the rights of man with the rights of nations, the equality of man with the equality of states. Let them found their relations on the state instead of man as unit. Let the citizens of each of the forty-eight and of each of the twenty-two democracies seek their individual freedom in establishing seventy national sovereignties where there now are two, and in guarding these seventy sovereignties as jealously as the fifteen democratic peoples guard theirs now. Who needs human guinea pigs to know that the seventy healthy organisms would then at once suffer the ills of the fifteen?

Consider more closely the effects of injecting the virus, *absolute nationalism,* into the forty-eight. They must then have not merely forty-eight flags where now they have one, but forty-eight armed forces, forty-eight currencies to keep stable by equalization funds, forty-eight national industries, farming classes, internal price levels and standards of living to protect by tariffs, quotas, subsidies, currency, depreciation, —all for the sake of the one thing left them in common: The Rights of Man.

The citizen of the sovereign republic of New York, when

he crosses the Hudson to the sovereign republic of New Jersey, must then stop to have his baggage searched and his money changed. He must have a passport and a visa—for the republic of New Jersey seeks to protect its workers from the immigration peril that cheap Harlem labor forms. To cross this line in his automobile he must first get a customs paper and stop at the frontier to get it stamped. To send a letter, he must pay double postage.

What of the freedom of the individual to do as he pleases with the money he earns? The same 129,000,000 men must then pay enough taxes to maintain not one but forty-eight national governments, foreign departments, diplomatic and consular services, customs and immigration services, armies, air forces, and navies. What would it cost New York to protect its precious corridor to the sea against Connecticut and New Jersey making an alliance against it with the support of Pennsylvania? How big an air fleet would New York need to keep off bombers then? How many Holland tunnels would it need to dig—not under the river for commerce and pleasure but in Manhattan's rock for shelter in war time? What would it cost New Yorkers to seek safety in invading and annexing New Jersey—and thus coming face to face with powerful Pennsylvania?

This injection of nationalism causes the people of the forty-eight to sacrifice their liberty and prosperity in other ways, too. It involves them in all sorts of costly and dangerous political, economic and financial quarrels,—quarrels that centre in mad, maddening, mystic questions of the ratio of one sovereign people to another. By identifying a man's self-respect with what he imagines is the standing of his state in the world, this nationalistic virus turns into a curse even the sense of dignity that freedom gives a man.

We see how the ills of the fifteen can be produced at will among the healthy forty-eight by injecting in them the same nationalism. Suppose we now inject into the fifteen our serum, *unionism.* Suppose the Americans, British, French, Australians, Belgians, Canadians, Danes, Dutch, Finns, Irish, New Zealanders, Norwegians, South Africans, Swedes, and Swiss all begin to think and act toward each other in terms of men and no longer in terms of nations. Suppose that by some miracle we could inject simultaneously into these fifteen peoples, as doctors can inject serum into patients, the simple idea that their freedom requires their union instead of their national independence. They gain by this one costless priceless change all they are now vainly struggling to gain by deepening their dugouts the higher they fly. Does any one

need human guinea pigs to believe that this serum would
effectively cure the fifteen of all those ills which it has already cured among the forty-eight?

CHAPTER X

The Union

When we are laying the foundation of a building,
which is to last for ages, and in which millions are
interested, it ought to be well laid.—*James Wilson* in
the American Union's Constitutional Convention.

American genius does not show itself in its Fords
and Wall Streets; it appears in its vital force only in its
political constitution which balances so well decentralization and unity.—*Count Sforza.*

To balance a large State or society . . . on general
laws is a work of so great difficulty that no human
genius, however comprehensive, is able by the mere
dint of reason and reflection to effect it. The judgments
of many must unite in the work; experience must guide
their labor; time must bring it to perfection, and the
feeling of inconveniences must correct the mistakes
which they inevitably fall into, in their first trials and
experiments.—*Hume.*

To what degree should the democracies in organizing inter-state government apply the union principle of government of the people, by the people, for the people?
Government of the people: Here the principle must be
fully applied: The inter-state government where it governs
at all must govern people, never states. It must have the power
to maintain itself by taxing all the people of The Union. Its
revenue must not depend in any way on the governments of
member states. It must have the power to raise and rule
directly the armed forces of The Union and be entirely independent of the state governments in this field, too. Whatever laws it makes must never bear on the member states as
states but only on all the inhabitants of The Union as individuals. It must have its own independent machinery for
enforcing these Union laws throughout The Union. Insofar

as it governs it must, in short, govern the people, the whole population divided as individuals, not as states.

"Insofar as it governs"—that brings another question. The union principle, we have seen, requires the fields of government to be divided between The Union and member states. Just which shall be the fields where The Union shall govern the people and which those where the nation shall govern them is, of course, a great and abiding federal problem. The answer depends on which government, Union or National, will best promote in any given field at any given time the object for which both were made, namely, the freedom in every sense of the individual. We shall therefore consider this question later when we reach the third point, *government for the people*.

Government by the people: Herè again no exception to the union principle must be allowed in favor of the National government, but some exceptions may well be allowed in favor of the nations as peoples. That is, all the organs of The Union government, legislative, executive, judicial, and the machinery for amending The Union constitution, must be based directly on the people. Their National government must have nothing to do with these organs. But the Union government does not need to be based entirely on the population with the individual taken as equal unit; it can be based partly on the population divided by nations. It must however be based predominantly on the former, as, for example, in the American Union. How the balance between the two should be struck is one of several questions in constitutional mechanism raised by the principle of government by the people; these will be discussed when we reach the problem of method.

Government for the people: This must be fully applied. The constitution should make explicitly clear that The Union is made for the sake of the people themselves, for the individual freedom of each person equally. Practically, this means the constitution should provide (a) a list of individual rights that the people retain and that the government is made to preserve, and (b) a list of the rights which the people give to The Union to enjoy exclusively or to share with the National governments,—the division of powers, in short, between The Union and National governments.

The Bill of Rights which The Union would guarantee all inhabitants would contain those rights of the individual which all the founder democracies now separately guarantee. The people of member democracies that guarantee rights not included in the Union Bill would continue to enjoy them. Union would prevent no nation in it from giving new rights to its citizens. Instead new rights would be expected to grow and spread among the member nations just as woman suffrage spread from one state to another in the American Union till it became general.

THE GREAT FEDERAL PROBLEM

What shall be the division of rights or powers or fields of government between The Union and the National governments?

If to each field of government we apply the test, *Which will serve our individual freedom best, to give The Union or leave the Nation the right to govern in this field?* we find five main rights that we need to give to The Union. They are:

1. The right to grant citizenship.
2. The right to make peace and war, to negotiate treaties and otherwise deal with the outside world, to raise and maintain a defense force.
3. The right to regulate inter-state and foreign trade.
4. The right to coin and issue money, and fix other measures.
5. The right to govern communications: To operate the postal service, and regulate, control or operate other inter-state communication services.

Manifestly, The Union must provide citizenship in The Union. Obviously this brings each of us an enormous gain in individual freedom. Since we remain citizens of our nations in becoming citizens of The Union we lose nothing and only gain. Union citizenship must involve inter-state citizenship in the sense that a citizen in moving from one state to another retains all his Union rights and can change his state citizenship easily. The case for giving the other four rights to The Union is no less clear. We are seeing every day in all these fields that the rights we have granted our National governments to maintain separate armed forces, separate customs areas, separate currencies and separate communication systems have become not simply unnecessary to individual freedom but increasingly dangerous interferences with it.

It is easy to imagine any of the free peoples going to war again to maintain their rights as men. But can one imagine the American, British, French, or any other free people flocking to the colors merely to defend their present practice of taxing without representation each other's citizens who happen to live with them? Can one imagine any of their governments being able to raise an army to fight simply for its right to impose tariffs against the other free peoples?

No free people lacks a proud record of heroes who gave their lives at the stake so that men might have religious freedom. Is there among them any record of heroes who burned alive so that men might have military discipline and wear military uniforms? Do we call liberators or militarists those who fight for the sake of an army or navy, to whom armed force is a glorious end in itself, not a means to freedom, dreadful even when necessary? The free whatever language they speak hold dear the memory of martyrs who died for freedom of speech and of the press. If there be men among them who would sacrifice their lives merely to establish and maintain different kinds of bits of paper representing money or postage, who would hold them dear?

Common sense, however, advises strongly against giving The Union even minor rights that the older and most successful existing unions do not have. The essential thing now is to get The Union established, not to draw a perfect line between the things that belong to The Union and those that belong to the nation. Our immediate aim must be to remove the most immediate dangers to our freedom, and the easiest way to do this is to make no change that is not urgently or clearly needed. Once The Union is established time will remain for other changes.

Our object in uniting, we need to remember, is not to see how much we can centralize government but rather how much we can decentralize it or cut it out entirely as unnecessary. Though over-decentralization in five fields drives us now to Union, it by no means follows that centralization is the friend of freedom. The fact is, paradoxically, that what little centralizing we would do in uniting would really be done in order, on balance, to have more decentralization; we transfer five rights to The Union in order to curb the centralizing tendency in each of our nations which its possession of these rights now causes. We create some new government in order to get rid of much more existing government, to gain on balance more freedom from governmental interference in our lives.

We create The Union to free ourselves from some fourteen governmental barriers to our selling dear and buying cheap, to reduce the expense of booming bureaucracy and monstrous armaments, to cut our way out of government gone jungle. *The acme of decentralization is, after all, complete individual freedom.* It is to come nearer to the democratic ideal where each man governs himself so perfectly that no other government is needed that we make our Union.

The five rights we would transfer to The Union are merely means of defending those individual, local and national rights that democrats hold dear,—means, that is, of defending what decentralization we have attained. Far from weakening these dearer rights, we protect and strengthen them by this transfer. Failure to make this transfer forces each democracy to centralize, to reduce individual and local rights so as to keep these five national rights, to sacrifice the end to the means.

The Union will give *de jure* status to all the existing decentralization that democrats value—to national home-rule for national affairs by whatever system of government, republic, monarchy, or whatnot that each nation desires, to each national language, each national education system, each distinctive trait that makes each nation, and to the whole distinctive system of local liberties and customs and individual rights within the nation for which each nation stands. All these things now really have only *de facto* status as regards the world outside each nation. Only by uniting to recognize and guarantee all these national, local and individual rights can the democracies legalize them even in the democratic world. The practical result of their doing this, moreover, is to make these rights much more secure as regards the outside nations to whom they would remain only a *de facto* claim until these nations themselves entered The Union.

In connection with centralization we need to remember that The Union would be unique among unions because of its colossal material strength. The strongest existing union, the United States, needs now to have much stronger central governmental powers and to develop much more homogeneity in its population than does this Union. The United States needs to insist on more and more homogeneity among Americans, to invade more and more the fields reserved to their states, to put more and more power in the hands of one man, and to provide a growing array of costly meddling central government organs, if its aim is not merely to defend the individual freedom of Americans against foreign centralizers, but to keep the American Union constantly pitted against other powerful free peoples, such as the British and the French. The United States must centralize more and more if it aims to battle all the time economically and monetarily and financially with all the rest of mankind, and to prepare always to battle separately from them by sea, land and air, cannon, gas and bomb. There is no end to the amount of government required when the aim of government is not only to live in world chaos but to keep the chaos alive too.

Not only would our world Union, because of its unrivalled

strength, need homogeneity in its citizenry and centralization in its government much less than does the United States now, but it would gain added strength to protect the rights of its members by this very lack of homogeneity and centralization. By encouraging the existing diversity among the democracies The Union would protect the citizen from the danger of hysteria sweeping through The Union.

How Shall We Unite?

We come to the problem of method: How, concretely, shall we unite our democracies to this desired degree? We can divide this problem in two. There is, primarily, the underlying political problem of putting these general principles into constitutional form, establishing The Union and its governmental machinery. There is, secondarily, the practical problem of meeting the various transitional and technical difficulties raised by transfer of each of the five rights to The Union. The better to distinguish between first things and matters of secondary importance we shall consider the former here and the latter in Annex 2.

The Constitution of the Union

The only detailed or concrete plan that The Union can need is a draft constitution. For the establishment of The Union eliminates many of the problems for which we now think we need plans and planned management, and it provides itself the mechanism—government—for solving the various problems of transition.

The Convention that framed the Constitution uniting the Thirteen American democracies not only framed no plan except the Constitution, but it had no draft even of a constitution when it began, nothing but the broad outline of the Virginia plan for one—and New Jersey and Hamilton soon produced opposing plans. Unlike us they had no existing federal constitution on which to base their planning.

Those who would constitute unions can turn now to many time-tested successes. For reasons that will be seen when we study carefully the American Union I believe that we should turn particularly to the American Constitution and experience for guidance.

The drafters of the constitution of our world Union, however, will have the great advantage of including authorities from every successful democratic union, each of which has its own valuable contribution to make. The Swiss themselves are best fitted to tell what they have learned in uniting solid geographical and historical groups of Germans, French and Italians. The Canadians can tell of their union of French and English, the South Africans of their union of Boers and English,—and in the United Provinces and the United Kingdom the Dutch and English have a much older experience to relate.

These examples may suffice to indicate the rich store of constitutional experience which, since Hamilton cited the passage from Hume heading this chapter, has been placed at the disposal of union constitution-makers. They may indicate too the long tradition and discipline and training in self-government on which our democracies can count to aid them in uniting. We have only to organize The Union of unions. Our constitutional problem is not so much the difficult one of creating as the relatively easy one of selecting, adapting, consolidating, perfecting. It is not the venturesome task of sowing but the safer task of reaping the crop already grown by reason and chance, trial and error.

It would seem now practically necessary to distinguish in The Union territory between the parts that are already fully self-governing and those that are not, and restrict the right to vote in Union elections and to hold elective Union office to those born or naturalized citizens of the former. This would not mean that those born in the rest of The Union would be deprived of the other rights guaranteed individuals by the constitution, nor of the right to vote and hold office in their country. Instead, The Union's policy should be to train them for admission to The Union as fully self-governing nations. It is true that one can destroy democracy by seeking to spread it too quickly and over-loading the state with too many voters untrained for self-government. It is also true, however, that the only way to acquire such training is to practise self-government, and that an old and well-trained democracy can safely and even profitably absorb a much greater proportion of inexperienced voters than seems theoretically possible.

This whole problem is one of striking a balance, of deciding what proportion of the peoples that for one reason or another are politically weak shall be admitted at the outset to full citizenship. Common sense would seem to suggest both that we start with a low proportion, and that we explicitly state at the start that The Union's aim shall be to increase this proportion thereafter as much as prudent experiment justifies. A policy that deliberately and unequivocally aims at preparing everyone in The Union for full citizenship should transform existing colonial psychology and make the colonial problem much easier to handle. It would be treating the politically inexperienced peoples much the same as we treat politically our own immature sons and daughters. These know that when they come of age they will enjoy full citizenship rights, and this great section of the unfranchised has never rebelled against the state nor taken the attitude the colonially unfranchised often do.

The Union Legislature

The chief technical problem in drafting the Union constitution is the organization of its governmental machinery, its legislative, executive and judicial departments, and its mechanism for amending the constitution.

Practice is strongly in favor of a two-house Union legislature with one house based completely on the population and the other modifying this principle of equal men in favor of equal states. If the constitution allows one representative for every half million or million citizens, the result would be roughly:

Australia	13	7	Norway	6	3
Belgium	16	8	Sweden	12	6
Canada	21	11	Switzerland	8	4
Denmark	7	4	Union of So. Africa[1]	4	2
Finland	7	4	United Kingdom	93	47
France	84	42	United States	258	129
Ireland	6	3			
Netherlands	16	8			
New Zealand	3	2	Totals	546	280

Those who fear this would give Americans too much weight in the House need to remember two things. One is that this weight would diminish with every new democracy that entered The Union. The other is that there is no more danger of the American deputies or those from any other nation voting as a bloc when elected individually by the people of separate election districts than there is of the New York members of Congress or the Scottish members of Parliament voting as a unit now. Party lines would immediately cut across national ones in this Union as in all others.

As for the Senate, its main purposes are to safeguard the less populous against the more populous states, the state governments against The Union government, and the people of The Union against over-centralization. In the American Union the method of achieving this purpose consists partly in

[1] Based on the white population since Negroes there lack the right to vote.

allowing two senators to the people—not the government—of each state, no matter what the number of people in it may be. This might be copied in our Union. The difference in population between the United States and New Zealand, the most and the least populous democracies in our Union, is proportionately about the same as the difference between New York and Nevada.

For my part, however, I would favor a slight modification of this part of the American system. I would allow two senators to every self-governing nation of 25,000,000 or less population, two additional senators for every additional 25,000,000 or major fraction thereof up to a total population of 100,000,000, and thereafter two more senators for each 50,000,000 or major fraction thereof. This would give two senators to each of the fifteen democracies except France, the United Kingdom and the United States, the first two of which would have four and the third would have eight. The results of the two systems may be seen below:

Australia	2	2	Norway	2	2
Belgium	2	2	Sweden	2	2
Canada	2	2	Switzerland	2	2
Denmark	2	2	Union of South Africa	2	2
Finland	2	2	United Kingdom	2	4
France	2	4	United States	2	8
Ireland	2	2			
Netherlands	2	2			
New Zealand	2	2	Totals	30	40

The American method would give the small democracies a preponderance of five-sixths. The other would give them three-fifths the Senate at the start, and these proportions would grow with the admission of new member nations since nearly all potential members have less than 25,000,000 population. It would seem wise to allow the government of so vast a Union as ours to draw more than the American system permits on the experience of the democracies most accustomed to government on a big scale, so long as the Senate's function of safeguarding the small democracies and decentralization is not thereby endangered. Either way the Senators would be elected at large by each nation, and each senator would have one vote.

PARLIAMENTARY OR PRESIDENT GOVERNMENT?

There are obvious arguments for the parliamentary and for the presidential system of government. The former is more responsive, the latter more stable. One can argue that in this new venture of establishing union on a world scale, and among so many historic nations, the first aim must be stability. Once The Union is firmly established its government can be made more responsive when the need becomes insistent, whereas if The Union is so responsive at the start as to be unstable it may be too late to remedy this defect and keep The Union together. It is safer to cut cloth too long than too short. Moreover, the establishment of The Union eliminates so much of the work of government today as to make responsiveness less necessary.

On the other hand, one can argue that by eliminating all the burden and waste of unnecessary government and by generally freeing the individual we stimulate enormously the most powerful sources of change. The drafters of the American Constitution had no way of knowing how rapidly the United States would grow under the free conditions they provided. We know now from this experience how conducive individual freedom is to rapid growth, invention, discovery, change in everything. We need only look back to see how the tempo of change has been accelerating every generation since government began to be made on the principle of the equality of man and for the Rights of Man. We cannot make this Union without speeding proportionately the tempo of change. Prudence once required for freedom stable rather than responsive government. Now prudence demands greater provision for adaptability.

My own view favors a combination of the responsive and the stable, of the parliamentary and presidential systems,— a combination aimed at keeping the advantages of each, meeting the peculiar needs of our Union, and insuring that its government will not seem too strange to any of the democracies. This brings us to the problem of the executive power. Only here do I think that we need to invent or innovate in making this constitution, though not very much even here.

The Executive

My suggestion is that instead of establishing a single executive we vest executive authority in a Board of five persons, each selected for five years, one each year, or each elected for ten years, one every other year. This would assure constant change in the Board and constant stability. I would have three elected by direct popular vote. I think it highly essential that there be some officer or officers in The Union elected by and responsible to the people of The Union as a whole, as is the American President. The other two members of the Board I would have elected in between the popular elections, one by the House of Deputies, the other by the Senate. This should assure a more representative Board. The Board would establish a rotation whereby each member would preside over it one or two years. Three should form a quorum of the Board and it should act normally by the majority of those voting.

The Board, I would further suggest, should delegate most of its executive authority to a Premier who would exercise this power with the help of a Cabinet of his own choosing until he lost the confidence of either the House or the Senate, whereupon the Board would name another Premier. I would give the Board power to dissolve either house or both of them in order to call new elections, and I believe it should also have a power of veto somewhat similar to that which the American President has. I would make the Board commander-in-chief of the Union's armed forces, and empower it with the consent of the Senate to conclude treaties and name all the Union judges.

I would also have it report to the people and the Legislature from time to time on the state of human freedom and of The Union, and on the effects and need of change, and to recommend broadly measures and policies. In short, I would entrust the more general and long term duties of the executive to the Board and leave the more detailed and short term duties to the Premier and Cabinet.

The aim of this system is threefold: First, to assure the supremacy of the people and to provide strength, continuity, stability and foresight in the executive while keeping it responsible to and representative of the people. Second, to reassure all those who would be fearful of any one man having too much power in The Union, or of all executive authority being in the hands of, say, an American, or an Englishman, or a Frenchman. Third, to avoid the unhealthy burden now placed on one man by the American system, while enabling the head of The Union to fulfill the liaison functions which the British royal family do to some extent in the smaller British Commonwealth, and which would be much more necessary in The Union. All members of the Board would be expected to travel through the Union. It would be easy for the Board to arrange rotation whereby one would be visiting the more distant parts of The Union while another was visiting the less distant parts and the other three were at the capital.* Such, broadly, are the aims of the system I suggest. I believe few will object to these

* Where should be the Union's capital? There would be advantages in having a permanent one, and also in having the Legisla-

aims, and certainly I would not object to any other system that promised to secure them better than mine, or nearly as well.

The essentials to me here are that there be an independent Supreme Court, that no controversies among member states be excluded from its jurisdiction, and that the constitution be made explicitly the supreme law of The Union. To attain these ends I would favor copying broadly the method followed in the American Constitution. No doubt there would be controversy over whether the Supreme Court should have the right to invalidate laws as unconstitutional. I believe it should have this right. The essential purpose of this right is, however, to keep the constitution supreme—to keep intact the division between the more fundamental law which can be changed relatively slowly, the Constitution, and the less fundamental law which can be changed relatively quickly, the statutes. It would seem wiser to accept any system that gives reasonable promise of attaining this purpose than to delay or sacrifice The Union by controversy over the question of method.

Connected with the problem of the judiciary is the problem of how the constitution shall be amended. Many of the objections made to the American Supreme Court would be more justly aimed at the American Constitution's amending mechanism. It makes that Constitution too hard to change, too rigid, and it has for me the further disadvantages of being based too much on the states as corporate bodies. All that has been said of our Union's need to adapt itself more quickly to change than the American Union needed to do when it began applies with special force to the present problem. I would suggest that the constitution be amended by majority vote of the voting citizens on proposals that had gone through some preliminary scrutiny, with several choices open as to the kind of scrutiny.

It would be expressly stipulated in the constitution, however, that certain constitutional guarantees, such as the right of each nation to conduct its own affairs in its own language and the right of each citizen to freedom of speech and of the press, could not be lessened without the consent of each nation.

Such are the main lines on which The Union could be constituted. Those who desire to see how these proposals look when actually applied will find in the annexes an illustrative draft constitution containing them. It may give a better idea

ture alternate sessions there with sessions in each of the main parts of the Union. This is one of the many questions best left to the Union to decide.

of them as a whole, and it provides an easy means of indicating how various minor constitutional problems not treated here might be solved.

CHAPTER XII

To Get The Union Now

> The people gave their voice, and the danger that hung upon our borders went by like a cloud. . . . The Statesman declares his mind before the event, and submits himself to be tested by those who have believed in him. . . . The adventurer is silent when he ought to have spoken.—*Demosthenes.*

LET UNIONISTS UNITE

To get The Union the first thing those who want it should do is to say so, and unite for it. The way not to get it is to think: "This idea of The Union is all right, and I'm for it, and though there are lots of difficulties no doubt they can be overcome some way, but you'll never get most peoople to believe in it, they're too prejudiced and unreasonable for it to have a chance, and so what's the use of my doing anything about it?" Individuals who take this condescending view of their fellows condemn themselves and form the main obstacle to their own desires. No one can express the individual's will but himself, and so long as individuals do not at least express their will for The Union it remains unknown, isolated, lost. So long as most men wait for the majority to make known their will for The Union that majority can not possibly be formed.

The Union has this great advantage: Its supporters do not need to wait on diplomats to get it. They need only turn to themselves and their neighbors,—but they must do that. The first necessity then is that Unionists wherever they are should make known their will for The Union and organize their neighborhood, and state and nation, and keep on uniting for The Union, and coordinating their work in all the democracies, until they form the majority needed to get The Union.

Democracy, however, allows policy to be promoted by men individually as well as collectively. Its true source of power is the free individual, and collective action is only one of the ways open to him. Each individual has an interest in

The Union, and democracy has freed individuals to advance that common interest by each putting behind it his own peculiar power. Some individuals have a gift for organizing men, others for organizing thoughts; one can express things in writing, another is excellent in impromptu public debate; there are men with special talent in every field,—trade, production, finance, defense, communications, research, popularization. For the establishment of The Union there is a need and a place for the special talent and special experience of every individual.

The essential is that each individual, without waiting for any one else, begin devoting some of his individual talent to The Union. Let those with a gift for organizing remember that the right of free assembly, which allows them to do the thing they best can do, was established only by union of democrats; let them begin using their gift for the safeguarding and extension of that right by organizing their neighbors for The Union.

There was a time when men with the gift of writing or speaking went to the stake so that other men with such gifts might freely use them. To preserve these rights today those with the gift of writing or speaking need only lend to The Union some of their gift. Each needs but lend a bit of the thing he is richest in and can best afford to lend. If each who profits from the rights of Man gives now his mite as he sees best for the cause that made possible these Rights, he will soon have world Union, and its greater rights for men.

We can get The Union still more quickly by working not only through our individual selves and through our organizations, but simultaneously through our governments. There is much complaint among us that autocracy allows men to act more swiftly than democracy. Autocracy, however, does not allow a people to do more swiftly what *they* will; it allows one man to do *his* will swiftly with the power of millions whom he keeps from even knowing what their will is. Democracy allows no individual the autocrat's speed and power of personal action, but it does allow the majority of men to form their common will and execute it swiftly. Democracy's speed of action is in direct ratio to the common sense of its citizens.

Though we usually form and express our will by votes on election day, we can form and express it any day in letters to the press, and more directly in messages to the representatives we have already elected. We can be certain that as soon as we make known to them our majority will for The Union we shall have our existing organized power—our governments—acting forthwith for The Union. Democracy is not simply government that bears always on the individual, it consists just as much in the individual bearing always on the government.

The democracy that permits a book such as this one to be freely written by any simple citizen and freely read by any individual. makes the speed with which the common will can be formed depend only on the book's truth and clarity, and the need for action. Men will not reject truth that they see clearly,—certainly not when need is opening their eyes. Democracy makes the speed with which the common will is then expressed and executed depend only on the majority of individuals using a microscopic fraction of their energy and money. It provides the citizen with a cheap and simple means—even less bothersome than the vote—of bringing his will to bear at once on his government.

He need only write, telegraph, telephone his Representative. Senator, Deputy, Member of Parliament, Premier, President.

The raindrop on the window seems powerless, but the crudest mill-wheel moves if only enough raindrops take the same canal. It is easier for the democrat to move his government to make The Union than for the raindrop to spin a turbine. Surely democracy which lets the individual do so much so easily is worth the effort that it requires from any man to save it and extend it.

The more advanced democracy is. the less effort it requires of each citizen. but the greater the responsibility on each to do that little promptly. How great a responsibility for man's vast future we each now bear, we may see by first looking backward.

In Man Our Trust

"Ours is not the first modern world—there was Rome." Of all I heard Dean Carlyle say at Oxford this I remember. There was Rome (it came to me long after) and had the men of Rome held the ground that Man had won then for Man. where might not we be now? Had Rome not fallen, would Man have needed 2,000 years to step from Aristotle on to Descartes. and seven generations more to step from Descartes on to Darwin?

Had the men of Rome only held this ground—but Rome fell, and when Rome fell, then fell not only civilized man, but all the barbarians whom they were civilizing, and American Redskins of whose existence they were not aware. When Rome fell, truly you and I and all of us fell down, for then fell down our species. It has not reached today the point it could long since have passed had Rome not fallen.

Fifty generations have lived and toiled and died since Rome fell, and slowly, coral-like, man has raised another and a far better Rome. It is the freest and the most extensive and the most marvelous and the most delicate civilization our species yet has known. Beside it Rome seems as barbarous as the world Rome ended seemed to Rome, and as unfree as our civilization should seem to our children.

With the fruits of past labor, with the slavery fruits of war, Rome bridged streams with massive stone. With the fruits of future labor, with the fruits of plants unplanted, we have flung strong spans of steel across great harbors. In the first Rome men knew how to make one hundred do the work of one hundred. Our Rome has been made possible because, with our greater freedom, we have found how to make one hundred do the work of one thousand by credit—which is to say by faith in our future, by faith in Man.

Thus Man has freed the power in his arm until a child's finger on a button in London can start gigantic machines in Australia. Man has given his legs the seven-league boots he dreamed of in his fairy-tale age. He has come to throw his voice across oceans of which the first Rome never dreamed, to attune his ear to voices coming at once from the same room and from the antipodes, to sharpen his eye until he has discovered and had to name worlds of tiny animals and enormous stars that Adam never saw. Man has freed himself not only to enter the heavens alive, but to fly upside down as the birds themselves can not fly.

Thus have men built up a civilization that seems too solid now to fall. And it is at once the strongest and the most fragile civilization that Man has ever made, the one in which the individual is most independent and dependent. We have not placed our world on the shoulders of an Atlas; we have pyramided our world on credit—on faith, on dependence on our neighbors (and we have for neighbors men not only next door but next continent), on dependence on ourselves, on dependence on Man and freedom for Man. Democracy is based on faith in free and equal Man, faith in Man's vast future.

For ten years now this confidence, this credit, this faith upon which our Rome is built has been crumbling away. Who can guarantee us that this crumbling can go on and our world remain? And if it fall? If it falls, then we can prophesy with certainty. If our democratic civilization falls, then will fall not only Germany, or France, or Russia, but Europe, not only Europe but America, Asia, Africa. The fat and the famished, the advanced and the retarded, the capitalists and the communists, the haves and the have-nots, the unionists and the nationalists,—they will all go down together into new dark ages, they and their children's children, for how many generations?

MAN'S WORST WEAKNESS

Our Rome need not fall. To live and grow to greater marvels it needs but the faith that made it, the faith in Man. Man's worst weakness is that he is always underestimating Man. He has never seen too large, he has always seen too small, too small. He has never had too much faith in what Man could do; he has always had too little.

Since time began, the western world lay there across the sea, but even when Columbus came he saw himself as the discoverer not of a new world but of a new route. The kettle steamed through thousands of years of human slavery; then came Watt—and which would amaze him most today: The automobile, or the Negro owning one? Once a man believed that Man could make a ship go without sails against a river. Other men called his ship *Fulton's Folly*. But he kept faith in Man, in one man,—himself,—and *Fulton's Folly* went paddling up the Hudson. Fulton saw far for his time, but doubtless he himself would have called it folly to believe the oil he used to cure a cold in the head could ever drive gigantic ships across the Atlantic in a hundred hours.

The fathers of the American Republic, the leaders of the French Revolution, the authors of the Bill of Rights, the political liberators of men everywhere had faith in Man— but they had no idea of all the forces they were freeing. They had no idea of all the rapid growth in civilization, all the transformation of the world, all the victories of men over autocracy and Nature that would come from freeing those then called *la canaille*. Washington, Jefferson, and Hamilton, all voiced despair of the American Union even after its establishment, but they are not remembered for their doubts. They are known for what faith they showed in Man.

Man has still to find the limit of what he can do if only he has faith in himself. And yet each generation has seen wonders done by men who believed in Man. Man's greatest achievements have been the work of some obscure man or handful of men with faith in themselves, helping mankind against mankind's stubborn opposition. These inventors, discoverers, artists, statesmen, poets,—each of our benefactors has always had to overcome not only Nature but his own species. And always these lone men with faith have worked this wonder. As Andrew Jackson said, one man with courage makes a majority.

We have seen a village unknown through all the ancient Roman era become in a century Mecca to a world greater than Rome ever ruled, because one man lived there then with faith in himself. We know what marvels one single simple individual with faith in Man can work—one Mohammed, one Joan of Arc, one Gutenberg, one Paine, Pasteur, Edison. What we do not know is what marvels could be done if the fifteen elected leaders of the 300,000,000 free men and women once worked together with the faith of one Columbus. We know that, working together,—which means depending on each other,—the Wright brothers did one of the many things that Man had always dreamed and failed of doing. But the Wright brothers were two simple citizens; they were not fifteen leaders in whom millions of men already trusted.

As I stand aloof and watch [Walt Whitman wrote] *there is something profoundly moving in great masses of men following the leadership of men who do not believe in man.*

Yet the leaders who have believed in Man and have appealed not to his lowest but to his highest instincts have always in the end been not only followed but alone remembered by all mankind. There is nowhere a monument to those who burned Bruno at the stake; there is in Rome a monument raised, in 1889, which says:

To Bruno, the century he foresaw, here where he burned.

As is the dust are all those of our species who said that Man could never bring the lightning down against his other natural foes. Green still is the name of Franklin. Who were those twenty-seven men who, preferring the freedom of New York to the freedom of New Yorkers, came so near to preventing the American Union? It is their opponent, Alexander Hamilton, whose name still evokes eloquence in Europe as in America.

The difficulties that now seem so certain to keep us apart, —will men remember them a generation hence more than they now remember those that seemed to make the Union of Americans impossible in 1787? Will our own children be the first to honor those who kept Man divided against himself, at war with himself and a prey to ignorance, disease, premature death?

DECLARATION OF DEPENDENCE

If we are to save our own world, we need The Union, and we need it now. If we are to save ourselves none of us can dodge or divide his individual responsibility, or delay. But the individual on whom the most responsibility must lie in each democracy is the one who has asked and received from his fellow citizens the post of guardian of their liberties. Among these few, the most responsibility must lie upon the one freely chosen and freely trusted by the most men and women.

For the condition of the whole human species to change immensely for the better, the American President need only invite the fourteen other leaders of democracy to join him in declaring the undeniable: That their common supreme unit of government is the individual free man, that their common supreme end of government is the freedom of individual man, and that their common means to their common end is the union of free men as equals; that Democracy and Union are one and the same; that the responsibility facing 300,000,000 free men today is the one that faced 30,000,000 in 1861 and 3,000,000 in 1787—the responsibility of choosing for themselves and their children whether to slip backward with the misery-making absolutist principle of the sovereignty of nations, or to continue forward with the richest political principle men have ever found, the principle of free union through the equal sovereignty of man. The American President need only ask the others to join him in making this Declaration of the Dependence of free men on themselves and on each other, and in convoking then our Union's constituent assembly.

If he fears that even now men will call his move premature and will not see in time what nationalism means he can recall Isaiah: "A people . . . which remain among the graves and . . . which say, Stand by thyself, come not near to me, for I am holier than thou. . . . These are a smoke in my nose. . . . Ye shall all bow down to the slaughter . . . ye shall be hungry . . . ye shall be ashamed . . . and leave your name for a curse. . . . He who blesseth himself in the earth shall bless himself in the God of truth . . . For behold, I create new heavens and a new earth."

If he fears that men will call him mad, he can reply with Lafayette: "If it be a wild scheme, I had rather be mad that way than to be thought wise on the other track."

He can ask as Lincoln asked on the eve of war: "Can aliens make treaties easier than friends can make laws? Can treaties be more faithfully enforced between aliens than laws can among friends? Suppose you go to war, you can not fight always; and, when after much loss on both sides and no gain on either, you cease fighting, the identical old questions as to terms of intercourse are again upon you."

He can turn then to Washington's Farewell Address, and repeat: "These considerations speak a persuasive language to every reflecting and virtuous mind, and exhibit the continuance of the Union as a primary object of patriotic desire. Is there a doubt whether a common government can embrace so large a sphere? Let experience solve it. To listen to mere speculation in such a case were criminal. We are authorized to hope that a proper organization of the respective sub-divisions will afford a happy issue to the experiment. It is well worth a fair and full experiment."

The President has his responsibility, but we each have ours, too. He must depend on us, as we on him.

There is no need, and there can be no excuse, for democracy and its great civilization to crash from failure to act in time. There is no need whatever for millions more to bow down to slaughter, hunger, shame. We can escape these. We can leave our name for a blessing. We can hasten man's vast future. There is need only that you, too, stand up for The Union now.

*   *   *   *   *   *   *

> *Our cause is ripe:*
> *The enemy increaseth every day;*
> *We, at the height, are ready to decline.*
> *There is a tide in the affairs of men,*
> *Which, taken at the flood, leads on to fortune;*
> *Omitted, all the voyage of their life*
> *Is bound in shallows and in miseries.*
> *On such a full sea are we now afloat;*
> *And we must take the current when it serves,*
> *Or lose our ventures.*
>
> Then, with your will, go on.
> Shakespeare, *Julius Caesar*, IV-iii.

PHILOSOPHY

Of Freedom and Union

One's-self I sing, a simple separate person,
Yet utter the word Democratic, the word En-Masse.

Of physiognomy from top to toe I sing,
Not Physiognomy alone nor brain alone is worthy
   for the Muse,
I say the Form complete is worthier far,
The Female equally with the Male I sing.

Of Life immense in passion, pulse, and power,
Cheerful, for freest action form'd under the laws
   divine,
The Modern Man I sing.

Whitman, opening Leaves of Grass, *1867*

CHAPTER XIII

Of Freedom and Union

If you would be freer than all that has been before, come
listen to me . . .

I swear I begin to see the meaning of these things . . .

I swear nothing is good to me now that ignores
individuals,
The American compact is altogether with individuals,
The only government is that which makes minute of
individuals,
The whole theory of the universe is directed unerring-
ly to one single individual—namely to You . . .

I am for those that have never been master'd,
For men and women whose tempers have never been
master'd,
For those whom laws, theories, conventions, can never
master.

I am for those who walk abreast with the whole earth,
Who inaugurate one to inaugurate all.

I will not be outfaced by irrational things,
I will penetrate what it is in them that is sarcastic upon
me,
I will make cities and civilizations defer to me,
This is what I have learnt from America—it is the
amount, and it I teach again.
> —*Whitman*, By Blue Ontario's Shore.

OF FREEDOM
One can not repeat it too often: There is nothing
so fertile in marvels as the art of being free.—*De
Tocqueville.*

We have too petty a notion of freedom. We are bound to,
since freedom is so great and growing. And yet our under-

standing of it need not be so petty.

We talk as if freedom of trade were simply a problem for the legislator and economist, a matter of freeing trade from this or that tariff or other legal or theoretical barrier. We talk as if neither the steamship that freed man from the accident of wind and the accident of calm, nor the express train that freed the producers of perishable foods from the tyranny of time and northern tables from the monotony of winter, had done anything to free trade. We forget the air-driven drill and the dynamite that enables us, when a mountain bars our road, to take a short cut through it. We forget a host of things that free us from the limitations of tongue and ear and eye, and let seller and buyer find each other swiftly anywhere on earth. Yet trade can lose its statutory freedom and be encumbered by politicians and economic experts with all sorts of man-made barriers, and still grow greater because other men have been freeing it from more stifling natural barriers.

As it is with trade, so it is with everything. The story of the freedom of man, of the freeing of man by man, is the whole story of man. It is the story of the invention of language, of the freeing of man's tongue to tell his thoughts to his neighbor and of the freeing of his ear to understand his neighbor's thoughts, of the freeing of his thoughts from space and time and the tricks of memory and death by the invention of writing. It is the story of the freeing of his tongue, ear, eye, mind by the invention of grammar, and still more by the invention of paper, and still more by the invention of printing, and still more by the discovery of America and of electricity and rubber, and by such political inventions as the freedom of the press and democracy and Union and such mechanical inventions as the steam engine and the locomotive and the high speed newspaper press, and the telegraph, photograph, phonograph, and the telephone, airplane, moving picture, wireless, talking picture and television.

This is not even a meagre outline of the freeing of man (insofar as he is free) in respect of his mind and thoughts and tongue and ear and eye. There is no word in this about the freeing of the eye to peer into the worlds of microbes and of stars, nor the freeing of the ear to the harmonies of music, nor the freeing of the mind from error thanks to logic and from terror thanks to the accumulated experience of generations, nor the freeing of the mind to think honestly about anything regardless of the taboos of society or the self-interest of the body. And when we have outlined this vast field we have only begun.

We have still to tell of the freeing of the power in the

arm of man from the time he extended it with a club or rock on through to where he extends it with a bullet or electric button, the freeing of his lungs until he can cross the ocean in a submarine, the freeing of his skin from cold and heat, of his stomach from famine, of his body and mind from disease,—and when we have told all this our tale of the freeing of man by man remains a fragment. It is a tale that can never be told. This is not only because of its vast range and the intricate inter-relation of every detail to the others and to the whole. It can never be told because in the telling it is growing; somewhere, wittingly, unwittingly, some of the two billion of men and women are at work freeing man, adding to a glorious tale new glories that men will not be free enough to recognize or use, perhaps, for a hundred years to come.

It is a myriad-sided, never-ending task and tale and joy, the freeing of man by man; and it is the myriad-sided, never-ending variety among individual men and women, the rich resources given mankind by the fact that no two individuals are precisely the same, that each forms a distinct combination of character, talent, knowledge, skill, tastes, curiosity, heredity, environment and physical, moral and mental strength,—it is this that allows the task to be advanced and the tale to be faintly imagined and the joy enjoyed. It is because the democratic principle of the equality and rights of man allows mankind to free all this power it has in men, and to let men enjoy themselves freeing mankind still more, that it is the most fertile and powerful political, economic, social, and philosophical principle that men have ever discovered.

The power in this principle lies in its guarantee by society to the individual of the right to do freely that which most interests him, and its guarantee to all other men of their right to judge freely his work.

Government of gasoline and electricity by the people does not consist in every man being able to build an automobile or dynamo, any more than the government of microbes by men consists in every one of us having a thorough medical and scientific knowledge. Hardly more does government of the people by the people consist in every man interesting himself deeply in political problems and trying to work them out himself.

We govern the power in gasoline, first, by insuring any man who is interested in the problem of governing that power the freedom to tackle it as hard as he pleases, and, secondly, by remaining free to pass judgment broadly on his solutions.

One of these engineer-minded men has it clear in his mind that gasoline can be so governed as to run a wagon, but he can not make it clear to the rest of us who are not so engineer-minded. And so to make it clear he makes us the first automobile. When we see it running we then see clearly that he was right. But it still is not at all clear to most of us that his automobile is safer than a horse, or cheaper, simpler, better. The more engineer-minded men, however, see that all this is true, too; in a widening circle they become interested in the problem of man governing gasoline. They fight out among themselves the technical questions, and when and as long as they all agree, we readily follow them. No buyer demands solid tires on a pleasure car, now when all engineers favor pneumatic ones.

But when these men of technical sense disagree they come to us, the men of common sense, and ask us not to solve their problems, but to pass judgment on their different solutions. And through purchase we accord our highest prize in the long run to the engineer who has solved the problem most clearly—for that means he has solved it in a way that those of us who are least mechanically endowed can understand is the best solution.

The government of gasoline by man began with a contraption so simple in its structure that one could see or hear its every organ, but so complicated in its operation that even the genius who contrived it could never be sure of getting home without a horse. Then by the democratic process of freedom mankind developed a machine so amazing that it makes the gasoline not only drive it far faster than a mile a minute but light its way at night, herald its arrival, and stop it shortly,—a machine so complicated structurally that no one genius could ever have developed it and so simple to run that a child can run it. Gasoline is being governed by the people when any man without engineering knowledge can make it take him where he wants to go with a touch of the finger, a touch of the foot, and a few simple rules.

The thing to note is that the human freedom that government of gasoline by the people brings is achieved, first, by freeing all engineer-minded men to tackle this problem, and second, by keeping the rest of mankind free to pass judgment on their work. This system discourages the engineer from turning to the best engineer as his supreme judge. It forces the best engineer to make himself so clear that a moron can see his solution is the best. It insures him that the greater his technical achievement is, the more he will gain the votes of the simplest laymen.

This is noteworthy because this system is the one through which government by the people for the people has been established, insofar as it is established, over everything they govern, whether it be gasoline, electricity, microbes, animals, music, fire, water, wind, earth or light. It is, too, the system whereby government of the people by the people for the people has been or is being established. This last is the most difficult and the most productive of man's problems in government. It means the government of the most powerful of the elements by the most marvelous and unaccountable among them, the government of man himself by man himself for man himself.

The way to solve this problem of self-government is to follow these free principles, while carefully avoiding an error, tricked out as truth, on which despotism, benevolent or malevolent, is based.

So well hidden is this trap that Plato himself fell victim to it. In his argument for government of all men by the wisest men, Plato seems to base his reasoning on the government of sheep by men. The statesman, he said, is the shepherd of the human flock, and since it would be absurd to reason that the sheep should elect and direct the shepherd, the conclusion seems to follow that the democratic theory is absurd. And so Plato divided his ideal state into three specialized classes,—rulers, fighters and farmers. He thought out elaborate machinery to make sure that the human shepherds shall never be responsible to the human sheep but only to other shepherds,—that the philosophers need answer only to the philosophers. And so men less wise and generous defend the principle of government through dictatorship by a single autocrat, or by an hereditary despot, or by some single class of men, whether the propertied or the proletariat, the oldest families or the *giovinezza,* the chosen Aryans or the chosen Jews.

The error in all this is the same. There is a difference between the shepherd and the statesman, a fundamental difference. The shepherd is a man governing, for men, a different animal, the sheep. The statesman is a man governing, for men, these same men.

The fact that in all cases, except that of man himself, the government by man of whatever he seeks to govern, whether sheep or gasoline, is invariably marked by his refusal to obey the governed, does not make this refusal the *sine qua non* or cause of success; it makes it simply a worse trap for human reason. It is not this negative detail that the shepherd and engineer are not answerable to the sheep and gasoline that is essential, but the positive principle that the shepherds and engineers are answerable to other men,—in last analysis to all other men, and not simply to shepherds and sheep-owners, or to engineers and owners of oil wells. Under this principle the supreme judges of the specialists are not the best of specialized minds but the commonest of lay minds. It results that the specialists must bring the government of sheep and gasoline by men to that point of perfection where a child can govern them. Thus does this principle lead to success.

The way, then, to solve the great central problem of freedom,—that of government of the people by the people for the people,—is neither to depend on the bulk of men to work out the solution, nor to make those who are the best political engineers or philosophers, or statesmen or rulers, answerable only to themselves, but to insure man, alone and in society, equally the rights of man. This means allowing any one who is politically-minded to devote himself freely to political problems, while allowing the rest of men,—the engineer-minded, farmer-minded, artistic-, financial-, economic-, business-, doctor-, research-, artisan-, manual-, and other-minded men, the right of passing judgment freely and frequently on his work.

These men do not want to think out their political problems for themselves any more than the man with a bend for governing men wants to work out for himself the problem of the automobile. The man who delights in making the soil grow two ears of corn where one grew before does not want to stop and fumble with the problem of how to distribute the extra ear, or of how to make his own body cease growing a cancer. The cry for leadership in politics is simply the demand by us all that our political inventors and explorers invent and discover for us as all our other inventors and explorers are doing—as each of us who is following his natural bent is doing. We are tired of seeing politicians blame our stupidity when we reject their truths, we want them to get down to their business of making their political truths so clear that a child can understand them.

They need not worry then about our verdict. They need only fear that we will vote so overwhelmingly for their truth as either to handicap by our gratitude their further search for truth, or to cause us to overreach their truth and fall again into error. When our vote is expressed by purchase we vote so readily for the man who makes his truth most clear in automobiles, or oil, or steel, or other things, that we load him now with a tremendous fortune liable to give him a diseased idea of his own importance, or dull his children's enterprise. Or we force them to leave the thing he can best do and try to solve a problem for which he may have no aptitude,—the problem of the distribution of wealth, of making the most of it to bring more freedom to himself and children and everyone by encouraging art, scholarship, medicine, industry, men. When the vote is by applause instead of purchase we give our Lindberghs so much applause that we deprive them of that freedom to live and act as simple folk which allowed them to do their greatest work.

When a Washington's firm grasp of truth liberates us our gratitude is such that, to show our pious respect, we make it heresy to follow his example and meet the problems of our time so boldly as to rebel against the "thus far and no farther" of the past. When a Lincoln makes the equality and rights of man clearer, we are so grateful that we make a myth of a man who was proud of being common; we forget that in so doing we fall into the very fault from which he sought to save us—that of disprizing or dishonoring members of our own species. What Jesus rebuked the Jews for doing to Abraham, the Christians soon were doing to Jesus, and for the same reason, to show their gratitude.

We are so ready to admit any man's truth if it is only made clear enough, so grateful to those who make it clear and so cursed with an inferiority complex about our species, that great teachers and liberators who seek to bring men to a truer concept of the equal dignity and rights of man need to guard against our deifying them more or less, or otherwise emotionally clouding over their central truth,—that Man, as Paine said, is Man's "high and only title, and a higher cannot be given him."

There is no more effective way than this democratic way for each of us to free ourselves from the tyranny of poverty, and disease, and ignorance, and matter, and time. There is no simpler, safer, cheaper way. No elaborate machinery is required: This is simply a question of freeing men so that their nature can most naturally take its own course. Everyone wants to do what gives him joy, and everyone is doing best his share in society when he is doing that which gives him the most joy.

The profit motive? True, it exists, and it is a mistake to rail at it or try to remove it. Whether he measures it in money, power, or whatnot, man will seek profit, and he should, for it is the fuel that moves perhaps the greatest force on earth, individual enterprise. Profit is but the surplus difference between what one puts into a thing and what he gets out of it, and nothing living grows except by getting back all it expends and something more. It is not profit we need weed out but the three evils, too much profit, too little profit, and dead loss,—for each of these dulls or kills individual enterprise. Provide a condition of freedom and security for the individual to develop his natural talent, and let him profit enough materially from his work to live fairly well, and usually he needs little or no further encouragement to bring us the best he has. When he is really bringing us his best, he is not working for money beyond what he needs to live comfortably and do his work.

The proof is that when he finds some way of further freeing us we cannot keep him silent with bribes or even with comforts. He will do without comfort, spend all his money, borrow all he can, slave through day and night, wear himself out, risk his life; he will do anything he needs to do simply to solve a problem he has freely set for himself and force us by our common sense to agree that he is right,— that we *can* free ourselves from malaria by killing a certain mosquito, that we *can* free ourselves from earth and fly. We do not need to encourage with millions in money men who are doing what they can do best; we can not contrive to discourage the men who are doing what they were made to do.

Every revolution, every great human crisis invariably shows that there is far more talent scattered through our species, and in the most unexpected places, than we imagine. There seems to be no limit to the power of individual enterprise, and there is no resource in which we are richer than individual men and women, and none we use less or waste so appallingly.

All manner of means for freeing men are to be found widespread among men. We had no way of divining that the man who could give us paper would be born in China, that an Arab would bring it to us, an Englishwoman would give us a Turk's idea of vaccinating against smallpox, an Italian would give us wireless, a German Jew would find the cure of syphilis with the help of a Japanese, and that Negroes instead of white men would be the first slaves to establish an enduring republic of self-freed slaves. No one could have predicted that a Pole would be the writer who would bring the salt of the sea best in English to the English, or that a Dutch dry-goods merchant would be the man to make the lens that freed our eyes to discover the microscopic world. We can no more tell today what bargeman on what river will rise to steer our freedom through a dangerous conflict than our great-grandfathers could tell that a lanky Mississippi raftsman would be the man to save the first great union of the free.

We have no way of telling from what family, nation, race or class our future liberators will come, or from what farm, village, city, country, empire. We have no way of knowing that our cook will never change one day into a poet, our miller into a chemist, our farmer into a flier.

Yet there are some things we know, for they have been proved a million times. We know that men will not stay put, that great changes are continually happening in them, that the liberating genius of man is concentrated in no family or place but is scattered generously through the whole species. We know a ray of it was here yesterday, there today. We can divine only that it may be somewhere else tomorrow. We know that not even one beam of it is the monopoly of any man.

We know that out greatest liberators are those who make their liberating truth most clear to all of us. Their greatness is in proportion to the speed with which they can get us voluntarily to absorb and assimilate their truth as fully as they have themselves. The sooner they can free us from the need of their expert services, the more they allow us to build further on the top brick they have laid, until that top brick becomes indistinguishable from all the bricks above and below and around it.

We are beholden the least to those who seek to maintain themselves longest in a position of superiority to us and convert a truth they have found into a permanent source of tribute to themselves. Our true benefactors never seek to impose themselves or their children on us, never seek in any field, political or other, to be answerable to us only once for all time, or to alienate in the slightest those inalienable rights of man that allowed them to do themselves whatever they have done. The mark of the spurious liberator, of the autocrat in every field, is the desire to make oneself more indispensable to mankind. We know that our true liberator frees us more and more from dependence on him and seeks only to enable others to outstrip him,—he is a man of the great, proud line of Whitman:

> I am the teacher of athletes;
> He that by me spreads a wider breast than my own
> proves the width of my own;
> He most honors my style who learns under it to destroy
> the teacher.

We know all this, and in our hearts we know, too, that for each of us to gain the most freedom we must all keep all the doors to life forever freely open to every man and woman.

At the heart of our freedom, then, lies the democratic principle of the equality and rights of man, the freedom of the individual to follow his natural bent and to bring his findings to mankind for judgment, and to pass judgment on the findings of his fellows. And at the heart of the rights of man lies the freedom of speech and of the press. Do you still think that freedom of speech and of the press is concerned simply with politics and words? Read then this letter written by the School Board of Lancaster, Ohio, in 1826 and unearthed in 1920 by the *Cleveland Press*:

> You are welcome to use the schoolhouse to debate all proper questions in, but such things as railroads are impossibilities and rank infidelity. There is nothing in the Word of God about them. If God designed that His intelligent creatures should travel at the frightful speed of 15 miles an hour by steam, He would have clearly foretold it through His holy prophets. It is a device to lead immortal souls down to hell.

The glory of Elizabethan England to me is Peter Wentworth. He was the one who reminded the House of the rumors of what the Queen would do to those who opposed certain bills, and of her messages commanding Parliament not to consider certain measures, and who then spoke out: "I would to God, Mr. Speaker, that these two were buried in hell, I mean rumors and messages." For this the House itself sent him to the Tower. When he came back a year later he spoke again for the right to speak freely in at least the House of Speech, and again he was sent to the Tower.

The glory of Elizabethan England is likewise John Stubbs and his printer, and those who stood with them. John Stubbs wrote a pamphlet protesting against Elizabeth's proposed marriage with Alençon, and for this he and his printer were condemned to have their right hands cut off. The lawyers and judges who protested were put in the Tower, and the right hands of John Stubbs and his printer were cut off at the wrist by a knife driven through with a mallet. With his left hand John Stubbs then waved his hat and cried, "God save the Queen!" And though her Star Chamber might a little while continue to assert the need of limiting "the excessive multitude of printers," her cruelty shocked and his fortitude encouraged people, and their children rose up in one hundred years and made the first king subject to the first Bill of the Rights of Man.

And now their children's children and all of us may go freely to the National Portrait Gallery in London and find one small room on the top floor big enough not only for Elizabeth and the great men of her time (not Wentworth, not

Stubbs), but also for Henry VIII and the greater of those whose heads he had cut off. But as we go on down chronologically through the rooms and centuries, and the crude absolutist method of men governing men by cutting off their heads and hands gradually gives way to men governing men by the free speech principles of the Wentworths, and by the free press principles of the Stubbses, and by the other rights of man they led to, the scene changes.

Where there were only a few portraits for each reign, and these, mainly of rulers, generals, priests, the number and the variety of portraits grows more and more, until on the ground floor we find the nineteenth century needing room after room to house the great of England. There the rulers, generals and priests become a minority amid the Shelleys and Jane Austens and Butlers, the Disraelis and Gladstones, the Benthams and Mills, the Stephensons and Faradays and Listers and Huxleys and Darwins.

Such is the great flowering of the genius of man that every people has enjoyed and is enjoying as they have enjoyed and are enjoying equally the rights of man.

In another gallery I looked at Leonardo's works after coming up through the centuries at the Italian Art Exposition in Paris in 1935, and it dawned on me that before his century the best eyes in Italy had been blind to the beauty in the play of light, blind to shadow. I walked back then through the centuries seeking shadow: Cimabue, Giotto, blind to shadow; Uccello discovering perspective but ignoring shadow; then here and there a painting with here and there a shadow,—the shell in Botticelli's *Birth of Venus* casting a shadow, but not Venus nor any of the figures nor the trees, no real perception of shadow there. Shadow always everywhere, and everyone blind to it until somehow one man saw shadow clearly, and then everyone thereafter seeing shadow.

Why did we need so long to make the simple, invaluable wheel? Could man ever help but see the circular? Nature is all curves. It would seem that man must have made the wheel long before achieving that miracle of abstract reason, the brick. For men could not see so easily the square, cube, or straight line in Nature. These man created. Yet America knew the square before Columbus came, but not the wheel. Ages before mentioning the wheel, the Bible celebrates in the tale of Babel not only the confusion of tongues but the discovery of how to "make brick" and all it meant to men. To understand what a marvel the common brick is, one needs to read the Bible afresh: Since "this they begin to do . . . now nothing will be restrained from them" while "the people is one" and "have all one language,"—not even the achievement of the great ideal that mankind then at once magnificently set out for: The building of "a city and a tower whose top may reach unto heaven."

The wheel, despite all Nature's hints, also required a miracle of pure reason. To turn the first natural disk into the first wheel one had to see something that was there no more and no less than the straight line. Something invisible, abstract, yet so tangibly there that one needed only to put finger and thumb on it to make all men see—the axis, and wheels everywhere.

The marvelous thing about us is not simply that it took so many men for one to see the axis. It is perhaps even more marvelous that it took only one to see it and demonstrate it clearly for each of us to see it at once, and for all of us to keep it forever after. It is this marvelous power in our species that democracy harnesses through its equal interest in and equal freedom for every individual.

Underlying alike the brick and the wheel is a greater miracle—Man's creation of the straight line. How could it have taken us eras to see a truth so simple and precious as the straight line? How many simple things of truth, of beauty, of priceless value, lie today around us all, unseen, awaiting the marvel of sight by some one becoming sight by all?

Surely in such a world we can not fail to keep building on the simple truth of which we have had such proof: That Man's vast future lies in the democratic philosophy that would give every one an equal chance, an equal freedom to tell us all whatever truth he alone has seen or believes that he has seen, an equal obligation to express his truth with that clarity and simplicity that makes us all see it and thereby proves it true, and an equal right to refuse to accept whatever one alone still doubts is true, an equal veto against whatever one alone believes is false.

OF CAIN AND ABEL, SOCRATES, JESUS AND MOHAMMED

To understand is what is hard. Once one understands, action is easy.—*Sun Yat Sen.*

We learn to understand the new by studying the old.—*Confucius.*

We shall now combine our individual power into one great power which is this confederacy and we shall therefore symbolize the union of these powers by each nation contributing one arrow, which we shall tie up together in a bundle which, when it is made and completely bound together, no one can bend or break . . .

> This bundle of arrows signifies that all the lords and all
> the warriors and all the women of the Confederacy
> have become united as one person.—*Laws of the
> Confederacy of the Five Nations, or Iroquois Indians.*

Man's freedom began with men uniting. Both love of kin
and love of country have served our species as a means of
freeing man by uniting men. Blood patriotism built the family into the nomad tribe and allowed man, through the
taming of the horse, sheep and cow, to free himself from
some of his natural limitations. As he freed himself from
subjection to the accidents of the hunt, he settled down
and land patriotism rose to free him and his beasts from
Winter's hunger and cold and from the accidents to which
the hunter and nomad herdsman are prey. It grew through
blood barriers, brought tribes together, tied the nomads not
only to the land but packed them together and built the
City. It grew through centuries of warfare between nomad
and husbandman, which (as I learned from George Cram
Cook one day in the ruined temple of the Delphic oracle)
are compressed in the tale of Cain and Abel.

Cain was the first man known to love his country. Before
his time there was no fatherland. There was only father.
The nomad patriot abhorred the thought of being bound to
the land where he happened to be born. He roamed the earth.
Love of a common father and common aversion to the land
held together the nomad tribe. Then came Cain.

Cain settled down. "Cain was a tiller of the ground." He
brought to the Lord Judge the fruits of the soils as his offering. But Abel remained "a keeper of sheep," and "brought
of the firstlings of his flock and of the fat thereof. And the
Lord had respect unto Abel and to his offering: But unto
Cain and to his offering he had not respect. And Cain was
very wroth." Neither the Judge who in favoring the conservative had promised the innovator, "If thou doest well, shalt
thou not be accepted? and . . . thou shalt rule over him," nor
the tribal bond of blood could prevent the conflict. "Cain
rose up against his brother, and slew him . . . and builded a
city."

The city united more men in a closer compass than the
flock or farm, and with it rose great empires, Nineveh,
Babylon, spreading through mankind the fruits of the
city's work in freeing man from his limitations. So it was
that human wisdom grew strong and brave enough in Athens
to take "Know thyself" for motto and to begin to think and
talk in terms of individual freedom and universal union. It
looked upon the slaves tilling the earth and revolted against

the dogma that man's freedom must remain bound to the soil. It questioned the love of country on which the city's civilization was based, and asked, as did the philosophers whose horrified countrymen called them Cynics, dogs, "Why should I be proud of belonging to the soil of Attica with the worms and slugs?" And it realized primitively, as Plutarch said of Alexander, "the Cynic ideal on its political side by the foundation of universal empire."

"The Cynics," says Professor Barker, "were descended from Socrates; and the Cynics were cosmopolitans, who found their own reason and knowledge sufficient for their needs, and, craving no guidance or instruction from any city, took the world to be their home." With them, as he points out, "two new ideas are entering the world, both destined to a long history—the idea that all men are naturally equal, and the idea that they are all by nature brothers in a single human society."

Then came Jesus teaching men to render unto Caesar the things that are Caesar's and unto God the things that are God's,—to decide each in his own conscience which things are Caesar's and which things are God's, to decide each for himself what he owes to the gods of other men and what he owes to the god within himself.

> Jesus went unto the mount of Olives . . . saying, I am the light of the world: he that followeth me shall not walk in darkness, but shall have the light of life.
>
> The Pharisees therefore said unto him, Thou bearest record of thyself; thy record is not true.
>
> Jesus answered . . . Though I bear record of myself, yet my record is true . . . And ye shall know the truth, and the truth shall make you free.
>
> They answered him, We be Abraham's seed, and were never in bondage to any man: how sayest thou, Ye shall be made free?
>
> Jesus answered them, . . . I speak that which I have seen with my Father: and ye do that which ye have seen with your father.
>
> They answered . . . Abraham is our father.
>
> Jesus saith unto them, If ye were Abraham's children, ye would do the works of Abraham. But now ye seek to kill me, a man that hath told you the truth, which I have heard of God: this did not Abraham . . . Your father Abraham rejoiced to see my day.
>
> Then said the Jews . . . Thou art not yet fifty years old, and hast thou seen Abraham?
>
> Jesus said unto them, Verily, verily, I say unto you, Before Abraham was, I am.

Then came Mohammed to be hailed too as a liberator, and first by the slaves, and first of all by woman. He came into a society where a man inherited his mother as part of his father's property, wore sackcloth and ashes when a girl-child was born, and buried alive in the sand the sex that brought poverty-ridden men more mouths to feed. Mohammed stood out against that society "in the name of the Compassionate, the Merciful, the most Beneficent, who hath taught the use of the pen." He freed the girl-child from burial alive, and her mother from slavery, and through him tens of millions of women received economic rights that Christendom did not allow until modern times. He freed not only man from the myth that he was made of earth but woman from the myth that she was made of man. Mohammed rationally taught, "He hath created the sexes, male and female, from the diffused germs of life," and he preached a single standard of morality for man and woman.

The truth that Jesus brought to make men free was so misunderstood that his followers soon converted one of the most liberating of doctrines into an authoritarian institution and a dogma that has kept many men and women from striving after and enjoying truer and freer lives by promising them paradise when they die if only they suffer till then the evils of this world. The freedom Mohammed brought was corrupted until Mohammedan came to connote the seclusion of woman, and Islam, which means "to make peace," came to connote Holy War.

Yet the teaching of Jesus with its appeal to the individual and to all mankind, instead of to the rulers of men, or to this or that tribe or nation of men, survived to do great service to human freedom. So, too, with the teachings of Mohammed: They led to the wisdom of many of the Cynic and other Greek philosophers being saved from the Christians, and to the printed Bible being made possible by the bringing of paper from China to the West, and to Voltaire pointing to the Turks, when he wrote his *Essay on Tolerance,* as an example for the world to follow.

Like the means of uniting men that preceded it the modern dogma of nationalism is but an idea of men, no more, no less. It is a combination of the patriotism of blood and patriotism of land, of the ideas of *jus sanguinis* and *jus soli* as the lawyers who try to separate them say,—a confused and confusing mixture of our throwback to the nomad bound to his beasts and to the peasant bound to the soil.

It is historically a *parvenu.* It was not known in the time of Jesus nor during the long centuries when what a European believed about God mattered more than his blood or land. As for the Moslem world, until the Turkish Republic was established Islam asked the traveller for his religious belief rather than his nationality; it organized men politically in its empires by religions and not by nations. There was so little nationalist patriotism in the great century of discovery that scarce an important explorer sailed under the flag of his birth, and a Portuguese captain, Magellan, angry when refused an increase in pay in Portugal, went over to Charles V of Spain, and, to prove to him that the Spice Islands were not in the zone the Pope had given Portugal, set out on the voyage that proved the world is round.

Nationalism really began to flourish only in the nineteenth century when it did for freedom the great service of uniting the numerous petty states of Italy and Germany into two great peoples. It rose as a means of securing those wider and stronger political organizations which the steam engine and other inventions were making more and more necessary. It rose too as a democratic offshoot, as a lever for supplanting absolute royal sovereignty with popular sovereignty, and alien rule with home rule.

Nationalism reached its crest early in our century when the major nations were united to the point where further application of this principle was bound, because of the multiplicity of small nations in such states as Austria, Russia and Turkey, to begin dividing the world more into small compartments than integrating it on the greater scale that the gasoline engine and electrical and other inventions were making increasingly necessary. Since nationalism united men by making all-important, not Man's need of union, but things separating one group from others, it could not possibly unite into one state the groups it had united as nations, except by the imperialist methods to which the greater nations turned. Its stress on points of difference between nations, once this stress had brought most of their nationals together, could only keep mankind divided and make for greater misunderstandings, quarrels and wars.

Nationalism's main positive, constructive, integrating work being done, all the human force and sentiment and gratitude which its liberating work had gathered behind it could only pour into and operate the negative, destructive, disintegrating principles inherent in it from the start. And so we had the World War of Nations, for the place in the sun of big nations, for the rights of small nations to independence and self-determination, and, as the need of organizing the world to prevent a return of this nationalist inferno grew more imperious, for a league of nations.

This period of transition was marked, as all such periods must be, by both the forces involved, by the one ending and by the one beginning. The constructive, liberating side of nationalism in its death agony served human freedom by creating in the League and International Labor Organization and Court and Bank the first such world institutions to live, and by thus preparing the way for The Union of free men.

It served human freedom in other ways too. It replaced the remaining hereditary autocracies in the West—Russian, German, Austrian and Turkish—with more democratic governments. It restored to the human equality and dignity that all men crave such peoples as the Poles and Czechs, whose position became intolerably inferior once the theory of nationalism succeeded religion and dynasty as the basis of politics and the popular criterion of liberty. It gave new life to other peoples such as the Chinese and Turks and made them a better medium for their own westernization than imperialism could possibly have been.

But when all is said, it remains true that in our generation nationalism reached its logical limits, its constructive elements began to wane and its destructive ones to wax, until its spiral definitely turned downward. It is operating less and less to bring men together and more and more to keep men apart. It has turned against both society and the individual, it has changed masters and quit serving the freedom of man to serve the freedom of the state—as was shown so strikingly when 3,000,000 Sudetens were deprived of their individual freedom and delivered to autocracy in the name of democratic self-determination. Like everything that has outlived its usefulness nationalism has changed from a beneficent into a maleficent force.

The political theories which the tribesman and the countryman and the nationalist represent have the same motive and method. They seek to free men from the tyranny of accident by uniting them, and they try to unite men by subjecting them to the accident of how or where they happened to be born. They make this accident the all-determining tyrant for each individual by circling it with magic or mysticism.

Nationalism was saved for a while from its basic irrationalism by its early connections with democratic rationalism. Its rapid degeneration now may be seen from the way it is galloping back behind Guide Hitler to the nomad's belief in the superiority of the tribal blood and tribal gods. Such priestcraft may still be necessary among the more backward peoples—and it is for each people to say for itself through its institutions and its leaders how politically backward it is.

But while nationalism was growing, there was also growing up another means of uniting men, democratic Union. It stemmed from Socrates and Jesus rather than from Cain and Abel. It grew out of the Renaissance of that democratic appeal to reason that produced Greek philosophy and made Athens great in the days when Pericles said, "These things are made for men, not men for them." It rose too from the Reformation that sent the individual back from authority to the Word itself, to its doctrine that "the sabbath was made for man, and not man for the sabbath," and its insistence on the equality of the soul of man and the importance of the humblest person.

It came up with the English and the American and the French Revolutions to unite men for their *Bill of Rights,* for the principle that *all men are created equal,* for the ideals of *Liberté, Egalité, Fraternité.* The men it has freed no longer need mysticism to keep them together. They need only Union now to bring them all together to free mankind still more. They have now enough experience behind them and intelligence in them to understand that freedom lies in free men freely uniting, trusting in each other and depending on each other. They are mature enough to understand that the way to man's freedom can not possibly lie in worshiping the accident of birth. They know that freedom for each can lie only in men freeing all the billion possibilities that the billions of men can alone supply for the billion-sided task of freeing man from accident's arbitrary rule. They know that to free man from the accident of death they must begin by freeing his mind from the accident of birth.

OF UNION

Liberty and Union, now and forever, one and inseparable.—*Webster.*

There never was an independent man, or nation, or empire, and there never will be. To think these possible is foolish. It is worse to believe that one has achieved them, to glory proudly in one's independence or his nation's. It is shameful.

There is no shame in admitting one's dependence on his fellows, and the dependence of one's nation on one's species —dependence not only on the living but on the billions and billions of men who have brought us painfully up. We need not blush to remember that in the sweat of arms like ours was paved the path on which we stroll, that through a human patience perhaps surpassing ours our enemy the wolf was made our friend the dog, that we owe much to the boldness of Xerxes in defying the gods by throwing the first bridge across the Hellespont, and to the courage of the Spartans at Thermopylae, and to the wisdom that Socrates by his way of dying carried far beyond the grave.

We need not hang out heads in recognizing that minds and hands like ours are somewhere in nearly everything we see, and are protectingly around us wherever we may be, that they discovered the microbes that cling to fingers and made the waxed paper and invented the machines to put it round the food we announce "no human hand has touched." There is no shame in being mindful of our dependence on the men who today are tapping the rubber tree in the tropics, braving the explosive gas of the coal mine, feeding the hungry silk-worm, watching the whirring spindles, cleaning the streets and the surgeons' lances, tracking storm to its Arctic lair and fever to its African marsh, guarding the thoroughfare we crowd and the lonely reef that lies in ambush for us.

The shame lies instead in forgetting all we owe our species, exaggerating what little mankind owes to us, combining ingratitude, conceit and usurpation to make a patriotic virtue and profess that we are self-made and independent. The shameful thing is for a man to think that mankind is in his debt when the balance is struck between what mankind has done and is doing every day for him, and what he has done to make his species freer and happier. It is still more shame-ful to act as if mankind were so much in his debt as to justify his receiving, and his children and his children's children receiving, millions more than other men, or political, social or other title and position whose possession needs no further justification—no matter how many other benefac-tions other men confer thereafter on society. The shame is not lessened when such delusions of grandeur are enjoyed by masses of men instead of by individuals, when a whole nation assumes that it has given more than it has received, that there is something naturally superior and peculiarly sacred in it, that it is the Elect of God or the Chosen People, that it was meant to be the lord of others. These are the things that are shameful in men, and they are shameful be-cause they are so tawdry and false and unworthy of a species whose name gives us the adjective, *manly*.

The freedom of man goes hand in hand with the inter-dependence of men, whether organized or tacit. This is true in every field, it has always been true, and the more our free-dom and self-reliance have grown, the more inter-dependent we have become, and the more we have needed union with more men.

It is a common thing to find a man who treats all the rest of us as stupid, as obstacles in his path from which he longs to be free. Each of us has sometimes felt that way about some, or all, of the rest of us. It is natural that each man should always be ready to indict the mass of mankind as stupid. We are all ignorant and awkward and stupid in far more ways than we are skilled and wise. That makes us esteem more our own wisdom where we have it. The fewer the things in which we are wise, the more value we set, of course, on our wisdom, and the more irritating becomes the stupidity of our fellows in the field where we are wise.

But the interesting side of this is the other side of the medal, for it is the positive side. Though a man may be stupid in no matter how many things, he is almost certainly more skilled or wiser than most of us in some few things, or at least in some one thing. "In every god there is something divine," Anatole France remarked, and we can add that in every man there is some of Man. I once had a cook who I thought was a hopeless moron until one day she made an apple pie. It was the one thing she knew how to do, it was her specialty, but she could do it so succulently well that one forgave her a heap of other things.

The man who was no good at piemaking would be a fool not to depend on her for apple pies, and the one who could make pies, but not so well, would be a fool not to depend on her for instruction. This example being typical, we can smile while minorities of different experts nearly 2,000,000,-000 strong accuse our (and their) species of a hundred million stupidities. We can be sure our species will survive and each of us will grow richer, wiser, freer, so long as we enjoy this wealth in minorities of experts—and are not so stupid as to try to be independent of any of them.

Put in other terms, the wildest reactionary is never 100 per cent conservative, and the wildest revolutionary is never 100 per cent rebel. Our Neville Chamberlains are the first to rebel at the cut-and-dried methods of diplomacy, our Lenins are conservative not only in their habit of dress but in a host of other things. Conservatism and radicalism partly result from men differing in the velocity of their adaptability to change, and from this standpoint the most hide-bound among us would appear a flighty revolutionist to his own great-grandfather. Some of course in every generation welcome change in general relatively more than others, but usually we are each conservative about many things and actively rebellious against only a few.

But the result of our division into conservatives and rebels is that we each can depend absolutely on our species never lacking plenty of men either to rebel against every conceivable obstacle to the freedom of man, or to conserve every bit of the freedom won by yesterday's rebels until those of today prove the new bit of freedom that they bring is really worthy of acceptance. This may not conduce to our independence, but can we have a better way than this to free ourselves?

It is not our greatest men who think it beneath them to acknowledge their dependence on others. They teach us not to depend on ourselves alone if we would free what is individual in us, but to study diligently other men who are masters, for, as Sir Joshua Reynolds said, "The more extensive your acquaintance with the works of those who have excelled, the more extensive will be your powers of invention . . . and what may appear still more like a paradox, the more original will be your conceptions."

As it is with those lonely venturers, our great men in every field, so it is with those who are pioneers in the narrower sense of the word. If any man can be called independent it is the pioneer who goes out into the wilderness and carves out his home, the man of the type of Mr. Bulow, the Connecticut farmer who took Brillat-Savarin on a turkey hunt in 1794 in the forest near Hartford. . . .

These pioneers of Connecticut were among the first to sacrifice the sovereignty of the state and ratify the Constitution of the United States. Their forebears, the first men to pioneer in Connecticut, Lord Acton notes, "possessed so finished a system of self-government in the towns, that it served as a model for the federal Constitution."

It was precisely in these conditions, when in the American wilderness civilized man was thrown most upon his own resources, that his dependence on his fellows was most driven home to him, and men came to realize that their freedom lay in trusting in each other, in uniting freely on the basis of the equal rights and dignity of each of them. It was in these pioneering conditions that the men of these American colonies, before they constituted their Union, united under state constitutions that form the first written constitutions in history superior to and limiting the government and alterable only by the people themselves.

As the pioneers moved westward for 200 years men had to depend on women to do not only a woman's work but a man's work too,—to seize the reins and drive the covered wagon while the man stood off the Indians, to take his rifle and defend the children when he fell or was away. Pioneering conditions made so clear the dependence of men and women on each other that there finally began in the Rocky Mountains the liberation of half the human race. There never were men more independent than the cowmen and prospectors and homesteaders of Wyoming in 1868, and they were the first to recognize and extend their dependence on women by giving them the vote.

Our freedom has always been inseparably bound to our faith in our fellows, and the more of them we have trusted, and the more implicitly, blindly, we have depended on each of our fellow-men—no matter what race, nation, class or sex —the more we have been rewarded with freedom. Truly of the stuff of dreams is our species made.

Two hundred, one hundred, fifty years ago one finds everywhere in every field far less dependence of men upon each other, and far less freedom. Then perhaps ten or a dozen men entrusted themselves for fifty miles to a stage-coach driver with four or six horses, after making inquiry, and scrutinizing their man. Now a thousand men rush into a train and are whisked off sixty miles in an hour. They may do it twice a day through every year or they may cross a continent without ever going up to the locomotive to see what manner of man is there with his hand on the reins of hundreds of horses, with his eye now on his watch and soon searching vigilantly through the mist for the signal lamps.

They may do this all year without it once occurring to them that they are all trusting their lives to a man at the throttle, and to the unknown men who made his watch, and to the man at the throttle of the train hurtling toward them, and to the maker of his watch, and to distant train dispatchers and their watches and clocks, and to the signal men, and to the brakemen, and to the long line of men who made the brakes and the wheels and the cars and the locomotives, and to the men who made and inspected and laid the rails, and to the section hands, and track-walkers, the bridge-builders, the tunnel-makers. We can not enjoy the freedom from the horse's limitations that a train gives without trusting our lives blindly to the good faith of thousands of unknown men.

And they, in turn, have to trust in millions of passengers having faith enough in the railway to use it. The *Great Eastern,* that forerunner of our Atlantic liners, failed not from lack of room for passengers,—she was longer than nearly all the ocean greyhounds afloat sixty years later,—but because she lacked passengers. She failed because ocean travellers in 1857 lacked faith in steamships, in their makers and their crews and in men generally.

The train and the ocean liner are two of many wonders that are possible only through the willingness of men to depend utterly on their fellow-men. Wherever we go, whatever we do, we need but keep our eyes open to see the same phenomenon of freedom for each man through faith in every man.

It is in every item in our newspaper as it is in every bed in our hospital. Our newspapers, now that they reach to the ends of the earth for men who are interested in and need to know everything on earth, require for their functioning far more confidence all round than ever before, far more faith in unknown men. The statesman, the banker, the businessman who closes his door on the press, who impatiently tries to dodge when the newsmen surround him may not realize, when he suppresses or distorts or falsifies to them the news of what he has been doing, that he is hurting most himself. Yet, however important he may be, he has only a few items of news to give compared to all those he needs to get, and the more he handicaps the newsmen in their work of accurately and quickly reporting the essentials in every field to everyone, the more he contributes to a condition that poisons the air which he himself must breathe.

Our great-grandfathers rarely trusted their lives to men they did not know, our grandfathers did so only sparingly, but we are doing it all the time, many of us nonchalantly many times a day. Yet it is now, and especially among the more trusting peoples, which is to say the freer peoples, that the death rate is far lower and the span of life is growing. We eat and drink almost anywhere on earth without the fear that man once had that strangers might poison him. We pile into elevators and go dizzily down, we dodge through streets crowded with cars more powerful than the monsters of antiquity, we jump into taxicabs without worrying whether the driver may possibly be drunk—and we never suffer half the qualms that grandfather did.

In his time there were never on the roads nearly so many horse-drawn vehicles as there are now horseless ones. When he was out driving in the buggy he did not need to trust that the men driving the few buggies he met would keep to their side of the road and not run into him and kill him. He could depend on the other man's horse and his own horse not colliding even if both drivers went to sleep, and he could be reasonably sure that an accident would not be fatal.

Paradoxically, the more that men depend upon machines, the more they must depend on men, and on more men. The number of slaves who labored up the Great Pyramid is small compared to the world-scattered, ungeneralled army of free men who now help bring each tourist to see that work of autocrats and slaves.

The doing of a book may seem an independent enterprise,

one requiring few hands compared to those needed to bridge the Golden Gate. Yet I would sooner try to count the hair of my head than the men and women who have lent a hand merely on the mechanical side of the writing of this book: The men who felled the trees, who brought them to the paper mill, and mined and smelted its minerals and provided it with chemicals and fuel and grease, who loaned the money to build the mill and provide the machinery for it, who ran the mill and distributed the sheet of paper on which these words are now being written by a typewriter,—and all the world-scattered men who put that typewriter on this desk, among them far away natives who helped bring it bits of rubber and provided its inked ribbon (we must count in, too, the cotton-pickers).

And then there is the host of men behind this desk, this chair, this house, this fountain pen, this ink, and behind the universal postal system that carries this "manuscript," and the machines that set in type every letter in it, and the presses that print that type,—and the tale is neither finished nor complete as far as it goes.

And when we have finished with the mechanical side there would remain the substance of the book. That seems to be something independent, personal, but the book is studded with allusions to only some of those who have lent me a hand. If I sought merely to list all the men and women, great and obscure, known and unknown to me, whom I thank for encouraging me and helping give this book what substance it has, there would be no space left in it. Even to express my thanks I must depend on Lincoln who solved the problem so well when he wrote in his letter to Conkling and the "unconditional Union men" of 1863:

Thanks to all—for the great Republic, for the principle it lives by and keeps alive, for man's vast future,—thanks to all.

I can not even number the individuals, living and dead, upon whom I have had to depend, and upon whom I am glad to depend to bring before your eyes these words:

Let us then all keep clearly in our minds and tightly in our hearts that in Union there is freedom, and that each shall be the freer and happier the more we all recognize our dependence on the individual, on each other and on all our species. We are all the losers when one of us is not doing the work that is joy for him. We are all the gainers when he is doing what he loves to do, for he is then doing his share best. The more deliberately and fully and trustingly we unite with each other and depend upon each other for our freedom, the more we shall solve the problem of so arranging our society that each lives in it more happily and freely. For freedom is like love, the more of it we give, the more of it we can enjoy, and love is like union, too. True love can not do without union, nor can there be full union without love, nor freedom without either, nor either without freedom.

We have too long forgot that freedom and love were born together, and we have yet to learn that they can not live and grow without each other. As a child sometimes sees deeper than a man, so Man, when he was making words for those ethereal solid things that he has never touched and always reached for, saw into them more deeply than we do, and he made his word for *love* his word for *free*. We have too long forgot that we began *to free* with the Gothic *frijon* and the Sanskrit *pri*, which means, *to love*; we have yet to learn that not simply through the Gothic *frijonds* up from the Sanskrit *priyon* for *beloved* but from the very nature of things stem together *friend* and *freedom*.

Man has on earth no one but Man to help him, and what a mighty, what a generous, what a kindly and abiding and dependable friend and liberator is Man to Man. Man has already wrought miracles of Man by Man for Man. These are great, and they are but a hint of those that will be done when our Union opens Man's vast future as each Man pledges each:

Thy freedom is my freedom as is my freedom thine.

Man

Here in a thimble
seed of Man
enough to fill every womb in the land
womb within womb
seed within seed
all in a thimble
Say
what shall we say
of Man?

Myriad myriad
seed of Man
born and dead and back in the land
myriad myriad
still to be sown
and then one day Man shall be grown
Man who shall be
finally free
Then he shall say
        who he is
        why he is
        all he is
        Man.

ANNEXES

Annex 1: Illustrative Constitution

The draft constitution that follows is meant to make the proposed Union clearer by illustrating how the democracies might unite. This draft is not intended to be a hard and fast plan. Practically all of its provisions, however, are time-tested.

The draft is drawn entirely from the Constitution of the American Union, except for (1) a few provisions that, although not drawn from it, are based on American practice (notably Art. II, sections 1, 2, 4, 5), and (2) a few innovations: These latter are given in italics so that they may be seen at once. Most of the draft taken from the American Constitution has been taken textually, though its provisions have sometimes been re-arranged with a view to greater clarity and condensation, and once or twice they have been made more explicit and somewhat expanded. The Preamble is the only serious example of this last. In the American Constitution the Preamble reads:

We the People of the United States, in order to form a more perfect Union, establish Justice, insure domestic Tranquility, provide for the common Defence, promote the general Welfare, and secure the Blessings of Liberty to ourselves and our Posterity, do ordain and establish this Constitution for the United States of America.

No important element in the American Constitution has been omitted. The draft follows:

ILLUSTRATIVE CONSTITUTION

We the people of The Union of the Free, in order to secure freedom equally to every man and woman now and to come, to lessen ignorance, poverty, and disease, to insure our defense, to promote justice and the general welfare, to provide government of ourselves, by ourselves, and for ourselves on the principle of the equality of men, and to bring peace on earth and union to mankind, do establish this as our Constitution.

Part I

The Rights of Man

Article I.—In the individual freedom this Constitution is made to secure we include:

1. Freedom of speech and of the press and of conscience.
2. Freedom to organize ourselves for any purpose except to change by violence this Constitution and the laws made under it; freedom to assemble peaceably and to ask redress of grievances and make proposals.
3. Freedom of our persons, dwellings, communications, papers and effects from unreasonable searches and seizures, and from warrants unless issued upon probable cause, supported by oath or affirmation, and particularly describing the place to be searched and the persons or things to be seized.
4. Freedom from ex post facto law and from bills of attainder.
5. Freedom from suspension of the writ of habeas corpus except when public safety may temporarily require it in case of rebellion or invasion.
6. Freedom from being held to answer for a capital or infamous crime except on indictment of a grand jury— save in the armed forces in time of war or public danger— and from being twice put in jeopardy of life or limb or liberty for the same offence, and from being deprived of life, liberty, or property without due process of law and from having property taken for public use without just compensation.
7. The right when accused of any crime to have a speedy public trial by an impartial jury of the country and district wherein the crime shall have been committed, as previously ascertained by law, and to be informed in good time of the nature and cause of the accusation, to be confronted with the witnesses against one, to have compulsory process for obtaining witnesses in one's favor, to be under no compulsion to be a witness against oneself, and to have the assistance of counsel for one's defense.
8. Freedom from excessive bail or excessive fines or cruel and unusual punishments.
9. Freedom from slavery, and from involuntary servitude and forced labor except in legal punishment for crime.
10. The right to equality before the law and to the equal protection of the laws.
11. The preceding enumeration is not exhaustive nor shall

it be construed to deny or disparage other rights which we retain.

PART II

THE GOVERNMENT OF THE UNION

ARTICLE II.—THE PEOPLE OF THE UNION.

1. All persons born or naturalized in the self-governing states of The Union are citizens of The Union and of the state wherein they reside. So, too, are their children, wherever they may be born. All citizens above the age of 21, except those in institutions for the feeble-minded or mentally deranged or in prison, are entitled to vote in all Union elections, and to hold any Union office for which their age qualifies them.

2. All other persons in the territory of The Union shall enjoy all rights of citizens except the right to vote in Union elections. The Union shall seek to extend this right to them at the earliest time practicable by helping prepare their country to enter The Union as a self-governing state.

3. *The self-governing states of The Union at its foundation are Australia, Belgium, Canada, Denmark, Finland, France, Ireland, the Netherlands, New Zealand, Norway, Sweden, Switzerland, the Union of South Africa, the United Kingdom, and the United States of America.*

4. The non-self-governing territory of these states and of all states admitted later to The Union is transferred to The Union to govern while preparing it for self-government and admission to The Union.

5. *Before casting his or her first vote each citizen of The Union shall take this oath in conditions to be prescribed by law:* "I do solemnly swear (or affirm) that I will preserve, protect and defend the Constitution of The Union of the Free against all enemies, foreign and domestic."*

6. Treason can be committed only by citizens against The Union and can consist only in levying war against it or in adhering to its enemies, aiding and comforting them. No one shall be convicted of treason unless on the testimony of two witnesses to the same overt act or on confession in open court.

---

* The American Union requires this oath only of naturalized citizens or of citizens entering the Union service or applying for a passport.

ARTICLE III.—RIGHTS OF THE UNION AND OF THE STATES.

1. The Union shall have the right to make and execute all laws necessary and proper for the securing of the rights of man and of The Union and of the states as set forth in this Constitution, and to lay and collect income and other taxes, duties, imposts, and excises, provided these be uniform throughout The Union, and to incur and pay debt, provided that no money shall be drawn from the treasury except by lawful appropriation and that an account of all receipts and expenditures be published regularly.

2. The Union shall have the sole right to

a. grant citizenship in The Union, admit new states into The Union and regulate immigration from outside states and from the non-self-governing territory of The Union;

b. treat with foreign governments, provide for The Union's defense, raise, maintain and control standing land, sea and air forces, make war and peace, regulate captures, define and punish piracies and felonies committed on the high seas, call forth the militia to execute the laws of The Union, suppress insurrections and repel invasions, organize, arm, discipline, and govern such part of the militia as The Union may employ, and punish treason;

c. regulate commerce among the member states and in The Union territory and with foreign states;

d. coin and issue money, regulate the value thereof and of foreign money, provide for the punishment of counterfeiting, fix the standard of weights and measures;

e. own and operate the postal service and own, operate or control all other inter-state communication services;

f. grant authors and inventors exclusive right to their work for limited periods;

g. provide uniform bankruptcy laws throughout The Union;

h. govern any district The Union may acquire for its seat of government or for forts, magazines, arsenals, dockyards, and other needful Union plant.

3. The Union shall have no right to establish a Union religion, grant hereditary or noble titles, levy any tax or duty on inter-state commerce, subject vessels bound to or from one state to enter, clear, or pay duties in another, grant preference by any regulation of commerce or revenue to one state over another.

4. The rights not expressly given to The Union by the Constitution nor forbidden by it to the states or the people are reserved by it to the states respectively, or to the people.

5. The Union shall guarantee to every state in it a demo-

cratic form of government and shall protect each of them and all the territory of The Union against invasion; and on application of the state legislature or executive The Union shall protect each state against domestic violence.

6. Each state has the right to maintain a militia and a police force, but may engage in war only if actually invaded or in such imminent danger as will admit of no delay.

7. Each state has the right to guarantee to the people in it greater rights than those enumerated in this Constitution.

8. No state has the right to

a. abridge the rights, privileges and immunities of citizens of The Union;

b. exercise, except temporarily by consent of The Union, any of the rights given by this Constitution to The Union alone;

c. raise any barriers to inter-state commerce or communications without the consent of The Union;

d. adopt any law impairing the obligation of contracts;

e. enter without the consent of The Union into any pact or agreement with another state or foreign power.

9. Full faith and credit shall be given in each state to the public acts, records and judicial proceedings of every other state in The Union.

10. The citizens of each state shall be entitled to all privileges and immunities of citizens in the several states.

11. A person charged in any state with crime who shall flee and be found in another state shall on demand of the executive authority of the state from which he fled be delivered up to it.

ARTICLE IV.—THE LEGISLATIVE POWER.

1. The legislative power of The Union is vested in the Congress, which shall consist of a House of Deputies and a Senate. Each shall choose its own officers, judge the elections, returns, and qualifications of its own members, determine its rules of procedure, have the power to punish its members for disorderly behavior, to compel their attendance, and to expel them by two-thirds majority; keep and publish a record of its proceedings, meet and vote in public except when two-thirds shall ask for a private meeting on a particular question, vote by roll call when one-fifth of the members ask this, form with a majority a quorum to do business though fewer may adjourn from day to day, act by majority except where otherwise stipulated in this Constitution.

2. The Congress shall meet at least once a year at a regular date it shall fix. During a session neither branch shall

adjourn more than three days or to any other place without the other's consent.

3. Members of Congress shall not be questioned outside their branch of it for anything they said in it, nor shall they be arrested on any charge except treason, felony, or breach of the peace, during attendance at a session of Congress or while going to and from it.

4. No member of Congress shall hold other public office in The Union or in a state during his term, *except in the Cabinet*.

5. The Deputies shall be at least 25 years old, and shall be elected directly by the citizens every *third* year.

The number of Deputies from each state shall be determined according to population, a census being taken at least every ten years, and shall not exceed one for every *1,000,000* inhabitants or major fraction thereof, though each state shall have at least one.

6. Senators shall be at least 30 years old, shall have resided since at least 10 years in the State by which elected, and shall be elected at large from each state directly by the citizens every *eight* years, except that in the first election half the Senators of each state shall be elected for only four years. There shall be two Senators from each state *of less than 25,000,000 population, and two more for each additional 25,000,000 population or major fraction thereof.*

7. To begin with the apportionment of Deputies and Senators shall be:

Australia	7	2	Norway	3	2
Belgium	8	2	Sweden	6	2
Canada	11	2	Switzerland	4	2
Denmark	4	2	Union of So. Africa ..	2	2
Finland	4	2	United Kingdom	47	4
France	42	4	United States	129	10
Ireland	3	2			
Netherlands	8	2			
New Zealand	2	2	Totals	280	42

8. To become law a bill must pass the House and the Senate and be approved and signed by *a majority of the Board.** If *a majority of the Board* shall return the bill with its reasons for not signing it, the bill shall become law only if passed again by House and Senate by two-thirds roll-call majority, and if a *member of the Board* shall ask to be heard by House or Senate during its debate thereon he

* The executive, see Art. V. The United States Constitution gives to the President the powers this paragraph gives to the Board.

shall be heard. A bill not returned by the Board within fifteen days (holidays and Sundays excepted) after presentation to it shall be law, as if signed, unless adjournment of Congress shall have prevented its return. This shall also apply to every order, resolution, or vote to which the concurrence of the House or Senate may be necessary, except on a question of adjournment, and to every expression of The Union's will, unless otherwise provided herein.

9. The Congress shall have the power to declare war, make peace, and exercise all the other rights of The Union unless otherwise provided herein.

10. The Congress shall have the right to admit new states into this Union; but no new state shall be formed or erected within the jurisdiction of any other state nor any state be formed by the junction of two or more states or parts of states without the consent of the state or states concerned.

ARTICLE V.—THE EXECUTIVE POWER.

1. The executive power of The Union is vested in the *Board. It shall be composed of five citizens at least 35 years old. Three shall be elected directly by the citizens of The Union and one by the House and one by the Senate. One shall be elected each year for a five-year term, except that in the first election the citizens shall elect three, and the House shall then elect one for two years and the Senate shall then elect one for four years, and the Board shall then by lot assign terms of one, three, and five years respectively to the three Members elected by the citizens.*

2. *A majority of the Board shall form a quorum, and it shall act by majority thereof unless otherwise provided herein.*

3. *The Board shall establish a system of rotation so that each Member may be President of it one year.*

4. The *Board** shall be commander-in-chief of all the armed forces of The Union, shall commission all officers of The Union and appoint ambassadors, ministers and consuls, may grant reprieves and pardons for offences against The Union, shall have the power to make treaties by and with the advice and consent of the *Premier and Congress*,† and to appoint with the advice and consent of the Senate the justices of The High Court and of all lower Union Courts, and to make any other appointments required of it by law.

The *Board** shall from time to time report to the people

* President, in the United States Constitution.
† Senate, in the United States Constitution.

and Congress on the state of The Union, *its progress toward its objectives, and the effects and need of change,* and shall recommend to their consideration such policies and measures as it shall judge necessary and expedient; it may require the opinion of any one in the service of The Union on any subject relating to the duties of his office.

The *Board** may convene extraordinarily Congress, adjourn it when its two houses cannot agree on adjournment, *or dissolve it or either branch of it for the purpose of having it elected anew as shall be prescribed by law.*

The *Board** shall receive ambassadors and other public ministers.

5. *The Board shall delegate all executive power not expressly retained by it herein to a Premier, who shall exercise it with the help of a Cabinet of his choice until he loses the confidence of House or Senate, whereupon the Board shall delegate this power to another Premier.*

ARTICLE VI.—THE JUDICIAL POWER.

1. The judicial power of The Union is vested in a High Court, and in such lower courts as The Union may from time to time establish by law. All Union judges shall be appointed for life. The number of High Court judges shall be fixed by law, but shall not be less than *11*.

2. The judicial power extends to all cases in law and equity arising under this Constitution, the laws of The Union, and treaties made by it; to all cases affecting ambassadors, other public ministers, and consuls; to all cases of admiralty and maritime jurisdiction; to controversies between two or more states; between a state and citizens of another state; between citizens of different states, and between a state, or citizens thereof, and foreign states, or persons.

3. The High Court shall have original jurisdiction in all cases affecting ambassadors, other public ministers, and consuls, and those in which a state or a foreign state shall be party; in all the other cases before-mentioned it shall have appellate jurisdiction, both as to law and fact, under such regulations as shall be made by law.

ARTICLE VII.—THE AMENDING POWER.

1. The power to amend this Constitution is vested in *the citizens of The Union acting by a majority of those voting on proposals made by two-thirds majority of the House and of the Senate with the approval of three-fifths of the Board, or by two-thirds majority of either House or Senate with the*

unanimous approval of the Board, or by a special constituent assembly established by law, *or by petition signed by at least one-fourth the voters in one-half the states. No state, however, shall be deprived without its consent of its right to have its own language and its own form of democratic government.*

ARTICLE VIII.—GENERAL.

1. This Constitution, and the laws of The Union which shall be made in pursuance thereof; and all treaties which shall be made under the authority of The Union, shall be the supreme law of the land; and the judges in every state shall be bound thereby, anything in the Constitution or laws of any state to the contrary notwithstanding.

2. All persons in the service of The Union, and the legislative members and executive and judicial officers of each state, shall at the beginning of each term renew their oath to support this Constitution.

3. All Union elective offices, unless otherwise stipulated herein, shall be filled on the same day throughout The Union, to be fixed by law; the exact date when their terms shall begin and end shall also be fixed by law, as well as the manner for filling vacancies.

4. All persons in the service of The Union shall be paid from The Union treasury as shall be fixed by law, but the compensation of no judge shall be decreased during his term nor shall that of any elected officer of The Union be increased during the term for which he was elected.

5. Any one in the service of The Union, on impeachment for and conviction of treason, bribery, or other high crimes, shall be removed from office and may be disqualified from holding office again, and if convicted remains liable to indictment, trial, judgment, and punishment according to law.

The House shall have the sole power of impeachment and the Senate the sole power to try an impeachment, and it shall convict only by two-thirds majority of the Senators present sitting under oath or affirmation. The Chief Justice shall preside when a President *or Member of the Board* is tried.

6. No religious test shall be required as a qualification to any office or public trust under The Union, nor shall there be any official Union religion.

ARTICLE IX.—RATIFICATION.

1. The ratification of this Constitution by *ten states, or by*

France, the United Kingdom, and the United States, shall suffice to establish it among them.

Annex 2: My Own Road to Union

The world must be made safe for democracy. Its peace must be planted upon the tested foundations of political liberty.—*President Wilson,* April 2, 1917.

It may be useful to retrace briefly the road by which I have come to dissent now when "it is generally conceded that we should not have entered the last war," and were duped into it mainly for economic motives, when it is the fashion to jest bitterly of "making the world safe for democracy," as if it were "a matter of no overwhelming importance to the United States"—when "my brethren," as in the time of Job, are "ashamed because they had hoped." If I can not accept the basic premises and conclusions of this school it is not from failure to give its arguments consideration. It is rather because I happened to go through long ago the evolution which many have undergone only recently, and because I have had more time and been under greater pressure to evolve further.

On April 4, 1917, the Associated Students of the State University of Montana where I was then editor of the college paper, *Montana Kaimin,* sent this telegram to President Wilson:

Monster patriotic demonstration today by students of State University. A united Student body, who, having faith and confidence in your wisdom and judgment, pledges its enthusiastic support of your every undertaking.

The next day the college paper published under my signature the following:

BLIND DEMOCRACY

I have been asked why I voted against sending the telegram to President Wilson which was to say that the University students "stand behind him in whatever he undertakes." I was opposed to it because I object to the all-inclusiveness of the wording which I have just quoted.

When the war first began we condemned that very attitude among the Germans. We criticized severely their blind obedience to the Kaiser. Now at the first shadow of war, although we are not in the danger the Germans were with hostile countries on both sides, shall we lock up our brain and throw the key away?

To say that we are behind the President in everything he undertakes, especially at this stage of the international situation, is to undermine the very foundations of democratic government. It is an indication of mob-mindedness and is least to be expected and most to be deplored when found in our colleges.

Instead of being a "glittering generality" the telegram should have said something definite. If it had said, "We are behind you in every move you make to aid the cause of democracy against autocracy, and we urge you to make the entrance of the United States into the war dependent upon the definite agreement of the allies to establish a league to enforce peace after the conflict is over and while overpowering the German government to oppose dismembering and economically crushing that nation and thus sowing the seeds of future warfare"—if the message had been of that order, I would have been among the first to say aye.

When the college term ended I volunteered in June, 1917, in one of the engineer regiments which Marshal Joffre on his visit to Washington urged the United States to organize and dispatch at once to France; it was called at first the 8th and later the 18th Railway Engineers. (I had been working summers as transitman in the United States Public Land Surveys in Alaska and the Rockies.) Six weeks after the regiment was organized we were sent to France where I remained until discharged from service June, 1919. In June, 1918, I was transferred to the Intelligence Service (G. 2, S.O.S.) and in December was attached in a confidential position to the American Peace Commission in Paris where I remained for six months.

I had access there to many highly secret official documents, not only the daily record of the secret meetings of Wilson, Lloyd George, Clemenceau, etc., but daily despatches between the President and American generals on all fronts, our diplomats, and Washington (on the home and Senate situation). I was in an unusual position to see daily what was really happening, and how little the press or public knew of this, and to see, too, from the inside how propaganda was being handled abroad and at home. I was also one of those chosen to guard President Wilson on his return to Paris from Washington until the secret service men he brought with him could take over, my job being mainly to "smell" the bouquets sent him to see they hid no bombs. I mention these details to show the degree to which my functions encouraged a skeptical attitude—in one already born a Missourian.

My mental evolution during the war and armistice period does not need to be reconstructed now from memory; it can be followed in these excerpts from what I wrote then:

March, 1918, [Letter published in the Missoulian,
Missoula, Mont.]

"I can not understand the wave of intolerance, with its determination to suppress the least expression of non-conformity, which seems to have spread over the country which has always acclaimed its freedom of speech and press," writes Private Clarence K. Streit, formerly of the Missoulian staff, from "Somewhere in France." "I suppose the country is only going through the same psychological stage as that experienced by England and France at the beginning of the war. May they pass through it quickly. When they have, they will realize that in a country fighting to make the world safe for democracy, intolerance, hate and forced conformity are among the enemies of the cause."

Oct. 26, 1918. [Letter]

It is going to be mighty easy to lose this war in winning it. By that I mean that I think the war will have been lost to democracy no matter what the decision on the field if the prime motive in the making of peace is not the safe-guarding of the world against another catastrophe such as this war. If only a quarter of the zeal paid in each country to the protection of its "national interests" were devoted to the interests of humanity!

Dec. 22, 1918. [Paris, Letter]

I reached Paris about 9 a.m. Saturday Dec. 14th. . . . Soon came the boom of a cannon. The President had arrived. . . . I arrived at the *Champs Elysées* just in time to hear the cheers and see the handkerchiefs and hats waving. . . . He received a magnificent reception.

. . . The French recognize the greatness of Wilson, even if a portion of the American public, perhaps too close to him and certainly too far distant from the late front, can't seem to appreciate him. . . .

Dec. 23, 1918. [*Diary, Paris, Record Room,*
American Peace Commission]

I made the usual inspection to see what important papers had been left out. Found a great deal of valuable information lying around. Also all the keys to the filing cabinets. Among other things, a document dated Nov. 29,1918, from the French Republic to the U. S. Government giving plans for Peace conference drawn up by French Govt.

One learns a great deal at this station. Surprising the way things are left accessible. This record room contains all the files and documents of the Peace Commission. . . . It is enough to give one an idea of the immensity of the problems confronting the coming conference—to see the universal scope of the documents and books in this room.

Jan. 9, 1919. [*Diary, Paris*]

So many diverse peoples of the world are expecting so many diverse benefits from Wilson and America at the Peace Conference that the many inevitable disappointments are likely to have a boomerang effect in the world's opinion of the U. S. There is such a thing as setting up too great expectations.

Before the Armistice the Allied press was filled with stories of the lack of food and raw materials in Germany, paper suits, etc. Since the Armistice the press is filled with stories of the comfortable situation of the Germans, of the plenitude of food in Germany, and no one has yet spoken of seeing a paper suit. The answer is—Propaganda. Germany is menaced by famine, yet the idea of feeding their enemies grates upon some Christian folk and they try to prove that said enemies need no food. . . .

No doubt German historians will prove the war was a victory for Germany or, at least, that she was not beaten. And millions of Germans will be brought up to believe that. Just as millions of other children will be brought up to believe another "truth." Each group of belligerents used its press for four years to instill into the majority of its people its own particular "truths," these "truths" being as absolutely opposed to each other as the soldiers of the two camps during a bayonet charge.

It would be idle to suppose that the effects of this persistent propaganda should die out with the Armistice and that now Truth should shake off her shackles, reveal herself to all people of the world so that no one could longer doubt her identity. Even in times of continued peace we cannot decide just what is this much referred to "Truth." What chance is there for her to be recognized now?

Jan. 18, 1919. [Diary, Paris]

The grand conference of Paris has at last opened, ushered in with some well chosen platitudes from the mouth of President Poincaré . . . . Surround the peace conference with a halo of high and noble thoughts, and then do your dirty work behind closed doors. Same old scheme that they worked in Vienna in 1815. . . . Read the stenographic report of the afternoon's session.

Jan. 25, 1919. [Diary, Paris]

Gave the peace conference the once over . . . from the outside. *Populo* is not very popular with the peace commissioners. He is useful as a background for the splendid limousines which roll by and up to the door of the Quai d'Orsay, carrying his "servants." . . . There were two or three hundred of *populo*, representing most of the Allied nations, many soldiers anxious to see the "fathers of the victory," the "premier poilus," the select few who "won the war."

Many of them, I gathered from phrases overheard, were waiting especially to see Pres. Wilson. . . . I recognized Balfour, and I think I saw Winston Churchill. . . . Marshal Foch . . . drew a cheer. . . . The President . . . also drew a cheer, and the crowd pressed to the fence to see him descend from his car. . . . They could only get a glimpse of him. Cold weather, nipping wind. But crowd stuck. I see in the morning papers that Pres. Wilson made an important speech on the Society of Nations at this session.

Feb. 19, 1919. [Paris, Letter to a French girl]

President Wilson's speeches were all that reconciled me in the least toward this war as a war. The patriotic speeches only disgusted me. The men who were the strongest supporters of the United States entering the

war "for democracy," why, they were all the worst
reactionaries in America, men who all their lives had
bitterly opposed democracy at home. And the men,
most of them at least, who protested against our entering the war and were called traitors and maligned in
the press—they were the men who had been abused
for years by the same press because they advocated
democratic reforms.

I detested the German government and the German
idea, wherever I found it. And I found plenty of Prus-
sianism in the U. S. I put little faith in the Allied
protestations of democracy. And, in the last three
months, I have seen enough of the secret inside workings to know that the heads of the Allied Governments
are not sincerely democratic, they are only as democratic as they feel compelled to be by public opinion.
Some of them are cynically un-democratic, though in
their public speeches they usually hide this.

[I would here give a general warning to the reader. I
was only 21 when I enlisted and had never been east of the
Mississippi. I was much impressed in Paris by the fact that
I was then in a better position to judge what was really going
on than most contemporaries, more impressed by this than
by the facts that the picture was, even so, very incomplete
and that I was young and inexperienced.

Nor did I then realize what strange chameleons documents are. A passage in a document read when it is fresh
and in the light of one's impression of the whole situation
then may seem to one cynical and significant, while if read
years later when quite removed from the context of events
it may seem innocent and ordinary. Conversely, documents
that raised no eyebrows when written can take on a most sinister meaning when read years after the contemporary at-
mosphere has gone, and facts not common knowledge then
have come to light, or viewpoints have changed.

We tend to assume that the picture we get of a given
event will be the one the future will get of it or that the past
got. Yet how many of the factors that influenced President
Wilson and other leaders of his day are lost to us, and how
many factors that we know now were unknown to them?]

March 3, 1919. [Paris, Letter]

Part of the Louvre museum is now open. . . . I've
visited it twice. What did I go back to see the second
time? Especially the Venus de Milo. And also the Vic-

tory of Samothrace. . . . The Victory of Samothrace has no head. Did Victory ever have a head? Perhaps. But it always loses it. . . .

No doubt these letters of mine from Paris are rather disappointing to you. So little about this epoch-making Peace Conference—this great historical assembly. . . .

I might say, however, that this is not a Peace Congress but an inter-allied Victory meeting, with indignation as the guiding general force and Individual Economic Interest as the chief counselor of each nation. If you want to cling to your opinion of the greatness of a number of gentlemen much in the public's eye, why, stay home and read the newspapers. Don't hang around here.

But still, this conference is an enlightened body compared to some of the vociferous Senators back home, for whom political thinking ended when the Constitution was written and the Monroe Doctrine enunciated. The world is moving mighty fast these days, but just where it is going I would not venture to say. Ah, these piping days of—the armistice.

But I'll re-iterate that President Wilson, in my opinion, is far ahead of the others. But he is handicapped by lack of support at home and I doubt if he will be able to accomplish much.

March, 1919. [Paris, Letter]

The opinions of the American press these days show a lamentable ignorance of world conditions. To read the papers, and the speeches of . . . [various] . . . senators, one would think that they have been asleep for the last five or ten years. They talk about . . . keeping out of European affairs. Were we able to keep out of this war? The world isn't as big as it used to be. And it is getting smaller all the time.

I don't think the proposed League of Nations is by any means perfect. . . . What discourages me with so much of American criticism of the League—it is so plainly caused by nothing more than personal or party hostility to the man Wilson. Or it is urged by a selfish nationalism. It is not helping the cause of future world peace.

March 20, 1919. [Paris. Letter to a French girl]

I think parents are rather under obligation to the child. . . . The same reasoning I apply to man's relation to the state. A man owes a state nothing because of the fact that he happened to be born in it. It was through no choice of mine that I am an American. I could be naturalized now as citizen of some other country? True, but the state, in educating me, was fitting me for a life within that state, its object was to train me into being a good citizen of it. And the very accident of birth gave me dear associations, friends, memories in America, made me prejudiced in her favor. I would not change. With all her faults, I prefer America to any other country.

But—had I been born in France, say, of French parents—I would no doubt prefer to be French, would be proud of my French nationality just as you are. And if the fates had willed that I should have been born an Englishman, a Russian, a German, a Chinaman, a Turk or any other nationality, I would undoubtedly be just as happy in my state and prefer it to any other.

And yet, this simple accident of birth under one flag instead of another colors the mental attitude and distorts the intellectual processes of most men, including most of the men whom I used to look up to as intellectuals, men of science and philosophy, men whose sole concern was the truth. This war showed the stuff of which the world's "élite" or "intelligenzia" is made —and it a sight enough to make one despair.

For my part, I love America—aside from the accident of birth—because of the ideals on which the Republic was founded (not all of them, however), I love American life for its boundless energy, its freedom from tradition, because it is facing the future and not the past. But that isn't going to keep me from trying to see things as they really are. I am an intelligent man first, an American afterwards. The United States is now undoubtedly the most powerful single nation on the globe. All the more need then for men in America whose allegiance is to the human race.

*   *   *   *   *

MY EVOLUTION AFTER 1919

My evolution, then, has not been from unthinking acceptance of the war to disillusioned belief that it was a monstrous mistake into which we the people were led through no fault of ours but through sinister influences. My evolution has been from doubtful acceptance of the war as being, on balance, more right than wrong, to a bitter feeling as early as 1919 that it had been botched. After this interlude of disillusionment I have slowly grown to the deep conviction that with all their mistakes Wilson and the American people chose the lesser evil in all their essential choices.

Though I went into the war favoring a league to enforce peace, I thought of it then only vaguely. When President Wilson talked of making the world safe for democracy I did not then understand that the real problem was not that of doing justice at once, but of providing the means of doing justice, the machinery of world self-government. I lost interest in his League in 1919 because it was coupled with so bad a treaty and because I thought it was too weak. I have since become convinced that, considering all he had to face and choose between, President Wilson showed high statesmanship in tying the Covenant to the Treaty of Versailles, and that he got as strong a world organization founded as was practically possible then. Though I have since come also to believe that the League is no solution for us because its basic working principle—which I never questioned then—is wrong, I am nonetheless convinced that this League was practically essential for the necessary transition to world organization on a sound basis. But when I left the army I was so disappointed with Woodrow Wilson and his works, and so opposed to the irreconcilables, that I took no part in the ensuing fight over the League at home.

I went to work as a reporter and then in January, 1920, returned to Europe as a Rhodes Scholar. After covering the Turco-Greek war, during vacation, for the Philadelphia *Public Ledger,* I left Oxford in the Fall of 1921 to become the *Ledger's* Rome correspondent. My interest in the League had so ebbed that though I was in Lausanne for months in 1922-23 reporting the Turkish peace conference I never bothered to make the trip of only one hour needed to visit Geneva. I never saw the League in action, in fact, before *The New York Times* sent me in 1929 from New York to Geneva to be its correspondent there. Meanwhile, however, my life and work in many parts of Europe and especially in the territory of the Central Powers had helped persuade me that we had not made a mistake in entering the war.

The reasons that split Americans for and against the League in 1920 were, of course, paper reasons, for the League then existed only on paper. Yet to this day only a relative handful of Americans have had or taken occasion to test their theories by studying on the spot how the League of Nations really works in practice. Most of the leading American opponents of the League have such faith in pure theory that they have never so much as laid eye on a League meeting. My own theories about the League have had to face the facts.

Unlike most of those who have been in close contact with the League and its problems, I have never been responsible for any part of the League machinery or for producing results in any of its fields for any government. My responsibility, instead, has been that of reporting objectively, accurately and understandingly to all who cared to read what these others were doing. This function required close continual contact with the permanent officials of the League, I. L. O. and Bank, with the policies and special problems and delegations of all important member and non-member countries, and with all big world questions, political, economic, monetary, social—and yet sharp detachment always from each of these. No one present but the reporter had this function. Nor was any one under more pressure to see each day's development in every field in terms of living men and women, and to judge correctly the essentials in it interesting laymen and experts far removed in distance or occupation. I have enjoyed the further and immense advantage of reporting for *The New York Times*. Mr. Ochs said to me, as my only instructions on being appointed League correspondent in early 1929: "Remember always to lean backwards in being fair to those whose policies *The New York Times* opposes."

Such, briefly, was the road which I took at the age of 21, and by which I have come in 21 years to propose Union now.

Last Word

On all great subjects much remains to be said.—*Mill.*

One must not always finish a subject so completely
as to leave nothing for the reader to do. The object is
not to make others read but to make them think.—
Montesquieu, De l'Esprit des Lois.

When Aristide Briand proposed his European Federation
the similarity of many of the responses impressed me. They
applauded, they said: "This is noble, this is what we all
want," and they added, "But there is this difficulty and that
difficulty, and how is he going to meet them?" They acted as
if the veteran French statesman, though in a much better
position than they to see the difficulties his proposal faced,
had not foreseen them and needed their help in seeing
rather than in solving them. They implied that all these difficulties were for him to overcome; they assumed the role of
spectators who would not be affected if his project came
to naught through his failure to overcome every difficulty
himself. These waiters-for-a-perfect-plan could not see that
in this enterprise they were willy-nilly involved, that they too
would be punished—swiftly, mercilessly, increasingly—for
failure to solve in time the problems on which Aristide
Briand had made so brave a beginning.

I am aware of many of the difficulties confronting The
Union, and I have no doubt that there exist more than I
realize. I know that this book has led me into fields where
others have a much greater knowledge than I. No one needs
to take time to convince me that this book falls far short of
what it should be, that it is weak indeed compared to the
great enterprise it would promote. I regret that this book is
not as clear, short, complete, well-organized, free from error,
easy to read and hard to controvert on every page as I—
perhaps more than any one—desire it to be. I feel, however,
that I have reached the point of diminishing return for isolated work on its problem, and that time presses for an
agreed if imperfect answer. My hope is that the book can
now make at least the friends it needs, for if it can then I

am sure that they can do far more than I to correct its faults and advance its purpose.

One can not believe as I do in democracy and fail to believe that the surest way to bring out the true from the false and to accomplish any great enterprise is to get the greatest number of individual minds to working freely on it. The variety in our species is so rich that one can be sure in any such undertaking that one can do almost no detail in it so well as can some one else.

Democracy taps this rich vein. It recognizes that Man can not foresee which obscure person or lowly thing may suddenly become of the greatest value to Man. And so it sets an equal value on every man and on every thing, and seeks to give equal freedom to every man to do the thing he best can do and trade it in the commonwealth for all the billion things he can not do so well. That is the meaning of democracy's great declaration, *All men are created equal,* and the reason why the rise of democracy has led to the discovery of more and more truths and to the doing of greater and greater enterprises.

And so I ask you not merely to make known any error you have found in this book but to try yourself to solve the problem that it leaves. Since it was you who found the fault how can you know that you are not the one who can overcome it better than I, better than anyone?

After all, are not your freedom, your prosperity, your security, your children at stake as well as mine? Is not the problem of world government your individual problem as well as mine? Can I alone organize the world for you any more than you for me? Can any dictator do it for us? If you and I and the other man and woman working freely and equally together can not gain our common end, then how on earth can it be gained?

For Man's freedom and vast future man must depend on man. It is ours together, or no one's and it shall be ours.

The votaries of liberty will lay this book [Union Now] *aside with a sigh. . . . It will have conjured up a vision of the greatest political and economic opportunity in history, by comparisons with which the opening of the North American continent was a modest beginning . . .*

Gigantic opportunities would be opened up. A rise in the standard of living of millions of consumers would result from the expansion of markets and the consequent lowering of prices for mass-produced goods. Even a relatively slight expansion in their known market would enable U. S. automobile manufacturers (to take only one example) to cut prices, and cars would thus become available to more persons, not only in the other states of the Union but also at what we call "home." The economic history of the U. S. demonstrates that this process is cumulative and that it would almost certainly result in lower automobile prices than even Mr. Ford has dreamed of. There would be an inevitable revival in shipping and in railroads, and hence in the capital-goods industries behind them. Industrial unemployment might, therefore, almost disappear.

A genuine union of the democracies, then, opens up a vista of industrial growth to which the only enlightening parallel is the growth of the United States itself. At the time the American Union was formed the eighteenth-century libertarian economists were preaching free trade. And the abolition of tariffs within the borders of the United States provided for this doctrine the most spectacular practical demonstration that any economic theory has ever had.

Fortune, April 1939 (editorial on *Union Now*)

Index

Absolutism, 212
  basic conception of, 211
  in democracy itself, 198-99
  and sovereignty, 90-99
  See also Dictatorship, Totalitarianism, Tyranny
Acheson, Dean, 21
Acton, Lord
  quoted, xi, 69-71, 77, 100-1, 120, 158-59, 213, 281
Adams, James Truslow, quoted, 28
Adams, John, 63
Adenauer, Konrad, 21, 24
Africa, federation of, 11, 19, 162
Alaska, 79
Allais, Maurice, quoted, 160-61
Alliances, 196n., 203
  defined, 62
Aly, Bower, vii
American Peace Commission (Paris), 297
American Revolution, 2, 100-1, 126
  as two revolutions, 101-3
Arabia, federation of, 82
Armed power
  balance of, 44-45
  in Union, 43, 45-49, 199, 240
  See also Defense
Articles of Confederation (League of Friendship), 58, 60, 121, 193-94, 224
  chaos under, 71-73
  powers of, 63-65
  prohibited diplomatic relations by states, 59, 64-65
  stronger than NATO, 63-65
  See also Federal Convention of 1787
Asia, federation of, 19, 162
Atlantic Community (Atlantica), 62, 188
  common culture of, 165-72, 173-77

Atlantic Community—*Contd.*
  "the country without a man," 166-67
  creation of, 5
  struggle with Communism, 176-177
  See also Community, Union
Atlantic Congress
  composition of, 4
  Final Declaration quoted, 1, 62
  recommendations of, 4-5
  weakness of, 151
Atlantic Convention (Convention of Citizens of North Atlantic Democracies), 22, 33, 56, 79, 180, 188
  approved by Congress, vii, 4, 18, 128
  opposed by "patriotic" groups, 136
  task of, 6, 149-56
Atlantic Federal Union, *see* Union
Atom bomb, 15, 41, 45
  French expenditure on, 47
Atomic power
  international control of, 96n.
  of Union, 45-49
Atomic secrets, 48-49
Auriol, Vincent, 20
Australia
  admission to Union, 36
  a federal union itself, 81
  a founder of Union, 33, 197
Austria, admission to Union, 36

Balance of power theory, 204
"Balance of terror," 44-46
Balkanization, 10, 19, 25, 86, 127, 176
Barker, Ernest, quoted, 274
Belgium, 20
  a founder of Union, 33, 35, 197
Benelux, 20, 34
Berlin blockade, 21, 54-55
Bevin, Ernest, 21

Beyen, J. W., 20
Bible, quoted, 3, 149, 157, 173, 274
Bidault, Georges, 20
Billotte, Pierre, 20
Bloc, defined, 62
Borah, William, 170, 216
Brandt, Willy, 21
Briand, Aristide, 86, 306
Bruges Conference, 62
Brugmans, Henri, 20
Brundage, P. F., 46n., 70
    quoted, 136-37
Burnaby (English traveller), quoted, 68-69

Cain and Abel, 273
Canada, 169
    a federal union itself, 81
    a founder of Union, 32-34, 197
Capitalism, Marxist theory of competition within, 52-53
Cavour, Camillo di, 213
Charles I, 100n.
China, 7, 13, 16, 30, 45, 50
    and Russia, 164-65
    and Union, 162-65
    and United States, 164
Church, Frank, 170
Churchill, Winston, 20, 24
    a "puzzle," 82-83
    quoted, 80
Citizen, as basic unit of government, 177, 210-12, 226
"Citizen sovereignty," 161, 174
    See also Sovereignty
City republics, 101-2
Civil rights, Lincoln quoted on, 121
    See also Freedom
Civil War, 77, 119-26, 236
Clayton, Will, 21, 24n.
Clinton, George, 72-73
Coal and Steel Community, 9, 20, 65
Coalition, defined, 62
Collective security, 96n.
Collective will, 26
Colonies
    effect of Union on, 246-47, 289
    liberation of, 9, 16-19
    See also Balkanization

Comintern, 13
Common Market, 9, 20, 62, 65, 86
    lack of experience in free government within, 34
Communism, 43
    attitude toward Union by, 51-56
    goal of world government by, 95-96, 148
    policy of disruption by, 45
    Russian vs. Chinese, 164-65
    satellite nations and, 162-65
    strength of, 7-8
    struggle with Atlantica by, 176-177
    underdeveloped nations and, 10, 159, 162
    weakness in, 165
    See also Russia
Community, defined, 62-63
    See also Atlantic Community
Confederate States of America, 58, 60
    constitution of, 121-23
    a "federation," not a "confederation," 121
Confederation
    defined by author, 62
    defined by Webster, 60-61
    discussion of meaning of term, 58-63
    See also Articles of Confederation
Conference on Atlantic Community (Bruges), 62
Confucius, quoted, 272-73
Congo, 18
Congress of the United States
    Act calling for Atlantic Convention, vii, 4, 128
    resolutions favoring Union introduced into, 33
Connally Amendment, 98
Constitution (Confederate), 121-123
Constitution (United States)
    balance between Senate and House in, 131-32
    Confederate constitution and, 121-23
    a "discovery" in political science, 118

Constitution—*Contd.*
  Preamble to, 74, 122-23
  a protection for smaller states, 131-34
  semantic confusion in, 117-18
  See also Federal Convention of 1787
Constitution of Union, 79, 193
  amendments to, 251, 294-95
  Bill of Rights in, 193, 288-89
  draft of, 287-96
  executive power in, 248-51, 293-94
  judicial power in, 251, 294
  legislative power in, 247-48, 291-93
  ratification of, 295-96
Constitutional Convention, *see* Federal Convention of 1787
Convention of Citizens of North Atlantic Democracies, *see* Atlantic Convention
Cook, George Cram, 273
Coolidge, Calvin, quoted, 24
Courage, statement by Andrew Jackson, 256
"Courage grows as a rose . . . ," 173
Cuba, 45, 50
Curtis, Lord, 81
Cynics (of ancient Greece), 274-275

Daughters of the American Revolution, 136
Davis, Jefferson, 122
De Gasperi, Alcide, 20, 24
De Gaulle, Charles, 24, 46-47
  appeal to, by the author, 87-89
  urges Franco-British union, 20, 86
De la Fouchardière, Georges, 29
De Tocqueville, Alexis, 27, 73, 85
  quoted, viii, 2, 22-23, 80, 118-119, 129, 261
Debate squads, vii
Debré, Michel, 68n.
  quoted, 86-87
Declaration of Independence, 72, 108, 193-94
"Declaration of Liberty-and-Union," 177-80

Defense, savings through Union, 136-38, 141
  See also Armed power
Democracy
  absolutistic practices within, 198-99
  allows citizens to promote policies, 252-54
  American knowhow in, 38-40
  based on the individual, 210-13
  defined, 195
  experience among nations in, 34-36
  freedom and, 216-18, 263-66, 269-70, 307
  materialism and, 22-23
  sovereignty and, 25-27, 92-93, 216-18
  states' rights in, 217
  in unions, 216-18
  weakness of, 164
  See also Freedom
Democratic party, platform, 4, 56-57
Demosthenes, quoted, 252
Denmark, a founder of Union, 33, 35, 197
Depression, 127, 154
  avoidance by rearmament, 8
Dickinson, John, 114-16
Dictatorship
  furthered by leagues, 215-16
  Plato's advocacy of, 265
  world, 96
  See also Absolutism, Totalitarianism
Dictatorship of the proletariat, 26
Diefenbaker, John G., quoted, 9
Disarmament, x, 145-46, 199
Divine right of kings, and sovereignty, 91
Dulles, John Foster, 21, 70
Dunham, Lord, 81

Eastern Europe, 163
Economist, The, 82
Education, in Union, 139, 172, 244
Einstein, Albert, 96n.
Eire
  admission to Union, 36
  a founder of Union, 33, 197

Eisenhower, Dwight D., 4, 21, 84
  quoted, 43, 54
English Revolution, 100
Ethiopia, war with Italy, 228-31
Euratom, 20, 65, 86
European Defense Community, 62
European Economic Community, *see* Common Market
European Union, 15
  first step to Atlantic Union, 47
  possible domination by Germany, 163
  proposed by Briand, 83, 306

Faure, Maurice, 4
Federal Convention of 1787, vii, 5-6, 15, 54, 153, 155, 207-8, 245
  discussions of sovereignty in, 73-76, 110-18, 133-34
  simplicity of, 152
  See also Articles of Confederation
Federalist, The, 118, 155, 189
  British apostles of, 81
  quoted, 2
Federation
  a British method, 80-85
  defined by Webster, 60-61
  discussion of meaning of term, 58-63
  opposed by Lenin, 95
  regional, 11, 19, 30
  by states not connected by land, 79
  success of principle of, 194
Finland, a founder of Union, 33, 197
Fiske, John, quoted, 206
Fortune, quoted, 308
Founders of Union, 192, 196-97, 289
  to depend on current situation, 33
  ideal list of, 32
  NATO membership and, 32-34
  requirements of, 31-32, 197
France, 80
  attitudes toward Union, 85-89, 169
  democracy in, 34

France—*Contd.*
  a founder of Union, 32-33, 35, 197
  nationalism in, 47
France, Anatole, quoted, 280
Franklin, Benjamin, 102
Freedom (liberty), 26, 261-78
  anarchy and, 164
  in democracy, 263-66, 269-70, 307
  etymology of, 285
  as goal of Union, 107-8, 170-172, 177-80, 200-2
  history of, 273-78
  interdependence and, 279-85
  in the minority, 40-41
  peace and, 41-42
  as a political ability, 40
  sovereignty and, 104-6, 124-5, 127
  of speech and the press, 270, 288
Freedom Against Itself, 7n., 39n.
Freedom and Federation, 8, 26n.
French Revolution, 85, 158
Fundamental Orders of Connecticut, 75

General will, 26
Germanic Confederation, 60
Germany, 20-21, 36, 54, 94, 299, 301
  a founder of Union, 33, 35-36
  lack of experience in free government within, 34
Gerry, Elbridge, quoted, 113
Gillette, Guy, 22
Goodman, Elliot R., quoted, 90, 95n., 96
Government
  basic units of, 177, 210-12, 226
  democratic, 216-18
  of "gasoline and electricity," 263-65
  "by the people," 73-74, 241
  "for the people," 74-75, 241-42
  "of the people," 73, 76, 240-41
  by philosophers, 265-66
  purpose of, 177
  See also World government
Great Britain (United Kingdom), 19-20

Great Britain—*Contd.*
   American union with, 12
   attitudes toward Union in, 80-85, 169
   a founder of Union, 32-34, 197
   Labour party in, 46, 84
Great Republic, *see* Union
Greece, 36
   ancient, 37, 101-2, 169, 274-75
   a founder of Union, 33, 35-36
Grew, Joseph, 24n.
Gromyko, Andrei, 96n.
Gross Union Product, 160
Gruenther, Alfred M., 21

Hamilton, Alexander, 73, 118, 189
   opposition to state sovereignty by, 110, 134, 225-26
   quoted, 113, 191, 222, 226
Harding, Warren G., 24
Hawaii, 17-18, 79
Hays, Wayne, 22
Henry, Patrick, 102n., 112, 116-118, 216
   quoted, 99-100, 130
Herriot, Edouard, 20
Hitler, Adolf, 212-14
Hobbes, Thomas, 210
House of Deputies (Union), 247, 292-93
House of Representatives (United States), 131-32
Hume, David, quoted, 240
Hungarian Revolution, 97n., 163

Iceland, a founder of Union, 33, 35
Ideals, aiming toward one's, 32
Inonu, Ismet, 37
Interdependence of man, 278-85
Ireland, *see* Eire
Iroquois Confederacy, 102, 272-273
Ismay, Lord, 21
Isolationism, 203-4
Italy, 20, 36
   a founder of Union, 33, 36
   lack of experience in free government by, 34
   sanctions of League of Nations and Italy, 228-31, 236

Jackson, Andrew, 98, 236, 256
   quoted, 119
Jaszi, Oscar, "Introduction" to 1949 edition by, 189-90
Jay, John, 118, 207
Jeanne d'Arc, 181-82
Jefferson, Thomas, 89, 98
Jesus, 274-75
Johnson, Gerald W., 24
Johnson, Lyndon B., 1, 57
Judd, Walter, 153

Kefauver, Estes, 22
   "Introduction" to 1960 edition by, 187-88
Kennedy, John F., vii, 57
   quoted, 1
Khrushchev, Nikita S., 28, 53-56
Koch, Robert, quoted, 237
Kolonji, Albert, 58
Korovin, E. A., 95

Lafayette, Marquis de, quoted, 258
Lamb, F. Gilbert, vii
Languages, in Union, 139, 192, 244
Lansing, John Jr., 112
Latin America, federation of, 19, 60, 162
Law
   conscience and, 93
   enforcement by leagues and unions, 226-36
   as supreme in society, 92-93
League of Friendship, *see* Articles of Confederation
League of Nations, 12, 71, 203, 212, 224, 277, 302, 304-5
   author as correspondent at, 152, 304
   sanctions by, 145, 228-32
   as "super-state," 66, 216
Leagues
   cannot enforce law, 226-32
   defined, 62, 195-96
   failure as type of political organization, 202-3
   ineffective, 222-24
   public opinion and, 222-23
   unanimity rule in, 223-24
   undemocratic, 215-16

Lee, Richard Henry, 207
Leeuwenhoek, Anton van, quoted, 237
Lenin, Nikolai, opposition to federations, 95
Liberators of mankind, 268-69
Liberty, *see* Freedom
"Liberty-and-Union," *see* "Lincoln Law of Liberty-and-Union"
Lincoln, Abraham, 98, 123-26, 182
  quoted, 2, 6-7, 29, 73, 119-20, 179, 181, 258, 284
  quoted on equality, 121
"Lincoln Law of Liberty-and-Union," 124-5
Litvinoff, Maxim, 96n.
Lothian, Lord, 81
Luxemburg, a founder of Union, 33, 35

MacDonald, John A., 81
Macmillan, Harold, quoted, 1
Madison, James, 98, 110-11, 118
  quoted, 2, 15, 71, 150
Malenkov, Georgi, quoted, 55
Man (a poem), 286
Marquand, David, quoted, 129
Marshall, George C., 20, 21
Marshall Plan, 21
Martin, Luther, 76, 112
  quoted, 112-13
Martino, Gaetano, 20
Mason, George, 73, 74, 99, 114, 115-17
  quoted, 191
Materialism, as danger to democracy, 22-23
Mazzini, Giuseppe, 213
Mill, John Stuart, quoted, 215, 306
Missouri Compromise, 120, 126
Moe, Finn, 22
Mohammed, 275
Mollet, Guy, 20
Monick, Emanuel, 68n., 87
Monnet, Jean, 20, 86
Montesquieu, Baron de, quoted, 306
Morgan, Thomas E., 153

Morley, Felix, 26n.
  quoted, 8
Mussolini, Benito, 213-14

Nation, ambiguity of term, 212-214
National character, and Union, 169
National interest, 26
Nationalism, 14, 25, 302-3
  a balkanizing force, 86
  economic, 10, 154-55, 171
  as force for Union, 85
  in France, 47, 85
  freedom and, 212-14
  as a "germ," 237-40
  growth of, 200-1
  history of, 275-78
  inefficiency of, 221
  sovereignty and, 105
NATO, *see* North Atlantic Treaty Organization
Nehru, Jawarharlal, quoted, 1
Netherlands, 20
  a founder of Union, 33, 197
New Federalist, The, 17n.
"New frontier," 1
New Jersey Plan, 112
New York Times, 304-5
New Zealand
  admission to Union, 36
  a founder of Union, 33, 197
Newton, Isaac, 27, 182
  quoted, 181
Nixon, Richard M.
  proposes North Atlantic Confederation, vii, 4, 54n., 57-60, 66
  quoted, 1
Nkrumah, Kwame, 11
Noblesse oblige, in a nation, 19
North Atlantic Confederation, proposed by Rockefeller and Nixon, vii, 4, 54n., 57-60, 66
North Atlantic Treaty Organization (NATO), vii, 21-22, 54, 152, 187-88
  as "alliance" or "league," 63
  a basis for Union, 32-34, 66-69
  Council of, 63
  excessive duplication in, 136-137

North Atlantic Treaty Organization—*Contd.*
Parliamentary Conferences of, 4, 22, 62, 188
population of, 40
power of, 63-65
responsibility of, for building stronger institutions, 5
weaker than American Confederation, 63-65, 69
Northwest Territory, 65
Norway, a founder of Union, 33, 35, 197
Nullification, 119, 236

Paine, Thomas, 68n.
quoted, 53-54, 193, 206, 215, 267
Parkes, Henry, 81
Patterson, William, quoted, 112
Peace, 15, 26, 40n.
importance of freedom to, 41-42
sovereignty and, 176
Peace Conference (1919), 299-301
Pearson, Lester, 21
Philippines, admission to Union, 36
Pinckney, Charles, 111
Plato, 265
Poincaré, Jules, 300
Point Four, 38
Political history, landmarks in, 189
Population
of NATO, 40
of Union, 35
Portugal, a founder of Union, 33, 35-36
Profit motive, 267-68
Public opinion, effect on leagues and unions, 222-23

Randolph, Edmund, 102n.
Rayburn, Sam, 57
Read, George, 114-15
quoted, 112
Republican party, 105
Reuter, Ernst, 21
Reynaud, Paul, 20
Reynolds, Joshua, quoted, 281

Richards, James P., 22
Roberts, Owen J., 24n.
Robertson, Wishart McL., 22
Rockefeller, Nelson
proposes North Atlantic Confederation, 4, 54n., 57-60, 66
quoted, 70
Roman civilization, 254-57
Roosevelt, Franklin D., 83
Rousseau, Jean Jacques, 26
Russia, 7-16, 45, 50
"dropped" from League of Nations, 228n.
satellite nations and, 162-65
sovereignty and, 90-99, 104, 133
Rykens, Paul, 20

Schuman, Robert, 20
Schumann, Maurice, 20
Secession, in American history, 119-26
Self-determination of nations, 86
Sudetens and, 277
Senate (Union), 247-48, 292-93
Senate (United States), 131-32
Sforza, Count, 20
quoted, 240
Shaw, Bernard, 85
quoted, 182
Shub, David, quoted, 53
Slavery, 268
Civil War and, 122-24
"Snooper state," 221
Socrates, 274, 278
Sovereignty, 212
as anarchy, 13, 198
"citizen" vs. "national," 161, 178
in Civil War, 123-26
Communist attitude toward, 90-99, 104, 133
confusion over concept of, 25-27, 103-7, 119, 126-29, 136
considered as danger, 104-5
democratic concept of, 25-27, 92-93, 100-3
diplomatic, 176
discussed in Federal Convention, 73-76, 110-18, 129-31
divine right of kings and, 91
false concept of, 90-92, 94-99, 103-4

Sovereignty—*Contd.*
  in federations and confederations, 61
  freedom and, 105-6, 124-25, 127
  gain in, through Union, 134, 138-42
  opposed by Washington in American history, 109-10, 116, 133
  of the people, 92-93, 118-19
  and Russia, 90-99, 104, 133
  "sacrifice" of, 216-17
  three concepts of, 116
Soviet Union, *see* Russia
Spaak, Paul Henri, 20, 21, 64
Stalin, Joseph, 52
State
  development of the, 106
  freedom and the, 91-93, 100-101, 174, 213-14
  as unit of government, 210-12
  See also "Super-state"
State High School Debate Leagues, vii
States rights, defined, 217
Stimson, Henry L., 24-25
Streit, Clarence
  Kefauver's estimate of, 188
  at League of Nations, 152, 189
  his "road to Union," 296-305
Stubbs, John, 270
Suez crisis, 56, 84
Summit meetings, 84
Sun Yat Sen, quoted, 272
"Super-states," 59, 65-68, 216
  meaning of term, 220-22
Sweden
  admission to Union, 36
  a founder of Union, 32-33, 197
Switzerland, 202
  admission of Union, 36
  a founder of Union, 32, 33, 197

Tariffs, 154-55
  between American states, 208, 308
Teller, Edward, quoted, i
Tocqueville, *see* De Tocqueville, Alexis

Totalitarianism, 26
  concept of sovereignty in, 91-93, *See also* Absolutism, Dictatorship
Trade barriers, 10, 105, 154-55, 171
"Trooper state," 221
Truman, Harry S., 21
Tucker, Josiah, 68n.
  quoted, 207
Turkey
  a founder of Union, 33, 35-36
  history of, 37, 37n.
Tyranny, not dependent on size of state, 221

U-2 spy plane, 43-44
Unanimity rule, of League of Nations, 223-24
Underdeveloped nations
  aid by Union to, 161-62
  Communism and, 10, 159, 162
  fear of Atlantic Union by, 159-62
Union
  admission to, 36, 192-93, 246
  alternatives to, 202-4
  armed forces of, 43, 45-49, 199, 240
  atomic weapons and, 45-49
  capital city of, 250n.
  colonies and, 246-47, 289
  common culture of, 165-72
  Communism and, 51-56
  Communist satellites and, 162-165
  defense savings from, 136-38, 141
  economic advantages of, 52, 141-42, 154-55, 160-61, 171-172, 308
  economic power of, 43, 50, 197, 199-200
  education in, 139, 172, 244
  experience in democracy needed for, 34-36, 208
  fear of, by other nations, 157-162
  freedom as goal of, 107-8, 170-172, 177-80, 284-85
  intangibles in, 36-38, 165-72
  languages in, 139, 192, 244

Union—*Contd.*
moral power of, 43, 156
national governments within, 139, 192, 201, 241, 244
objections to, 13, 68, 108
personal fulfillment through, 170-72
population of, 35
powers of, 192, 242-45, 290-91
provisional, 32
purpose of, 107, 177-78, 192
self-governing and non-self-governing parts of, 246
sovereignty and, 134, 138-42
steps toward, 4, 252-59
strategic advantages of, 46
subsequent growth of, 43-51
tax power of, 240
underdeveloped nations and, 159-62
United Nations and, 142-46
See also Atlantic Convention, Constitution of Union, Founders of Union, Unions (in general)
Union Now
comment by Kefauver on, 187-188
editions and printings, viii
editorial by *Fortune* on, 308
offer to supply to debate squads, vii-viii
where author would alter, 30-31
1939 edition, 3, 11
1940 concise edition, basic chapters, 187-308
1943 edition, 12-14
1949 (Postwar) edition, 7-8, 11, 15-16, 187, 189-90
Union Now with Britain, 12, 32
Union of South Africa
a federal union itself, 81
a founder of Union, 33, 197
racist policies of, 33, 197
Unions (in general)
defined, 195-96
democratic as compared with leagues, 215-18
disputes between states in, 235-236

Unions (in general)—*Contd.*
enforcement of law by, 232-236
increase of citizen's power in, 218-20
public opinion and, 222-23
rapidity of action by, 224-25
United Kingdom, *see* Great Britain
United Nations, 12-15, 19, 40, 71
as a league, 12, 63
police force of, 144-45
and Union, 142-46
veto in, 41, 144-45
United Nations Association, 149
United States
attitudes toward Union in, 89-90
contributions to Union by, 21-22
disunion in 1760 in, 68-69
economic success of, 78
extension of suffrage in, 77
a founder of Union, 32-34, 197
gain to states by formation of, 134-36
"impossibility" of union of, 207
isolationism in, 203-4
knowhow about democracy in, 38-40
See also Articles of Confederation, Constitution (United States)
United States Citizens Committee on NATO
United World Federalists, 149
Urey, Harold C., 44-45, 48-49

Van Cauwelaert, Frans, 20
Vandenberg, Arthur, 21
Van Zeeland, Paul, 20
Virginia Plan, 111-12, 117
Voltaire, François de, 275

Washington, George, 71, 98
Convention of 1787 and, 6, 67, 99
opposition to state sovereignty by, 109-10, 116, 133
quoted, 89, 99, 258-59
Webster, Daniel, quoted, 278

Wentworth, Peter, 270
West Germany, *see* Germany
Wheel, invention of, 271-72
Whitman, Walt, 189
    quoted, vii, 257, 260, 261
Wilson, James, 134
    quoted, 54, 113, 240
Wilson, Woodrow, 21, 24, 86,
    296-301, 303-4
    quoted, 296

Winsor, Curtin, 58
Woman suffrage, 169, 242
World government, 144
    as alternative to Union, 91n.
    as goal of totalitarianism, 95-
        96, 148
    as long-range goal of Union,
        146-49, 192-93

Yalta, 47-48

TO HELP UNITE THE FREE

THE FEDERAL UNION ORGANIZATION

originated when readers of *Union Now* began joining together in 1939 to achieve its purpose. It was incorporated in 1940 as a non-profit membership association, "to promote education in the basic principles of federal union as exemplified in the Constitution of the U.S., with a view to attaining world order by a Federal Union of the Democratic Peoples." Anyone favoring such work is invited to join. Membership does not commit you to details, but makes your name count for the basic principles of freedom and union this book sets forth, and helps provide the means to advance them. Officers: president, Clarence Streit; chairman, Melvin Ryder, publisher; vice-presidents, Roy B. Chipps, truck line executive, and Charles H. Prange, manufacturer; secretary, Edgar G. Shelton, Jr., radio-TV executive; treasurer, Leo H. McCormick, insurance executive.

FREEDOM AND UNION MAGAZINE

has been published by Federal Union since 1946 for the general public. Edited by Clarence Streit, it is indispensable to anyone who would follow this field. On its 10th anniversary, General Marshall, General Gruenther, John Foster Dulles, Lord Ismay, Clare Boothe Luce and many other distinguished readers testified to its "stimulating," "creative" character.

The Atlantic Union Committee was incorporated in 1949 to supplement the educational work of Federal Union with the action which Congress finally took in 1960 when it authorized a convention of delegates from NATO nations to explore how to unite them more strongly. Its founder-president, the late Justice Owen J. Roberts, was succeeded by Elmo Roper. W. L. Clayton, former Under Secretary of State, is vice-president; Lithgow Osborne, former Ambassador to Norway, secretary; John Q. Robinson, insurance executive, treasurer, and Gerald B. Henry, manufacturer, executive committee chairman. Its Council includes 800 widely known leaders.

THE INTERNATIONAL MOVEMENT FOR ATLANTIC UNION

formed in 1958 and incorporated in 1959, coordinates the work of national organizations, such as the above two. Chairman, General Pierre Billotte, Paris; vice chairman, Lord Shawcross, London; president, Clarence Streit, Washington; vice-presidents, Frans van Cauwelaert, Antwerp, and W. McL. Robertson, Ottawa; secretary-treasurer, Ambassador Robert de Dampierre, Paris; North American secretary, Mrs. Chase Osborn, Washington.

For More Information About Any of These Write
FEDERAL UNION, INC.
2700 Ontario Rd. N.W. Washington 9, D. C.